VALLEY OF THE KINGS

THE TOMBS AND THE FUNERARY TEMPLES OF THEBES WEST

EDITED BY
Kent R. Weeks

PHOTOGRAPHS BY
Araldo De Luca

PROJECT EDITORS
Valeria Manferto De Fabianis
Laura Accomazzo

GRAPHIC DESIGNER
Clara Zanotti

ISBN 88-8095-712-0
1 2 3 4 5 6   05 04 03 02 01

Printed in Italy by Officine Grafiche De Agostini
Color separation by Fotomec, Turin

INTRODUCTION

In our country's illustrious past, no city reigned as supreme over Egypt as did Thebes. The mention of the name evokes a golden age of history: a thriving culture exemplified by its accomplished architecture and sophisticated artistic canon. Although the modern bustling city of Luxor now overlies much of the remains of Thebes, in many places her glories still shine, in particular in the tombs, temples, and treasures west of the River Nile.

The Theban Necropolis is one of the richest archaeological sites in the world, with hundreds of fascinating sites excavated and studied, and with hundreds more still to be opened. This area, once called "The Great West" by the ancients, provides us with some of the most glorious examples of Egyptian art. From the austere beauty of the tombs in the Valleys of the Kings and Queens, the measured geometry of Queen Hatshepsut's funerary temple of Deir el-Bahari, and the regal colonnades of the Ramesseum to the always edifying and sometimes witty depiction of daily life in the private necropolises, the art and architecture of the Theban West Bank presents us with the panorama of Egyptian life in the glorious New Kingdom 3,500 years ago.

The experience of visiting these monuments is not easily forgotten. I will always remember my first visit to the exquisitely painted tomb of Queen Nefertari. After making the steep descent from the entrance, I was rewarded with the breathtakingly vivid colors of the first chambers. Lost in wonder, I felt as if I had taken a step back in time and was a participant in an ancient sacred mystery. The clarity with which I recall that moment is testimony to the power of the images and the experience.

I also remember the liveliness of the scenes in the private tombs of the important officials of the state. The images of weaving, tending animals, sowing and harvesting crops, and other household chores are not so different from scenes of daily life in the countryside of Egypt today. The spectrum of vivid art in Thebes testifies to the continuity of tradition from the ancient period until today.

This book, the most spectacular visual record ever of the monuments, tombs, and temples of Egypt's ancient capital, will go far in aiding the memories of those of us who have been fortunate to visit Thebes and its West Bank, as well as providing a glimpse of Egypt's wonders for the armchair traveler. The combination of superior photographs and authoritative scholarship make this volume a valuable record and gift from a visit to the Theban Necropolis. In addition, it captures for posterity and for our enjoyment the tombs and temples that are not always open to visitors due to the need to protect them from the elements and the sometimes harmful effects of too many visitors in such restricted spaces.

I enjoin everyone to take a journey through the pages of this book, to relive the personal wonder of a visit to Egypt or to experience it for the first time. It truly captures the awe and majesty of the Great West.

H.E. Mrs. Suzanne Mubarak

Suzanne Mubarak

PREFACE

No ANCIENT CIVILIZATION HAS GENERATED MORE ENTHUSIASTIC INTEREST FOR A LONGER PERIOD of time than ancient Egypt. In recent decades, every year has seen dozens of books, fiction and non-fiction, television productions, films, tours, posters, and fake antiquities pour onto the market to be lapped up by a public with an insatiable appetite for things pharaonic. And of all the sites in Egypt, Thebes gets more than its share of attention. With its great monuments, tales of gold, mummies, colorful explorers, and a fascinating cast of ancient characters, it is one of the most enticing parts of the story of ancient Egypt. Indeed, given all that Thebes has to offer, it would be hard to imagine people not being fascinated by it.

Thebes has been continuously inhabited by humankind for thousands of years. But it was to the five centuries of the New Kingdom that most of the monuments that today fascinate the public belonged. Royal tombs in the Valley of the Kings, temples larger than any other religious structures on earth, statues weighing a thousand tons each—its dozens of monuments cover hundreds of hectares. Discoveries of *objêts* of staggering worth, crafted in gold and stones and minerals with unsurpassed skill, inspire craftsmen even today. Wall reliefs and paintings that convey more clearly than data from any other ancient civilization how an ancient people lived offer a virtual tour of the ancient landscape. Papyri and *ostraca* show how similar in their hopes and dreams and concerns the ancient Thebans were to us who live today. No culture, no archaeological site, offers more material of more aesthetic or scholarly value than Thebes. None provides data that allow us to see with greater clarity into the hearts and mind of a people who lived a hundred fifty generations ago.

Designed to be visually pleasing, this book's photographs are also intended to inform. Designed to be readable, its articles are also intended to be accurate, thorough, and up to date. The contributors are certainly well qualified to write about Thebes; between them, they have worked for centuries at Thebes and most are currently working there on important ongoing projects.

The ancient Egyptians considered Thebes to be the world's most perfect city. Few today would disagree that it has become one of the world's most important and fascinating archaeological treasures.

Kent R. Weeks

CONTRIBUTORS

KENT R. WEEKS

Kent R. Weeks is professor of Egyptology at the American University in Cairo and Director of the Theban Mapping Project. He is the discoverer of KV 5, the tomb of the sons of Rameses II in the Valley of the Kings, and the author of numerous books and articles.

ARALDO DE LUCA

Araldo De Luca was born in Rome in 1952. Considered one of the greatest photographers of statuary and jewelry in the world, De Luca has developed sophisticated lighting techniques that allow his seductive images to communicate the passion that the artists invested in their work. He is the author of the photos published in the books *Egyptian Treasures* (1999), *Tutankhamun, Splendor of the Boy Pharaoh* (2000), *Treasures of Ancient Egypt* (2001).

HARTWIG ALTENMÜLLER

Hartwig Altenmüller was born in 1938 in Saulgau/ Württemberg. Since 1971 he has been professor at the Archäologischen Institut der Universität Hamburg. He has worked in the Valley of the Kings and is also author of many titles related to the tombs in the Valley of the Kings.

MORRIS L. BIERBRIER

Morris L. Bierbrier was educated at McGill University, the University of Toronto and the University of Liverpool. He is the author of many books and articles including *The Tomb-Builders of the Pharaohs, Community of Deir el-Medina*, and *Historical Dictionary of Ancient Egypt*.

PETER BRAND

Canadian Egyptologist Peter Brand received his doctorate from the University of Toronto in 1998. The subject of his dissertation was the monuments of Seti I. He is currently Director of the Karnak Hypostyle Hall Project of the University of Memphis.

BETSY M. BRYAN

Betsy M. Bryan is the Alexander Badawy Professor of Egyptian Art and Archaeology at Johns Hopkins University in Baltimore, Maryland. Her primary research interest is in the New Kingdom, largely the 18th Dynasty. She has written on the reigns of Thutmose IV and Amenhotep III and has turned her attention recently to issues of artistic production. She has copied and excavated the tomb of the royal butler Suemniwet, where unfinished paintings allow her to study techniques of the artisans.

EDWIN C. BROCK

Edwin C. Brock has worked in Egypt since 1983, mainly in Thebes and the Valley of the Kings. He served for 10 years as Director of the Canadian Institute in Egypt and is now a member of the Theban Mapping Project at the American University in Cairo. He studied Egyptology at the University of Toronto and is completing a doctoral dissertation on the royal sarcophagi of the New Kingdom in Egypt.

MOHAMED A. EL-BIALY

Mohamed A. El-Bialy was born in 1953 in a village near Mansura and studied Egyptology at Cairo University. He has worked with different missions in Saqqara, Fayum, and he has been on the West Bank since 1984. In 1997 he became General Director of the Antiquities of the West Bank at Thebes.

RITA E. FREED

Dr. Freed is the Norma-Jean Calderwood Curator of Ancient Egyptian, Nubian, and Near Eastern Art at the Museum of Fine Arts and Adjunct Professor of Egyptian Art at Wellesley College. She is a specialist in Egyptian art and has participated in archaeological excavations in Egypt, Israel, and Cyprus.

MELINDA K. HARTWIG

Melinda K. Hartwig is the Curator of Egyptian Art at the Institute of Egyptian Art and Archaeology, and a Member of the Graduate Faculty of Art at the University of Memphis in Memphis, Tennessee. Dr. Hartwig received her Ph.D. from the Institute of Fine Arts at New York University, and specializes in Theban tomb painting.

ERIK HORNUNG

Erik Hornung was born in 1933 in Riga (Latvia), and was Professor of Egyptology in Basel (Switzerland) from 1967 to 1998. He has published extensively on the Valley of the Kings and its religious texts.

T.G.H. JAMES

T.G.H. James wa born in 1923 in Neath, South Wales. Educated at Oxford University, he spent his professional life in the British Museum, where he was keeper of Egyptian Antiquites from 1974 to 1988. He worked in Egypt on different excavations. He has specialized in the publication of texts on stone and on papyrus, and in writing history; among his publications are *Howard Carter: The Path to Tutankhamun* (1992) and *Tutankhamun: The Splendor of the Boy Pharaoh* (2000).

CHRISTIAN LEBLANC

Christian Leblanc graduated in Literature and Human Sciences, and is a researcher at the CNRS. He has directed the French Archaeological Mission of the Laboratory of Archaeology and Theban History (LAHTES) at the Louvre Museum since 1995. Having explored the Valley of the Queens, his work presently centers on the royal families of the New Kingdom. In cooperation with the Egyptian Supreme Council of Antiquities, he coordinates the researches of the Ramesseum and is excavating the tomb of Rameses II. He is also the author of many scientific works.

LYLA PINCH-BROCK

Lyla Pinch-Brock, a Canadian, lives in Egypt and has worked in Egypt and Greece for the past 12 years as an archaeologist specializing in epigraphic work. She cleared KV55 from 1993 to 1996 and is presently Co-director of the Royal Ontario Museum's Theban Tombs Project and Assistant Director of the Tell el-Borg Project in Sinai.

The Publisher would like to thank:
H.E. Farouk Hosny - The Egyptian Minister of Culture;
Gaballah Ali Gaballah - Secretary General of the Supreme Council for Antiquities;
Nabil Osman - President of the Egyptian Information Center;
Gamal Morsi - Director of the Cairo Press Center;
Sabry Abd El Aziz Khater - General Director of Antiquities of Luxor and Upper Egypt;
Mohamed A. El-Bialy - General Director of Antiquities of Thebes-West;
The Mena House Oberoi Hotel, Cairo;
Angelo Sesana; Gamal Shafik of the Cairo Press Center; Francesco Zanchi

The Publisher would also like to acknowledge Eni and its Egyptian subsidiary Ieoc, which have supported and promoted the publication of this volume.

The Editor would like to thank staff members of the Theban Mapping Project:
Francis Dzikowski, Edwin Brock, Nathalie Walschaerts, Walton Chan,
Lamis Gabr, Ilka Schacht, Susan Weeks, and Magdy Ali;
Mark Linz of the American University in Cairo Press, for suggesting
that we take on this project in the first place.

The wife of Menna in a pose of
adoration. Note the perfumed cone
on her head and her elaborate
collar and coiffeur, bracelets, and
painted fingernails. Tomb of Menna,
TT 69, inner hall.

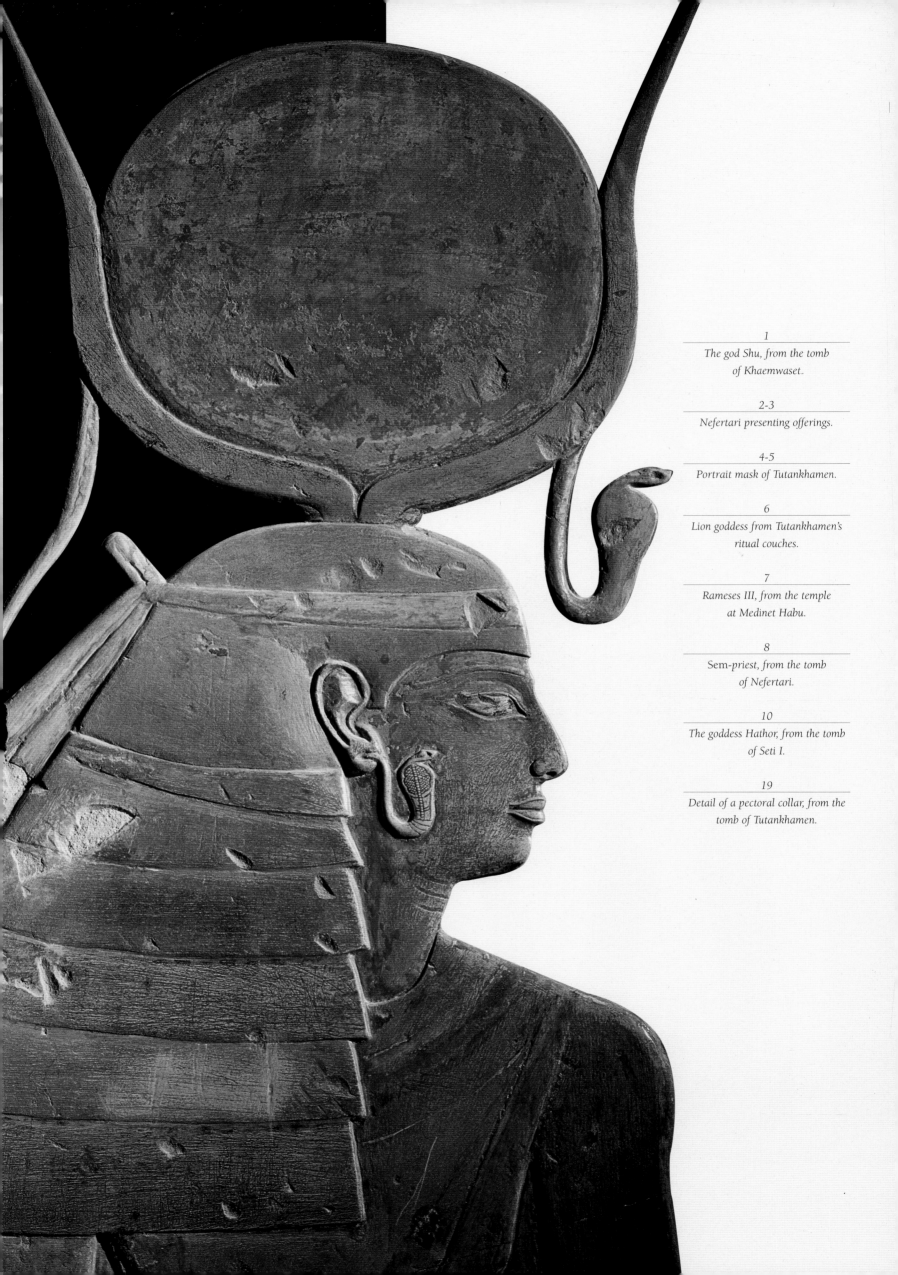

CONTENTS

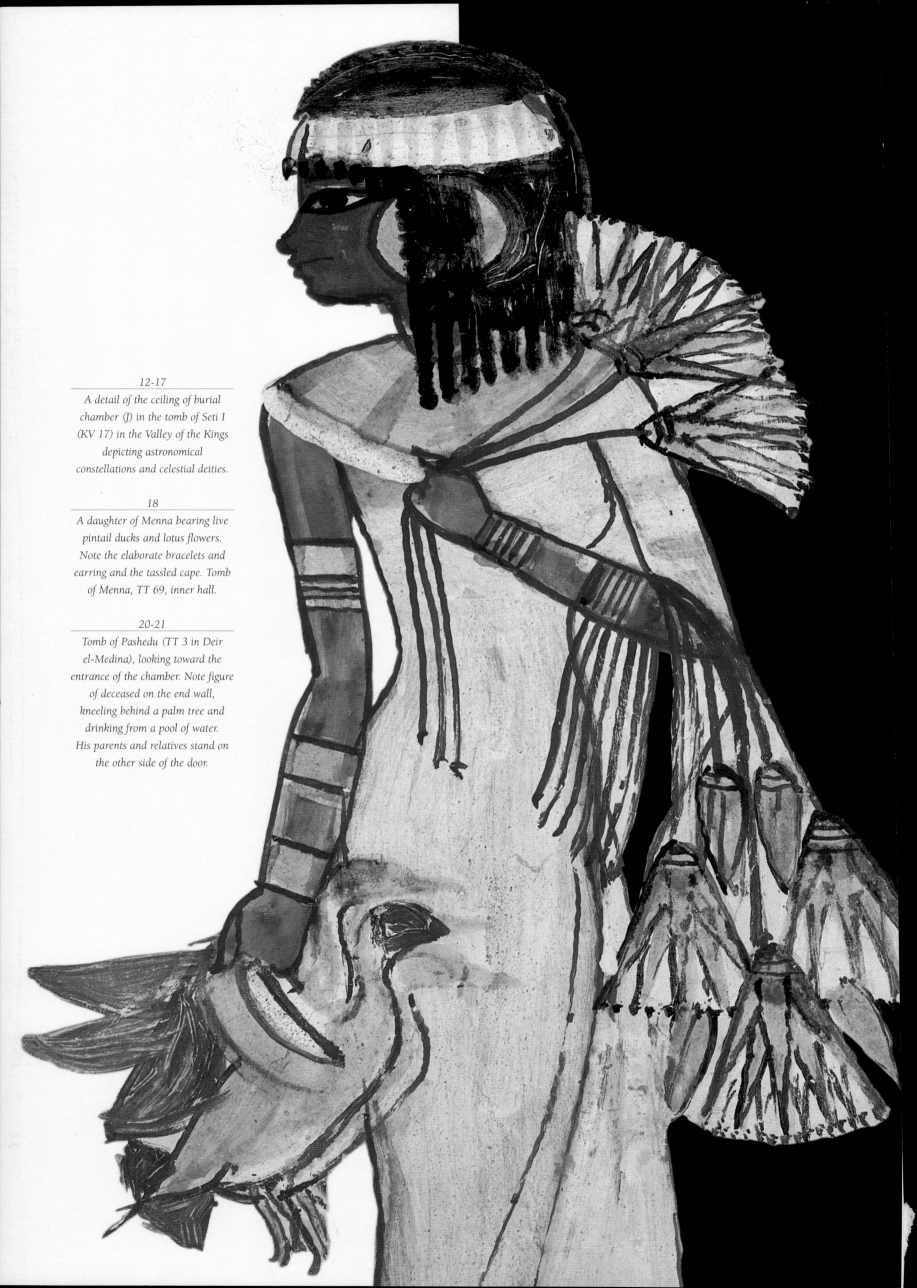

12-17

A detail of the ceiling of burial chamber (J) in the tomb of Seti I (KV 17) in the Valley of the Kings depicting astronomical constellations and celestial deities.

18

A daughter of Menna bearing live pintail ducks and lotus flowers. Note the elaborate bracelets and earring and the tassled cape. Tomb of Menna, TT 69, inner hall.

20-21

Tomb of Pashedu (TT 3 in Deir el-Medina), looking toward the entrance of the chamber. Note figure of deceased on the end wall, kneeling behind a palm tree and drinking from a pool of water. His parents and relatives stand on the other side of the door.

THEBES: A Model for Every City

by Kent R. Weeks

22 left

Satellite view of the Upper Egyptian Nile looking west from above the Red Sea. Thebes lies south (left) of the great bend in the river.

22 right

The River Nile makes a great bend eastward in Upper Egypt. The area on the bend shown here extends from near modern Nag Hammadi (top left) to Armant (bottom). Luxor/Thebes lies north of Armant, where the valley floor widens.

22-23

The River Nile shown in a satellite photograph looking northward. The Mediterranean Sea is at left, the Red Sea at right.

THEBES IS ONE OF THE LARGEST, richest, and best-known archaeological sites in the world. It lies about 900 kilometers (560 miles) south of Cairo on the banks of the River Nile. On the East Bank, beneath the modern city of Luxor, lie the remains of an ancient town that from about 1500 to 1000 BC was one of the most spectacular in Egypt, with a population of perhaps 50,000. Even in the Middle Kingdom, four centuries earlier, Thebes had earned a reputation as one of the ancient world's greatest cities. Within it the Egyptians had built the huge temple complexes of Karnak and Luxor, two of the largest religious structures ever constructed and the homes of priesthoods of great wealth and power. On the West Bank lay the Theban Necropolis—covering about 10 square kilometers (4 square miles)—in which archaeologists have found thousands of tombs, scores of temples, and a multitude of houses, villages, shrines, monasteries, and work stations.

Thebes has been inhabited continuously for the last 250,000 years; the first evidence of the Palaeolithic in Africa was found here. But the most important period in the history of Thebes was the five-century-long New Kingdom, when what the ancient Egyptians called this "model for every city" achieved unrivalled religious, political, and architectural stature. Every New Kingdom pharaoh—there were thirty-two of them—and many before and after that date added to the site's huge architectural inventory. The monuments erected during dynasties 18, 19, and 20 have ensured that even today, thirty centuries later, Thebes is one of the world's foremost archaeological sites. Not surprisingly, Thebes was one of the first sites listed by Unesco as a World Heritage Site (in 1979).

The name "Thebes" was given to the town by early Greek travelers. Some historians believe the Greeks misheard the local name for an area around Medinet Habu, *Djeme*; others that it came from *Tapé*, or *tp*, meaning "head" in ancient Egyptian. In the Bible, Thebes was called "No", from the ancient Egyptian word *niw*, meaning "city." The Egyptians also called it *waset*, the name of the nome (administrative district) in which it lay, or *niwt 'Imn*, "city of Amen", which the Greeks translated literally as *Diospolis*, "city of Zeus," (the god with whom Greeks equated Amen). The Egyptians had many epithets for Thebes: "City Victorious," "The Mysterious City," "City of the Lord of Eternity," "Mistress of Temples," "Mistress of Might," and others. The more recent name for Thebes, "Luxor," derives from the Arabic *Al Uqsur*, which in turn may derive from the Latin word *castra*, meaning a military garrison.

The Theban West Bank extends from el-Tarif in the north to Deir el-Chelwit in the south, a distance of about eight kilometers (5 miles). Its archaeological zone lies adjacent to a three-kilometer (2 miles) wide floodplain that in turn

24 top

Deceased harvesting wheat in fields in the Afterlife. East wall of burial chamber, tomb of Sennedjem, TT 1, in Deir el-Medina.

24 bottom

Trees and plants growing along canals that define fields ploughed by the deceased in the Afterlife. East wall of burial chamber, tomb of Sennedjem, TT 1, in Deir el-Medina.

lies on the Nile. This zone, extending the length of the Theban West Bank, varies in width from a few hundred meters (feet) to several kilometers (miles). We shall deal with each of these areas in turn.

Between the river and the desert edge the floodplain consists of a thick layer of nutrient-rich Nile silt deposited by millennia of annual Nile floods. Today, perennial irrigation waters fields of sugar cane, clover, wheat, and vegetables, and produces two, even three crops annually. Before the completion of the Aswan Dam in the 1960s, which ended the annual Nile flood, the river rose every year in June and then for the following four months covered the floodplain with 30-50 cm. (12-20 inches) of water. The water filled shallow, natural

'basins' that were a product of uneven silt deposition across the floodplain. About six such basins lay on the Theban West Bank, each covering several square kilometers (miles). After the floodwaters receded, these now water-saturated basins were planted and their crops harvested in late autumn and winter. In dynastic times, farmers grew wheat, barley, sorghum, pulses, onions, garlic, and melons. These were vegetables of such quantity and quality, grown with such ease, that European visitors constantly remarked about wondrous Egyptian agriculture. Some Greek travelers believed that life generated spontaneously in this rich Nile mud and that simply drinking Nile water would cause a woman to become pregnant. The valley's richness

became for Europeans proof of the special place Egypt occupied in the hearts of the gods. Nowhere but in Egypt were the silts so rich, the crops so ripe, the fields so easily tended. Even today, the Theban area has a great reputation for agricultural excellence, and tourists who come to admire its monuments often leave equally impressed by its landscape. Azure skies, green fields, dark blue river, golden hills, crimson sunsets, and florescent afterglow give Thebes the appearance of an over-imagined painting. Europeans were certain that here was the landscape in which God had created the Garden of Eden.

The ancient Egyptians, too, waxed eloquent about its attributes:

"What do they say everyday in their hearts,
Those who are far from Thebes?
They who spend their day blinking at its name,
If only we had it, they say—
The bread there is tastier than cakes made
of goose fat
Its water is sweeter than honey,
One drinks of it till one gets drunk
Oh! That is how one lives at Thebes."

24-25
Aerial view of the Valley of the Kings looking east across the Theban hills and West Bank fields to the Nile and modern Luxor.

25 bottom
Deceased inspecting fields of wheat; recording quantities of wheat harvest. South end of east wall, hallway in the tomb of Menna, TT 69.

In dynastic times, several man-made canals were dug across the West Bank floodplain. One extended westward from the Nile across from Luxor Temple to Medinet Habu; another ran from Karnak Temple to the Temple of Seti I. At the edge of the desert these joined a north-south canal connecting small harbors dug in front of temples built in the New Kingdom. Each year, these canals played a role in "The Beautiful Festival of the Valley." This ceremony, one of the most important in the New Kingdom Egyptian calendar, was held annually in the second month of summer. Statues of gods and the pharaoh were taken in a procession of boats from cult temples on the East Bank to each of the memorial temples lining the west. The temples were places where priests and royalty celebrated the union of the living pharaoh with his ancestors, around which peasants celebrated their ancestors' arrival in the Netherworld. Because of their role in this festival, to call the temples on the West Bank "mortuary temples" does an injustice to the important part they played in the royal cult. Many Egyptologists therefore prefer to call them "memorial temples." The ancient Egyptians called them "temples of millions of years."

The Beautiful Festival of the Valley was a joyous one. Texts relate that these were days of music and dancing, when people, rich and poor, visited their ancestors in local cemeteries, drinking and feasting and singing. It was a festival celebrating the continuum of existence that joined this life with the next, this generation with its ancestors.

Most of the nearly thirty memorial temples lay on low-lying desert at the edge of the cultivation and, for the first time in dynastic Egypt, were separated—often by several kilometers (miles)—from the royal tombs to which they were ceremonially and theologically connected.

Part of a procession for the Beautiful Feast of the Valley. Statues of the pharaoh and gods were taken by boat from Karnak across the Nile to each of the memorial temples built there along the edge of the cultivation. From Karnak Temple.

Nile deities offering fowl, fruits, flowers, and other foods from the rich harvest of the Nile Valley. Paintings realized by Ippolito Rosellini from the tomb of Rameses III and published in his Monumenti dell'Egitto e della Nubia (Monuments of Egypt and Nubia).

The Beautiful Festival of the Valley explains why this was so: the temples had to lie adjacent to the floodplain for the procession of boats to reach them and the requisite religious ceremonies to be performed. The tombs lay in desert wadis to take advantage of limestone bedrock and a dry, preservative environment. The first to be built along the cultivation was the 18th Dynasty temple of Amenhotep I and Ahmose-Nefertari; the last were erected in the 20th Dynasty. The Middle Kingdom temple of Nebhepetre Mentuhotep II and the 18th Dynasty temples of Thutmosis III and Hatshepsut were built farther to the west, at the base of a sheer cliff, still in the low desert but nearly a kilometer (mile) from the floodplain. Some temples, like that of Rameses III at Medinet Habu, are extraordinarily well preserved; some, like the Ramesseum of Rameses II, have become among the best-known monuments in ancient Egypt. One, the memorial temple of Amenhotep III, is arguably one of the largest religious structures ever built: it covered over 350,000 square meters (3,800,000 square feet). But all of them are being threatened today by rising ground water.

This is the downside to the agricultural richness of Thebes. In recent years, the growing of sugar cane, a crop that demands huge quantities of water, has raised the water table on the West Bank to the point that most memorial temples have become embarrassing ruins, buried in waterlogged silts and mounds of rubbish. Many of them simply will not survive even a few decades more. Parts of many temples have already been destroyed by agriculture that has illegally expanded into the archaeological zone. The resulting rise in ground water levels has seriously weakened temple foundations and turned mud brick walls to mud. Hundreds of low-lying shaft tombs have been flooded, their decorated walls destroyed. Several small hamlets today lie between and upon the remains of these memorial temples, and there was also a thriving community here three thousand years ago. Papyrus British Museum 10068 includes a census of buildings on the edge of the Theban cultivation taken in the 20th Dynasty. It covers the area from the Temple of Seti I to that of Rameses III at Medinet Habu, and lists the houses that lay here and the names of their owners. The houses varied from substantial residences of priests and prophets to smaller mud structures of stablemen, beekeepers, and brewers. Geophysical surveys of this area one day may reveal the extent of the ancient buildings and locate temple-related structures now buried beneath agricultural land. Perhaps we will be able to reconstruct, on paper, what the area looked like three millennia ago. Unfortunately, we probably will not be able physically to save these important and fascinating structures.

Beyond the low-lying desert plain a series of hills and wadis extends as much as four kilometers (2 miles) westward from the edge of the cultivation. This terrain was formed twenty million years ago when a pre-Mediterranean sea called Tethys receded, exposing the limestone seabed that would become North Africa. For several million years, torrential rains eroded this landscape, gradually cutting an intricate drainage system that included the Nile Valley and hundreds of tributary wadis. In dynastic times, the resulting web of limestone hills and wadis gave Egyptians the ideal medium into which Theban officials, courtiers, priests, and pharaohs could cut their tombs. From the Old Kingdom onward, but especially during the five centuries of the New

Kingdom, these hills and wadis became Egypt's foremost cemetery. The size and quality of the tombs and the large quantity of grave goods they contained have made the Theban Necropolis one of the richest archaeological sites in the world.

Immediately west of the memorial temples, a series of low hills comprise an area sometimes called the "Tombs of the Nobles." In fact, there are five zones here. Farthest north is el-Tarif, where huge, uniquely Theban *saff* (meaning "row") tombs were cut in the late Second Intermediate Period and early Middle Kingdom. South of el-Tarif lies Dra Abu el-Naga, a rough hillside with about 80 numbered tombs, many belonging to priests and officials of dynasties 17-20 and to the rulers of the Dynasty 17. El-Assasif lies in the area in front of Deir el-Bahari and contains 40 numbered tombs, most of the New Kingdom and later. El-Khokha is a small hill with five Old Kingdom tombs and 53 numbered tombs of dynasties 18 and 19. Sheikh Abd el-Qurna,

named for a mythical Muslim sheikh, has 146 numbered tombs, most of the 18th Dynasty, including some of the most beautiful and frequently-visited of all West Bank private tombs. The southernmost nobles' tombs lie in Gurnet Murrai: 17 numbered tombs, most of them of Ramesside date. In all, there are about 800 tombs in the Theban Necropolis to which Egyptologists have assigned numbers, but in fact there are probably thousands more lying undug in these hillsides.

Looming over the necropolis stands a mountain, the highest peak in the long chain of Theban hills, called the "Qurn," an Arabic word meaning "horn" or "forehead." At the northern base of the Qurn, from where the mountain bears a striking resemblance to a pyramid, lies the Valley of the Kings, "the Great Place." In rock-cut tombs that the Greeks called *syringes*, long corridor-like chambers lead deep into the hillside to elaborately decorated chambers in which the Egyptians buried their New Kingdom rulers.

Sixty-two tombs have been found in the valley (plus a number of unfinished "commencements"), about half of which were cut for pharaohs.

South of the Valley of the Kings lies the Valley of the Queens where about eighty smaller rock-cut tombs were used for the burials of royal family members (male and female) and high officials. Nearby, the village of Deir el-Medina was home to the craftsmen and artists responsible for cutting and decorating royal tombs and many other Theban monuments. Evidence from this village has provided detailed glimpses of the lives of these workmen, their families, and their work.

About a kilometer (mile) south of the village lies Malkata, "the place for picking things up." Amenhotep III built a huge complex of palace buildings here to serve as his residence. It may also have been the residence of many of his successors. To its east, now buried beneath the floodplain, Birket Habu, a huge lake or harbor was dug for use in Amenhotep III's *Heb-Sed* (jubilee) festivals.

30

The goddess Maat protectively embracing the name of Nefertari who stands at right presenting offerings to her, Selket and Hathor. South wall of corridor 2 in the tomb of Nefertari, QV 66, in the Valley of the Queens.

31

Ra-Horakhty before Seti I. On pillar D, chamber J, tomb of Seti I, KV 17, Valley of the Kings.

The close proximity of limestone cliffs
and the richness and extent of adjacent
agricultural land helped maintain the wealth and
prestige of ancient Thebes. But the reasons that it
grew from a sleepy Old Kingdom hamlet to a
substantial Middle Kingdom town and a
formidable New Kingdom city were political and
religious. The reunification of Egypt after the
defeat of the Herakleopolitans at the end of the
First Intermediate Period was largely the work
of Theban rulers and they appointed Theban
officials to high government positions, thus
assuming control of the entire country. During the
Second Intermediate Period, Theban rulers again
achieved prominence; with the expulsion of the
Hyksos in the 17th Dynasty, they again governed
the Two Lands.

Thebes was inconveniently located too
far south to rule a country increasingly tied
economically and politically to western Asia. The
town of Pi-Ramesse was built in the Nile Delta to
ease problems of international communications,
and it assumed importance as Egypt's diplomatic
and military center. Memphis, at the apex of the
Nile Delta, served as the headquarters of the
Egypt's internal bureaucracy. But inconvenient

location notwithstanding, Thebes prospered and was revered. In part, this was due to the religious, political, and economic power wielded by Amen, the principal god of Thebes. Credited with having freed Egypt from its enemies, making it the wealthiest and most powerful country in the ancient world, establishing Thebes as "the queen of cities," Amen, joined with the Heliopolitan solar deity as Amen-Ra, became "king of the gods," the leader of the Egyptian pantheon. The Theban temples of Amen, their huge landholdings, and the large cadres of priests that managed them, ensured that Thebes was Egypt's pre-eminent religious center. It remained the perceived capital city of Egypt long after actual bureaucratic authority had moved away. This state of affairs continued into the Late Period. But, as Egypt's wealth and power declined, so invariably did that that of Thebes. There are Late Period, Greek, and Roman references to Thebes, and a large number of Christian monasteries, churches, and

hermitages on the West Bank. But from about the 11th century AD until its "rediscovery" by European travelers in the late 18th century, Thebes virtually disappeared from history. With the coming of European visitors, however, Thebes, now Luxor, resumed its place as one of the most famous cities in the world.

Tourism at Thebes can be traced back to Late Dynastic times, but it remained a relatively minor activity until late in the 20th century AD. Since the 1990s, it has become a major component of Egypt's economy and the largest employer of the citizens of Luxor. In the 1950s, no more than one or two hundred tourists visited Luxor each day; in 2000 there were about 5,000 daily. The Ministry of Tourism is working to increase that number and hopes to have 25,000 tourists in Thebes daily by the year 2015. This will pose great problems. Only in the last few years have Egyptologists and bureaucrats come to accept that the monuments of Thebes are a

fragile and finite resource that must be actively protected if they are to survive. But only now are plans being made to record, manage, and preserve them. For some monuments, it is certain that these plans come too late.

Many Egyptologists believe that a significant percentage of Theban monuments will disappear within the next fifty years, victims of rising water tables, uncontrolled urban growth, tourism, and improper maintenance. Others believe that they will last only one or two decades. Let us hope that these dire predictions are wrong and that major conservation projects will be undertaken on an urgent basis. No archaeological site on earth is more admired than Thebes. None has so captured our interest or spurred our imagination. None has offered us more information about the lives of our distant ancestors. For the treasures of Thebes to be lost to future generations would be a cultural and human tragedy.

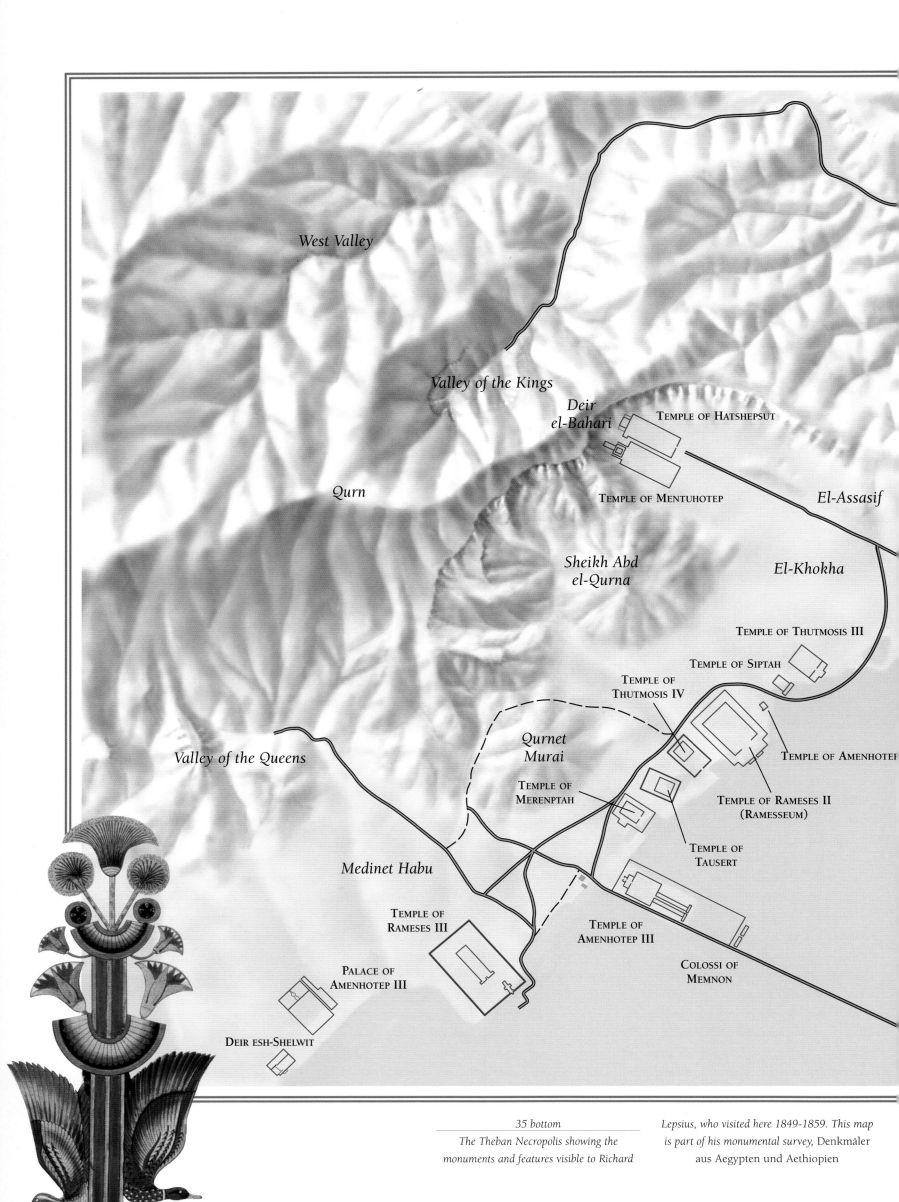

West Valley

Valley of the Kings

Deir
el-Bahari

TEMPLE OF HATSHEPSUT

Qurn

TEMPLE OF MENTUHOTEP

El-Assasif

Sheikh Abd
el-Qurna

El-Khokha

TEMPLE OF THUTMOSIS III

TEMPLE OF SIPTAH

TEMPLE OF
THUTMOSIS IV

Qurnet
Murai

Valley of the Queens

TEMPLE OF AMENHOTEP

TEMPLE OF
MERENPTAH

TEMPLE OF RAMESES II
(RAMESSEUM)

TEMPLE OF
TAUSERT

Medinet Habu

TEMPLE OF
RAMESES III

TEMPLE OF
AMENHOTEP III

COLOSSI OF
MEMNON

PALACE OF
AMENHOTEP III

DEIR ESH-SHELWIT

35 bottom
The Theban Necropolis showing the
monuments and features visible to Richard

Lepsius, who visited here 1849-1859. This map
is part of his monumental survey, Denkmäler
aus Aegypten und Aethiopien

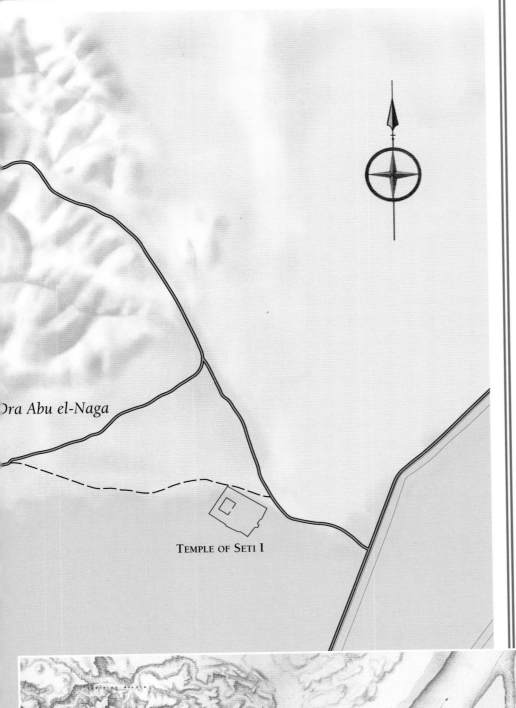

Dra Abu el-Naga

TEMPLE OF SETI I

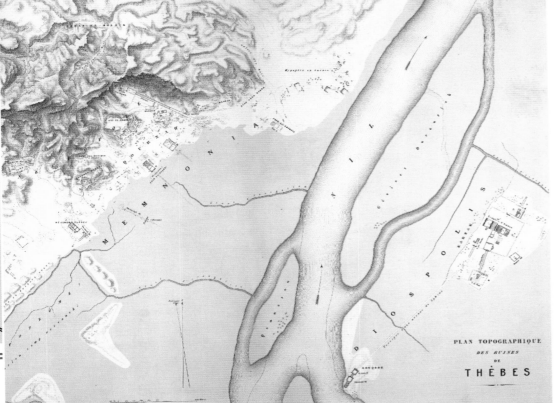

PLAN TOPOGRAPHIQUE
DES RUINES
DE
THÈBES

CHRONOLOGY

EARLY DYNASTIC PERIOD *3100-2700 BC*
(1st - 2nd Dynasties)

OLD KINGDOM *2700-2184 BC*
(3rd - 6th Dynasties)

FIRST INTERMEDIATE PERIOD
2184-2040 BC
(7th - 9th Dynasties)

MIDDLE KINGDOM *2040-1782 BC*
(9th - 12th Dynasties)

SECOND INTERMEDIATE PERIOD
1782-1570 BC
(13th - 17th Dynasties)

NEW KINGDOM *1570-1070 BC*

18th Dynasty *1570-1293 BC*
Ahmose I 1570-1546
Amenhotep I 1546-1524
Thutmosis I 1524-1518
Thutmosis II 1518-1504
Thutmosis III 1504-1450
Hatshepsut 1498-1483
Amenhotep II 1450-1419
Thutmosis IV 1419-1386
Amenhotep III 1386-1349
Amenhotep IV / Akhenaten 1349-1334
Semenkhkara 1336-1334
Tutankhamen 1333-1325
Ay 1325-1321
Horemheb 1321-1293

19th Dynasty *1293-1185 BC*
Rameses I 1293-1291
Seti I 1291-1278
Rameses II 1278-1212
Merenptah 1212-1202
Amenmeses 1202-1199
Seti II 1199-1193
Siptah 1193-1187
Tausert 1187-1185

20th Dynasty *1185-1070 BC*
Setnakht 1185-1182
Rameses III 1182-1151
Rameses IV 1151-1145
Rameses V 1145-1141
Rameses VI 1141-1133
Rameses VII 1133-1126
Rameses VIII 1126
Rameses IX 1126-1108
Rameses X 1108-1098
Rameses XI 1098-1070

THIRD INTERMEDIATE PERIOD
1070-664 BC
(21st - 25th Dynasties)

LATE PERIOD *664-332 BC*
(26th - 30th Dynasties)

GRAECO-ROMAN PERIOD
332 BC-395 AD

The Exploration of THEBES

by Kent R. Weeks

36 top

Richard Pococke's 1738 view of the Theban West Bank. Clearly visible are the Colossi of Memnon (center bottom), Medinet Habu (center left), the Ramesseum (center right), and scores of nobles' tombs (hillside, far right).

36 bottom

Richard Pococke visited Thebes in 1738 and was one of the first Europeans to explore the site and record what he saw. This map of the Valley of the Kings clearly shows the Qurn and the doors of tombs open at that time. Although parts are fanciful or mis-remembered, most of the tombs shown can be identified by their location.

36-37

Claude Sicard's map of Egypt, drawn in 1717, was the first to correctly identify Thebes.

37 bottom

Frederick Norden's drawing of the Colossi of Memnon with the Ramesseum in the background.

Tourism has been a part of Theban life since antiquity. Dynastic visitors were commonplace. Graffiti carved on monuments and hillsides indicate that Thebes was visited frequently during the Ptolemaic period. The graffiti aren't especially profound; for example, one carved on the foot of a colossus of Memnon reads: "From Trebulla. Hearing the holy voice of Memnon I missed you, O my mother, and I prayed that you might hear him too." But they are useful indicators of the kinds of tourists who visited Thebes two millennia ago: most were not scholars but Greek and, later, Roman businessmen from Alexandria and the Fayum. Their tour was motivated by tales of the wonderful Colossi of Memnon and the tombs in the Valley of the Kings. They would have agreed with Diodorus Siculus (ca. 59 BC) that Thebes, filled with "huge buildings, splendid temples, and other ornaments . . . [was a city] more opulent than the others in Egypt or anywhere else." But Diodorus disappointedly noted that the opulent remains could have been even more so: "while the structures themselves have survived until our era, the silver, gold, and ivory, and a king's ransom in precious stones, were carried off by the Persians in the time when Cambyses burned the temples of Egypt." (There is no evidence of this.)

During the Ptolemaic Period, Thebes was in frequent rebellion against Egypt's Greek and Roman

rulers. Battles were fought in 200 BC, 130, 88-85, 30 and later between forces from Alexandria and Thebes. Although Thebes never decisively won these skirmishes, it did manage to maintain a substantial degree of autonomy throughout most of its post-dynastic history. These revolts continued during Roman times and records indicate that many monuments at Thebes were damaged during ensuing battles.

By the 2nd century AD, Christianity was the predominant religion in Egypt, and between 451 and 1065, when a great famine hit Egypt and decimated its population, many Theban tombs and temples were converted to monasteries or churches and statues and scenes of pagan gods were defaced. This was the beginning of the desecration of dynastic monuments at Thebes that unfortunately continues even today. In 390, Constantine removed two obelisks from Thebes to Alexandria, then to the Circus Maximus in Rome and Istanbul, two of the first shipments of Theban monuments abroad. Many more shipments would follow, although not immediately: for more than a millennium after the Coptic period, Thebes was in a dramatic political and economic depression. There is virtually no mention of the city in any text until the 18th century, and even knowledge of its precise location was lost. The first modern European to "rediscover" Thebes was the Jesuit priest, Claude Sicard, who came in 1726 and realized that the monuments he gazed upon were those of the fabled ancient city. Earlier travelers to Upper Egypt had mistaken Memphis, Antinopolis, and other sites for Thebes, and failed to recognize the town itself. But once it had been rediscovered, it again became a major source of antiquities for the European markets. The number of European visitors to Thebes in the 18th century was small; but these travelers published journals and commentaries that contributed greatly to the rise of 19th century interest in ancient Egypt and to the rapidly increasing popularity of Nile Valley travel. Egyptian art and architecture became popular in Europe and interior decorators and architects clamored for drawings of ancient monuments. One of the first visitors to sketch what he saw at Thebes was the Danish artist and engineer, Frederik Ludwig Norden (1708-1742). Norden sketched in the Ramesseum and gave the first description of a temple relief, albeit an erroneous one. Of a scene showing Rameses II seated under a persea tree while gods write his name on its leaves, Norden wrote it is "an allusion to the fall of Adam and Eve."

Another early visitor, Richard Pococke (1704-1765), made the first map of the Valley of the Kings and drew plans of nine tombs. He also sketched plans of the Ramesseum and the Ptolemaic temple at Deir el-Medineh. James Bruce (1730-1794), who discovered the tomb of Rameses III in the Valley of the Kings (KV), later called "Bruce's Tomb," also accurately described how the relief decoration in the temple of Medinet Habu had been carved.

The most important early attempt to record Theban monuments was prompted by Napoleon's desire to learn more about the country that he sought to conquer. His army was in Egypt in 1799-1801, accompanied by over 130 scholars from all fields of science and the arts. They had instructions to record everything from modern costume to natural history to ancient monuments. The results of their surveys, published as the *Description d'Egypte*, appeared between 1809 and 1828. Two of the 19 folio volumes of plates were devoted to the antiquities of Thebes and gave Europeans their first (mostly) accurate description of its monuments. Two members of this scholarly brigade, Prosper Jollois and Edouard de Villiers, prepared a remarkably accurate map of KV, and plans of several KV tombs and many other Theban monuments.

The French were deeply impressed by Thebes. Vivant Denon, French scholar and a senior expedition member, describes the moment he and a detachment of Napoleon's soldiers first saw the Theban West Bank: "At nine o'clock, in making a sharp turn round the point of a projecting chain of mountains, we discovered all at once the site of the ancient Thebes in its whole extent; this celebrated city, the Size of which Homer has characterized by the single expression of "with a hundred gates," . . . This illustrious city . . . the whole army, suddenly and with one accord, stood in amazement at the sight of its scattered ruins, and clapped their hands with delight, as if the end and object of their glorious toils, and the complete conquest of Egypt, were accomplished and secured by taking possession of the splended remains of this ancient metropolis." (Denon, Travels, 1803; quoted By P.A. Clayton, *Rediscovery of Egypt*) . The *Description* and other early 19th-century works on Egypt whetted Europe's appetite for things Egyptian and encouraged large numbers of explorers, adventurers, merchants, and scholars to visit Thebes both to study the monuments and to take them home. So, too, did such popular books as Amelia Edwards' (1831-1892) *A Thousand Miles Up the Nile*, and paintings of the Theban landscape (real and imagined) by such artists as Alma Tadema (1836-1912), David Wilkie (1785-1841), Edward Lear (1812-1888), John Frederick Lewis (1805-1876), and especially David Roberts (1796-1864).

One of the most successful early travelers was Giovanni Battista Belzoni (1778-1823) who had come to Egypt to sell a water-lifting device to the government. He failed at this, but quickly found employment carting antiquities from Theban sites to Europe. He described searching private tombs at Qurna for antiquities: "Surrounded by bodies, by heaps of mummies in all directions . . . the blackness of the wall, the faint light given by the candles or torches for want of air, the different objects that surround me, seeming to converse with each other, and the Arabs with the candles or torches in their hands,

naked and covered with dust, themselves living mummies, absolutely formed a scene that cannot be described."

In the course of his work at Thebes, Belzoni discovered the tombs of Mentuherkhepeshef, Rameses I, Ay, and, most importantly, Seti I. His exhibition, in London in 1821, of the decoration from Seti I's tomb was wildly popular and encouraged great general interest in ancient Thebes and contributed to an increase in Egyptian tourism. Others who worked at Thebes during the first half of the 19th century included James Burton (1788-1862), Henry Salt (1780-

1827), Bernardino Drovetti (1776-1852), Giovanni Anastasi (1780-1860), and Giovanni d'Athanasi (1799-1850).

John Gardner Wilkinson (1797-1875), who worked at Thebes in 1824 and 1827-28, copied scenes and inscriptions in the private tombs that eventually led to his hugely successful study of life in ancient Egypt, *The Manners and Customs of the Ancient Egyptians*, a masterful ethnography of dynastic times. Wilkinson also surveyed the known tombs in the Valley of the Kings, assigning numbers to the 20 tombs then visible and establishing the numbering system still used today.

40-41 top	40-41 bottom
Workmen of Giovanni Belzoni hauling away a statue of Rameses II from the Ramesseum. It now stands in the British Museum, the Museum's largest piece of sculpture.	Belzoni's documentation of the tomb of Seti I (KV 17) was the first complete record ever made of a Theban royal tomb. The drawings were exhibited to huge audiences in London. Belzoni discovered the tomb on 18 October 1817.

41 top left
Giovanni Battista Belzoni, one of the 19th century's most successful excavators and dealer in Egyptian antiquities. At Thebes, he discovered the tombs of Rameses I, Seti I, and Mentuherkhepeshef, among others. He also made significant discoveries at Giza and Abu Simbel.

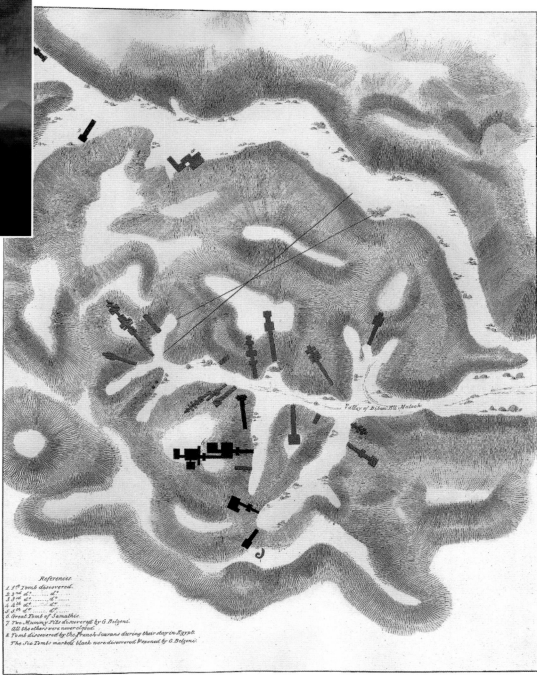

41 center right
Belzoni's map of the Valley of the Kings. The valley's entrance is at the right (north is in the upper right corner). Tombs shown in black were discovered by Belzoni; they include KV 16, 19, 21, 23, 25, 30, and 31.

It was Champollion's correct assumption that royal names were written within enclosures called cartouches that enabled him to read such names as Cleopatra (shown here) and Ptolemy. Those readings ensured Champollion's decipherment of Egyptian hieroglyphs.

After Egyptian hieroglyphs were first deciphered in 1822, the demand for accurate copies of Egyptian texts grew rapidly. Jean Francois Champollion (1790-1832), who was responsible for the decipherment, himself recorded texts and scenes at Thebes and was the first to recognize that royal tomb inscriptions were religious texts, not autobiographical ones. Niccolo Francesco Ippolito Baldessare Rosellini (1800-1843) worked with Champollion and published volumes of 400 folio plates of Egyptian texts and scenes. Together with the *Description* they were Egyptologists' principal reference works for many decades and still

42 bottom
Example of the epigraphic work
of the Franco-Tuscan mission:
pharaoh Merenptah stands
before Ra-Horakhty to receive
life and stability.
From Monumenti dell'Egitto
e della Nubia (Monuments
of Egypt and Nubia)
by Ippolito Rosellini.

42-43
Another example of the
epigraphic work of the Franco-
Tuscan mission published in
Rosellini's Monumenti
dell'Egitto e della Nubia, from
the tomb of Rameses III (KV 11).
At right, the king pours a
libation and offers incense
before Ptah-Sokar and Isis.

43 bottom
King Charles X of France and
Grand-Duke Leopoldo II of
Tuscany established a Franco-
Tuscan expedition to record the
monuments of Egypt in 1827.
Its members are shown here
and included Ippolito Rosellini
and Jean-Francois
Champollion.

remain valuable sources. Champollion's interest
in Thebes was not entirely benign, however.
He also worked to cut pieces of wall decoration
from the tomb of Seti I and have it installed in
the Louvre. In reply to a complaint from Joseph
Bonomi, Champollion wrote: "... one day you
will have the pleasure of seeing some of the
beautiful bas-reliefs of the tomb of Osirei [Seti I]
in the French Museum. That will be the only
way of saving them from imminent destruction
and in carrying out this project I shall be acting
as a real lover of antiquity, since I shall be
taking them away only to preserve and not
to sell."

44 bottom right

Robert Hay whose early work at
Thebes included clearing and
recording in the Valley of the Queens
and whose precise (but still
unpublished) journals are valuable
records of many monuments that
today have vanished.

44-45

The Valley of the Kings from
Lepsius's Denkmäler. Lepsius
worked here in 1844-1845; he
examined and described parts of
twenty-five KV tombs. This view
looks southward toward the Qurn
from near the entrance of KV 11.

45 bottom

Carl Richard Lepsius, whose Denkmäler
aus Aegypten und Aethiopien still stands,
nearly 150 years after its publication, as
one of the most important epigraphic
works ever published. Its 900 plates and
accompanying text comprise the largest
Egyptological publication ever made.

The greatest of the 19th-century
epigraphic expeditions was that of Carl Richard
Lepsius (1810-1884), which resulted in the
Denkmäler aus Ägypten und Aethiopien (1859),
894 folio plates of Egyptian texts, reliefs,
architectural drawings, panoramas, and maps,
including two volumes on the monuments of
Thebes. It is the largest Egyptological work ever
published and today, as Egyptian monuments
deteriorate, it is an increasingly valuable record of
ancient sites. Other epigraphers and artists who
worked in Thebes include Hippolote Antoine Nestor
l'Hote (1804-1843), Achille Constant Theodore Emile
Prisse d'Avennes (1807-1879), and Robert Hay
(1799-1863). Edouard Henri Naville (1844-1926)
published four tombs in the Valley of the Kings in
1887 and (assisted by Howard Carter) the temple
of Hatshepsut at Deir el-Baḥari in 1894-1908.

Photography was used at Thebes by Maxime du Camp (1822-1894), Francis Frith (1822-1898), and other early photographers, but they did not try to produce systematic records of the monuments. Perhaps the first to do so was Felix Guilmant, who produced a complete photographic record of the tomb of Rameses IX. The Metropolitan Museum of Art's photographer Harry Burton (died 1940) was responsible for several major photographic surveys at Thebes including complete coverage of the excavation of the tomb of Tutankhamen and its objects.

The meticulous painted records by Norman and Nina de Garis Davies (1865-1941) of several Theban private tombs resulted in superb publications of ancient scenes. The work of Jan Assmann in Theban tomb 389, Gertrude Thausing and Hans Goedicke's color photographs of the tomb of Nefertari, the work of the Deutsches Archäologische Institut, and the Institut Français d'Archéologie also stand as exemplary publications of tomb relief and painting. Since 1924, the University of Chicago's Epigraphic Survey has been working with a combination of photography and drawing to record Theban temples. Work on the complex of structures at Medinet Habu has

occupied that expedition for much of its history and continues to this day. There have been many other epigraphic missions, most of them concerned with private tombs, working at Thebes over the last century, but much still remains much to be done.

Unfortunately, the recording of Theban monuments, ambitious and accurate though much of it has been, has not kept pace with the deterioration, vandalism, and theft that has plagued Thebes for centuries. One of the first visitors to express concern for the preservation of Theban monuments was Richard Pococke. He lamented that, "They are every day destroying these fine morsels of Egyptian Antiquity, and I saw some of the pillars being hewn into millstones." Auguste Mariette (1821-1881) decried the all-too-common tourist who came to Thebes "with a pot of tar in one hand and a brush in the other, leaving on all the temples the indelible and truly disgraceful record of his passage." And he begged his colleagues to "preserve Egypt's monuments with care. Five hundred years hence Egypt should still be able to show to the scholars who shall visit her the same monuments that we are now describing." Mariette's plea

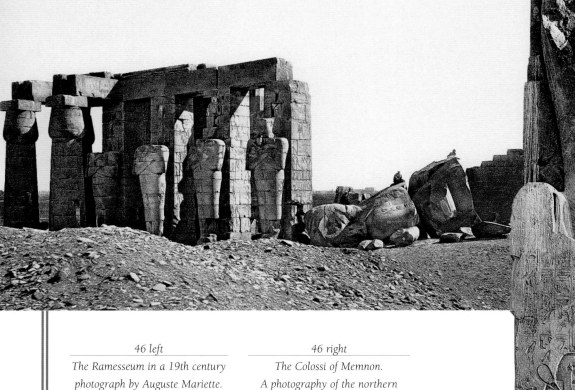

was largely ignored, however and, if anything, the destruction of the monuments became even more common in the later 19th century.

From the 19th century onward Egyptian antiquities were much sought after by European collectors and museums. Many tales have been told about gun battles fought between rival expeditions and diplomatic rows over objects. But by the early 20th century, this Wild West Bank image had ended and the number of objects stolen or sold dramatically declined. It didn't stop completely, however: theft and vandalism still occur at Thebes in spite of the best efforts of the authorities to prevent it. The passing of strict antiquities laws in Egypt has helped, as has the listing of Thebes in 1979 as a Unesco World Heritage Site, and Unesco declarations controlling international trade in antiquities, but as long as there are customers there will be people willing to supply the market.

Archaeological work in Thebes has varied greatly in methodology over the last 150 years, from highly destructive, slipshod ransacking of tombs and temples to the meticulous analysis of microscopic remains. Unfortunately, the former approach has been by far the most common. The Abdel Rassul brothers of Qurna, Ali, Mohammed, Ahmed and Soliman, illicitly dug several Theban sites from 1871 to 1926, including the Deir el-Bahari cache of royal mummies. Inexplicably, the family obtained formal permission in the 1950s to clear a tunnel at the rear of the tomb of Seti I. (Their hopes of finding a gold-filled chamber were still unrealized when funds ran out and the work was abandoned after two years of digging.)

47 bottom
View of the Deir el-Bahari Cirque, 19th century photograph by Auguste Mariette, looking to the north. The temple of Queen Hatshepsut is not visible.

Excavations funded by the American businessman Theodore Davis (1837-1915) in the Valley of the Kings included work by Howard Carter, Edward Ayrton, Arthur Weigall. Carter later cleared the tomb of Tutankhamen (discovered in 1922, worked on until 1932), an enormous undertaking that still is not fully published. William Mathew Flinters Petrie (1853-1942) in 1898, assisted by James Quibell, cleared six of the memorial temples that lie on the edge of the cultivation. Ernesto Schiaparelli (1856-1928) began work on the workmen's village at Deir el-Medina, a project taken over by the French

48 top left

The entrance TT 320, the Deir el-Bahari cache, in a photograph taken by Emile Brugsch in 1881. It was from this tomb that the Abd el-Rassul family plundered royal mummies until apprehended by the Egyptian Government.

48 bottom left

Mr and Mrs Arthur Weigall, the Inspector of Antiquities, Theodore M. Davis, financier and sponsor of excavations in the Valley of the Kings, and Edward Ayrton, archaeologist, at the entrance to the tomb of Rameses IV (KV 2).

48 right

The outer coffin of Queen Ahmose-Nefertari, mother of Amenhotep I, and Ahmed Kamal, an Egyptian inspector of antiquities.

49 left

Outer coffin of Yuya, found in KV 46, the tomb of Yuya and Tuya, by James Quibell, working for Theodore Davis, in 1905. KV 46, tomb of the parents of Queen Tiy, was small but found virtually intact.

49 top right

49 top right

Ernesto Schiaparelli, Italian
archaeologist whose work in the tomb
of Nefertari (QV 66) and at Deir el-
Medina made significant contributions
to the history of New Kingdom Thebes.

49 bottom right

A member of the Italian mission
recording a painted wall in the tomb
of Nefertari (QV 66).

shortly after it began. The French mission also is
working at the Ramesseum and in the tomb of
Rameses II. The Germans have worked at the
temples of Seti I and Amenhotep III, the Swiss at
the temple of Merenptah, the Japanese in the
West Valley of the Kings and at Malkata.
Edouard Naville (1844-1926) worked on
Hatshepsut's temple and those of Thutmosis III
and Nebhepetre Mentuhotep II at Deir el-Bahari
from 1893 to 1907. That work was taken over by
the Metropolitan Museum of Art in New York
from 1911-1932 under the supervision of Herbert
E. Winlock (1884-1950), a highly skilled excavator
and Egyptologist. Restoration work at Deir el-
Bahari, begun by Winlock and Emile Baraize, has
been continued since 1962 by a joint Egyptian-
Polish expedition. Winlock also was responsible
for excavating the burial of slain Middle Kingdom
soldiers, the tomb of Meket-Ra, that of
Hekanakhte, the palace at Malkata, and
Hatshepsut's quarry. The Metropolitan Museum
also cleared and published an important Coptic
monastery at Thebes. At Medinet Habu, epigraphic
work of the University of Chicago in the 1930s
was accompanied by extensive excavations at the
site by Uvo Hölscher.

50 top

Lord Carnarvon, supporter of the excavations of Howard Carter at Thebes. The two men are best known for the discovery of the tomb of Tutankhamen (KV 62).

50 bottom

The entrance to the tomb of Tutankhamen (KV 62) lies below the rectangular stone walls in the center, immediately beside the entrance to KV 9, the tomb of Rameses VI. The pit at the left is part of Carter's excavations of the valley floor.

50-51

Carter at work in the tomb prior to the removal of the second coffin of Tutankhamen

Arguably, there have been seven excavations that are the best-known of the many at Thebes. Each of them thrust Thebes into international headlines and helped to shape people's image of the ancient site. They are: the discovery of the tomb of Seti I by Giovanni Belzoni (1817); the discovery of caches of royal mummies in 1881 (in Deir el-Bahari tomb 320) and 1898 (in the tomb of Amenhotep II); the discovery of the tomb of Nefertari by Ernesto Schiaparelli in 1903; James Quibell's discovery of the tomb of Yuya and Tuya, the parents of Queen Tiy, in the Valley of the Kings in 1905; the 1922 discovery of the tomb of Tutankhamen by Carter; and the 1995 discovery by the Theban Mapping Project of KV 5, a tomb of sons of Rameses II.

But it is the many less publicized projects working to clean, conserve, study, and protect the monuments that provide details of life at Thebes three millennia ago and that will help ensure their survival. Today, over three dozen projects annually work on the Theban West Bank. There are nearly ten projects in the Valley of the Kings alone. Some projects work briefly to clear and record small private tombs; others undertake large-scale clearing of whole sites or record and geophysically survey temples to protect ancient foundations from encroaching agriculture. Aerial and satellite photography is used to map the Necropolis and

create site management plans for Thebes. Today,
there is more emphasis on cleaning and
conservation than ever before and, while it comes
too late for many monuments, new technologies
offer hope for the protection of ancient Thebes.
After generations of pillaging, destruction,
vandalism, and environmental deterioration,
archaeological projects are finally working to
ensure the survival of at least parts of Thebes. It is
to contemporary archaeological and epigraphic
missions that we must look for assurances that
the monuments of Thebes–long taken for granted,
long assumed to be safe and inexhaustible–will
survive even long enough for our children to
learn from and enjoy.

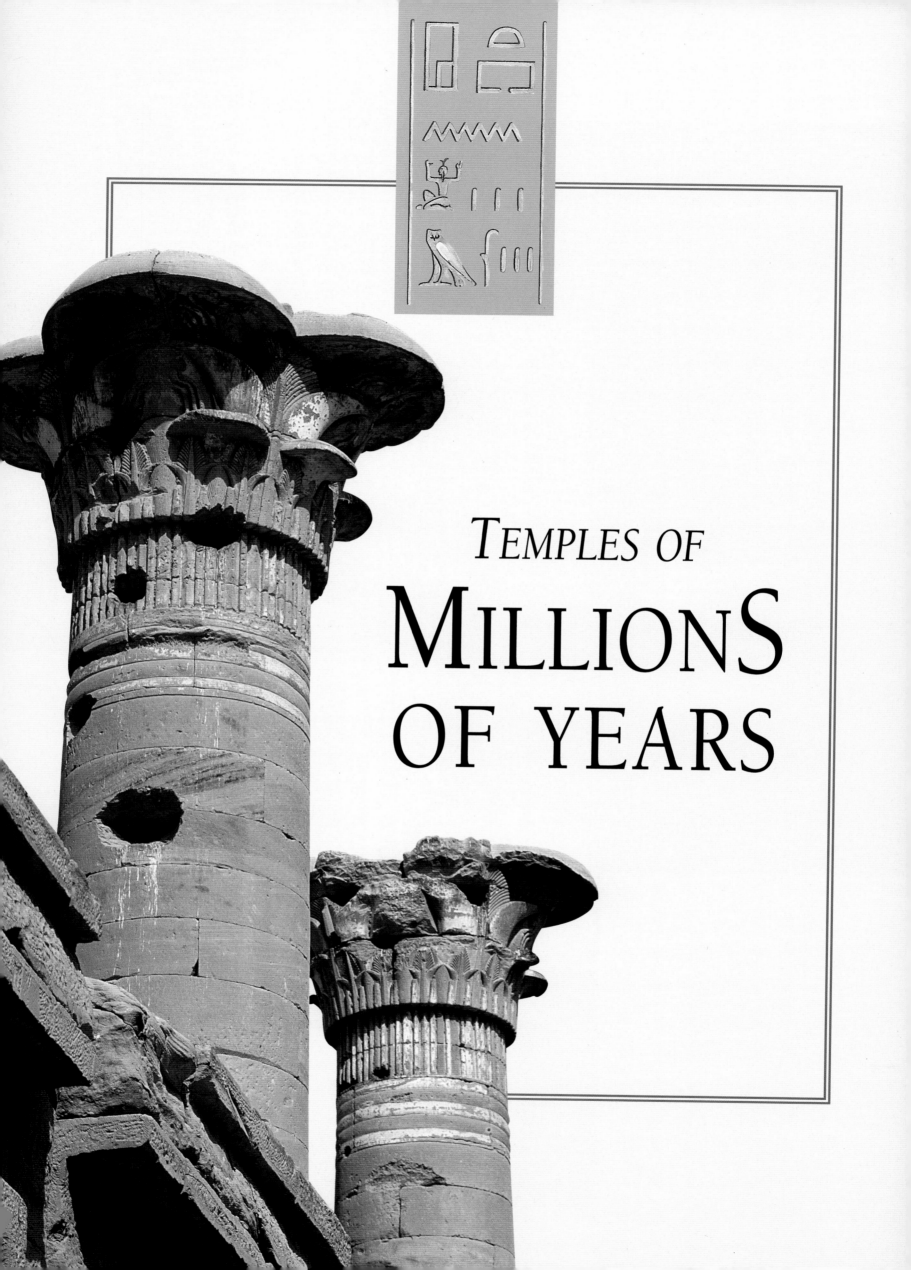

TEMPLES OF
MILLIONS
OF YEARS

Temples Of Millions of Years in Western Thebes

by Betsy M. Bryan

EGYPTIAN BELIEFS ABOUT THE CONTINUITY of life required the provision of offerings—food, drink, clothes, cosmetics—for the statues of any king. These statues, designed to serve as containers for the rulers' spirits, were housed in shrines within cult rooms in temples. Temples associated with specific rulers were characteristic of ancient Egypt from the earliest known kingships. Enormous mud brick enclosures containing cult areas were built for kings of the 1st and 2nd Dynasties at Abydos, while the tombs of these rulers were placed to the southwest further into the desert. These early mud brick temples were succeeded by the funerary temples placed against the

pyramids of the Old and Middle Kingdoms. The funerary temples were approached by causeways, or roads, that linked the temple and tomb with the agricultural valley and, often, a Valley Temple, whose function may have simply been that of a reception area—first for the body itself and then for offerings arriving by boat. In the First and Second Intermediate Periods, lines of kings were buried at Thebes in rock-cut tombs cut into the hills of Dra Abu el-Naga and Deir el-Bahari. Although only the complex of King Mentuhotep II of the 11th Dynasty preserves most of its original elements, the enclosures of all these rulers must once have included a Valley Temple, causeway, temple and

tomb. As Mentuhotep's temple shows us, even the early royal burials at Thebes were designed to include large processional ways and open courts for festival activities. Both Amen of Karnak and Hathor of Thebes were provided for in Mentuhotep's temple, and Hathor's chapel was likely a festival focus even in these early days. Indeed, the features of New Kingdom Temples of Millions of Years all occur in this late 11th Dynasty complex. The developments in religious notions between the 11th Dynasty (ca. 2000 BC) and the 18th to 20th Dynasties (ca. 1550-1070 BC) account for most of the architectural and decorative variations on Mentuhotep's model.

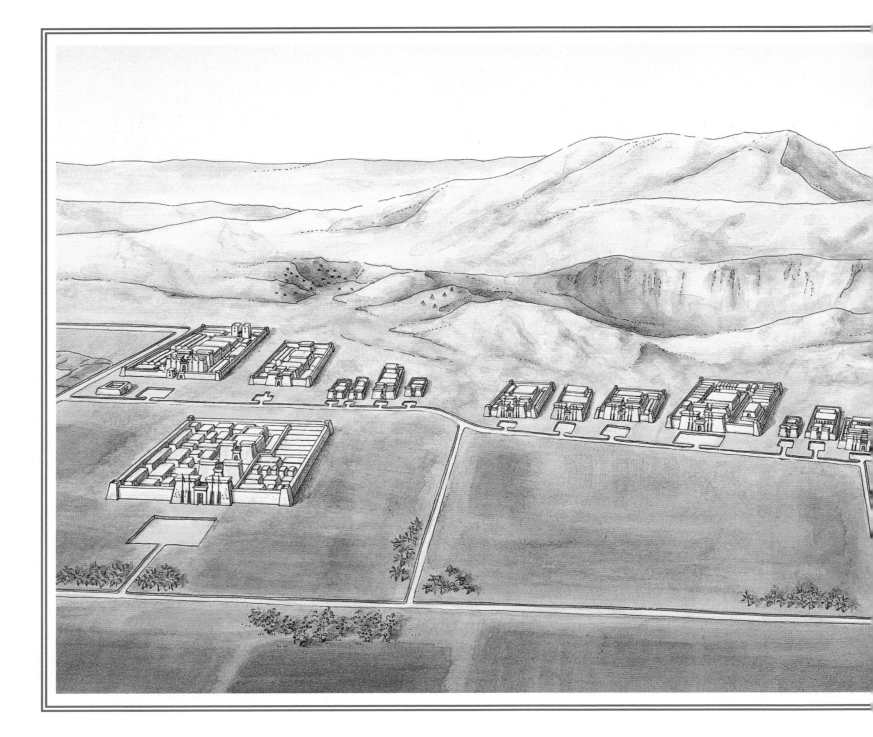

52
Columns from the Necanebo I portico at the Medinet Habu small temple of Amen.

53
The temples of Hatshepsut, Thutmosis III, and Mentuhotep II set against the limestone bay of Deir el-Bahari.

54-55
Drawing showing the temples of millions of years set along the edge of the cultivation at Thebes.

55 top
The Ramesseum in the foreground touching the sugar cane fields, and the bay of Deir el-Bahari at the back.

55 bottom
The Colossi of Memnon front the ruined temple of Amenhotep III.

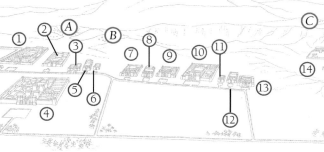

LEGEND

1	TEMPLE OF RAMESES III AT MEDINET HABU	11	TEMPLE OF AMENHOTEP II	
2	TEMPLE OF AY-HOREMHEB	12	TEMPLE OF SIPTAH	
3	TEMPLE OF THUTMOSIS II	13	TEMPLE OF THUTMOSIS III	
4	TEMPLE OF AMENHOTEP III AND COLOSSI OF MEMNON	14	TEMPLES OF MENTUHOTEP, THUTMOSIS III, HATSHEPSUT AT DEIR EL-BAHARI	
5	TEMPLE OF AMENHOTEP SON OF HAPU	15	TEMPLE OF SETI I	
6	TEMPLE OF THUTMOSIS I			
7	TEMPLE OF MERENPTAH			
8	TEMPLE OF TAUSERT	A	VALLEY OF THE QUEENS	
9	TEMPLE OF THUTMOSIS IV	B	DEIR EL-MEDINA	
10	RAMESSEUM, TEMPLE OF RAMESES II	C	VALLEY OF THE KINGS	

TEMPLES OF MILLIONS OF YEARS

The purpose of royal "Temples of Millions of Years" was not solely that of a funerary temple. That function, supplied by priests appointed to serve the ruler's cult, both during and after his lifetime on earth, was combined with several others. The theology of the New Kingdom, as interpreted for the ruler's cult, would guarantee the king's eternal deification and identification with the sun god and with Osiris. The temple shared the work of the tombs in the Valley of the Kings where the texts guaranteeing the king's rebirth with the solar gods were amplified. While the foreparts of the temples celebrated the king's close association with Amen-Ra, in the deepest sanctuaries the king's identification with Ra and Osiris was stressed to guarantee his dominion over the heavens and the netherworld.

As the cult of Amen-Ra of Karnak spread to the west bank of Thebes, rulers associated their Temples of Millions of Years and themselves to that god. We can better understand this idea by citing the titles associated with a captain of boats belonging to the temple of Thutmosis IV (ca. 1400 BC). The man Ipy referred to himself as "Overseer of boats for Menkheprura (Thutmosis IV's prenomen) in the Temple of Amen" and also "Overseer of boats for Amen for the Temple of the Lord of the Two Lands Menkheprura." His son was titled "Priest of

Menkheprura", meaning he served the cult in the same temple. Another man, Ra, served the cults of several temples. He was at one and the same time High Priest of Amen in Men-set (Temple of Amenhotep I), High Priest of Amen in Djeser-Akhet (Deir el-Bahari temple of Thutmosis III), High Priest of Amen in Henket-Ankh (Temple of Thutmosis III), and finally High Priest of Menkheperra (Thutmosis III). We learn several things from these titles. First, the fact of Amen-Ra's residence within the Temples of Millions of Years is clearly established; second it is a form of Amen-Ra specifically associated with the temple; third, the cults of the king and the god are separately defined and provisioned; and fourth, the duties associated with the priests of Amen on the west bank may not have been greatly demanding, since the priest Ra was able to service three different Amen cults simultaneously —in addition to his role as Thutmose III's High Priest. Indeed, the inclusion of Amen-Ra in the

Temples of Millions of Years was the result of festivals that brought the statues of Amen and his family to the west bank of Thebes from his home in Karnak. The Beautiful Feast of the Valley, celebrated in the second month of Inundation season each year, was an important event for the local population. The temple boats of Amen-Ra, Mut, and Khonsu in festal regalia oared across the Nile and were received, no doubt, by throngs of people who ran alongside the procession as it made its way from the quay and Valley Temple up the causeway to the temple of the ruler. Early in the 18th Dynasty these processions followed the old path to Deir el Bahri and rested at Mentuhotep's

complex, but each new Temple of Millions of Years provided a new terminus for the procession. In the tomb of the scribe Userhet (TT 56) mention of the Beautiful Feast of the Valley refers to two venues for the festival. Userhet's son sings to his father that he prays Amen-Ra will favor him when the god rests in "Ab-Akhet at his festival of the western Valley," while elsewhere the High Priest Mery invokes the favor of Amen "when he rests in Henket-Ankh." The first invocation places the Valley Feast in the temple of Amenhotep II, the second in that of Thutmosis III. We begin to envision the procession having numerous stops as the New Kingdom lengthened. In the 19th Dynasty Gurna Temple of Seti I, the Beautiful Feast of the Valley was emphasized by cult space and reliefs, even more than in the temple of Hatshepsut at Deir el-Bahari. Likewise, the Temple of Rameses III at Medinet Habu provides much space for and elaborate decoration illustrating the festival.

58 bottom
Partially reconstructed temple of Seti I at Gurna on the north end of Thebes. The ceremonial palace appears in the lower left of the image, and the pylons are indicated as long low rectangles in the middle of the picture.

59
View of Medinet Habu from the east taken early in the morning when the sun bathes the pylons with light making them into horizons for the sun god.

60-61
On the back of the first pylon at Medinet Habu, Rameses III in his chariot hunts wild bulls in the marshes. The king proved his worthiness to rule by curbing the violent forces in the world – whether this meant bulls and hippotami or Nubians and Asiatics was dictated by the choice for decoration in the temple.

58 top
Soldiers accompanying Rameses III on his hunt for wild bulls. Egyptian soldiers regularly carried shields as here, and axes or scimitars, as does the last soldier. Here, however, they also carry rope to tie up the captured animals.

58 center
Ancient Egyptian temples were painted with bright colors once the decoration was carved. Here at Medinet Habu the ceiling and tops of columns in the court behind the second pylon display bright colors still in pristine condition.

to us are somewhat staggering, as we learn that the storerooms of the Ramesseum were capable of housing grain for some 3,400 families, perhaps amounting to some 15-20,000 people. Clearly this amount of grain was not intended to support solely the bread and beer-making for the cult of Rameses II and the yearly festivals. Rather the royal temple's stores were the wealth used to pay for royal exploits and monuments, whether the building of new temples or, perhaps, the financing of diplomatic exchanges. As such, Temples of Millions of Years, in Thebes and elsewhere, were endowed with personal royal funds, some larger and some smaller.

However, it is important to note that the festival provisions of the temples—whether for the Beautiful Feast of the Valley or for festivals honoring Hathor of the West or Anubis—were tied to the annual religious calendar and could be celebrated independent of the cult of the ruling king. It is somewhat similar to the addition of favored saints and their feasts within the churches of medieval Europe. The king became the patron of Amen-Ra and other gods and built space for them to reside and celebrate.

A final discussion of the role of Temples of Millions of Years concerns their economic power. The royal institutions were endowed with land, people, mineral wealth, and numerous other commodities. The figures left

THE TEMPLE OF
AMENHOTEP III

by Kent R. Weeks

THE MEMORIAL TEMPLE BUILT BY
Amenhotep, son of Hapu, for his pharaoh, Amenhotep
III, was the largest temple ever constructed in ancient
Egypt. Today, it is also one of the most heavily damaged.
Built in the Nile flood plain on the Theban West
Bank, it was intentionally located so that all but its
innermost sanctuary would be flooded during the
annual rise of the river. The temple's reappearance as
the flood receded symbolized order and rebirth.
These floods severely damaged the temple after it
was no longer being maintained, and the damage was
made worse by the fact that many of its walls were of
mud brick. Worse still, its sandstone pylons and columns
were far too heavy for the weak and even non-existent
foundations on which they stood. By the 19th Dynasty
reign of Merenptah, when an earthquake caused
further serious damage, the temple became little
more than a quarry for building stone and statuary.
In the Ptolemaic Period, the entire temple compound
was covered by a dense grove of acacia trees and

almost nothing of its
buildings could be seen.
    Indeed,   the
only parts of the temple
certainly visible after
dynastic times were the
two Colossi of Memnon, seated figures of
Amenhotep III that flanked the first pylon, and a
large stela, originally one of a pair, that stood in the
inner court. The colossi alone were enough to
convince early Greek and Roman travelers that the
site had been a special place. After an earthquake
in 27 BC cracked the northern colossus, it emitted
a bell-like sound each morning as temperature and
humidity rose. Greeks believed that this was the
greeting of Memnon (a mythical African ruler killed
in the Trojan War and made immortal by the god
Zeus) to his mother, Eos, goddess of the dawn. To
hear this "song" was thought to bring good fortune.
(The crying stopped when Septimus Severus patched

62 bottom right

*Colossal head of Amenhotep III. The king
wears the crown of Upper Egypt. His facial
features are highly stylized and anticipate
characteristics of portraiture in the reign
of his son, Amenhotep IV. Red granite, ht.
215 cm (85 inches). From his memorial
temple at Thebes. Luxor Museum, J 133.*

62-63

*Aerial view of Kom el-Heitan, the memorial
temple of Amenhotep III. The central axis
of the temple extended from the Colossi of
Memnon (center bottom), parallel to the
road past a standing stela, eastward to
the modern edge of the cultivation.*

cracks in the colossus in 199 AD.) Greek and Roman visitors left graffiti on the colossi (61 in Greek, 45 in Latin, 1 bilingual) boasting of hearing the voice of Memnon. The emperor Hadrian heard the colossus sing on three different mornings–a sign, he believed, that the gods held him in especially high regard.

Ancient Egyptians called the southern colossus "Ruler of Rulers." Later travelers called the two of them "Shammy" and "Tammy" (perhaps a mishearing of the Arabic words for "left" and "right"). Local villagers today call them "El-Colossat," or "Es-Salamat." (The site as a whole today is called "Kom el-Heitan.") Standing 23 meters (75 feet) tall, each weighing a thousand tons, the colossi were carved from blocks of quartzite taken from quarries either near Giza or Gebel es-Silsileh (scholars are not yet agreed on which). They depict Amenhotep III with his mother Mutemwia (on the northern colossus) and his wife, Tiy (on the southern), and one of his daughters. The chairs on which the king sit have relief carvings on their sides showing Nile gods joining together plants

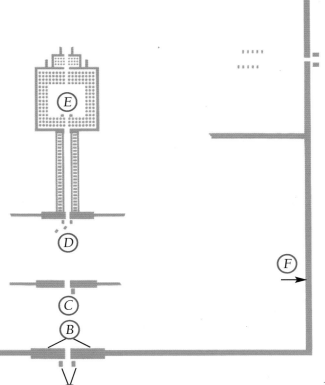

Legend	
A	COLOSSI OF MEMNON
B	FIRST PYLON, MUDBRICK, NOW DESTROYED
C	SECOND PYLON WITH QUARTZITE COLOSSI OF PHARAOH IN FRONT
D	THIRD PYLON WITH ALABASTER COLOSSI OF PHARAOH IN FRONT
E	SOLAR COURTYARD; GRANITE STATUES OF PHARAOH ON SOUTH, QUARTZITE STATUES ON NORTH
F	MUDBRICK ENCLOSURE WALL

symbolizing Upper and Lower Egypt.

The Colossi of Memnon were only two statues in what may have been the largest sculptural program ever undertaken in ancient Egypt. Everywhere in the temple lie fragments of colossal statues of Amenhotep III, of the goddess Sekhmet, of sphinxes (some with the bodies of crocodiles), and other deities. Of Sekhmet alone there were said to be one seated and one standing figure for every day of the year. The Colossi of Memnon stood before the temple's first pylon; two other quartzite colossal statues stood before the second; two more, of alabaster, stood before the third. A long avenue of sphinxes led from the third pylon westward to a large solar court that contained many more statues of the king, Osiride statues that stood 8 meters (26 feet) high. Those in the northern half of the court were of quartzite, those in the southern of red granite. There were many other colossal statues as well, such

as a pair of striding figures of the king that flanked the northern entrance to the temple complex, today barely visible in fields of sugar cane. Some Egyptologists believe that colossal statues of Rameses II in the Ramesseum, including the famous fallen statue of "Ozymandias," were originally carved by Amenhotep III and usurped.

Amenhotep III may have begun his memorial temple early in his reign, but most of it was built during his last decade, when the king celebrated three *Sed* (jubilee) festivals. Much of the temple was dedicated to Amen, but a large part of the northern sector was dedicated to Ptah-Sokar-Osiris. The temple, "The House of Amen on the West of Thebes," originally measured 700 by 550 meters (1800 feet), and covered over 385,000 square meters (4,200,000 square feet). Its grandeur can perhaps be imagined from Amenhotep III's description: "He did (it) as his monument for (his) father Amen, lord of the throne of the two lands, making for him a splendid temple on the right of Thebes; a fortress of eternity out of good white sandstone—worked with gold throughout. Its floors were purified with silver, all its doorways were of electrum. . . ." [B. Bryan, Egypt's Dazzling Sun, p. 91]

64 left

Detail of the Colossi of Memnon: the side of the throne on which Amenhotep III sits shows Nile gods uniting plants that symbolize Upper and Lower Egypt.

64-65

The Colossi of Memnon, seated figures of Amenhotep III accompanied by his wife, mother and daughters. The figures stand 23 m. (75 feet) tall and are among the largest sculptures ever produced in Egypt.

65

Seated figures of Amenhotep III and his wife, Tiy. Three princesses stand beside them but only Henettaneb, the eldest daughter, standing between the couple, is well preserved. The Queen and princess both wear a platform-like headdress that originally supported two tall plumes. From the king's memorial temple at Thebes. Standing 7 meters (23 feet) tall, this limestone statue group is the largest piece in the Egyptian Museum, Cairo. JE 33906.

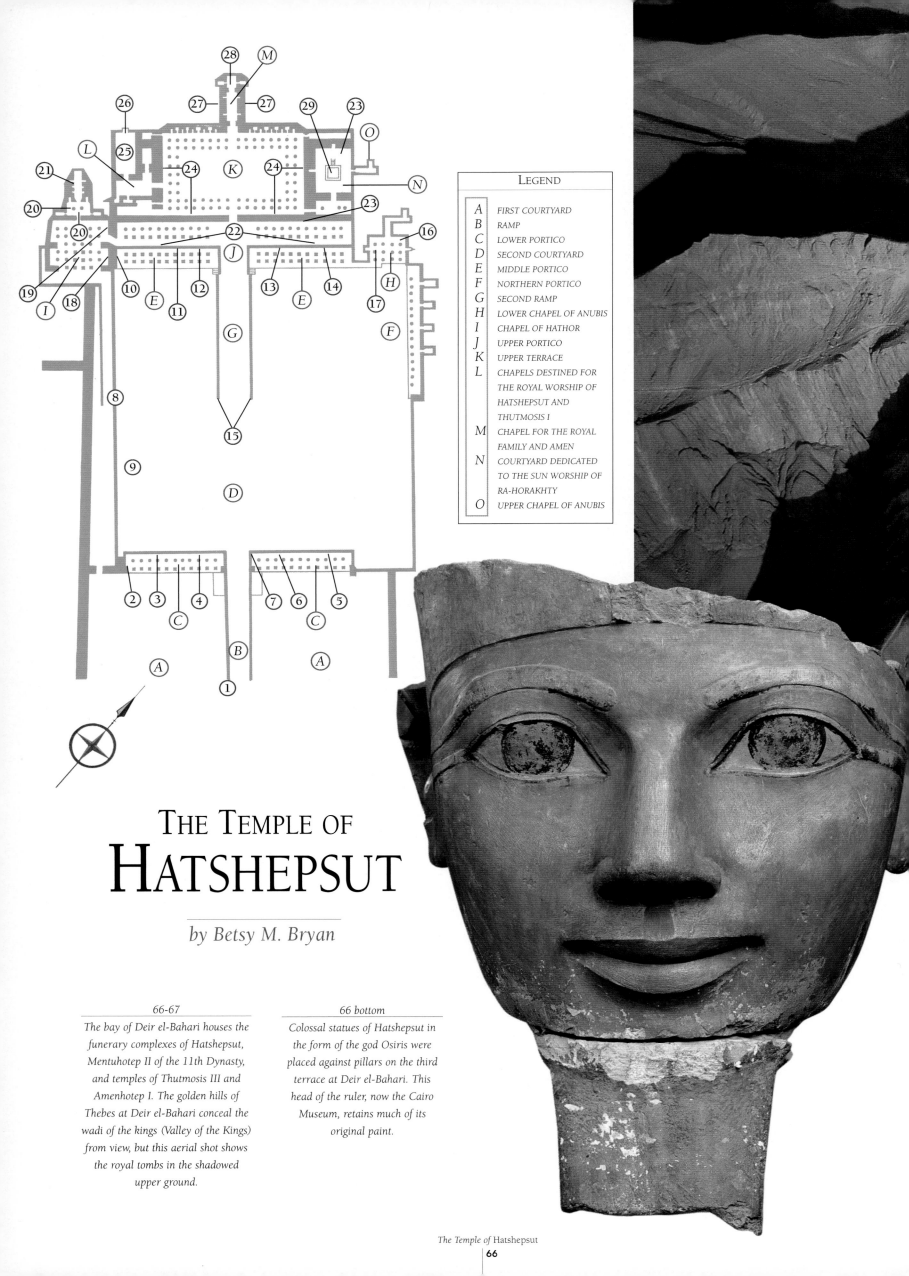

THE TEMPLE OF
HATSHEPSUT

by Betsy M. Bryan

66-67

The bay of Deir el-Bahari houses the funerary complexes of Hatshepsut, Mentuhotep II of the 11th Dynasty, and temples of Thutmosis III and Amenhotep I. The golden hills of Thebes at Deir el-Bahari conceal the wadi of the kings (Valley of the Kings) from view, but this aerial shot shows the royal tombs in the shadowed upper ground.

66 bottom

Colossal statues of Hatshepsut in the form of the god Osiris were placed against pillars on the third terrace at Deir el-Bahari. This head of the ruler, now the Cairo Museum, retains much of its original paint.

Main Scenes

1	Lion in relief on left side
2	Remains of Nubian campaign
3	Ships bringing obelisks
4	Queen offering obelisks to Amen
5	Fishing and fowling
6	Queen offering statues to Amen
7	Queen trampling as sphinx
8	Horus names of Queen in relief
9	(Not visible) Remains of Brick pyramid and temple of Amenhotep I
10	Journey to Punt in six registers
11	Queen before Amen
12	Queen enthroned with Year 9 text of Punt
13	Divine Birth series in lower registers
14	Coronation in upper registers
15	Coiled cobras in relief on balustrades
16	Queen and Thutmosis III before Sokar and Anubis
17	Queen presenting offerings to Amen
18	Hathor cow suckling Queen
19	Festival for Hathor with boats crossing Nile. Four registers
20	Thutmosis III with wine; Queen with milk before Hathor cow suckling Queen and Amen in front
21	Senenmut praising Hathor and Amen
22	Series of Osiride colossi
23	Queen before Thutmosis I with text announcing her coronation
24	South Procession of Opet Festival; north Beautiful Feast of the Valley
25	Priests offering to statue of Queen
26	Tympanums with Thutmosis III and Queen offering to Amen
27	Queen and Thutmosis III with Neferura before bark of Amen and Thutmosis I, Queen Ahmose, and Princess Nefrubiti.
28	Inner room Ptolemaic chapel to deified Imhotep son of Hapu
29	Alabaster altar dedicated to Ra-Horakhty by Queen

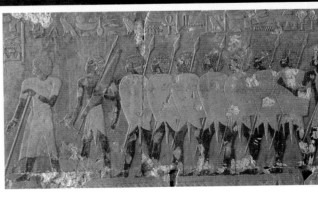

67 bottom
The Punt Reliefs. Here the Egyptian envoys and military escort arrive in Punt on the coast of Somalia to begin a trading mission for incense and other African products.

A view of Deir el-Bahari from the
south shows the temple of
Mentuhotep II (ca. 2040 BC) and
behind it the temple of Hatshepsut.
Both are designed around colonnades
set against platforms reached by
ramps. Mentuhotep's design, however,
led into the cliff where the royal tomb
was placed, while Hatshepsut's
several platforms terminated in
her temple cult rooms.

68 center
A view from the north showing the
second and third terraces of
Hatshepsut's temple. The reliefs
showing the Divine Birth of the
queen are behind the piers on the
lower of these terraces.

Among the favored tourist stops
in Thebes is the temple of Hatshepsut, built up against
the tall limestone cliffs of Deir el-Bahari that hide the
Valley of the Kings from the view of the Nile. Having
been restored over the last forty years by an
archaeological mission from Poland, the temple, which
was destroyed by the agents of Thutmosis III late in his
reign, once again displays three terrace levels,
monumental Osiride figures attached to square pillars,
and cult rooms dedicated to Amen-Ra and to
Hatshepsut herself. When the temple was excavated,
beginning in 1934 by the Metropolitan Museum of Art,
the remains of granite sphinxes, royal statues, and
colossal Osiride figures were found hacked up and
tossed aside for use as quarrying stone. Today the
patient work of excavators and restorers has brought
the temple back to resemble its form in the reign of
Hatshepsut herself.

Hatshepsut began to emerge as king soon
after her husband and half brother Thutmosis II died.
Although Thutmosis III, her nephew and step-son, had
ascended to the throne, Hatshepsut was his regent, as
well as the God's Wife of Amen, and Great Royal Wife.
She continued work on a temple for Thutmosis II in
Karnak, despite his death, and gradually she inserted
herself in it with royal titles and insignia. It is quite
probable that the site of her Temple of Millions of Years
was originally designated for Thutmosis II as well. If so,

that plan was soon abandoned as Hatshepsut's officials, including her Steward Senmut, began to oversee the building of her greatest monument, called in Egyptian "Djeser Djeseru," "The Most Holy of Holies." Although royal temples in Thebes in the 18th Dynasty were largely built of mud brick walls faced with stone relief, Hatshepsut's Djeser Djeseru was carried out from its inception entirely in limestone. The overall plan is one using terraces which lead into long shallow colonnades running north and south from a central ramp. Terraces are characteristic of Theban temple architecture, both before and after the reign of Hatshepsut; her design did not combine the building of pylon gateways into the layout, as did those of the kings who succeeded her. Rather Hatshepsut appears to have taken her cue from Mentuhotep II, whose neighboring complex, built in the 11th Dynasty, combined colonnades with a ramp and terrace as well.

A Valley Temple was planned for the complex, but it appears not to have been completed. Leading up from it, however, was a broad causeway, some 30 meters (100 feet) wide and punctuated by a bark shrine where

68-69

Osiride limestone statues of colossal proportions are set against the square pillars of the third terrace. The ruler appears as a mummy associated with the god Osiris but holds the insignia of kingship (crook and flail) and wears the double crown of Upper and Lower Egypt. This crown links the ruler to the solar deity Atum.

festival processions rested. Lining both sides of the causeway were granite sphinxes of Hatshepsut herself, in such large numbers as to invoke the image of the sphinx alley between Luxor and Karnak Temples on the east bank of Thebes. The causeway ended in an enormous forecourt at the back of which are the lowest level of colonnades. Although the walls of relief decoration behind these square columns are badly preserved, careful study has revealed the content of their scenes. On the south side was a text citing Hatshepsut's victories against the Nubians and next to this four registers showing land and water processions leading up to dedications by the queen to the god Amen-Ra. Ships are shown carrying obelisks quarried and transported from Aswan, and caged lions are brought as well. A military escort accompanies the procession as do priests who

assist in ritual sacrifice for the festival. Hatshepsut then presents the obelisks to Amen-Ra. On the north side of the central ramp are the remains of diverse scenes: the queen is shown fishing and fowling with the gods, offering statues and sacrificial cattle to Amen-Ra, and finally trampling enemies in the form of a sphinx.

On the second terrace are two more colonnades. That on the south records the famous diplomatic and trading mission to the land of Punt, located perhaps in modern Somalia on the coast. Beginning from the south end the relief illustrates the Puntite village built on stilts, and it shows the ruler of Punt, Parohu, and his wife Ity, shown with rolls of fat—a distinctively non-Egytian body type. The Egyptian military are shown arriving to meet the local ruler. The products of Africa appear in the continued reliefs, and the Egyptians take baboons,

70 top

On the south side of the second terrace are the reliefs of the Punt journey. The ruler of Punt, Parohu, raises his hands in thanking god for the visit from Hatshepsut's court.

70-71

Reconstruction of the temples of Hatshepsut, Thutmosis III, and Mentuhotep at Deir el-Bahari. All are placed to connect with the limestone cliff behind and all are designed from colonnades and terraces.

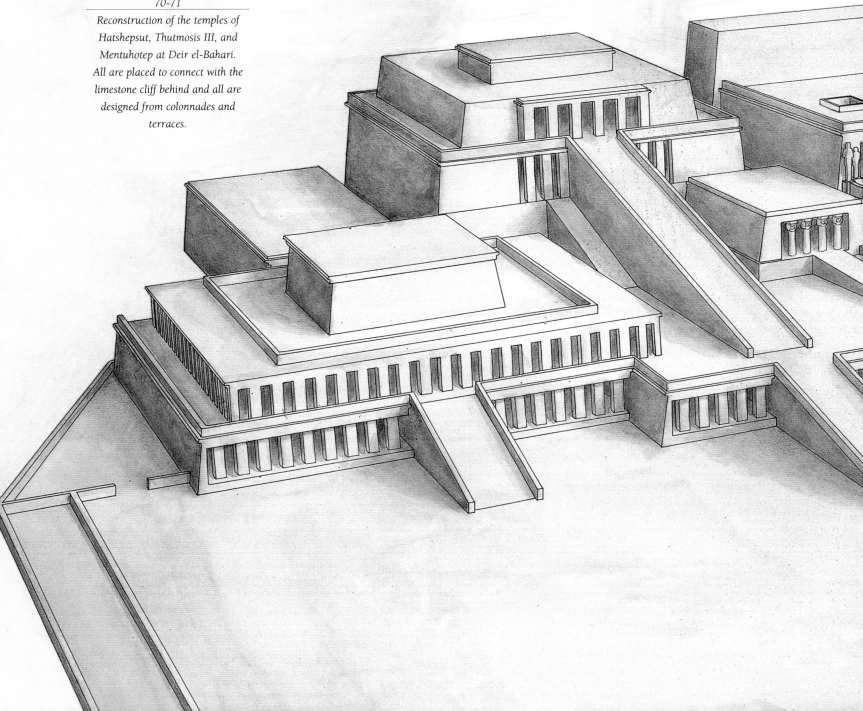

panthers, and incense trees onto their ships. Other reliefs show the ships in transit. The continued representation of incense trees, including ones with their roots preserved in baskets, appears, and finally badly mutilated scenes of the queen presenting the products of the expedition to Amen. North of the central ramp is a cycle depicting Hatshepsut's divine birth from the union of Amen and Queen Ahmose, wife of Thutmosis I. This is the earliest version preserved of the Divine Birth cycle, but it was renewed and usurped by Rameses II in the 19th Dynasty. Some of the scenes are repainted and sometimes difficult to see. The inscriptions are accompanied by scenes that show Amen asking the ram god Khnum to create Hatshepsut on his potter's wheel. The god Thoth is then entrusted to bring Ahmose to the palace. The queen meets Amen and is later escorted to the birth room. The child Hatshepsut and her *ka* are then shown being suckled by the queen and divinities. Hatshepsut is presented before the gods. In the upper register is a badly destroyed version of Hatshepsut's coronation and presentation to her officials by her father Thutmosis I.

South of the middle terrace is a chapel of Hathor, built independent of the temple proper. It is situated to be as close to the early Hathor Chapel in the Mentuhotep II precinct as possible, and it is fronted by a court with decorated walls. Originally this court was open and gave a view of the scenes of a festival associated with coronation when boats crossed the Nile and celebrations for Hathor took place. Later the court was filled with columns topped with large Hathor cow heads. Behind them on the west wall and on either side of the chapel's door are large reliefs of the living Hathor cow who was raised in the precinct. The king (here re-identified as Thutmosis III) hand feeds the cow in an exceptional duet of reliefs. Within the chapel the queen associates herself with Hathor's offspring Ihy. She takes the child/calf's place suckling from the Hathor cow in several scenes. In the inner sanctuary are niches where Senmut showed himself with texts of praise to Hathor.

To the north of the middle terrace is the Shrine of Anubis designed with a small hypostyle hall before two vaulted chambers. In the hall are scenes of the queen offering to Anubis and other gods. Within the first and second halls Hatshepsut offers to Amen, Osiris, and Anubis. The chapel may allude to a cult of Anubis in the region of Thebes. More hidden Senmut texts occur here.

72
Scenes from the Punt reliefs. Cattle
in Punt are shown near the village.
One cow leans over to reach a plant.

73 left
The ka, or spirit, of Hatshepsut joins
the ruler as she approaches the god
Amen to present the revenue returned
from the Punt journey. On the head of
the ka are two arms in the air, the
hieroglyph for ka. This is the divine
essence of the ruler.

73 top right
Puntites carrying bags of trading
materials approach the Egyptians
from the village. Their donkeys
accompany them.

73 bottom right
The ruler of Punt, Parohu, and
his wife, accompanied by bearers
with incense and other Puntite
products, come to greet the
Egyptian envoys.

The third terrace is marked by a series of colossal
Osiride statues of Hatshepsut placed against square piers
north and south of the central axis. A central granite
doorway leads into a pillared court with decorated walls
around its perimeter. Those reliefs illustrate the great
Theban festivals of the Opet, when Amen of Karnak
traveled to Luxor Temple to renew the divine kingship; and
the Beautiful Feast of the Valley, which brought Amen of
Karnak to West Thebes and to Deir el-Bahari annually.
North of this court is a smaller court containing an open
altar to the sun god Ra-Horakhty and smaller chapels to
Amen and Anubis. South of the central court are rooms with
vaulted ceilings where the cults of the queen and her father
are honored. Hatshepsut's place in the boat of the sun god
is depicted, while the hymns of the hours of the day and
night guarantee a cycle of eternity for her. On both the
north and south sides of the central court are niches that
contain images of Senmut who appears to have partaken
of the cult surreptitiously.

The Sanctuary area acts to effect a union between
Amen-Ra and Hatshepsut's family. The boat of the god,
apparently having arrived at the time of the Feast of the
Valley, is shown on the north and south walls with

The Temple of Hatshepsut

74 top left

South of the Punt reliefs is the Hathor Chapel, dedicated to the goddess who was often depicted as a cow. The ruler appears in a relief sculpture suckling the Hathor cow's milk, thus receiving sustenance directly from the goddess and making of her Hatshepsut's mother.

74 bottom center

The god Anubis, with a jackal head and human body, sits on a throne and receives food offerings in his chapel at Deir el-Bahari. Located north of the Divine Birth reliefs on the second terrace, the Anubis Chapel was associated with the netherworld and the gods of the Osirian cults.

74 right

The court before the Hathor chapel contains square piers with Hathor faces, as well as columns with Hathor capitals. The court received pilgrims to the Hathor chapel over many hundreds of years.

75

A column with a Hathor head capital in the court before the chapel. Atop the head of the cow-eared face is a shrine with two uraei cobras set in it. The shrine is framed by two volutes identified with the cow horns of the goddess. Taken together the column is a colossal image of a sistrum, or rhythmic rattle, used in temple cult to please gods, particularly Hathor.

Thutmosis I, Queen Ahmose, and a princess Nefrubiti standing behind it facing the outer doorway. Hatshepsut, Thutmosis III, and Princess Nefrura offer to Amen and the bark of the god and, as is implied by their placement, to Thutmosis I and the royal females. Elsewhere in niches Hatshepsut, Ahmose, and Thutmosis II receive offerings from priests. The rooms of the Sanctuary were also used in the Ptolemaic era and contain dedications to the deified Imhotep and Amenhotep son Hapu, as well as other gods.

The building of Djeser Djeseru was completed in fifteen years but perhaps only some twenty five years later Thutmosis III ordered the destruction of the monument. He built his own temple at Deir el-Bahari, "Djeser Akhet," "[Amen is] Holy of the Horizon" and designed it to be much higher, if smaller, than Hatshepsut's monument. Because Djeser Akhet was later robbed of its stone by temple builders of the Ramesside era, Hatshepsut's Djeser Djeseru and Mentuhotep's Hathor Chapel remained important sites of pilgrimage and festival procession throughout ancient Egyptian history.

THE GURNA TEMPLE
OF SETI I

by Peter Brand

76 right
This fine statuette of Seti I is typical of the high standards of art produced during his reign. The king wears a long pleated gown and a long braided wig with the royal cobra or uraeus on his brow.

76-77
An arial view of Seti I's memorial complex nestled in the modern village of Qurna from which it derives its name. Only the rear portions of the temple building are well preserved. The magazines, palace and enclosure walls are modern restorations.

THE MEMORIAL TEMPLE OF SETI I, second king of the 19th Dynasty, is the northernmost of a series of New Kingdom royal memorial temples on the desert edge where it meets the fertile valley. Seti chose a site in western Thebes called *Hefet-her-nebes*, "Opposite its lord," the "lord" in question being the imperial god Amen-Ra whose principle sanctuary at Karnak lay on the eastern bank of the Nile directly facing Seti's edifice. The temple faces east, towards Karnak. Today the site is known as Gurna, a reference to the Qurn or "horn," the Arabic name for the highest peak on the mountain that dominates Western Thebes.

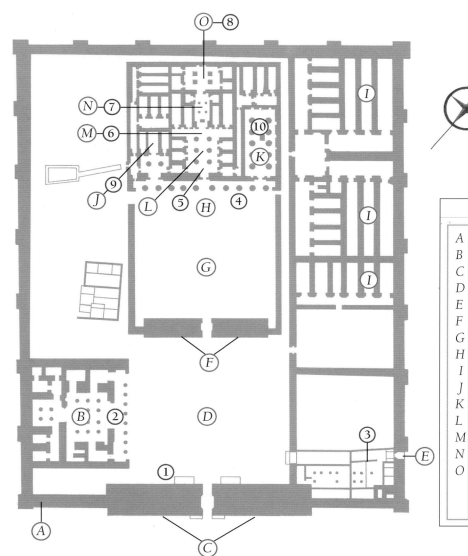

LEGEND		MAIN SCENES	
A	ENCLOSURE WALL	1	Damaged reliefs in the gateway and four votive stela of Seti I and Rameses II adoring the gods
B	ROYAL PALACE		
C	FIRST PYLON	2	A badly damaged "window of royal appearances" with Asiatic prisoners
D	FIRST COURTYARD		
E	NORTH ENTRANCE	3	Inscribed blocks from the ceiling and walls of the First Pylon gateway and outer court showing the king worshiping the gods
F	SECOND PYLON		
G	SECOND COURTYARD	4	Procession of barques of Theban Triad and the king in the Festival of the Valley
H	PORTICO		
I	MAGAZINES	5	Seti I and Rameses II worship the Theban triad and other gods
J	RAMESES I SUITE		
K	SUN COURT	6	Rameses II worships the gods and the divine Rameses I and Seti I
L	HYPOSTYLE HALL		
M	TRANSVERSE CORRIDOR	7	Seti I before the sacred barque of Amen-Ra
N	SANCUARY OF AMEN-RA	8	Seti I worships the gods. Funeral of Osiris in side room
O	FOUR PILLARED HALL		
		9	Thoth worships divine Seti I and the king's sacred barque
		10	Rameses II adores Ra, Amen and other gods

In antiquity, the temple was reached by a canal extending from the Nile and alongside the main overland road on the West Bank that led to Queen Hatshepsut's nearby memorial temple at Deir el-Bahari. This prime location ensured that Seti's temple would be an important setting for the Beautiful Festival of the Valley. During this annual feast, the cult statues of the gods Amen-Ra, his consort Mut and son Khonsu, were transported across the Nile in Amen-Ra's huge gilded river barge via canal to Deir el-Bahari with stopovers in the memorial temples of the reigning pharaoh and his most important ancestors. On land, the statues were carried on the shoulders of priests, enclosed within gilded boat-shaped shrines called sacred barques.

Seti I ruled at a time when the pharaonic office had lost some of its repute after the excesses of the "heretic" king

Akhenaten. After the death of Akhenaten's childless successor Tutankhamen, three non-royals came to the throne by appointment. The third, Rameses I, was followed by his son Seti I who restored the hereditary principle. Rameses I's reigned less than two years, not enough time to complete his own temple, and it fell to Seti I to provide for his father's cult within his own Gurna temple.

The temple was named "Seti I is Beneficent in the Domain of Amen which is on the West of Thebes." Gurna was a companion to Seti I's most impressive monument, the Great Hypostyle Hall he built within the Karnak temple complex across the river, which he called simply "Beneficial is Seti I in the Domain of Amen." By name, only the phrase "on the West of Thebes" distinguishes Gurna from the Karnak Hypostyle Hall and these similar names indicate that the two

monuments were linked together in their function; both were dedicated to the cults of both Amen-Ra and the divine king himself.

Today, only the rear third of the Gurna temple is still intact because it was built entirely of stone. The rest was constructed largely of mud brick, now mostly gone.

The whole complex was surrounded by a thick mud brick enclosure wall with tower buttresses set at intervals because Egyptian temples were considered divine fortresses whose walls protected the sacred world inside the precinct from the chaotic forces of the profane beyond. These walls have been restored and the precinct is now entered via a side gateway at the north east corner because the original main entrance on the east side is blocked by debris and by the modern village of Gurna directly abutting the facade.

Funerary temple complex of Seti I on the west bank of Thebes. Lying on the desert edge, the temple complex of Seti I is surrounded by imposing mudbrick walls resembling a fortress. Inside, the temple building proper includes two open courts fronted by pylon gateways. Only the roofed portions at the back are made of stone. Surrouding the temple is a complex of storage magazines, a symbolic palace and a sacred well.

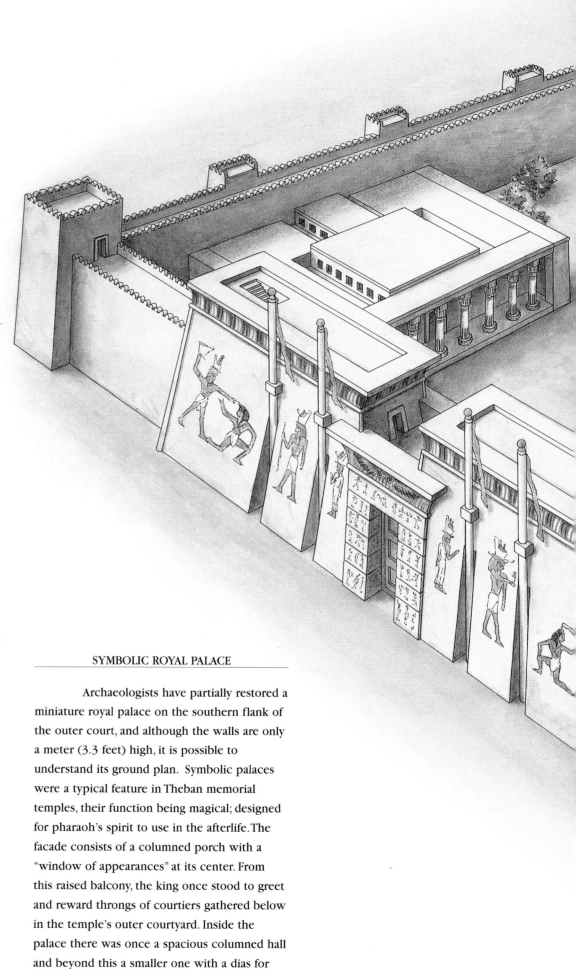

OUTER PYLON GATEWAY AND COURTYARD

Inside its precinct, the main temple is subdivided into three parts. The outer and middle sections consist of two open courtyards, each fronted by massive twin towers framing a monumental gateway, called a pylon. Only the lowermost courses of the outer pylon are preserved, including some badly decayed limestone reliefs lining the passage through the outer pylon. Just inside the outer courtyard a pair of colossal sphinxes abut the back of the first pylon with only their pedestals and fragments of their crowns remaining. The pedestals are inscribed with Seti I's titles and a series of "name rings." From the tops of these oval loops sprout the heads and torsos of bound prisoners; inside each ring there is the name of a foreign city, country or people considered to be Egypt's foes. Dozens of these rings formed a list of ancient place names that are an invaluable source for the history and geography of the ancient world. Nearby there are four round-topped slabs of sandstone inscribed with images of Seti I and Rameses II worshiping the gods. Today, the outer court resembles a sculpture garden since a number of inscribed blocks from destroyed parts of the temple have been set up here. They include part of the great sandstone lintel incised with images of Seti kneeling before the gods and massive ceiling slabs with the outstretched wings of vultures, all from the gateway of the outer pylon. Since they were built largely of mud brick, almost nothing survives of the inner and outer courtyards or of the second pylon gateway that once separated them.

SYMBOLIC ROYAL PALACE

Archaeologists have partially restored a miniature royal palace on the southern flank of the outer court, and although the walls are only a meter (3.3 feet) high, it is possible to understand its ground plan. Symbolic palaces were a typical feature in Theban memorial temples, their function being magical; designed for pharaoh's spirit to use in the afterlife. The facade consists of a columned porch with a "window of appearances" at its center. From this raised balcony, the king once stood to greet and reward throngs of courtiers gathered below in the temple's outer courtyard. Inside the palace there was once a spacious columned hall and beyond this a smaller one with a dias for the royal throne. The side rooms giving off these chambers included a royal bedroom, bath chamber, and storage magazines.

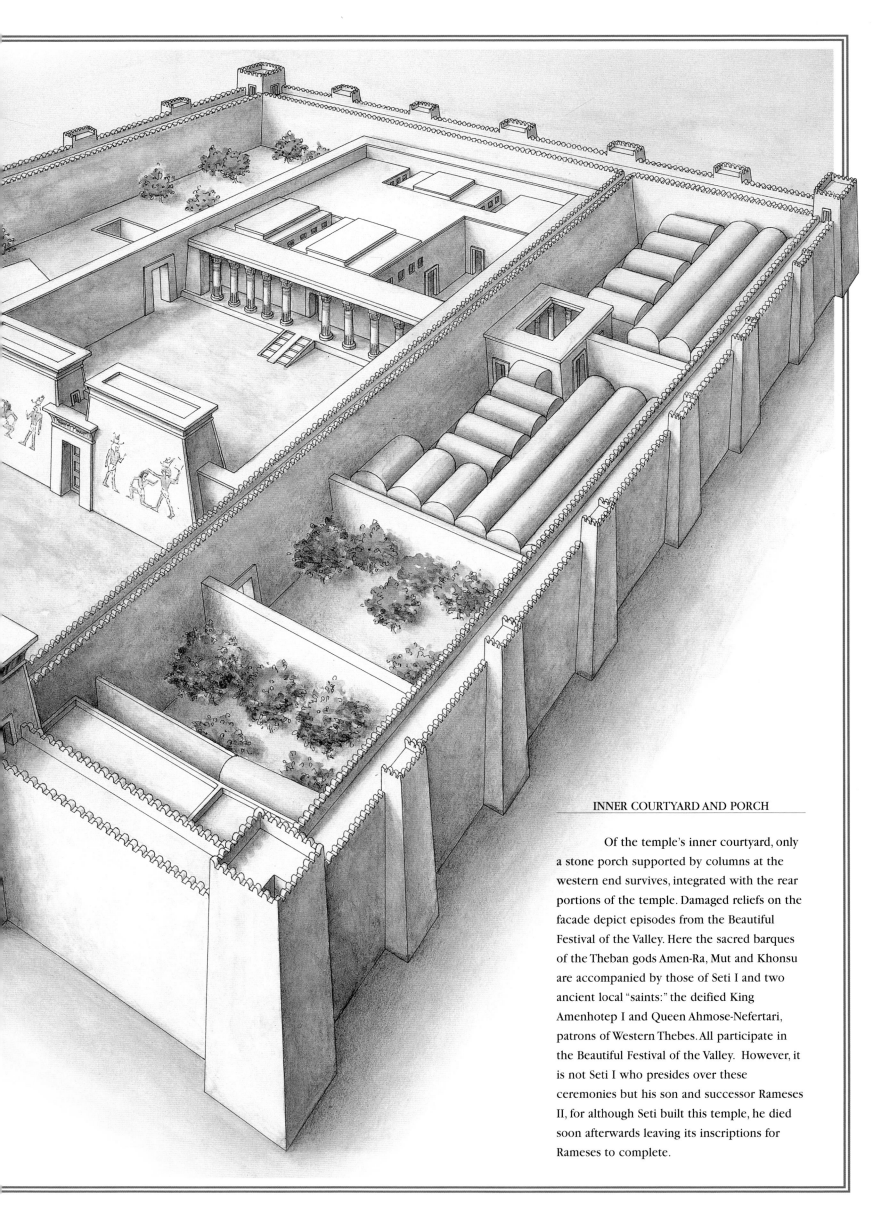

INNER COURTYARD AND PORCH

Of the temple's inner courtyard, only a stone porch supported by columns at the western end survives, integrated with the rear portions of the temple. Damaged reliefs on the facade depict episodes from the Beautiful Festival of the Valley. Here the sacred barques of the Theban gods Amen-Ra, Mut and Khonsu are accompanied by those of Seti I and two ancient local "saints:" the deified King Amenhotep I and Queen Ahmose-Nefertari, patrons of Western Thebes. All participate in the Beautiful Festival of the Valley. However, it is not Seti I who presides over these ceremonies but his son and successor Rameses II, for although Seti built this temple, he died soon afterwards leaving its inscriptions for Rameses to complete.

HYPOSTYLE HALL, SIDE CHAPELS AND TRANSVERSE CORRIDOR

The innermost part of the temple is further subdivided into three parts, accessed by separate doorways through the porch. The grand central gateway leads to the temple's hypostyle hall, a large chamber supported by six columns shaped like papyrus stalks. Six small chapels line the walls, three each on the north and south sides. The two eastern rooms are "dummy chapels," really passageways connecting to other parts of the temple.

The four westernmost chapels are dedicated to various aspects of the king's funeral cult. The central ones are the most important. On the north side, reliefs in the central chapel depict rites showing the pharaoh's identity merged with the god Amen-

Ra's. Its southern counterpart shows the divine king adored and attended by various gods. Reliefs in the south-west side chapel show the king's sacred barque, and here we also see him attended by a goddess wearing a tall rectangular hieroglyph on her head, with smaller ones inside it. These spell out the temple's name. The goddess herself, symbolically called Seti's mother, is a personification of the whole Gurna temple. The north-west chapel is dedicated to images of Seti's unification with Osiris, traditional god of the underworld.

The reliefs in these side chapels show only Seti I with the gods, but on the walls of the hypostyle hall which gives access to them, Seti is accompanied by his son Rameses II. Their titles are carefully balanced in inscriptions embellishing the doorframes, columns and ceiling. Seti completed the four side chapels, but he died before the hypostyle was inscribed, leaving that work for Rameses. Rameses commemorated his deceased father by showing Seti I alongside himself as though

his father were still alive.

Adjoining the hypostyle hall there is a transverse corridor. Its floor is raised slightly and is accessed via a short ramp. Traditionally, the floors of Egyptian temples gradually rise towards the innermost sanctuary in imitation of the primordial mound believed to be the first land to have arisen from Nun, the primordial ocean, at the dawn of creation. Upon this primeval mound, the sun god began to create the universe. Every temple, then, was a model of that creation, and its hypostyle hall represented the reed marsh sprouting at the edge of the primeval island.

80-81
Only the stone built hind portion of the temple survives fronted by the portico at the back of the second court. The courts and pylons were built of mud brick, but inscribed stone jambs and lintels from their gateways now line the approach to the portico.

81 bottom
One of the closed-bud papyrus columns from the hypostyle hall which supports one of the few intact roofs of any Theban temple. The fine bas reliefs covering the walls were inscribed by Rameses II after the death of his father Seti I, yet both kings are named in the reliefs and inscriptions as if Seti was still alive. The doorway leads into one of the four side chapels.

The Gurna Temple of Seti I

82 top
Fine bas reliefs from the four-pillared hall behind the sanctuary of Amen are among the only reliefs in the temple completed in Seti I's lifetime. The scenes depict him performing the daily cult ritual for Amen-Ra. Here Seti dresses the god in a cloth mantle.

82 center
Rameses II offers two bowls of wine to Amen-Kamutef and Isis from a wall relief in the Rameses I suite of cult rooms. The somewhat crude

sunk relief was favored by the king from the earliest days of his reign and compares poorly with the fine bas reliefs of his father.

83
The deified Seti I stands behind Khonsu in a relief of Rameses II in a room dedicated to the cult of his grandfather Rameses I. The crook folded across his chest and the ankh dangling by his side identify him as a god. Both Rameses I and Seti I were worshiped here by the pious Rameses II.

MAIN SANCTUARIES OF THE THEBAN GODS

The transverse corridor has five doorways through its western wall and the three central portals lead to the chapels for the sacred barques of the Theban Triad. The largest, given pride of place in the center, belongs to Amen-Ra. There are smaller chapels for Mut immediately to the south, and Khonsu to the north. These in turn, are flanked by two deeper ones on the extreme north and south, both of whose walls are so denuded that no inscriptions survive to identify their divine occupants. The chapel walls of the Theban gods have images of Seti adoring their sacred barques that were once lodged here during the Festival of the Valley. The most impressive and best preserved scenes are in the Amen-Ra chapel. Here the king, dressed in a long pleated gown, worships Amen-Ra's sacred barque with its ram-headed prow and stern pieces, this animal being sacred to him. The large cabin shrine housing the cult statue is embellished with a complex mosaic of hieroglyphs spelling out the names of both king and god in a kind of cryptogram.

Moving through a doorway at the back of Amen-Ra's chapel, we pass into a large rectangular hall supported by four square piers, all covered with scenes of the king worshiping various gods. In the center of the west wall, at the very back of the temple, there was the now destroyed "false door," a magic portal through which the king's *ka*, or spirit, once passed from the netherworld into this one to receive food offerings it needed to survive in the Afterlife.

False doors such as this are a standard feature of the mortuary cult, and there is an intact example in Rameses I's chapel elsewhere in the Gurna temple.

Four more side rooms give off the rear hall, most of them being largely destroyed. Fortunately, some interesting scenes have survived in the north-west room, where there are episodes from the funereal rites of the god Osiris. Here the murdered god's twin sisters Isis and Nephthys stand doubled over with their hands nearly touching the ground in mourning over him while Horus and the king kneel to either side of his bier. Osiris himself lies on a lion-shaped funeral bed.

SOLAR SHRINE

To the north of the temple's central axis, there is a large rectangular courtyard dedicated to the cult of the Egyptian sun god Ra. Niches line the four walls and an offering table in the form of a podium stands in the center. A roofed portico, once supported by ten columns, has entirely vanished. This type of "solar court" was a standard feature in royal memorial temples at Thebes. They are always located on the north side of the temple, so that they lie closest to the sun god Ra's principle sanctuary, far to the north at Heliopolis. Behind the solar court are four ruined storerooms containing some unfinished inscriptions. This whole northern wing was inscribed only after Seti I's death, by Rameses II.

At the south end of the portico facade, there is a suite of rooms dedicated to the cult of Seti I's father Rameses I who was unable to construct his own temple during his brief reign. An outer vestibule is supported by two columns, and its walls are decorated with scenes of Rameses II. In many of these reliefs he worships both his deceased

and deified father Seti I and grandfather Rameses I.

The decoration includes a combination of fine raised reliefs and cruder sunk relief. Rameses II inscribed the doorways, roof and columns with his own names and titles alongside those of his father. This combination of the names of both kings led many scholars to believe that they had ruled jointly in a coregency. It now seems likely that Rameses II piously completed his father's

rooms were engraved in a crude sunk relief by Rameses II. The central one was completed in fine bas reliefs by Seti I and is dedicated to the cult of his own father Rameses I. Here again, there are representations of the sacred barque of Amen-Ra with its distinctive ram-headed aegises. Behind these are twin images of Seti anointing the deceased Rameses I who is dressed in the guise of Osiris. The point of all this was to commemorate Rameses I's mystical union with both Amen-Ra and Osiris in the afterlife.

The back wall is Rameses I's well preserved false door by which his spirit came into the chapel to receive food offerings. Because space was limited, separate functions were crammed into this one room, whereas elsewhere, several chambers were dedicated to these differing aspects of the divine Seti I himself in his portion of the temple.

temple after Seti I died; such were the obligations of a dutiful son. But to enhance his own legitimacy as pharaoh, Rameses used the project to emphasize that he was both the son and grandson of kings when he himself and his newly founded royal house were still considered young and inexperienced.

Besides the main entrance, the vestibule has five other portals. The north and south doors lead to other parts of the temple, including a suite of ruined side rooms to the west, behind the Rameses I suite. On the west wall there are three long chambers. Two side

SACRED LAKE AND STORAGE MAGAZINES

Beyond the rear of the temple proper, on its the south side, lies the sacred lake, shaped more like a large open well with a sloping access ramp. Here the priests came to draw ritually pure water to wash themselves for the sacred rites. Finally on the north side of the temple some much ruined mud brick storage magazines were once stocked with grain, produce and other goods that supported the priests and workers connected to the temple.

Although Seti I's memorial temple was not as grand that of his son Rameses II, the Ramesseum, or of Rameses III at Medinet Habu, Gurna was the prototype for all the Ramesside memorial temples built over the next two centuries.

84 top
Male and female demi-gods march in procession laden with offerings. Each one of these "fecundity figures" symbolizes a different province of Egypt. Lotus plants on their heads identify these two as personifying Upper Egyptian locales.

84 center
Rameses completed only some portions of the temple in the years following his father's death. The rest of the work was not completed until years later. Beside a portal inscribed with Rameses' titulary, the barque of Mut is carried by priests.

84 bottom
Reliefs of Rameses II in the solar court may have been completed in his 30th year in preparation for his first jubilee. Here the king is shown making an offering to the sun god Ra-Horakhty. Beyond the missing side walls are the remains of the hypostyle hall.

84-85
View of the four columned hall and ruined side chambers behind the main sanctuary. This hall is supported, unusually, by square pillars. The pillars and walls are decorated with the fine bas reliefs typical of Seti I's reign. The ritual scenes on the walls were among the last carved before the king's death.

85 bottom
The portable sacred barque of Amen-Ra is portrayed in intricate bas relief on the side wall of the god's main chapel. The prow and stern are fitted with ram figureheads bedecked with gold collars. A mosaic of hieroglyphic designs on the walls of the cabin shrine honored the god and spelled out the king's name.

General bird's eye view of the Ramesseum, photographed from the west. Built of sandstone, the temple occupies the central part, surrounded on three sides by a huge economic complex in mud brick. Extending for several hectares, the religious, administrative and economic center of the foundation of Rameses II, was one of the largest at West Thebes, during the New Kingdom.

86 bottom

Usermaatra was Rameses' name when he was still a prince. He bore this name until the second half of year 2 of his reign, after which his coronation table bore the full version: "Usermaatra Setepenra" or "Powerful is the universal order of the God Ra," "He whom Ra hath chosen."

87

A statue of Rameses II stood to the left of the axial staircase of the second courtyard. Only the magnificent head in quartzdiorite of this statue still stands today. Still complete at the time of Diodorus of Sicily, this statue seems to have been taken apart later, probably during the Christian period. The king, who wears the nemes with the double crown or pshent, was depicted seated.

THE RAMESSEUM
THE TEMPLE OF RAMESES II

by Christian Leblanc

ONE OF THE MOST GRANDIOSE buildings on the west bank of Thebes, the Ramesseum was built in the 13th century BC by one of the greatest pharaohs of the New Kingdom: Rameses II. This vast complex, erected at the edge of cultivated land and the piedmont of the Libyan mountains, now stands partly ruined, although its original surface area is estimated to have covered over six hectares. It included a beautifully elegant temple, a mammisi, apparently the first of its kind, port facilities and a sacred lake, as well as a large complex of mud brick buildings that housed administrative and economic offices and the law courts. Two walls enclosed the *temenos* which was accessed from the east through a monumental gate that has not survived. The ground plan is classical, with forecourts, pylons, porticoed courtyards, vestibule, hypostyle halls and sanctuary. Originally the Ramesseum also included secondary chapels, crypts, a chthonian as well as a solar complex and a library. To the south of the first courtyard lie the remains of the royal palace that was used by the king and his family, especially during certain important Theban liturgies. The reception hall as well as the throne room can be identified from the still-preserved ground plan of the palace which, in its original state, was equipped with a façade featuring a large opening known as the window of appearance, a sort of balcony from which the king would hand out sumptuous rewards to the most deserving dignitaries. Adjoining the official part of the palace to the west, a long corridor led to the royal private apartments, the ruins of which, if they still remain today, are buried under the peasant dwellings that have taken over the land.

Several dependencies shared the area of the administrative and economic sector that flanked three sides of the temple. These included a school and a tribunal, workshops, warehouses for local agricultural produce or tributes paid to the king by foreign lands. These vaulted buildings, located to the north and the west served to store wine, beer, oils and fats, honey, wheat and a whole range of other commodities that were used not only to prepare offerings to the gods, but also to feed the staff of the complex and even to pay the craftsmen who dug and decorated royal tombs as a sort of salary in kind. Close to these warehouses stood a long columned hall, identified as a treasury annexe. This roofed area was well guarded since it was used to store the most precious items such as incense and balms, perfumes and perhaps also

certain furniture articles that were used mainly for religious ceremonies. The dwellings of the priests and temple staff were most probably located towards the north east, closer to the sacred lake and the luxuriant gardens, between the two walls enclosing the temple. Although excavations have so far not produced any results, it must be borne in mind that this area was ravaged by expanding agriculture and crop cultivation that has now extended up to the first pylon.

Similar ravages did not spare the kitchens and bakeries that have only been recently identified. These were located in two large building units situated in the south-eastern part of the Ramesseum. The buildings featured a large number of rooms fitted with ovens, small underground storage areas, sinks and work tables.

The long courtyard with two rooms to the south that separates these two building units was probably used for the slaughter of sacrificed animals. The temple complex was equipped with stables that housed an entire herd of cattle and sheep.

Built just after Rameses II's coronation, the Ramesseum is one of the Temples of Millions of Years, the first of which is thought to have been built at the end of the Middle Kingdom. It is not strictly a funerary temple, but more of a memorial glorifying the monarchy in the person of the king. The important events of his reign are masterfully depicted on the walls and perpetuate his perfect symbiosis with Maat, the entity that incarnates harmony, or rather universal, cosmic balance. The pharaoh who reached the divine sphere here, received a cult through his petrified

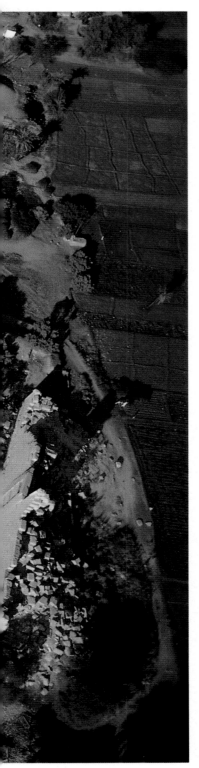

hypostases, in the form of statues and colossi, one of which, nearly sixteen meters (52 feet) high, that formerly adorned the first courtyard of the building, bore the name of 'Sun of Princes'.

Far from being absent, Rameses II's family is also depicted in certain areas of the sacred complex. Nefertari, the great royal consort, appears in the relief sculptures and in statuary, while the mammisi was consecrated to Tuy, the king's mother, whose gigantic statue stood in the first courtyard. A large number of fragments of this statue were uncovered during our excavations. Princes and princesses, on the other hand, were relegated in long processions in the lower registers of several walls, especially in the vestibule gallery and in the large hypostyle hall.

During Rameses II's lifetime, the temple served as a large religious and economic center. Offerings were made daily to Amen-Ra and the other divinities who resided in the 'Castle of Usermaatra Setepenra That Joins Thebes-City, in the Domain of Amen, to the west of the City'. Especially noteworthy in the vast pantheon venerated at the sanctuary were Mut and Khonsu, Ra-Horakhty, Isis, Ptah, Sekhmet, Osiris, Hathor, Atum, as well as Rameses 'the great god' and Ahmose-Nefertari, the mother of Amenhotep I,

who was deified after her death and venerated at least up to the 21st Dynasty.

Several rooms of the main building had been arranged to house small boats and it was precisely these vessels, which were portable and contained a *naos*-like shrine bearing the divine image of its owner, that were carried around in great pomp during feasts. The pilgrimage of the Beautiful Feast of the Valley, for instance, celebrated in the second month of the summer season for a full twelve days, was just one of the occasions for such processions. Joining the *userhat*, the large ornate boat from Karnak bearing the effigy of the 'King of the Gods' to the west of Thebes, the other boats left their respective sanctuaries in order to take part in this imposing feast celebrated not only in honor of the ancestor-kings, but also of all 'Those Who Had Reached Eternity'.

In fact, while the funerary aspect of the temple cannot be totally ignored, it must be borne in mind that it assumed tangible proportions only after the physical death of the king. As evidence available until the end of the Ramesside period indicates, even after the temple assumed its funerary role, liturgical and profane activities continued to be celebrated at the site, albeit at a more subdued pace. After the

88-89

The temple of Rameses II was known as the 'Castle of Millions of Years of Usermaatra Setepenra that joins Thebes-City in the domain of Amen, to the west of the city'. Hecataeus and Diodorus of Sicily called it the 'tomb of Ozymandias' while the geographer Strabo referred to it as the 'Memnonium'. In 1829, while studying the romantic ruins of this famous monument, J.-F. Champollion gave it a new name: the 'Ramesseum', under which it is still known to this day.

LEGEND		MAIN SCENES	
A	FIRST PYLON	1-2	The battle of Qadesh (5th year of the reign)
B	FIRST COURTYARD		
C	THE ROYAL PALACE AND THE PRIVATE APARTMENTS	3	The Peace Treaty (21st year of the reign)
D	THE COLOSSUS OF RAMESES II 'SUN OF PRINCES'	4	Feasts of Min (upper register). Battle of Qadesh (lower register)
E	SECOND PYLON		
F	SECOND COURTYARD	5	Amen-Ra breathing divine life and strength into Rameses II (upper register)
G	THE STATUE OF THE 'YOUNG MEMNON'		
H	THE VESTIBULE GALLERY		Procession of the sons of Rameses II (lower register)
I	THE GREAT HYPOSTYLE HALL		
J	THE ASTRONOMICAL HALL OR 'HALL OF THE BOATS'	6	Procession of divine boats
K	THE HALL OF THE LITANIES	7	Litanies and offering glorifications to the canonic sanctuaries of Upper and Lower Egypt
L	THE SANCTUARY		
M	TEMPLE-MAMMISI OF TUY AND NEFERTARI		

90 top

Partially broken down, then completely pulled down, the colossus of the 'Sun of the Princes', represented the king as a god. This monumental statue was nearly 16 m (53 feet) high, and stood in the first courtyard of the temple, against the southern end of the second pylon.

90 center

The colossus inspired Shelley who devoted the poem "Ozymandias" to it. Several fragments, including the feet that Vivant Denon wanted to bring to France during the Egyptian Expedition, still lie in the first courtyard.

90-91 and 90 bottom

The second courtyard of the temple, taken from the west. Originally it was flanked by colonnades to the north and south and included, from east to west, porticoes with Osiride pillars, of which only those to the north-east and north-west, still stand. Access to the hypostyle hall is by an axial staircase flanked by two beautiful statues of Rameses II. The upper part of the statue to the left now lies in the British Museum: the 'Young Memnon', removed from the Ramesseum in 1816 by Belzoni. Granodiorite and aplite. Height: 2.67 m (9 feet).

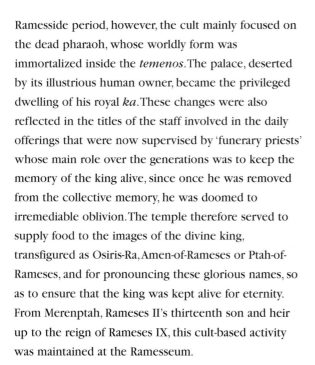

Ramesside period, however, the cult mainly focused on the dead pharaoh, whose worldly form was immortalized inside the *temenos*. The palace, deserted by its illustrious human owner, became the privileged dwelling of his royal *ka*. These changes were also reflected in the titles of the staff involved in the daily offerings that were now supervised by 'funerary priests' whose main role over the generations was to keep the memory of the king alive, since once he was removed from the collective memory, he was doomed to irremediable oblivion. The temple therefore served to supply food to the images of the divine king, transfigured as Osiris-Ra, Amen-of-Rameses or Ptah-of-Rameses, and for pronouncing these glorious names, so as to ensure that the king was kept alive for eternity. From Merenptah, Rameses II's thirteenth son and heir up to the reign of Rameses IX, this cult-based activity was maintained at the Ramesseum.

On the other hand, the economic aspect of the site was also preserved, at least for a time. The agricultural holdings of the family and the crown, continued to the supply the temple with income in kind. The granaries and warehouses were full of commodities that were gradually redistributed, in keeping with the needs of the cult or for the payment of salaries to the officers in charge of maintaining the temple. Towards the end of the reign of Rameses III, this aspect was so well acknowledged that it is before the

Million Year Temple of Rameses the Great that the craftsmen of Set Maat went to demand outstanding pay from the scribes. According to the Strike Papyrus of Turin, the demonstration took place in the second month of the winter season, on the 12th day of the year 29, precisely at the 'southern gate' of the temple, not far, in fact, from the very kitchens whose produce in terms of breads and cakes was so parsimoniously distributed to the workers in charge of the tomb, that they were pushed to dramatic revolt. Documents dating to the reign of Rameses IX, provide evidence that even at that time, the temple complex played an important role in local social life. A petition hall, located either inside or close to the royal palace, was set up to distribute copper biscuits to the population. Whether these copper biscuits were used as a sort of salary paid to temple officers is still open to debate. However, a little later, when Rameses XI ascended to the throne, the situation was drastically different. Not content with sacking the royal necropoleis, grave robbers seemed to have turned their attention even to memorial temples, and the

Ramesseum was no exception. The gold, copper and precious wood was stripped from chapels and doors. It was almost certainly during these incursions that that electrum panelling, mentioned in a band of text close to the door, that adorned the posts of the door separating the hall of boats from the hall of litanies was carried away by robbers. During the same period, cult objects as well as commodities and manufactured goods were carried away, sometimes under the very noses of the guards paid to ensure their protection, who all too often turned a blind eye. Official records of investigations or seizures of looted goods, often mention that such booty, like wood, was particularly prized by robbers, since it could be easily exchanged or transformed.

The close of the Ramesside period also marks the end of the sacred and profane activities in the Castle of Usermaatra Setepenra. Pillaged and sacked, the temple that no longer served as a place of royal cult was abandoned by its servants. Its warehouses, once overflowing with commodities, were devastated. All life seems to have taken flight. Only the memory of Rameses

the Great remained petrified in the monumental scenes that still covered the walls but soon they too would be dismantled to be used in the construction of new structures, elsewhere.

Transformed into a vast priestly cemetery at the beginning of the Third Intermediate Period, the temple of Rameses II entered a new phase of its history around 1000 BC. The economic area, especially, was broken up into hundreds of funerary lots that would soon overflow into the area separating the thick enclosing walls that once housed the wide processional routes, lined with sphinxes. Although the area was first used as a cemetery for eminent

members of the Osorkon and Takelot royal families, funerary concessions were later granted to humble priestly families that served in the various temples of the region. Tombs and chapels in mud brick were often built with material scavenged at the site. The former warehouses, kitchens and other dependencies were subjected to these changes and to the new function assigned to the site. The huge necropolis was entrusted to the care of priests who ordered funerals and maintained the cult of the 'glorified'. The tomb-chapels are more or less luxurious or spacious, depending on the rank of the deceased. It seems that those least rich in purse were assigned to wall sepulchers, modestly dug into the ancient Ramesside walls and then blocked off with a few large bricks. Others were put to rest in underground burial chambers, accessible through a well dug into the conglomerate of the piedmont of the Theban mountains. These 'eternal dwellings' were generally very simple, constructed to merely house the body of the deceased and minimal grave equipment, just sufficient enough to ensure survival in the netherworld. Bodies were held in simple sarcophagi or even just bindings, most often accompanied by *shawabtis*, papyri and pseudo canopic jars and a little pottery. Although this may seem a far cry from the solemn burials of preceding periods, the cult of the dead still maintained its role and importance and was celebrated in the open air for the poorest of the deceased, or in the case of the more fortunate, in little chapels that held commemorate

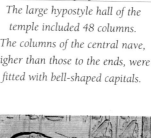

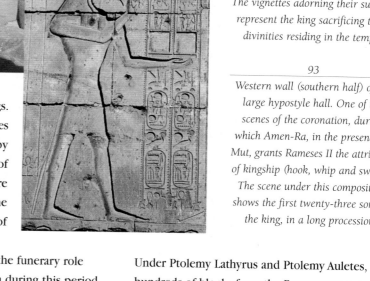

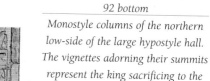

92 top left
The large hypostyle hall of the temple included 48 columns. The columns of the central nave, higher than those to the ends, were fitted with bell-shaped capitals.

92 top right
On the southern wall of the vestibule gallery, Thoth, the divine scribe, records the investiture of Rameses II at the royal coronation rites.

92 bottom
Monostyle columns of the northern low-side of the large hypostyle hall. The vignettes adorning their summits represent the king sacrificing to the divinities residing in the temple.

93
Western wall (southern half) of the large hypostyle hall. One of the scenes of the coronation, during which Amen-Ra, in the presence of Mut, grants Rameses II the attributes of kingship (hook, whip and sword). The scene under this composition shows the first twenty-three sons of the king, in a long procession.

stelae and altars for offerings. Demarcations between graves were sometimes indicated by colorfully painted statues of the gods, some of which are still fairly conserved in the vast treasure-annex hall of the temple.

Side by side with the funerary role relegated to the Ramesseum during this period, the temple complex underwent its first major ravages. The sphinxes built along the procession route flanking three sides of the temple were broken up in the early Third Intermediary Period, while the mammisi was dismantled during the 29th Dynasty, under the reign of Achoris, who scavenged the stone to extend the peripteral monument commenced by the Thutmoside pharaohs at Medinet Habu. Later, especially during the Ptolemaic Period, the very walls, columns and pillars of the temple itself were broken down.

Under Ptolemy Lathyrus and Ptolemy Auletes, hundreds of blocks from the Ramesseum were used to build the huge pylon that stands before the complex commissioned by Taharqa and Nectanebo I, at Djeme. Other local temples, such as that dedicated to Hathor-Maat at Deir el-Medina, almost certainly were built from stone scavenged from the Ramesseum that had become a full-fledged quarry. If, during his visit to the 'tomb of Ozymandias' in the 1st century BC, Diodorus of Sicily describes a monument that seems more or less intact, he was one of the last historians to contemplate the Ramesseum in the waning days of its glory. For obvious economic reasons, from the Roman Period through to the Middle Ages at least, sandstone and limestone were pillaged from the ruins of the Ramesseum, up to its very foundations.

In the early centuries of our era, the Ramesseum, once again, sprang to life as a religious centre, when zealous believers in nascent Christianity not only took possession of the Theban mountain but also occupied the ancient, abandoned sanctuaries, setting up monasteries and churches through Thebaid, transforming several Pharaonic memorial temples on the west bank of the Diospolis Magna into centers of ascetic Christian worship. For instance, the temple of Hathepsut, with its high watchtower in mud brick became the 'Deir el-Bahari' (the Northern Monastery) consecrated to Saint Phoebammun, while the memorial of Rameses III, at Medinet Habu, honored St. Menas in a church set up inside the second courtyard. Close to the New Kingdom craftsmen's village at Deir el-Medina, the 'Convent of the Town' was dedicated to St. Isidore the Martyr, while another close sanctuary was set up in honor of St. Mark.

A very common theme in the iconographic repertory of the Ramesseum: several coronation scenes. On the southern wall of the vestibule gallery, Rameses II, escorted by Atum-Ra and Montu, is presented before Amen-Ra, his divine parent, from he receives the atef-crown and innumerable jubilees.

The faces of the Osiride pillars are decorated with scenes depicting Rameses II with gods. Here, the king consecrates an offering of white bread to Khonsu-Neferhotep, falcon-headed moon-god.

95 center

Detail of a scene of the 'royal ascent', sculpted on the southern wall of the vestibule gallery. The god Montu breathes divine life into Rameses II.

Certain orthodox monasteries were set up on the very slopes of the sacred mountain, such as the sanctuary that dominates the Valley of the Queens (Deir er-Rumi) or the church nestled in the curves of Dra Abu el-Naga (Deir el-Bekhit). Not only new layouts, but also hammered deformations and graffiti dating from the time of the Christian take-over still mark what remains of the Ramesseum today. The large hypostyle hall as well as the boat room were the central point of the new religious focus, and required modifications to accommodate an architecture more in tune with the Christian liturgy. The times have changed and there is no place for compromise or syncretism allowed for under the old pharaonic religion, a few centuries previously. After Christianity, 'pagan' effigies were mutilated, if not totally destroyed and the more provocative depictions, such as the monumental sculptures of the king-god, were taken apart or cast down. It was most probably during this period in the turbulent history of the Ramesseum that several statues of Rameses II —including the famous colossus in the first courtyard—were destroyed, while the Osiride pillars that originally adorned the porticoes of the peristyle of the second courtyard, were beheaded.

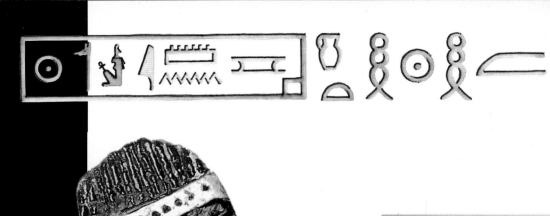

96

Faience plaques were used as inlays on the doors and the window of appearances of Rameses III's ceremonial palace that opened onto the first court of the Medinet Habu temple. On the left is a Libyan, with a tattooed body and a distinctive sidelock. On the right is a Syrian chieftain who wears an elaborate fringed cape wrapped around his garment.

Medinet Habu
The Temple of Rameses III

by Betsy M. Bryan

At the southern edge of the Theban cemetery region is a large complex of temples surrounded by well preserved high mud brick walls. Medinet Habu probably bears its modern name because as a village it is near the funerary temple of Amenhotep son of Hapu, a official from the reign of Amenhotep III who was deified and worshiped in the late dynastic era. Medinet Habu actually contains temple remains dating from the 18th Dynasty down to the Ptolemaic Period, but particularly it houses the small temple built by Hatshepsut and Thutmosis III

for Amen and the Temple of Millions of Years in western Thebes of Rameses III.

The visitor to Medinet Habu today enters through the pylon gateway of Rameses III, but in ancient times the first entrance was a few meters (feet) north and led to the small temple of the 18th Dynasty. That temple was built by Hatshepsut and Thutmosis III and was built to honor the cult of Amen-Ra Kamutef, a creator god associated also with Karnak and Luxor Temples. The small temple was believed to house the primeval mound from which Amen-Ra Kamutef emerged and to which

he must return to be renewed. A feast called "the decade feast" supposed that Amen crossed the river from Luxor Temple every ten days to be rejuvenated at the mound referred to in later texts as "Djeme". Medinet Habu had an important pilgrimage role as a result of the mythology associated with it, and in the later New Kingdom and following it became even more a focus for festival visitations. Perhaps the established association of the small temple with processions from the east bank influenced Rameses III to build his Temple of Millions of Year next to the chapel of Amen. By doing this the king tied the precinct to the Beautiful Feast of the Valley, making it the last stop on the procession. As was the case with other kings' Temples of Millions of Years, the festivals are prominently depicted on the walls of the temple's front courts. Both the side of the temple and the size of the endowment for the temple assured that Medinet Habu would remain a festival and pilgrimage site for the rest of Egyptian dynastic history.

The 20th Dynasty was a period during which Egypt's affluent light began to dim, as

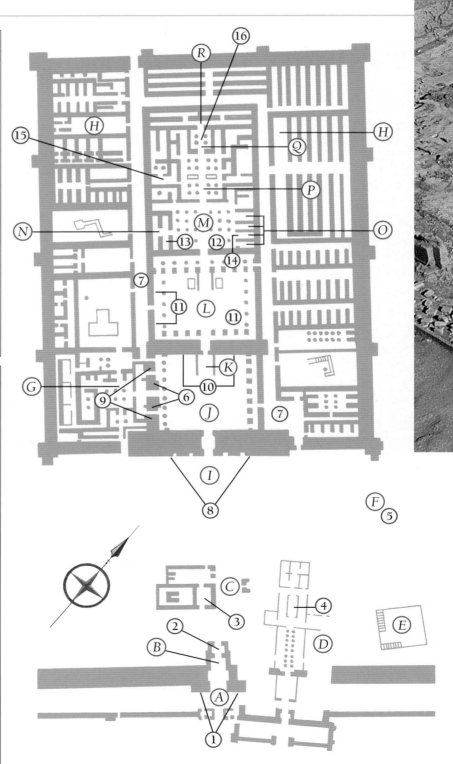

The Temple of Rameses III

The windows of the ceremonial
palace were made of sandstone but
inlaid with pigment and faience.
These window frames were two of
several found in the palace area.

Aerial view of Medinet Habu taken
from the southwest. In the upper
right foreground are the well
preserved remains of the ceremonial
palace and its entryway into the first
court of the Temple. Surrounding the
temple are the remains of storerooms
and, on the south side, houses of
priests and other officials.

100 top left
A view of the entrance to Medinet Habu taken from the south, slightly west. Visible is the "tower" punctuated with windows on two storeys above the ground level.

The roof of the "tower" has a frieze of horse-shoe shaped elements, borrowed from fortress architecture of the New Kingdom. The form probably originated in the Levant in the so-called "migdol" fort type.

100 top right
King Nectanebo I of the 30th Dynasty (ca. 380-362 BC) added a colonnade in front of the small temple at Medinet Habu. On the colonnade's entrance is the king smiting Asiatics in a traditional manner seen as early as the 1st Dynasty.

both internal and external stresses wore on the fabric of the society. Rameses III is often referred to as the last great warrior king of Egypt whose reign was something of a renaissance period, since the country had experienced both instability in the kingship and an interregnum in the period immediately prior to his rule. The thirty years of Rameses III's kingship, however, were notable for several successes in warfare and for a prodigious building campaign financed by the king's campaigns and by the god Amen. This appearance of strength and stability, as portrayed in the reliefs of Medinet Habu, was shadowed by continuing internal problems in the reign— perhaps the best known of which was the failed conspiracy within the king's own wives' apartments. Records of tomb robbing are also known from the reign of Rameses III, an indication of the effect of economic decline within.

100 bottom
Nectanebo I's lotiform columns front the 25th Dynasty pylon built by King Taharqa (690-664 BC) before the small temple at Medinet Habu. The central axis into the temple which was believed to hold the "mound of Djeme," or primeval hill of Amen's creation, is in the background.

101
The "tower" entrance to Rameses III's temple has colossal-sized scenes of the ruler smiting the enemies of the gods. Here, on the north side of the central axis,

Rameses III smites Asiatics with his scimitar as Ra-Horakhty observed and offers the king his own weapon. Scenes from the interior of the tower's upper storeys are visible above.

Even the enclosure of the entirety of Medinet Habu behind large walls late in the reign of the king may indicate the increasing insecurity in the Theban region. Still, within the precinct itself all appeared to be well.

The king's entrance tower built to resemble a fortress gateway contained rooms showing Rameses III and his daughters amid pleasurable activities, such as playing draughts. The rooms may well have functioned as leisure palace rooms, being on upper storeys where the air was cooler and well circulated. The ceremonial palace proper was located south of the first court of the temple, so the tower was perhaps a more functional area for the king and his family.

The first pylon of the temple is carved with scenes of Rameses III smiting enemies before a number of the national gods. If one follows the outside of the pylon around to the back on the north side

102 top
A "name ring" depicting a northern enemy of the king combines a bound Asiatic captive with a ring containing the name of the foreign region – here Kamaka. The rings appears on the First Pylon's outer face scenes of Rameses III smiting captive chiefs before Amen and Ra-Horakhty.

102 center
Bowmen of Rameses III's army shoot the Libyan enemies, whose fallen bodies are shown sprawled on the ground.

The Temple of Rameses III

102

102 bottom

The first pylon of Rameses III's Temple of Millions of Years preserves several scenes of the ruler smiting in front of the national gods. The pylon's flagstaff niches are visible across the front, and the windows placed as guard or observation positions within the pylon are also apparent.

102-103

The west side of the first court is the exterior of the second pylon. Here are the long texts of year 8 reporting Rameses III's war against the Sea Peoples. Rows of captives from that war are shown on the south side of the doorway. Here are shown a group of Peleset, or Philistines, wearing their distinctive feather-like headdresses.

103 top right

Interior face of the first pylon has the year 11 text of Rameses III's second Libyan war. Here Rameses receives the crown prince who presents the captives from the battle. A group of other officers appears below.

there begins a series of reliefs depicting the king's wars with the Libyans and the Sea Peoples. In the Libyan sequence on the exterior of the north wall the king is shown taking captives as his chariot awaits him. Archers and soldiers appear below this attacking Libyans. The king and the soldiers pursue Libyans from their chariots. The king is shown holding the foreign chiefs; then the ruler receives the crown prince who presents rows of captive Libyans, including the chief of the Meshwesh. Finally Rameses III presents the captives to the god Amen. The inscription states that the king spoke as follows: "Say to the defeated chief of the Meshwesh:'see how your name is destroyed forever and ever. Your mouth has ceased rebellion at the mention of Egypt, by the might of my father, the lord of gods'."

Also on the north wall is the Sea Peoples Battle. The king is shown inspecting troops before the battle and then in his chariot as he set out for the Levant. He appeared in his chariot amidst the battle against tribes traveling to Egypt bringing their wives and children in ox carts. A naval battle is shown after this, with the king standing on land shooting arrows at enemies on ships. The king and his entourage bring rows of captives, including Philistines, Tjekker, Sherden, Sheklesh, and others. At a fort the king receives captives brought by princes, and finally the recording of captives is shown. Rameses III presents the captives to Amen, Mut, and Khonsu.

103 bottom

The interior face of the first pylon looking back toward the "tower" entranceway.

104 top
Bowmen (left) accompanying the king fire arrows at the wild bulls in the marsh. Soldiers (right) carry rope to tie the bulls just felled in the hunt.

104 bottom
Soldiers of the ruler carry shields and spears as they accompany him on his hunt of wild bulls. The king had chased the bulls into the marsh behind which is open water. The bulls are trapped.

105
The rear of the first pylon, on the south side, preserves scenes of Rameses III hunting antelope and wild assess above and wild bulls below.

The king is shown in his chariot shooting arrows at the smaller game, while below he chases the bulls into the marsh and allows his military escort to shoot the animals.

The historical inscription that celebrates this battle is located on the exterior of the second pylon within the temple. Here Rameses III speaks to his children and soldiers as follows: "See the great power of my father Amen-Ra. The countries which came from their islands in the midst of the sea advanced to Egypt. . .A net was prepared for them, to ensnare them. As they entered secretly in the mouth of the harbor, they fell into it, being caught in their place. They were dispatched, and their bodies were stripped." The success apparently prevented a large scale settlement of people in the Egyptian delta—at a time when Egypt could least afford to support a greater population. The defeat of the Libyans on two separate occasions did not, however, deter those tribes from settling within Egypt. They came to inhabit large parts of the Egyptian delta and their descendants ruled Egypt in the 22nd Dynasty.

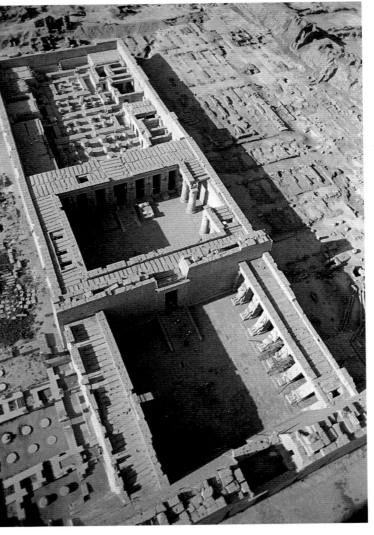

The front two courts of Medinet Habu were planned as festival spaces, particularly for the Beautiful Feast of the Valley. The procession is shown on the south wall of the first court and again on the north side of the second court. Here the boats carrying statues of Amen, Mut, and Khonsu are shown being carried and censed by priests. The festivals of Min and Sokar also appear on the walls of this second court. The first was associated with the king's coronation and the rejuvenation of his rule, while the second linked the reign with the resurrection of Sokar as a solar deity. In practice this meant that festivals were regularly celebrated within the temple, and they would have been occasions for great excitement. Indeed, Rameses III left a festival calendar inscribed on the exterior of the south side of the first court. Here he enumerated the daily feasts to be celebrated and the annual ones as well. In his introduction he outlined the dedications he made to the temple to supply the

107 top left
On the north side of the second court are scenes showing the festival of Amen at the Beautiful Feast of the Valley. The gods of Thebes attend the ceremony, and here is a portion of the boat containing the statue of Khonsu, moon-god son of Amen and Mut.

107 top right
The first court of the temple added before the second pylon is seen in the lower part of this aerial view. The ceremonial palace is to the left. The peristyle second court is visible behind this, and the hypostyle halls, now lacking their roofs appear in the background.

107 bottom left
A view of the western side of the second court, with the ramp up to the portico.

107 bottom right
The south and west sides of the first court of the temple. The open papyrus columns mark the entrance to the ceremonial palace. The second court portico is visible through the doorway.

106
The portico at the rear of the second court preserves relief with the colorful paint still visible. Papyriform columns support the porch's architraves and behind them can be seen Rameses receiving his insignia of rulership from the god Atum. Beneath are two of the thirteen sons of the king shown on this wall.

cult and the festivals and addressed the god Amen: "Let your provisions be brought into its [the temple's] midst and all offerings into the chapel... multiply its children that they might be priests and god's fathers for you, to call you to your food, to praise you; and others to direct the work in order to provide all daily offerings."

Beyond the first two courts are two hypostyle halls. On the north and south side of the

halls are rooms used to store cult furniture and also chapels for the major gods. There are chapels for Ptah, Sokar, Amen, and even the deified Rameses II off the first hall, but there are also rooms to hold ointments and luxurious materials such as stones and gold, as well as one for clothing. A slaughterhouse is also apparently included. Off the second hypostyle is a suite of rooms associating Rameses III with Osiris. Here the content of the scenes is connected with that seen on the walls of the king's tomb in the Valley of the Kings. Sections of the *Book of the Dead* are inscribed here, and the king is shown in the netherworld as he ploughs and harvests in the Field of Reeds. A similar association to the sun god occurs in a suite of rooms on north side of the hall. Here the king guarantees his inclusion in the boat of

108 top

Detail of the head of a Libyan prisoner on a faience tile from the palace of Rameses III at Medinet Habu. The palace doors and windows were inlaid with tiles of this type indicating the king's domination over all foreigners.

108 bottom

This aerial view of the back rooms of the temple shows two hypostyle halls with an area for a bark shrine behind. Small chapels flank both the north and south sides of the back rooms. Shrines associated with Osiris and Ra occur on the south and north respectively.

108-109

A view of the chapel of Ptah situated north of the first hypostyle hall. A headless statue of Ptah originally made of alabaster for Amenhotep III is placed in the chapel.

109 bottom left

In the chapel of Ra-Horakhty Rameses III offers food to the ka of Soped and another god.

109 bottom right

Statues of Amenhotep III associated with the moon god and the solar goddess Maat are reused by Rameses III in the temple.

Ra that travels the sky and the netherworld every day for eternity. The cult of the king's temple was therefore maintained in a manner traditional for the New Kingdom—combining the Osiris and Ra cults together to ensure the king's eternal existence.

Two palaces were built on the grounds of the temple during Rameses III's lifetime. Next to the second are also the remains of priest houses and outer installations built slightly later in the 21st Dynasty. By that time Medinet Habu had become the fortified center of Theban life and it continued as an active town through the Coptic period.

The Valley

OF THE

KingS

Introduction to the Valley of the Kings

by Kent R. Weeks

For ABOUT FIVE HUNDRED YEARS, during the New Kingdom (1550-1070 BC), most of Egypt's pharaohs were buried at Thebes in rock-cut tombs in the Valley of the Kings (KV). Of the 32 rulers of dynasties 18, 19 and 20, at least 26 were interred there. There are 62 numbered tombs in KV, 21 of them numbered in geographical order by John Gardner Wilkinson in 1827, the remainder numbered in order of discovery since then. In addition, there are about two dozen "commencements," tomb shafts that were begun but almost immediately abandoned for unknown reasons. The non-royal tombs in KV belonged to various officials, royal family members, and priests.

The Valley of the Kings lies about one kilometer (mile) west of the Nile floodplain at Thebes (modern Luxor). It is a small wadi that was cut by torrential rains and erosion during several pluvial periods in the Pleistocene into a thick layer of limestone that lies above a discontinuous stratum of Esna shale. The valley lies about 70 meters (230 feet) above the level of the River Nile (140 meters (460 feet) above mean sea level), and the immediately surrounding hills rise an average of 80 meters (265 feet) above the valley floor. It was probably chosen as the burial-place of royalty because of its geology, its relatively convenient access from the Nile floodplain, and the pyramid-shaped mountain, "the Qurn," or "forehead," that rises about 300 meters (985 feet) above its southern end and perhaps was seen as a symbol of the god Ra.

The selection of a KV site for a royal tomb was made by the vizier and the country's principal architects and later affirmed by pharaoh. Early in the New Kingdom, during the 18th Dynasty, preference was often given to sites at the base of the sheer cliffs that surround KV, ideally below gullys through which, in the rare event of rain, a "waterfall" would pour over the cliff and deposit debris over a tomb's entrance, burying it ever deeper over the centuries. In the late 18th and 19th dynasties, the preferred location was in lower-lying talus slopes; in the 20th Dynasty, it was one of the small spurs of bedrock that extended from the valley's sides into the center of KV. These changes in preferred location may indicate that 18th Dynasty tombs were intended to be completely and permanently sealed after the burial while 19th and 20th Dynasty tombs were to remain partially accessible so that ceremonies could continue to be performed in them long after the pharaoh had been interred. In this latter case, it is likely that only the burial chamber and its storerooms would have been permanently closed. The orientation of the tomb was apparently the result of geological considerations and not a desire to align the tomb to any particular cardinal direction (see table). Tomb axes run in compass directions from 68° to 357°. In order to correctly place decoration on its walls, artists arbitrarily assumed that a tomb's principal axis ran from east to west, from the rising to the setting sun, no matter what its actual direction.

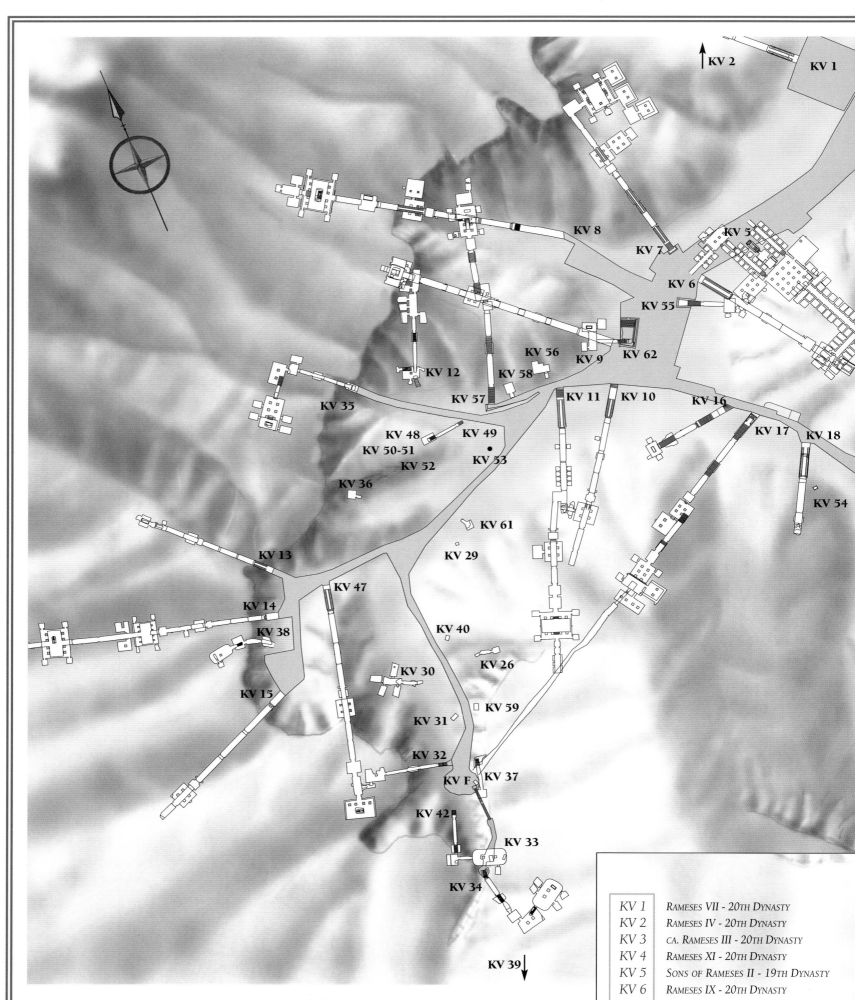

KV 2

KV 1

KV 8

KV 5

KV 7

KV 6

KV 55

KV 56

KV 9

KV 62

KV 12

KV 58

KV 11

KV 10

KV 16

KV 35

KV 57

KV 17

KV 18

KV 48

KV 49

KV 50-51

KV 52

KV 53

KV 36

KV 54

KV 61

KV 13

KV 29

KV 47

KV 14

KV 40

KV 38

KV 26

KV 30

KV 15

KV 59

KV 31

KV 32

KV F

KV 37

KV 42

KV 33

KV 34

KV 39

114-115

Map of the Valley of the Kings. Tomb
numbers 1-20 are in approximate

north to south geographical order;
numbers 21-62 were assigned more
or less in order of discovery.

115

Detail of lotus motif from lunar pectoral
from the tomb of Tutankhamen.

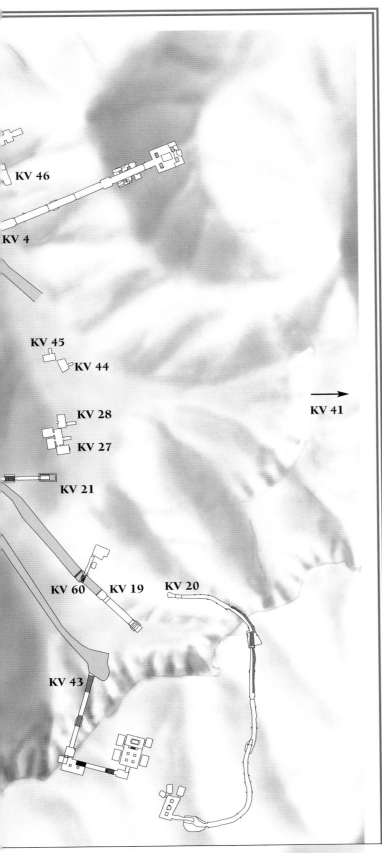

By the later New Kingdom, the Valley of the Kings was filled with tombs and there were fewer and fewer sites available in which more tombs could be cut. This crowding posed problems. It seems unlikely that ancient architects maintained a master plan of the valley showing the location of its tombs because we know of three instances in which quarrymen digging a new tomb collided with an earlier one. When such collisions occurred, the quarrymen presumably had three choices: immediately change the new tomb's axis and veer away from the earlier tomb; abandon the new tomb and dig elsewhere; or incorporate part of the earlier tomb into the new.

Once a site had been decided upon, rituals were performed to sanctify it. These included digging small pits, as many as four or five of them, into which were placed miniature construction tools, clay and stone vessels, religious symbols, and foodstuffs. These pits are called foundation deposits and they have been found associated with nine KV tombs, though some scholars believe that all the royal tombs had them.

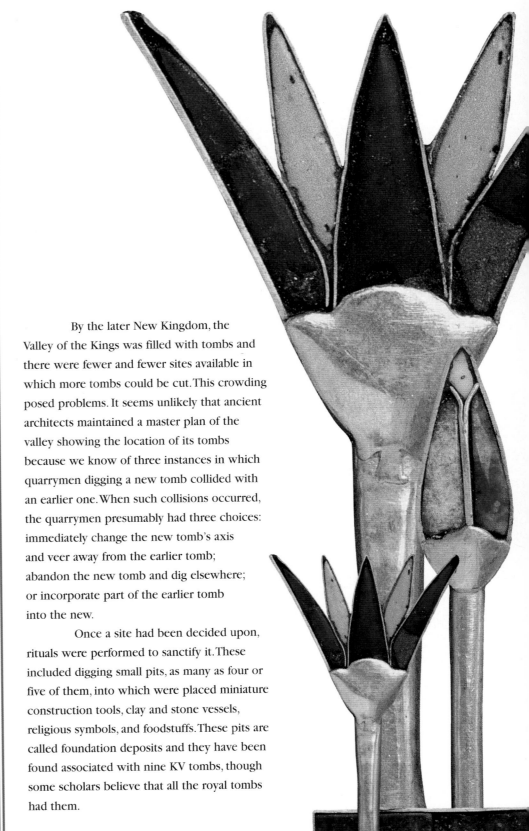

116 top

Builder's tools from the 18th Dynasty tomb of the architect Kha at Deir el-Medina, now in the Egyptian Museum, Turin. Shown are a wooden mallet, a mould for making mud bricks, a mattock for digging and mixing mud for brick-making, and an adze for cutting and shaping wooden objects.

116 bottom

Plan of the tomb of Rameses IV, KV 2, now in the Egyptian Museum, Turin. The measurements of the tomb given on the plan correspond to the measurements of the tomb itself. But it is not clear whether the men who dug KV 2 worked from this plan or whether it was a plan made after the tomb had been completed.

117

At the bottom of the aerial photo is Deir el-Medina, the New Kingdom village in which lived the artisans responsible for cutting and decorating the royal tombs in the Valley of the Kings. There were about 70 houses here, plus several workshops, built of stone along a central main street. North of the village lies a Ptolemaic temple. The path taken by the workmen each day to the Valley of the Kings ascends the hills to the left. Today, police security posts have been built at intervals along it. In the distance (top right) one can see the causeway of the temple of Hatshepsut at Deir el-Bahari.

We know a great deal about how KV tombs were cut and decorated in part because of thousands of objects and inscriptions found in the village of Deir el-Medina. Deir el-Medina lies about a kilometer (mile) south of KV and during the New Kingdom it served as the home and burial-place of the artisans and artists who carved and decorated KV tombs. The remains of about 70 houses can be seen in the village proper, and during the New Kingdom about 400 people lived here in small stone dwellings built along a narrow street. Many different specialists lived at Deir el-Medina: quarrymen, plasterers, scribes, sculptors, architects, draftsmen—all the skills needed for the preparation of the royal tombs. Their jobs were passed from father to son, and we have records of up to half a dozen generations of a single family employed in KV work. They were paid for their labor in kind: bread, beer, dried fish, onions and other vegetables. Texts found in the village include journals, love letters, business documents, inventories, shopping lists, legal papers—almost every aspect of life is discussed in them—and from them we have learned a great deal about work in the Valley of the Kings.

Quarrymen worked in the tombs in a "left gang" and a "right gang" of up to several dozen men each, each headed by a foreman. These gangs would begin cutting a royal tomb shortly after a new pharaoh ascended the throne and the tomb site was chosen. They worked with chert tools, one or two men in each gang cutting into the limestone bedrock, others forming basket brigades to carry the debris from the tomb. Their work was lit by oil lamps with linen wicks of carefully measured length; when a wick had burned up—they were designed to burn for four hours—it was time to stop for lunch or to leave for home. Salt was added to the oil to prevent it from smoking. The men worked eight hours a day for eight days, then took a two-day week-end. There were numerous other holidays throughout the year as well but digging must have been unpleasant work. We know from our own archaeological excavations in KV today that the tombs can be miserably hot and humid and filled with choking dust. There is an ever-present risk of being cut or bruised by sharp-edged fragments of limestone or of having ceiling blocks weighing several tons collapse on one's head.

It was difficult to cut tombs with precision and the ancient supervisors painted control marks on the walls and ceilings of tombs to help quarrymen ensure a straight axis or make a 90 degree turn or properly situate a doorway. Surveying tools were simple but effective: carpenter's squares determined right angles; plumb bobs assured vertical walls; and a length of string measured length. With patience and care, these elemental tools permitted highly accurate tomb cutting. There is a papyrus in the Egyptian Museum in Turin on which an ancient architect had drawn a plan of KV 2, the tomb of Rameses IV, and noted the dimensions of its chambers. We can convert the ancient measurements given there into modern metric units—1 cubit = 52.3 cm (20 inches) long, 1 palm = 7.47 cm (3 inches) or 1/7 cubit, and 1 digit = 1.87 cm (0.8 inches) or palm—and compare them with dimensions we can measure today. If we can assume that the plan was drawn before the tomb was cut, not after it—and this cannot be proved—then the quarrymen came within fractions of a centimeter (inche) of achieving what the specifications called for.

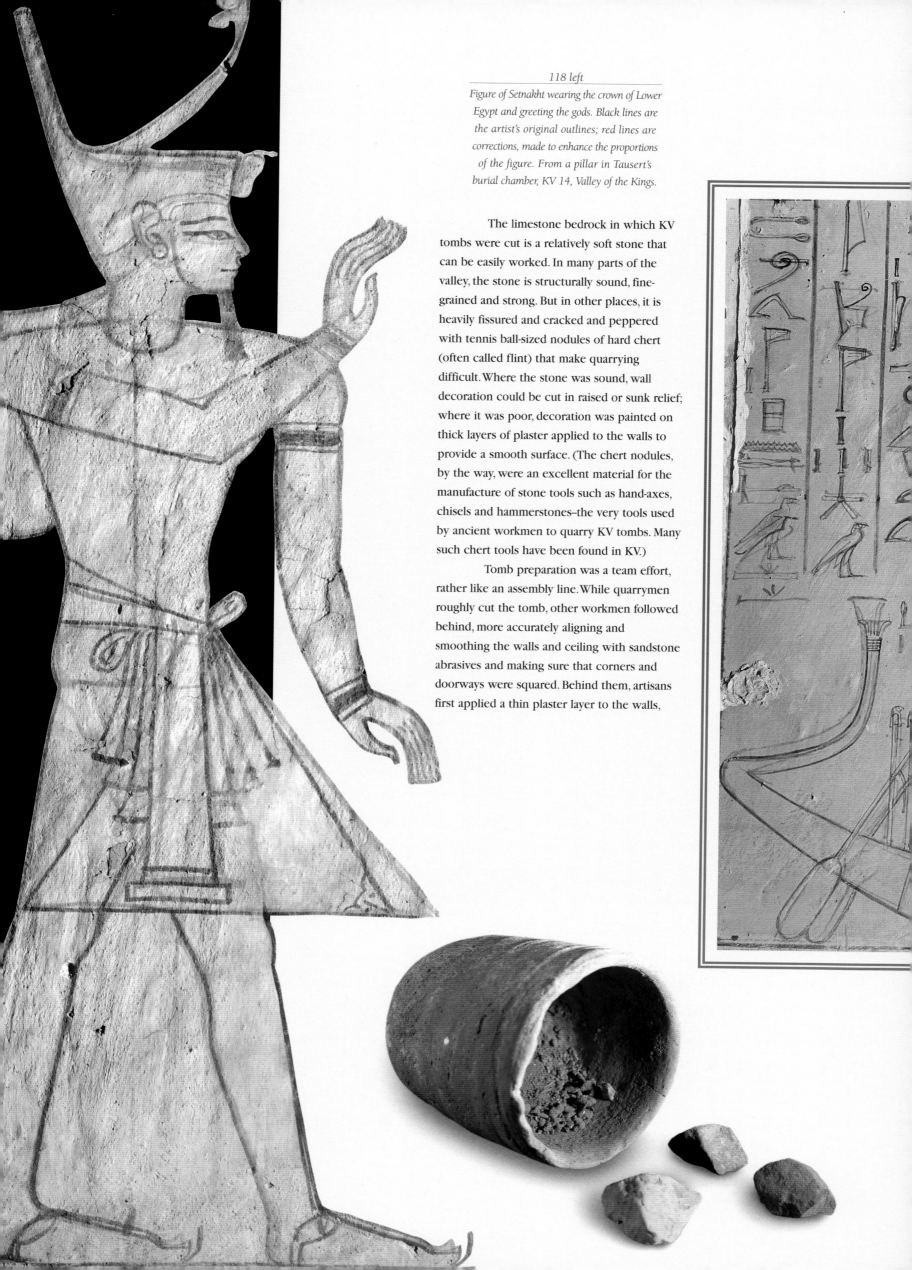

118 left

Figure of Setnakht wearing the crown of Lower Egypt and greeting the gods. Black lines are the artist's original outlines; red lines are corrections, made to enhance the proportions of the figure. From a pillar in Tausert's burial chamber, KV 14, Valley of the Kings.

The limestone bedrock in which KV tombs were cut is a relatively soft stone that can be easily worked. In many parts of the valley, the stone is structurally sound, fine-grained and strong. But in other places, it is heavily fissured and cracked and peppered with tennis ball-sized nodules of hard chert (often called flint) that make quarrying difficult. Where the stone was sound, wall decoration could be cut in raised or sunk relief; where it was poor, decoration was painted on thick layers of plaster applied to the walls to provide a smooth surface. (The chert nodules, by the way, were an excellent material for the manufacture of stone tools such as hand-axes, chisels and hammerstones–the very tools used by ancient workmen to quarry KV tombs. Many such chert tools have been found in KV.)

Tomb preparation was a team effort, rather like an assembly line. While quarrymen roughly cut the tomb, other workmen followed behind, more accurately aligning and smoothing the walls and ceiling with sandstone abrasives and making sure that corners and doorways were squared. Behind them, artisans first applied a thin plaster layer to the walls,

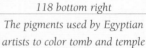

119

118 bottom right

The pigments used by Egyptian artists to color tomb and temple walls were made from locally available raw materials such as yellow ocher, red ocher, and ground Egyptian faience, crushed in a mortar and mixed with a binder such as gum arabic or oils.

118-119

The solar bark in the Book of Gates, third division, middle register, showing the sun god as a ram-headed man standing in a shrine protected by the mehen-serpent and preceded by the god Sia. From the tomb of Horemheb, KV 57, chamber "J."

119 top right

Book of Gates, second division, middle register, a detail of a scene called "The Bull of the Earth." From the tomb of Horemheb, KV 57, chamber "J."

119 bottom right

Two of nine gods shown in the Book of Gates, second division, lower register. From the tomb of Horemheb, KV 57, chamber "J."

painted lines to divide walls into scenes and registers, then drew in red ink outlines of the figures and hieroglyphs to be carved there. Senior artists and scribes used black ink to adjust the proportions of figures or correct spelling errors. Scenes and texts were either carved in raised relief or painted on plaster. Pigments were mixed from mineral compounds (red and yellow ocher, blue and green copper salts, black carbon, white gypsum).

It probably took only a few years to completely dig and decorate a royal tomb in the Valley of the Kings, even though only fifty or sixty workmen might be involved in the work. When a pharaoh's tomb was finished, the Deir el-Medina workmen would be free to work on other royal projects, on nobles' tombs or on tombs for themselves dug adjacent to their village until the next pharaoh was crowned and his tomb begun.

Royal tombs were sometimes, but by no means always, larger than nobles' tombs; they varied greatly among themselves in size. As the accompanying chart shows, there is no correlation between the size of a royal tomb and the regnal length of the pharaoh for whom it was cut. KV 5, the tomb of the sons of Rameses II, was largest of all, and the KV 5 chambers excavated to date cover over 1800 m_. (Until all its chambers are cleared, we are able to give only its area, not its volume, which is probably about 6,000m_). There is a strong likelihood that KV 5 will grow to perhaps 2500 mq when it has been completely explored.

The plans of KV royal tombs changed during the New Kingdom and, indeed, no two tombs are exactly alike. In some cases, size and plan may have been dictated by available time or resources. But many Egyptologists suspect that some changes in tomb plans were the result of ongoing discussions among Egypt's priests about the theological notions on which the interrelations between architecture, decoration, and religious beliefs were founded. As the priests' views of the Afterlife and the pharaoh's journey from this life to the next evolved, corridors or chambers might be added to the plan, chambers enlarged or reduced in size, or the tomb's axis changed from turning to straight. Put simply, the plan of a royal tomb might be seen as a road map

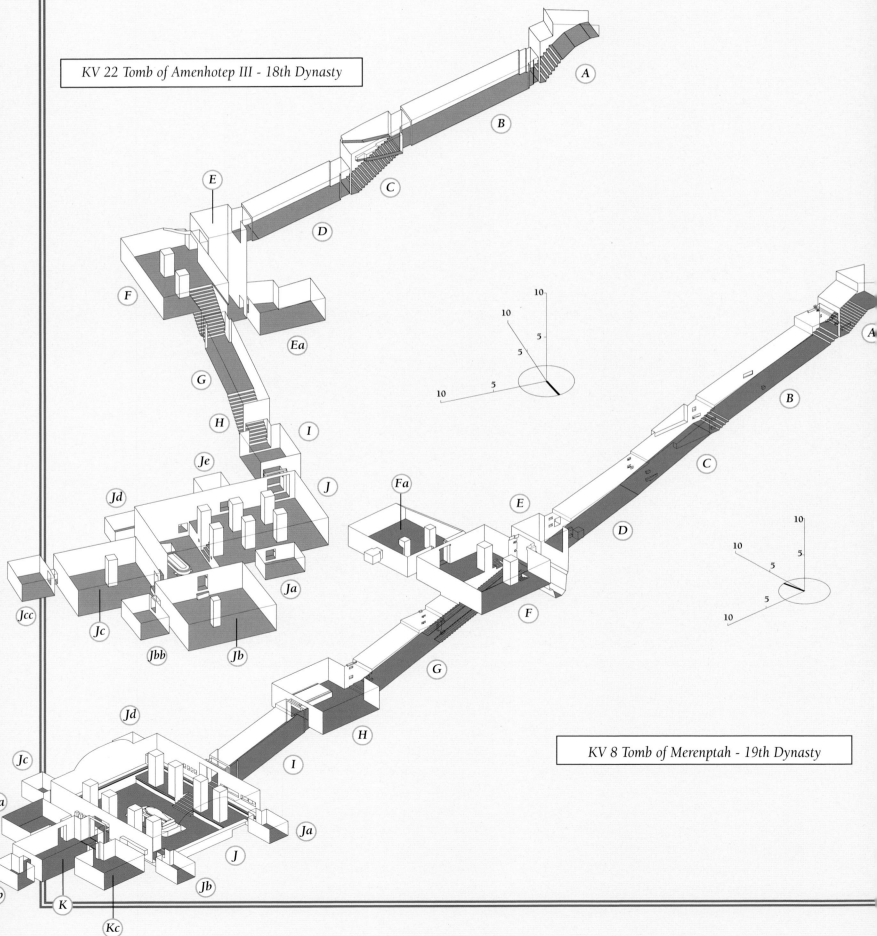

KV 22 Tomb of Amenhotep III - 18th Dynasty

KV 8 Tomb of Merenptah - 19th Dynasty

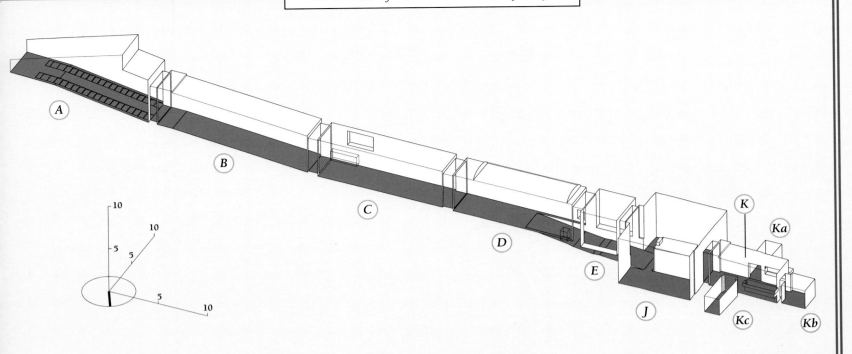

from this life to the next, its texts and scenes as a guidebook to the journey. When the priests decided that the route or its features changed, so would the tomb plan and its decoration.

The late American Egyptologist Elizabeth Thomas studied the component parts of New Kingdom royal tombs and assigned to them letter designations according to the function they were intended to serve. Not all royal tombs have all these chambers and some have more than one of each. The following table indicates these chambers and notes how some of them changed through time. Where known, the ancient name of each room is indicated, but keep in mind that these names are from Rameside texts and may have been different in earlier periods.

A. Tomb entrance, called the "Passage of the Way of Shu." Shu was god of air, and the entrance was fully open to the sky before the reign of Thutmosis IV, partly open after.

B. First corridor, called the "Passage of Ra," referring to the fact that this corridor was, in some tombs, depending on their orientation, descent and plan, the farthest that sunlight could penetrate. The *Litany of Ra* was often inscribed on its walls.

C. At first a chamber with a descent, later a stairwell with recesses, then a corridor, it (or the niches cut into its walls) was called the "Hall Wherein They Rest," "they" being statuettes of the thirty-seven gods mentioned in the Solar Litany.

D. A corridor whose ancient name may simply have been "Second Passage," and/or "Third Passage."

E. A deep pit or "well," called the "Hall of Hindering," was once thought to prevent .

flood water from entering the tomb or to thwart tomb-robbers. In 1817, Giovanni Belzoni found the corridor beyond the rear wall of the well in KV 17, the tomb of Seti I, to be blocked and painted. He also found that ancient thieves had used ropes to climb down into the pit and up the other side. They pierced the blocking, then continued into the tomb. If wells were intended as security devices, they seem regularly to have failed. Several wells have chambers cut off the bottom of their walls, and today Egyptologists believe that the wells served a religious purpose, as symbolic burial-places of the god Osiris.

F. This pillared hall is referred to as the "Chariot Hall," and remains of chariots have been found in the tombs of Thutmosis IV and Amenhotep III, and in other tombs as well, most notably in KV 62, the tomb of Tutankhamen. Some Egyptologists have argued that this hall marked a transition between the upper part of the tomb, equated with the "Upper Duat," (part of the Netherworld) and the lower part, or "Lower Duat."

G. The ancient names of this and the next two rooms are not known. Their functions were apparently simple: to provide additional wall surfaces for decoration and texts, and perhaps to offer storage space for funerary goods.

H. Originally a stairwell, "H" later became a corridor, then, at least in KV 57, 8, and 11, a chamber.

I. First a room, it became a corridor in later tombs. The Turin plan of KV 2 describes it as "the Ramp."

J. The burial chamber was called in ancient times the "Hall in Which One Rests," or

the "House of Gold," clearly a reference to the sarcophagus and shrines that were placed here. Another possible name was "The Hidden Chamber." The plan of this chamber changed through time, and is variously cartouche-shaped, rectangular, pillared, vaulted, and/or with two floor levels. Off it frequently lay four small side-chambers (designated Ja-d), two of them intended for storing food and drink, two for statuettes and ritual equipment. Occasionally, as in the tombs of Amenhotep III, Horemheb, and Seti I, there might be more than the usual four side chambers.

K. The "Passage on the Inner Side of the House of Gold," also called the "Second Passage Beyond the House of Gold," is found in some tombs, first as a corridor, later as a chamber.

L. This room of unknown designation was originally a corridor, later a chamber. It is not often found in KV tombs.

The accompanying table indicates which of the above chambers are to be found in individual KV tombs. The tombs are listed here in chronological order.

The axes of KV tombs changed several times during the New Kingdom. Eighteenth Dynasty tombs often had an L-shaped plan with one or two right angle turns to the left in it, and were usually cut at the base of sheer cliffs (type 1). They had rectangular or cartouche-shaped burial chambers with four small side-chambers for foodstuffs and funerary equipment. A second plan (type 2) has a right angle turn to the right and, for the first time, the appearance of chamber E. They date to the 18th and 19th dynasties. From the late 18th Dynasty and through the 19th, a third plan (type 3)

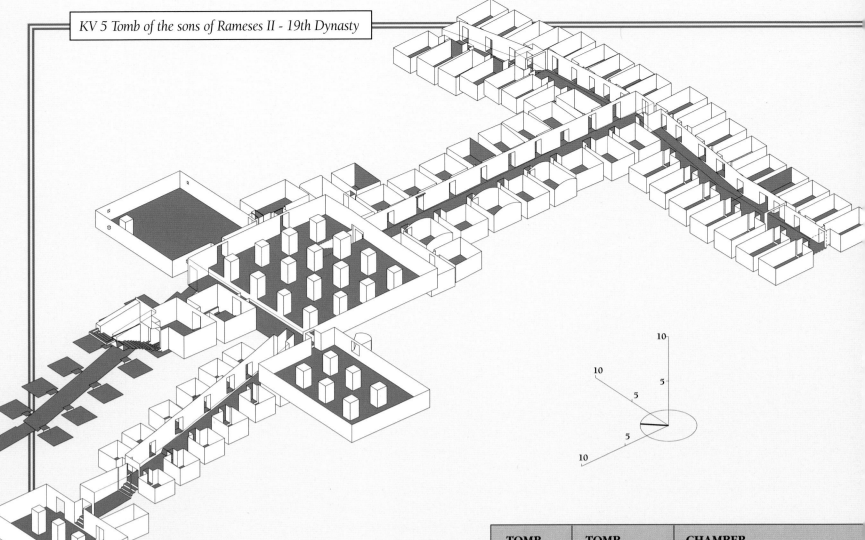

KV 5 Tomb of the sons of Rameses II - 19th Dynasty

TOMB NUMBER	TOMB NAME	CHAMBER		
		A	B	C
KV 20	HATSHEPSUT	YES	YES	YES, 2
KV 38	THUTMOSIS I	YES	YES	YES
KV 34	THUTMOSIS III	YES	YES	YES
KV 35	AMENHOTEP II	YES	YES	YES
KV 43	THUTMOSIS IV	YES	YES	YES
KV 22	AMENHOTEP III	YES	YES	YES
KV 62*	TUTANKHAMEN			
KV 23	AY	YES	YES	YES
KV 57	HOREMHEB	YES	YES	YES
KV 16	RAMESES I	YES	YES	YES
KV 17	SETI I	YES	YES	YES
KV 7	RAMESES II	YES	YES	YES
KV 8	MERENPTAH	YES	YES	YES
KV 10	AMENMESSES	YES	YES, 1C	YES
KV 15	SETI II	YES	YES	YES
KV 14	SETNAKHT	YES	YES	YES
KV 13	BAY	YES	YES	YES
KV 47	SIPTAH	YES	YES	YES
KV 11	SETNAKHT	YES	YES, 2C	YES, 4C
KV 2	RAMESES IV	YES	YES	YES
KV 9	RAMESES VI	YES	YES	YES
KV 1	RAMESES VII	YES	YES	
KV 6	RAMESES IX	YES	YES	YES
KV 18	RAMESES X	YES	YES	YES
KV 4	RAMESES XI	YES	YES	YES

NOTES TO CHART:

R	= rectangular plan;
S	= (approximately) square plan;
C	= cartouche-shaped plan;
V	= vaulted roof;
F	= flat roof;
c	= side-chamber;
p	= pillar;
var	= variant of type;
U	= well room is present but shaft is undug;
D	= dug;
B	= ledge on two sides of chamber;
L	= floor at rear of chamber is lower than floor at front.
KV 62	: a unique plan; chambers cannot be assigned standard letter or function designations.
KV 17	: "K" is a tunnel-like corridor at least 140 meters (460 feet) long.
KV 14	: Burial chamber J1 is RV/4c/8p/B; J2 is the same.
KV 47	: J1 was left unfinished after a break-through into KV 32; J2 is RV/4p.
KV 11	: D1 was abandoned after a break-through into KV 10; the tomb's axis was shifted and D2 was cut.

appeared. These tombs have a straight axis and descend steeply downward from entrances cut into sloping hillsides. They are usually larger than earlier royal tombs. A fourth plan (type 4) is similar to type 3 but with a jog in the axis about halfway between the entrance and burial chamber. They date to the 19th and 20th dynasties. In the 20th Dynasty, there were further changes in type 3 and 4 tombs: steeply sloping corridors were abandoned in favor of nearly horizontal ones and corridors became wider, ceilings higher.

There are more than 30 tombs in the Valley of the Kings that did not belong to pharaohs. Most are relatively small and often unfinished and undecorated. One of them is unique: KV 5, the tomb of the sons of Rameses II. Its entrance and first few chambers were visited by James Burton in 1822, but the tomb was later buried by flood debris and backdirt from excavations nearby. It was not until 1995, when the Theban Mapping Project relocated the tomb's entrance and explored its interior, that the tomb was found to be the largest ever found in the valley. So far, 150 chambers have been located, but the symmetrical plan of the tomb and the likelihood of more doorways in many walls mean that it is likely to contain at least 200 chambers.

The interest of Europeans in the Valley of the Kings can be traced back to Greek and Roman times. At times that interest has been intense. But only recently has it been matched by a concern for the protection of KV tombs. Many were filled with debris washed in by rain-fed flash floods that have poured into them perhaps a dozen times in the last three millennia. The clearing of that debris has often been slipshod, exacerbating the flood damage to decorated walls. Interest in the valley grew after the 1922 discovery of the tomb of Tutankhamen, but concern for the protection of KV tombs came about only in the 1990s. It has resulted in the careful excavation of KV 5, KV 10, KV 14, and KV 16, and in conservation studies of KV 17.

The Theban Mapping Project has published detailed maps of KV, hydrological studies of the valley, and plans of its tombs. But there is much more work to be done. Only a handful of tombs have been completely excavated, few have yet been adequately recorded and published, fewer still have benefited from adequate protective measures.

D	E	F	G	H	I	J	K	L	TYPE	AXIS	VOLUME	REGNAL YEARS
YES, 2						YES, 2			CURVE	94°02	1366,2	N/A
						C			CURVE	284°04	383,92	13
YES, 2P	YES/D	YES, 2P				CF/4c/2P			1	161°29	837,28	54
	YES/D+C	YES, 2P	YES			RF/4c/L			1	289°05	940,49	24
YES	YES/D	YES, 2P	YES	YES	YES*	RF/4c/6P/L			VAR. 1	196°55	1112,43	11
YES	YES/D+C	YES, 2P	YES	YES	YES	RF/7c/4P/L			VAR. 1	95°15	1463,77	38
									ODD	271°40	283,72	9
YES	YES/U					RF/1c			3	296°26	615,24	4
YES	YES/D	YES, 2P	YES	YES	YES	RF/9c/6P/L			4	357°43	1296,54	28
						SF/3c			3	240°24	253,86	1
YES	YES/D	YES	YES	YES	YES	RV/5c/6P/L YES	YES*		4	217°40	2429,11	15
YES	YES	YES, 2c	YES	YES	YES	SV8c/8P/B			2	324°45	1885,71	67
YES	YES/D	YES/1c/4P	YES	YES	YES	RV/4c/8PB	YES, 3c		3	280°51	2741,89	10
YES	YES/U	YES/1c/4P	YES	YES					3	191°02	939,78	3
YES	YES/U	YES/1c/4P				YES			3	223°44	866,88	6
YES	YES/U	YES	YES, 1c	YES	YES	J1+J2*	K1 + K2	YES	3	263°37	2148,57	N/A
YES	YES/U	YES	YES	YES, 2c	YES					292°54	419,59	
YES	YES/U	YES, 4P	YES	YES	YES	J1+J2*			3	172°02	1596,39	6
D1+D2*	YES/D	YES, 2P	YES	YES	YES	RV/4c/6P/L	YES*	YES	3	178°43	2039,28	N/A
YES	YES/U					SF/	YES		3	291°30	1116,29	6
YES	YES/U	YES, 4P	YES	YES	YES	RV/4P/B/PI	YES		3	290°20	1750,42	N/A
						R/V/N	YES		3	327°43	453,08	8
YES	YES/U	YES				SV			3	123°00	1124,85	18
										185°57	322,55	
YES	YES/U	YES				SV/4P/PIT			3	68°13	1634,75	28

Section from the 11th hour of the Amduat, *tomb of Thutmosis III. At the beginning of the upper register, is a double-headed god ('Ruler of Time'). At the side, Atum between two* wadjet-eyes. *He is grabbing a winged snake, which probably represents time. The scene refers to the task of seizing exactly the right moment for the 'morning renewal'.*

The first night hour of the Amduat in the tomb of Amenhotep II (left). It provides a list of important deities, who meet the deceased, beginning with the baboons, who are cheering the sun when it appears. The depictions are partly 'mutilated', especially the sun barge in the middle register. The texts are

written in hieroglyphs. The second night hour of the Amduat in the tomb of Amenhotep II (right). In the central one of the three registers, the sun barge is accompanied by a number of other boats, whose task is to carry provisions for the 'future life' of the dead. Also in the upper register, the gods provide ears of wheat to feed the dead.

Funerary Literature in the Tombs of the Valley of the Kings

by Erik Hornung

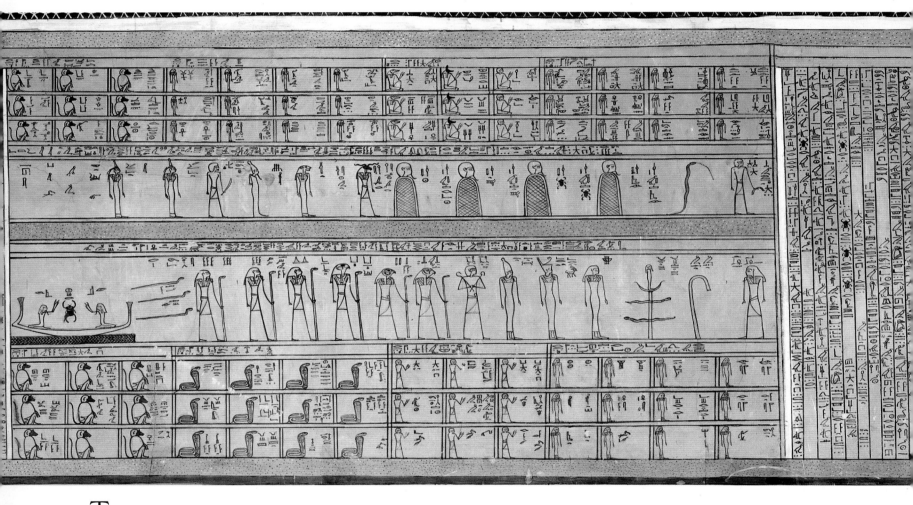

THE EARLIEST TOMBS IN THE VALLEY OF the Kings are very modest constructions, and in most cases only the burial chamber is decorated. No trace of the illustrated text used for these tombs can be found before the 18th Dynasty. Side by side with the further development of the traditional funerary literature (*Coffin Texts* and *Books of the Dead*), during the New Kingdom, a new, almost purely royal literary category emerged, known in Egyptian as *(Books of) that which is in the Duat (Underworld)*. Modern scholars first referred to these books as *Guides to the Beyond*, although in more recent times, this category of writings is generally referred to in English as the *Books of the Netherworld* (or Underworld), and in French as *Livres du monde*

inférieur or something similar. These are the earliest religious books that are not a compilation of unrelated, single instances, such as the *Book of the Dead*, but consist of a fixed, invariable body of text. As a result, even the drawings are not individual vignettes, but form an integral whole with the text. Save for a few exceptions, until the 21st Dynasty, these illustrated books constituted a tradition sent down only through the Kings. They apparently could not be used even by Queens, as can be seen in the tomb of Nefertari.

The older *Books of the Netherworld* (*Amduat* and *The Book of Gates*) unfold over the 12 hours of the night. At the mid-point of each hour stood the boat with the sun god in his nightly ram-headed form. In more recent books,

the boat of the sun god is almost totally absent and the presence of the god is indicated by the red sun disc, but even this is absent in scenes in which the damned are punished. In the *Book of Caverns*, the division into 12 parts according to the hours is replaced by a division into six portions, while the *Book of the Earth* adopts a division system that is still unclear.

All the *Books of the Netherworld* are constructed around the night voyage of the sun that is therefore viewed as the principle that creates and gives order to the caverns of the Beyond. The sun's nocturnal regeneration exemplifies the powers of renewal at work, on the other side of death. At the same time, this voyage leads into the rooms of the souls of men, where inner renewal is possible. That this is in fact a voyage of the soul can be seen in the fact that the sun god is depicted by the Egyptians as a *ba*-soul (that is to say, ram-headed since ram is *ba* in Egyptian), as he goes down into the depths; it is here that one can find the earliest important roots of modern depth psychology. The nocturnal path leads through space within the cosmos, that is not considered only as the Underworld or the depths of the earth, but also as Water (the primeval water Nun), the stygian Gloom and the Depth of Heaven. This also marks the origin of the symbolic depictions, so beloved since the time of Amarna, that try to represent the entire passage of the sun within a single complex image.

passive and throughout the entire *Amduat* does not utter a single word. Direct reference to the dead kings is only made at the 6th hour, during the decisive union between the sun-*ba* with his dead body, at the midpoint of the nocturnal journey. The ordered succession of some important netherworld creatures in the first hour of the night lays the foundation of an order and unfolding of the unknown in which the sun sets in the evening. Side by side with the sun-baboons (baboons that adore the sun) and the goddesses of the hours, other divinities of the upper and lower registers incarnate the general joy heralded by the appearance of the star (sun). Save for the damned (the enemies), all the inhabitants of the netherworld take part in this joy. In the middle register, the

fertile field, dominated by the lake *Wernes* in the second hour and in the third hour by the Waters of Osiris. During the second and third hours, the sun-boat is accompanied by other boats while during the remaining hours, it voyages alone. The god provides for the needs of the blessed souls that in the lower registers are depicted with ears of corn in their hands or in their hair. These are the "Peasants of *Wernes*," whose material needs are depicted here. During the third hour, the presence of Osiris is mentioned several times in the lower register and Ra addresses Osiris directly in the text at the end of the hour. Next, creatures in charge of punishment, armed with knives, meet up to neutralize all enemies.

With the fourth hour, the fertile, water-

The explicit preliminaries of the *Amduat* stress the knowledge that the book is supposed to transmit, such knowledge of netherworld phenomena is promised nine times. These introductory pages also give an overview of the contents of the *Amduat*. The book describes, in word and pictures, the voyage of the sun god through the 12 hours of the night, from sunset to sunrise. On the one hand the book describes the labors and discourses of the sun god, and, on the other, provides a description of netherworld beings and their functions. This is the first religious treatise that tries to consistently integrate the king into the daily passage of the sun. While Osiris is named constantly and depicted several times, he remains completely

goddess Maat, incarnation of order and harmony, appears, in her double form, directly in front of the sun-boat. She then opens the second hour, thus stressing that even here, in the netherworld, law and order reigns. In a second boat the sun-god appears already in his morning form of a scarab-beetle, worshipped by Osiris who is considered as his nocturnal form, already indicating the beginning of the journey towards its happy conclusion. At the end of the first hour, the *Amduat* deals with the opening and later sealing of the Netherworld that, because of its large population of underworld creatures, is also referred to as the Greatest City.

The following two hours open the netherworld proper, which is at first depicted as a

rich landscape is abruptly interrupted to open the way for the desert of *Ro-setjau*, the Land of Sokar, "He who is on his sand," a barren kingdom of sand, inhabited by snakelike creatures. Their extraordinary capacity of movement is symbolized by the legs and wings attached to their fantastic serpent bodies. A zigzag path, full of fire and frequently blocked by gates, cuts through this hour. At first the sun-boat must be pulled to make progress and it is later transformed into one of these serpent creatures that, with its fire breath, opens a path through the otherwise impenetrable darkness. At the precise mid-point of the hour, Horus and Sokar appear to defend the eye of the sun, the protection and renewal of which make up the subject matter of this part of the text.

The fifth hour departs somewhat from the usual structure of the text and at its midpoint stresses an intersection of the register. This hour incorporates the West and contains all the essential elements of the kingdom of the dead. The hill with the two mourning birds (Isis and Nephthys) is the burial mound of Osiris, from which the rejuvenated sun proceeds as a scarab. The killers and the large number of menacing snakes on the other side of the hill were exorcized so as to let the sun-god pass in peace, allowing him to travel through the narrow pass at the mid-point of the hour. The voyage goes over an oval that represents the Cavern of Sokar, in which the dual head of the Aker-Sphinx is imbedded. This is once again a depiction of the entire netherworld in which every night Osiris-Sokar mysteriously unites with the sun god. The Fire Lake is even more strongly represented as a place of punishment.

framed by Sobek and Nun as Lords of the Primreview Water, and Ta-tenen is referred to in the text as Lord of the Depths of the Earth.

At midnight the sun shines anew, but this self-generation of light is also a moment of great threat. At this point the seventh hour opens with the punishment of the enemies in the foreground, all ahead of the archenemy Apophis, depicted lying in his serpent form on his sand bank in front of the sun-boat, attempting to stop the renewed flow of light. He doesn't succeed in this endeavour as Isis and Seth cast a spell on him and Selkis throws her chains around his body, that is chopped up by Selkis' other helpers. Furthermore, the Sun is now also protected by the Mehen-snake. Similarly, in the upper register, Osiris triumphs over his enemies who are chained and beheaded by a demon in charge of punishment. Osiris is also surrounded by the protective Mehen-snake. Behind the sand bank

that represent the vaults throughout the realm of the dead, joyfully answer the sun god. The joyous sound of their answer can only be heard by human ears as animal cries and the sounds of nature (the buzz of the bees, banging of metal, etc.), while only the god can discern its true meaning. Conversely, the sounds of this world are also similarly distorted in the netherworld! In the middle register, the sun-boat is once again towed, so as to reach its goal speedily. The boat is followed by personified scheme-hieroglyphs, symbolizing the majesty as well as the suite of the god, including the four rams of Ta-tenen that at the end of the New Kingdom are depicted in the form of a four-headed run-ram.

In the ninth hour the crew of the sun-boat is presented, and it is the main subject matter of the middle register that also represents three divinities in charge of the material needs of the dead. Moreover, the upper and lower registers

After the desert of Sokar's land, at the sixth hour the sun reaches the watery hole at the Depths of the Netherworld, containing the primreview water Nun. This is the resting place of the Sun's dead body with which the ba-soul unites. The dead body is twice depicted at the end of the upper and middle registers. It is not depicted as a mummy but as the solar scarab that has just united with the rejuvenated morning form of the sun. This body also represents a Depiction of Osiris who is incarnated in the upper register as the lion-shaped Bull with the Thunder voice. Quite like ba and the dead body of the sun, Ra and Osiris also unite at the deepest point of the night voyage, and the nascent new life is heralded by the half-raised position of the divinities in the upper and lower registers. It is only at this crucial place that the Kings of Upper and Lower Egypt are depicted with the full splendor of the symbols of their power (scepter, crown and the snake on the top of the crown, known as uraeus), to help the dead pharaoh upon his resurrection. The lower register is

in the middle register, the tomb of the sun's dead body appears once again, protected by knives. In the lower register the sun god is enthroned as Horus of the Netherworld, in charge of looking after the passage of the stars, personifications of which fill the rest of the register. At the end, the helpful crocodile is depicted with the head of Osiris, whom he rescued from the water.

The regular construction of the eighth hour strikes the eye. Both the upper and lower registers are each organized in five caverns or vaults closed by portals that open at the invocation of the sun god. Almost all the creatures in these vaults are enthroned on Fabric-hieroglyphs that in the footnotes are identified as their clothing.

The subject matter of this night hour deals with clothing, that has from very ancient times held an important place amongst the needs of the netherworld. Upon rebirth, the dead must also be provided with new clothing. The texts also provide a detailed description of the how the ba-souls of the gods and the dead of these vaults,

continue with the issue of the provision of clothing, already dealt with in the eighth hour. The first upper group with its fabric-symbols is described as a court of law that brings down the enemies of Osiris while the following group of goddesses looks over Osiris, safeguarding him for his enemies. The twelve uraeus-serpents frighten attackers away, while the nine Field Gods with the stalk of grain in their hands continue to ensure the material maintenance of the dead.

The lower register of the tenth hour of the night highlights the rectangular pool of water with the drowned that is the main subject of the middle register of the ninth hour in the Book of Gates. The bodies adrift, like Osiris, shown in various positions, are depicted as being protected from putrefaction by Horus who later leads them to a blessed state of being, even though they were deprived of regular burial rites. Here the primeval water is represented as a re-generating element that covers the entire hour of the night that is described as having deep water and high banks. The overbearing darkness is illuminated by the four goddesses with snakes around their heads. The upper register deals with the protection and cure of the eye that represents both the eye of the sun and the eye of Horus. This task is entrusted to Thoth (the enthroned baboon), as well as to the lion-headed goddess of healing Sekhmet, represented in various forms. At the midpoint, the *ba*-souls of Sokar (falcon on the snake) and Osiris (the falcon-headed snake) appear in front of the sun-boat protected against enemies in the darkness, by the variously armed bodyguards of the sun god.

The eleventh hour deals with the preparations for the upcoming dawn or its rising from the Eastern mountain of the sky. The snake that surrounds the world depicted in front of the boat will in the next hour be miraculously rejuvenated. The serpent forms of Isis and Nephthys carry the two crowns of the land to the Eastern Gate of Sais guarded by four forms of the

goddess Neith. The upper register once again deals with time and the birth of the hours. It is important not to miss the precise moment at which the renewed dawn arises. In addition to the suite of the sun god, four goddesses mounted on dual snakes also appear at the end of the upper register, each holding a hand to cover her face. The fire breath of the snakes burns the enemies in the lower register as they are forced into the fire-filled caverns. The snakes that burn millions and the punishing goddesses execute the last judgement so as to protect the course of the sun against all threats.

In the twelfth hour of the night, the sun completes its rebirth. Since this is a repetition of the initial creation, it takes place in the presence of the primordial gods, a pair of whom are represented at the beginning of the lower register. The scene unfolds inside the snake that circles the world that was carried over in the

previous hour, and the intensity of the event is underlined by the extraordinarily large number of persons involved in pulling the boat: twelve men and thirteen women. All of them tow the boat with its millions of blessed souls through the body of the gigantic snake. The inverted direction of the towing, from the tail to the head, indicates the necessary inversion of time. According to the annotation, all the creatures enter the tail of the serpent as old and feeble, but leave the serpent's mouth as young children. At the end of the hour, the sun scarab, already on the bow of the boat, flies into the outstretched arms of the god Shu who lifts the sun into the sky. The scene unfolds in the midst of general rejoicing, represented by the divinities in the upper and lower registers. The rejoicing is not only for the sun but also for Osiris who is promised life, even if he still remains in the kingdom of the dead. The goddesses in the upper register drive away Apophis one last time with their fire-spewing snakes and give the dead further light with their burning torches after the sun has left the netherworld. For an instant, the netherworld remains open, but Shu seals it again, as the night journey comes to an end. Together with Osiris, depicted as a mummy at the end of the lower register, all the dead sink back into the sleep of death.

126-127

Barges in the middle register of the Amduat's second night hour, tomb of Seti I (burial chamber). In the first barge, we see a symbol for the moon and Maat's feather (representing justice and order); in the second barge, there is a symbol for the goddess Hathor (the waning sun) and a scarab. In the third one, we find a crocodile as 'master of the waters'; on the left, the sun god's barge.

127 bottom

The barge of the sun god in the Book of Gates (5th hour), upper pillar hall in the tomb of Seti I. Whilst in the Amduat there is a large crew on board, here only Sia and Heqa (magic) accompany the sun god. His ram-head characterises him as a ba-soul.

Characters from the Litany of Ra, on a pillar in the tomb of Thutmosis III. They illustrate various aspects of the nightly activities of the sun god. The 'Fiery One' is painted in red, the heads are black.

The nightly unification of Ra and Osiris in a symbolic depiction in the tomb of queen Nefertari. The ram-head represents the sun during the night, a mummy and the presence of Isis (right) and Nephthys is pointing to Osiris.

Together with the *Amduat*, the tombs of Thutmosis III and his vizier Useramen also depict the Solar Litany, that from Seti I fills the first two corridors of the tombs of the kings. Unlike the *Books of the Netherworld*, this book features an original title which may be translated as *Book of the Adoration of Ra in the West, of the Adoration of the United One in the West*. The text begins with the great litany that invokes the sun god 75 times with various names and under differing forms. Each invocation starts with the spell "Praise to thee, Ra, the powerful." The structure of the rest of the text is not very clear, only the litanies (nine), stand out with their uniform introductory spells.

The figures of the gods that illustrate each invocation of the great litany, belong to an ancient tradition. From the very beginning, these figures are divided into two rows, that in the Ramesside tombs, were placed facing each other on the walls of the second corridor. Up to the 51st invocation, the subdivision alternates rigidly, with one figure on the left (odd numbers) and one on the right (even numbers). In both rows, aspects of Ra and Osiris appear mixed, without any schematic distinction, representing the union of the two gods, one within the other, during this momentary transition. The names and figures that illustrate them refer to the most important functions of the sun god in the netherworld. So one finds the morning form Khepri (mentioned three times), the evening form Atum, the *ba* of Ra (as an additional figure), the forms as a ram, tomcat and child, the divine eye and the sun disc, as well as the accompanying figure of the baboon. The other gods and goddesses of the Ennead appear next to Atum, although Seth is replaced by Horus. Of the other gods, Nun and Taten are represented as well as the depths of the waters and the earth. Osiris appears only as Khentamnetiu, although two names refer to the union of Ra and Osiris, that is the central theme of the litany.

Furthermore, several names stress the close relationship between the god and the underworld kingdom of the dead. The god is therefore referred to as "He, of the Netherworld," "He, of the vault," "He who prays over tombs," "He who renews the earth," and even directly, "the West." Further names identify him as the wanderer through this sphere, and at the end of the great litany, he is known as the migratory bird that disappears and reappears. Rejoicing and mourning are both represented, since the text deals

with death and rebirth, and in some names refer to the dead body of the god, and even to the decomposition of his body that is followed by regeneration. The dual face of the night sun is depicted as a radiant light side by side with darkness. Lastly, the good deeds of the god in favor of the blessed souls are also represented, side by side with the punishment he metes out to the damned. From Seti I, a frontispiece in programmatic characters, was inserted between the title of the book and the great litany. The frontispiece depicts the scarab and the ram-headed god in the disc, in front of which the hostile powers, shown in animal form (snake and antelope, crocodile and antelope), flee from both sides. A representation of the union between Ra and Osiris was specifically prepared for the tomb of queen Nefertari. The representation depicts Osiris in his ram-headed mummy form and the Ra as the solar disc. This however is not part of the illustration of the solar litany itself, but refers to the beginning of spell 180 of the *Book of the Dead*, and has therefore also been found at the entrance to the tombs of certain dignitaries of the 19th Dynasty.

Since the book appears at the beginning of the decoration of the Ramesside royal tombs, it was considered obviously important. The book describes and praises the divinity that during the night descends into the netherworld to awaken the dead to new life, look after the blessed souls and punish the damned. The multiplicity of the aspects and functions of the nocturnal sun god in the great litany reveals the netherworld to the dead. At the same time, the text refers to the acceptance of the dead king in the passage of the sun, ensuring his daily regeneration. After the great litany, the dead king speaks for the first time, intimating that he has become very familiar with the nocturnal forms and names of Ra. The dead king expresses the hope that these nightly forms of Ra will open the netherworld to him and his *ba*-soul, since he has become the very image of the sun god his *ba*. Departing from the style of the *Books of the Netherworld*, in this text, the dead king speaks and is referred to in the third person. In the second litany that follows this text, the inhabitants of the netherworld are requested to open a path for the dead king, now part of Ra's entourage. Interrupted only by an invocation to the nocturnal sun that

shines in the Netherworld, the third litany closes with the prayer: "May you lead me along the path of the West." This formulates a primordial death wish that leads to the first direct inference that the dead king is equated first with Nun, then with Ra, his *ba* and his metamorphosis. The fact that Nun, the god of the primordial waters, is mentioned at the very outset, underlines the high regard with which he was considered, even in the *Book of the Heavenly Cow*, as well as his active role at the end of the *Book of Gates*. The next text invokes the United One, equating the dead king with *ba* and his body. The full meaning of this is underlined through the separate depictions on the ceiling of the second corridor of the royal tomb. A comment on recitation refers to the aspects of the gods and the sacrifices that are due to them. In his next invocation the dead king addresses them as Gods, who are in the West, and goes on to stress "I am one of you," identifying himself with the sun god, with whom he shares victory over all his enemies in heaven and on earth (even including the netherworld!). In the fourth litany that follows ("Joy to thee") even Osiris is invoked; Ra and Osiris greet each other and hold out their hands to each other. The fifth litany generally deals with the god's care for the dead king. This is followed by a prayer for protection from the killers of the underworld, their cauldrons, traps and ovens, since "I am Ra." After a description of the majestic aspect of the god as *ba*, the sixth litany opens with the prayer "O Ra, come to me, Guide" and continues with other self-identifications and conversations with the weak of heart in the netherworld. The seventh litany ("Truly, you have let me rise") is followed by the deification of the organs, through which the dead king becomes completely a god; each of his body parts is identified with a divinity. The dead king is also identified with Osiris, since he appears as the son of the god and assumes his authority. He addresses the inhabitants of the netherworld who are in charge of sacrifices. This section is brought to an end by the eighth litany of praises. The text ends with the adoration of the realm of the dead as the West (the ninth litany) and a last identification of the dead king with Ra, with the re-evocation towards the end, of the old formula that places the *ba*-soul in heaven and the body on the earth (adding the phrase under the gods).

A new *Book of the Netherworld*, the *Book of Gates*, appears instead of the *Amduat* in the tomb of Horemheb. As in the *Amduat*, this book also deals with the nocturnal voyage of the sun through the 12 hours. In this book the thematic content is only partly slightly rearranged (so that the drowned appear in the ninth instead of in the tenth hour). Departing from the *Amduat*, the *Book of Gates* distinguishes between the divinities and the blessed souls, and the dead seem to be limited to their respective regions of the hours of the night. Furthermore, the extraordinary representation of the pharaoh is particularly accentuated as he accompanies the sun god up to his rebirth in the morning, and his passage through the netherworld, symbolizes the path of the sun.

Upon entering the realm of the dead, the

depths of the earth. At the end of the register, even clothing is renewed, becoming shining white linen. In the lower register the Apophis appears for the first time, in the form of a huge snake, in front of Atum who supports two Enneads as they overcome the archenemy. The upper register of the fourth hour is dominated by two bodies of water, the lake of life (guarded by jackals) and the lake of *uraei*, both of which are variations of the lake of fire depicted in the third hour. In the middle register, shrines with mummies still immersed in the sleep of death appear before the boat. The sun god brings about their resurrection and salvation. The dead are only rarely depicted as mummies since, in the netherworld, they expect a new, perfect body. Their renewed life fills one hour of the night, until the

dead. The scene of the Osiris hall of judgement represented in a particular fashion heralds in the sixth hour and indicates its focal point. This is the only representation of the judgement hall of the dead in the *Books of the Underworld*, and is depicted using cryptography. Osiris, the judge, thrones over a gallery, while in front of him, the personified scales are empty, departing from the representation in the *Book of the Dead*. The Enneads of the acquitted blessed souls are depicted on steps, while the enemies are hidden, invisible, under the soles of his feet, and are condemned to destruction. Another hostile power is represented in the form of a pig. The hall of judgement of the dead is a prelude to the union between the *ba* and the body of the sun god as well as all the blessed souls in the sixth hour of the night, the deepest point

sun god is greeted not by individual divinities but collectively by all the dead who are referred to as gods of the desert and placed on the Western mountain. As in the *Amduat*, the first hour of the night is a transition point before the netherworld proper that starts with the first gate. Two ram- or jackal-headed poles represent the authority of the god who metes out punishment or rewards to the inhabitants of the netherworld. The second hour divides the inhabitants of the netherworld into blessed souls (in the upper register, the blessed souls have spoken with Maat and now live with Maat) and the damned (in the lower register, where Atum pronounces a punishment discourse against them). Besides the enemies, the lower register also contains the four sluggards that lie enfeebled on the floor, indicating that here in the netherworld, even the four points of the compass are enfeebled and invigorated. The third hour introduces certain central motifs of the nocturnal voyage, such as the resurrection of the mummies and their instatement in their shrines as well as the ambivalent lake of fire from which the blessed souls are saved, even though the waters of the lake become as fire for the damned. In the middle register, the sun god passes through the earth boat, a symbolic depiction of the entire voyage through the

sun god passes on to the next hour. The next scene represents the change of hour, with the snake of time, depicted as lying in many coils, and the 12 goddesses that personify the hours. In the lower register, Osiris in his shrine is surrounded on all sides and protected by the gods of his entourage. Horus, the faithful son, looks over his dead father, and, at the end of the register the enemies of the god are punished in the cavern of fire. The contents of the fifth hour of the night are very complex. The dead are here assigned space (in the form of fields that the gods measure with measuring tape in the upper register) and time (the gods with the body of the snake and the hieroglyphs for lifetime in the lower register). For this to take place without hindrance, the archenemy Apophis must be overcome, and is depicted as he who retreats in the form of a tamed captive in front of the boat. The lower register opens with a depiction of the four races of humanity, respectively represented by the Egyptians, Asians, Nubians and Libyans. All of them are assured life in the netherworld and they are entrusted to the care of Horus and Sekhmet. As in the great hymn of Akhenaten where Aten also takes care of foreign peoples, here too foreign races are afforded a place in the kingdom of the

of the voyage. As in the *Amduat*, the dead body of the sun is placed in the center, although it is still invisible. In the middle register, directly in front of the boat and its crew, the sun's dead body is carried by the gods, whose arms, upon touching the body, become as invisible and hidden as the body. In the lower register, the mummies of the dead lie on a long snake-shaped bier, as they take part in the union with the *ba* and the resurrection that follows. For this decisive process to take place without disturbance, Apophis must be kept way, and this is done by the gods with forked snake-staves in the upper register. Human heads appear out of the body of the snake-staves, and Apophis, who has devoured them, must now liberate them. Immediately to the side, time is represented by a dual coiled rope that unwinds out of the throat of the god Aqen. As in the *Amduat*, the theme of the seventh hour is the elimination of all the hostile powers, so that the re-birth of the sun is not endangered in any way. In the middle register, the jackal-headed pole of Geb appears in front of the sun, with two enemies of the gods, tied to it. Their punishment is meted out by demon-executioners with sinister names, as Ra looks on approvingly. In clear contrast with this scene, the upper register represents two groups of blessed souls, bearing baskets of sacrificial food as a sign of their material sustenance and the feather of Maat as a sign of their acquittal by the hall of judgement of the dead. All of them have a being up to his end hidden in the Maat, while the damned belong in the place of destruction. In the note, Osiris greets his new following. In the lower register, gods or blessed souls are shown looking after large ears of corn for the promised salvation. They are equipped with sickles to harvest the grain. Under the rays of the re-born sun, even corn grows in abundance! In the eighth hour, time is once again represented in the upper register as an endless rope that is unwound hour after hour (as in the sixth hour), together with the tow rope of the boat that brings forth the mysteries. In the middle register, the Lords of sustenance in

battle against Apophis, during which two sets of seven divinities hit him in the eye with nets. The nets, that they carry above them, hold, as though in a force field, the magic that renders Apophis powerless. Both the upper and the lower registers introduce particular forms of the sun god. He appears above as a griffin followed by two very complex snake-like creatures that take part in the punishment of Apophis and all the enemies. In the lower register, a continuous rope links all the figures. In the central part, the sun god is represented as a falcon but is also called Khepri (scarab). The accompanying text specifically refers to a going out and stresses that the voyage is moving upwards towards the sky. Even in the eleventh hour, Apophis, this time in the upper register, appears bound, dismembered and rendered

the West appear in front of the rope. At Ra's behest they look after the blessed souls and inflict evil on the enemies. The mummies in the lower register have turned around in the biers and are therefore already at the stage of resurrection. The rectangle of water with the drowned is the central motif of the ninth hour and appears in front of the sun boat. This is a reference to the *Amduat*, where the same scene appeared in the lower register of the tenth hour. Here there are four groups of the dead who in various positions push Nun into the primordial waters, and avail of her regenerative powers. For them water symbolizes refreshment. Their noses must breathe air and their *ba*-souls are not destroyed so that they can take part in the upcoming blessed existence. Ra is here depicted as he who is in Nun and in the last image, he has already ascended from Nun. The said *ba*-souls are depicted in the upper register next to a group that distributes bread and vegetables to them. By contrast, the lower register represents punishment. The fiery one is represented as a huge snake within whose coils the children of Horus lie as it spews its fiery breath against 12 enemies, that are tied up in three different ways. Horus accuses them of their misdeeds against his father Osiris and asks the fiery one to commit the enemies to fire. In the tenth hour, the middle register is entirely devoted to the

harmless. The rope that ties him and his helpers is held by a huge hand that reaches out from the deep. In the middle register Ra's face appears in a boat, so that the dead may be able to gaze at his face. The re-appearance of the god is heralded by stars. In the lower register the god's oarsmen appear together with the goddesses of the hours—time and energy (rowing)—act together to so as to bring the boat to the eastern horizon. Several divinities have the specific function of announcing the god at the horizon and their calls are a foretaste of the clamor that accompanies the sunrise. Through the gate with secret access the sun god reaches the twelfth and last hour of the night in which the miracle of re-birth is completed. The stars once again herald the appearance of the sun and goddesses enthroned on serpents surround the sun child. In front of the boat, Apophis lies already in chains and cannot stop the sunrise. He is kept in check by the gods with knives and crooks. Behind him, four baboons announce the sun god on the eastern horizon with joyful gestures using their fists. The lower register deals with crowns that are worn upon leaving the netherworld and with the upbringing of the new-born sun child through his nurses and the lament of Osiris who remains behind in the netherworld.

Isis and Nephthys, in the form of serpents guard the last door of the realm of death, through which the sun god passes to reach the horizon. This is followed by a closing image that is not divided into registers. The voyage of the sun is concentrated in a single image, as in a large number of illustrations of hymns to the sun, after the Amarna period. Half hidden in the deep, the god Nun raises the sun-boat out of the primordial waters (represented by lines of waves). In the boat, the sun, in the form of a suspended scarab is embraced by Isis and Nephthys, and he pushes the sun disk towards the goddess Nut who welcomes Ra. Her headfirst position represents the inversion of the passage of the sun that is now directed towards the netherworld, depicted by Osiris shown as a curved figure embracing the netherworld. Arms reach out towards the sun from above and below that hold him and push him forward through the space of the universe, day after day.

Seti I implemented a completely new decoration program, since, from the entrance up to the burial chamber, his tomb was adorned with relief sculptures. This allowed for decoration much richer than in previous tombs and his successors adopted his style of funerary decoration. Rameses VI, for instance, combined nearly all the funerary literature of the New Kingdom, in his tomb, including naturally the *Book of the Dead*, that is especially designed to give practical help in the netherworld: sustenance, resurrection and protection from danger. Spell 125 with its invocation of the hall of judgement of dead is especially important and since Merenptah, also appears in the tombs of the kings.

Since the reign of Rameses IV, the *Book of the Caverns* was also represented in funerary decoration. This book is divided into six sections that contain no reference to the hours of the night. It owes its modern name to the caverns or vaults that make up the realm of the dead. The representations contain a large number of ovals that refer to the sarcophagi. The contents once again deal with the sun's nocturnal voyage, during which the sun god, in both the first sections addresses a long monologue to the gods of the realm of the dead and in the third section, meets the body of Osiris in its coffin. All the sections also provide an exhaustive illustration of the punishment of the damned. The concluding image that was already found in the tomb of Merenptah, once again provides an overview of the entire voyage of the sun.

The *Book of the Earth* is also fully represented in the tomb of Rameses VI, while only some of its scenes have been found in later tombs. It stresses above all the gods of the depths of the earth such as Aker, Geb and Ta-tenen, and also describes the nocturnal rebirth of the sun, inspiring Piankoff to give the book the title of *La création du disque solaire*. The sun is raised, by several pairs of arms, from the depths where the damned are punished and destroyed.

The *Books of Heaven* describe the sun's voyage through the netherworld in the body of the goddess of heaven, Nut, who swallows the sun in the evening and gives it new birth in the morning. This is why this work is not represented on the walls but on the ceilings of the tombs, that even in the Old Kingdom symbolized the heavens, and from Seti I onwards symbolized the astronomical ceiling decorated with stars. The motifs of this heavenly night voyage are the same as in the books of the netherworld and even here, in the heavens, we find the primordial ocean Nun.

The *Book of the Heavenly Cow* features a special composition that is found on the outer golden shrine of Tutankhamen and from Seti I, is represented in a room adjacent to the burial chamber. At the mid point the book features the representation of the Heavenly Cow on which the sun god once left the earth because men rebelled against him as he was old and feeble. Some of the rebels escape punishment through the fiery eye of the sun, the goddess Hathor, but even their destiny now consists in deprivation of the presence of god, strife and death. In this way this myth explains the current, imperfect state of the world.

Since Seti I, not the walls of the tombs, but even the sarcophagi of the kings were richly decorated with scenes from religious books. Seti's famous alabaster sarcophagus contains the first complete version of the *Book of Gates*, while the increasingly larger sarcophagi of his successors featured various sections from several of the *Books of the Netherworld*. Furthermore, even these sarcophagi were enclosed in golden, decorated shrines as can be seen in the case of Tutankhamen.

When the Valley of the Kings was abandoned as a burial site at the end of the New Kingdom, the most important religious books were copied on sarcophagi and papyruses. From the 26th Dynasty onwards, these texts are also represented on the walls of sarcophagi, this time, not of kings but of dignitaries and priests. They therefore survived up to the Ptolemaic Period and it is quite possible that their content was known to Gnostic and Hermetic authors.

132

Depiction from the final scene of the Book of Caverns in king Merenptah's burial chamber. The picture summarises the nightly course of the sun (red disk); her smaller shape in the morning is represented by the scarab beetle.

132-133

The celestial goddess Nut, who swallows the sun every evening. During the night, the sun crosses her body, to be reborn by her in the morning. The goddess' head is placed between the red desert and the blue primordial waters. Ceiling of the burial chamber in the tomb of Rameses VI.

134-135

On the northern wall of the sarcophagus hall of the 'Great Royal Wife' Tausert, we see scenes from the Book of Caverns. The pillars are decorated with protective deities of the kingdom.

136-137

View of Thutmosis III's burial chamber with two pillars (visible: figures from the Litany of Ra) and the king's sarcophagus. For security reasons the walls are now behind glass. The room has an oval shape. The walls are decorated with the 12 night hours of the Amduat.

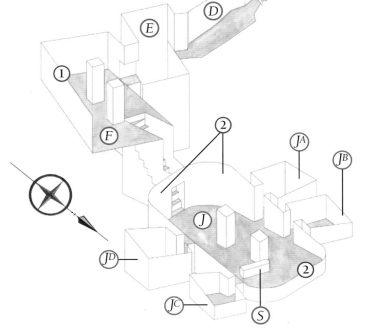

LEGEND	
A	ENTRANCE
B	FIRST CORRIDOR
C	FIRST CHAMBER
D	SECOND CORRIDOR
E	THE SHAFT
F	THE UPPER PILLAR HALL
J	THE BURIAL CHAMBER
JA-D	FOUR SIDE CHAMBERS FOR
	BURIAL OFFERINGS
S	THE SARCOPHAGUS
MAIN SCENES	
1	CATALOGUE OF GODS
2	BOOK OF AMDUAT

THE TOMB OF
THUTMOSIS III

by Erik Hornung

IN A RAVINE HIGH ABOVE THE VALLEY OF THE Kings lies the entrance to the tomb of King Thutmosis III (KV 34). For 20 years Thutmosis had lived in the shadow of his stepmother Hatshepsut, but with his victory at Megiddo he made Egypt the leading world power of his time. By those who lived after him he was remembered as a great conqueror, but his activities also included peaceful works, such as the construction of numerous temples. Kings' funerary temples were now separated from the tomb and lay at the edge of the fertile land of Western Thebes.

In February, 1898, workers from the Antiquities Department discovered the tomb's entrance and a few days later the Director, Victor Loret, arrived to oversee the clearing. The tomb's axis is not straight, but curved as in all early tombs in the Valley of the Kings. The entrance lies in the north, the burial chamber deviates to the east. This reflects the continuation of a tradition established in the Middle Kingdom under Sesostris II: the main corridor of

---

137 left

The upper pillar hall, with two undecorated pillars. On the walls, a catalogue of the Amduat gods. The ceiling is painted as a sky with yellow stars.

137 right

One of Thutmosis III's statues in the Cairo Museum, originally from Karnak temple. It is made from diorite. The king treads upon the enemies of Egypt, represented by the so-called Nine Bows. The royal head cloth carries the uraeus-serpent.

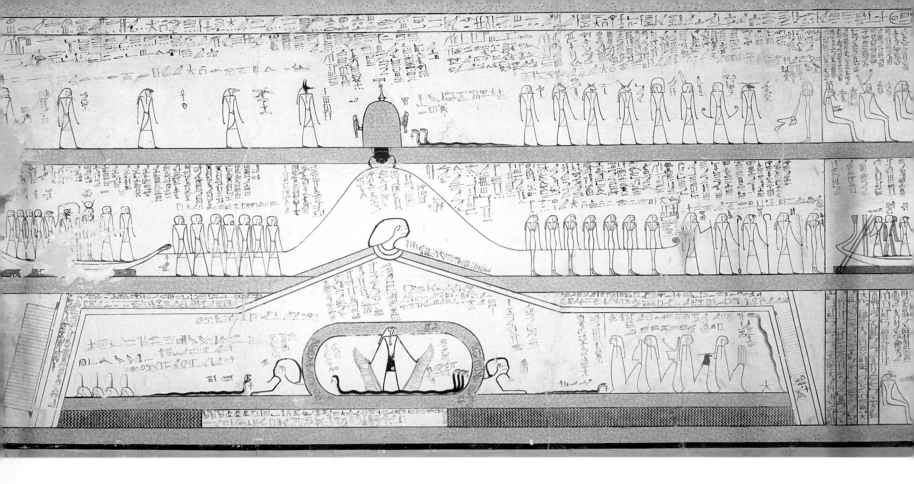

138-139

In the burial chamber, the fifth and sixth night hour of the Amduat, before the beginning of the book, with the title and first hour on the right. The fifth hour, between the heads of a double-sphinx, contains the oval of the god Sokar; the sixth hour contains the body of the sun god, protected by a snake with multiple heads.

138 center

On the front pillar, we find the damaged scene of Isis as a tree goddess offering her breast to the king, accepting him into the world of the gods. Next to her is the king with flail and scepter in his hands.

138 bottom

The punishing demon in the seventh hour of Amduat, tying down and decapitating enemies of Osiris. It has pointed ears like a cat, and symbolizes aspects of the sun god.

139 bottom left

Beginning of the seventh night hour of Amduat: the god Shepsi, the Praising One, with a lion's head, and an uraeus-serpent with a human head. Next to them, Osiris on his throne, protected by the snake, observing the punishment of his enemies.

139 bottom right

A wooden figure of the king, found by Loret in the Thutmosis III's tomb and now in the Cairo Museum.

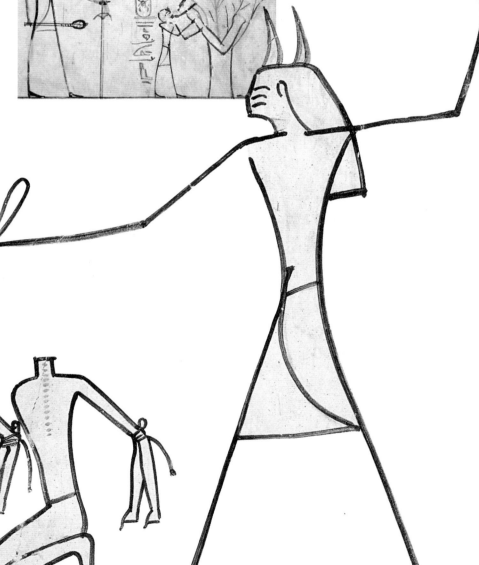

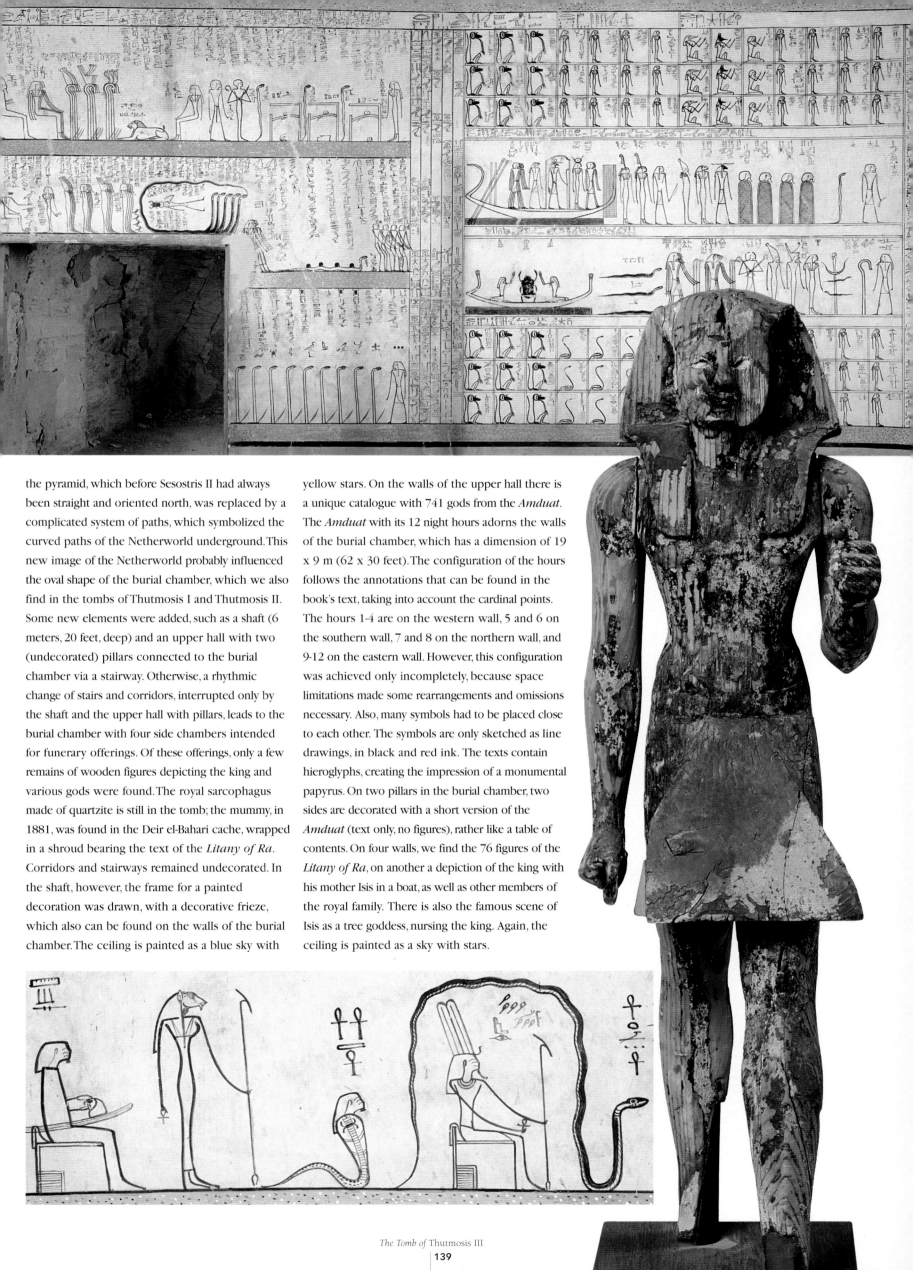

the pyramid, which before Sesostris II had always been straight and oriented north, was replaced by a complicated system of paths, which symbolized the curved paths of the Netherworld underground. This new image of the Netherworld probably influenced the oval shape of the burial chamber, which we also find in the tombs of Thutmosis I and Thutmosis II. Some new elements were added, such as a shaft (6 meters, 20 feet, deep) and an upper hall with two (undecorated) pillars connected to the burial chamber via a stairway. Otherwise, a rhythmic change of stairs and corridors, interrupted only by the shaft and the upper hall with pillars, leads to the burial chamber with four side chambers intended for funerary offerings. Of these offerings, only a few remains of wooden figures depicting the king and various gods were found. The royal sarcophagus made of quartzite is still in the tomb; the mummy, in 1881, was found in the Deir el-Bahari cache, wrapped in a shroud bearing the text of the *Litany of Ra*. Corridors and stairways remained undecorated. In the shaft, however, the frame for a painted decoration was drawn, with a decorative frieze, which also can be found on the walls of the burial chamber. The ceiling is painted as a blue sky with

yellow stars. On the walls of the upper hall there is a unique catalogue with 741 gods from the *Amduat*. The *Amduat* with its 12 night hours adorns the walls of the burial chamber, which has a dimension of 19 x 9 m (62 x 30 feet). The configuration of the hours follows the annotations that can be found in the book's text, taking into account the cardinal points. The hours 1-4 are on the western wall, 5 and 6 on the southern wall, 7 and 8 on the northern wall, and 9-12 on the eastern wall. However, this configuration was achieved only incompletely, because space limitations made some rearrangements and omissions necessary. Also, many symbols had to be placed close to each other. The symbols are only sketched as line drawings, in black and red ink. The texts contain hieroglyphs, creating the impression of a monumental papyrus. On two pillars in the burial chamber, two sides are decorated with a short version of the *Amduat* (text only, no figures), rather like a table of contents. On four walls, we find the 76 figures of the *Litany of Ra*, on another a depiction of the king with his mother Isis in a boat, as well as other members of the royal family. There is also the famous scene of Isis as a tree goddess, nursing the king. Again, the ceiling is painted as a sky with stars.

THE TOMB OF
AMENHOTEP II

by Erik Hornung

THE SUCCESSOR OF THUTMOSIS III pursued the same foreign policy as his predecessor, defending the Egyptian predominance in Syria against the attacks of the Mitannian empire and its allies. In his inscriptions he underlined his achievements in war and sports, but he also pointed out his role as a builder, especially at Karnak and in Nubia. Even his vizier, Amenemope, was permitted to have a tomb in the Valley of the Kings (KV 49). The entrance to his own tomb (KV 35) is hidden at the foot of a steep cliff. Victor Loret found it in March 1898, one month after the discovery of KV 34, the tomb of Thutmosis III. Again, the axis of the tomb is not straight. This time it makes a right angle turn. We see the same rhythmic change between stairs and corridors, and between the two pillared halls there is an additional corridor.

Only the burial chamber is painted; all other rooms are undecorated. To protect the painted walls from visitors, protective glass has been installed, as in many other tombs. The texts in the tombs of Thutmosis III and Amenhotep II were recorded by Paul Bucher and published in 1932.

In contrast to his predecessor, Amenhotep II returned to a rectangular burial chamber. Its design remained the common standard until the time of Seti I. After a section with six pillars there follows a lower part that contains the king's sarcophagus. Like KV 34, the tomb of Thutmosis III, there are four side chambers for the offerings, some of which (wooden figures) were found by Loret. In a figure of a king, a papyrus was concealed that contained the oldest version of Chapter 168 of the *Book of the Dead*, in which the 12 vaults of

140
Amenhotep II protected by a goddess in the shape of a snake. Behind, there is a sketch of a papyrus field. The cow horns and sun disk indicate Hathor, goddess of regeneration. The statue is in the Egyptian Museum in Cairo.

141 top
View of the burial chamber with the sarcophagus of Amenhotep II. At the foot end, Isis kneels down on the symbol for gold. On the sides are depictions of the sons of Horus. The pillars show the goddess Hathor, handing the symbol for life, the ankh, to the king.

LEGEND AND MAIN SCENES	
A	TOMB ENTRANCE
B	FIRST CORRIDOR
C	FIRST CHAMBER
E	SHAFT
F	UPPER PILLAR HALL
G	ROOM
J	BURIAL CHAMBER WITH THE SARCOPHAGUS (BOOK OF AMDUAT)
J A-B	SIDE ROOMS
J C-D	SIDE CHAMBERS WITH MUMMIES

141 bottom

*Panther figure from the tomb
of Amenhotep II, now in the
Egyptian Museum in Cairo
(CG 24622). The animal
symbolizes regeneration after
death. We also know this theme
of the king with a panther from
the tomb of Tutankhamen.*

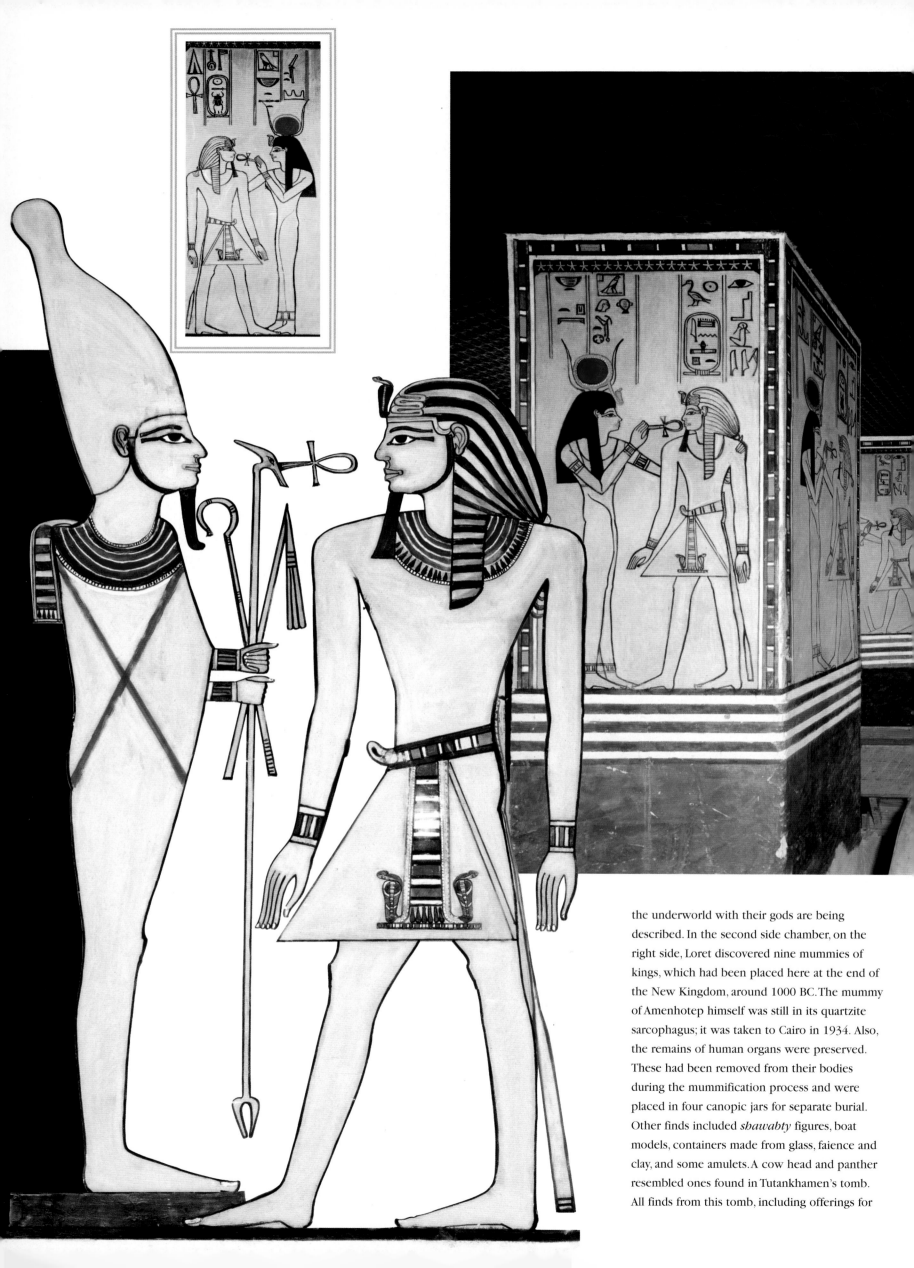

the underworld with their gods are being
described. In the second side chamber, on the
right side, Loret discovered nine mummies of
kings, which had been placed here at the end of
the New Kingdom, around 1000 BC. The mummy
of Amenhotep himself was still in its quartzite
sarcophagus; it was taken to Cairo in 1934. Also,
the remains of human organs were preserved.
These had been removed from their bodies
during the mummification process and were
placed in four canopic jars for separate burial.
Other finds included *shawabty* figures, boat
models, containers made from glass, faience and
clay, and some amulets. A cow head and panther
resembled ones found in Tutankhamen's tomb.
All finds from this tomb, including offerings for

142-143

View along the axis of the tomb through the upper part of the burial chamber. One can see the six pillars with their scenes with gods: Amenhotep symbolically receives life from Osiris, Anubis and Hathor. Everywhere he is depicted, the king wears the protectve uraeus-serpent on his forehead.

143 bottom left

Side of pillar with the king in front of Anubis, also called the master of the Afterworld and guardian of the necropolis. Here, too, the ankh is symbolically shown before the face of the king.

143 bottom right

One of the many amulets made from blue faience (others are made from wood) found by Loret all over the tomb (now Cairo CG 24348). It represents the hieroglyph for life (ankh), which the gods shown on the pillars hold before the king's face.

a prince, are now exhibited in the Egyptian Museum in Cairo.

The walls of the burial chamber are decorated with line drawings from the *Amduat*. The night hours are now depicted one after another without interruption of the sequence. The first are located on the back wall, then the 12 hours follow clockwise. A short version is placed at the end, on the left wall. The entire composition is surrounded by a broad red line representing the realm of the dead in the western desert into which the sun disappears every night. Such lines also separate the individual registers within the hours. The solar bark sails on a strip of water. On the right wall we see the transition from the third night hour with its ample water

142 top

Side of pillar with Hathor as goddess of the west and Amenhotep II. The goddess shows her symbol on the head, as well as cow horns and a red sun disk.

142 bottom

Amenhotep II in front of Osiris, from a pillar in his burial chamber. The god is wearing the White Crown (from Upper Egypt) and is holding the was-scepter, a shepherd's crook and a flail in his hands. An ankh-sign extends from the scepter to the king's face, to indicate his re-animation.

A winged snake of painted wood,
meant as a protective god for
Amenhotep II; now in Cairo
CG 24629. Such snakes also
appear in the Amduat.

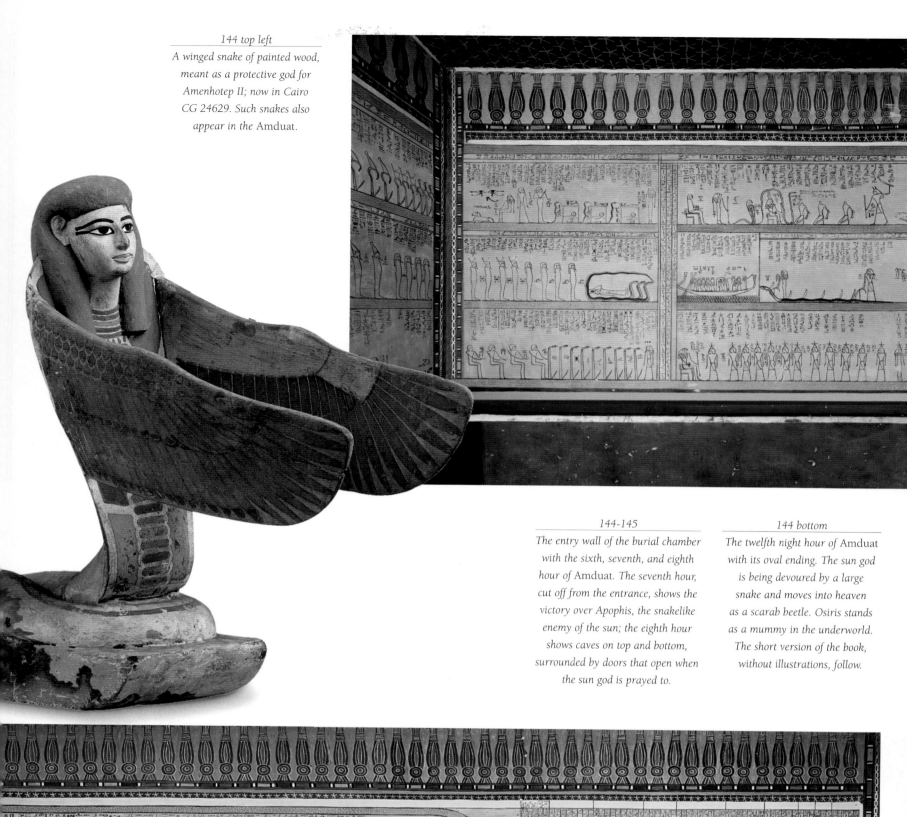

144-145

The entry wall of the burial chamber
with the sixth, seventh, and eighth
hour of Amduat. The seventh hour,
cut off from the entrance, shows the
victory over Apophis, the snakelike
enemy of the sun; the eighth hour
shows caves on top and bottom,
surrounded by doors that open when
the sun god is prayed to.

144 bottom

The twelfth night hour of Amduat
with its oval ending. The sun god
is being devoured by a large
snake and moves into heaven
as a scarab beetle. Osiris stands
as a mummy in the underworld.
The short version of the book,
without illustrations, follow.

supply to the desert landscape of Sokar's realm in the fourth hour. The final night hour, during which the sun is shrinking in a gigantic zigzag, has an oval end. At the top of the walls is a decorative frieze, similar to that used by Thutmosis III. The room's ceiling is painted blue, adorned with yellow stars.

All six pillars in the burial chamber are painted with scenes that show the king with a god or a goddess, holding an *ankh* sign to his nose. His partners in the scenes are Osiris, Anubis, and Hathor, who next to the sun god Ra (whose nightly voyage is described by the *Amduat*), are the most important personalities for the deceased. They ensure his survival in the Netherworld. Osiris is ruler of the dead and responsible for their judgement; Anubis cares for their bodily existence in their mummified form; and Hathor represents all aspects of regeneration in life and beyond. The first pair of pillars is entirely reserved for Osiris, the third for Hathor. On the second pair, decorations refer to both Anubis and Hathor. The gods have various nicknames: the king is generally called "beloved by Osiris." All scenes are drawn in black and red color only, as is the case in the *Amduat*. Paintings in others colors are found in the next tomb to be dug in the Valley, that of Thutmosis IV. The sky hieroglyph above all the scenes with gods (and above the *Amduat*), however, is painted in blue, and there is a multi-colored frame around each of the scenes. In the *Amduat*, water is also painted blue, especially in the tenth night hour, in which drowned persons float in the primordial waters.

145 bottom left

A cow head from the tomb of Amenhotep II, now Cairo CG 24630. The eyes are stylized as Horus-eyes (udjat); it represents to the cow-like goddess Hathor, who on the pillars appears as a woman with cow horns.

145 bottom right

One of the king's wooden figures, now Cairo CG 24598. Amenhotep II wears the royal headscarf and the ceremonial beard; other figures have a crown.

THE TOMB OF
TUTANKHAMEN

by T.G.H. James

Bᴇꜰᴏʀᴇ ᴛʜᴇ ᴅɪꜱᴄᴏᴠᴇʀʏ ᴏꜰ ʜɪꜱ ᴛᴏᴍʙ in 1922, Tutankhamen was a king known to have ruled towards the end of the 18th Dynasty, but about whom very little more was known. After his tomb was discovered, Tutankhamen became for a time the most famous of Egyptian royal names, and he and the wondrous treasures from the tomb have continued to fascinate the general public. Sadly, however, the tomb yielded very little historical information, and although a far clearer picture of his reign has been obtained through subsequent studies, there remains much to be discovered about the man and the happenings of his time.

There seems little doubt that the young prince, first named Tutankhaten, was the son of Akhenaten, the so-called heretic Pharaoh. He with his wife Nefertiti, abandoned Thebes and established a new capital at a place in Middle Egypt which he called Akhetaten, "Horizon of the Aten," now called El-Amarna. Here Tutankhaten was born, his mother very probably being a secondary royal wife, named Kiya. He was brought up in the royal court and in due course was married to the third daughter of Akhenaten and Nefertiti, Ankhesenpaaten. He was then possibly no more than seven or eight years old, while his wife was considerably older, perhaps fourteen or fifteen. Such marriages between half-brothers and half-sisters within the royal family were not exceptional. At the time of the marriage

146 left
Aerial view of the Tomb of Tutankhamen. To the right, the broad path leads to the tomb of Merenptah; to the left, the narrow path leads past the tombs of Horemheb and Rameses III to the tomb of Amenhotep II. Above is the entrance to the tomb of Rameses VI.

146 top right
Detail of the golden throne of Tutankhamen showing the young pharaoh's cartouche.

146 bottom right
The flail and the crook are symbols of royal authority.

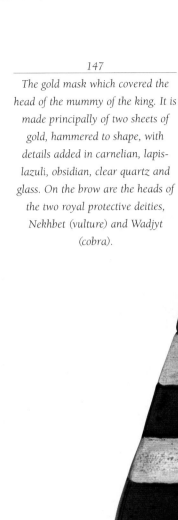

147
The gold mask which covered the head of the mummy of the king. It is made principally of two sheets of gold, hammered to shape, with details added in carnelian, lapis-lazuli, obsidian, clear quartz and glass. On the brow are the heads of the two royal protective deities, Nekhbet (vulture) and Wadjyt (cobra).

there may have seemed little chance of the young prince becoming king, but circumstances changed with the deaths in quick order of Akhenaten and of his successor Neferneferuaten, who may even have been Nefertiti herself.

Moves to abandon Akhetaten and to re-establish Thebes as a city of importance and the religious centre for the worship of the god Amen, seem to have started in the brief reign of Neferneferuaten, and they were accelerated after Tutankhaten's accession. The royal couple changed their names to Tutankhamen and Ankhesenamen, and the royal residence and administrative capital were established at Memphis, which had remained a place of importance throughout the Amarna years. The processes of religious rehabilitation and political renewal were in the hands of experienced administrators: Ay, formally the Regent, Maya the Treasurer, and Horemheb, the General. It seems certain that under the direction of these competent officials, the land of Egypt was restored to a settled state in which a fair return to the peaceful prosperity of the pre-Amarna reign of Amenhotep III was achieved. Some small military operations may have been conducted in the East where Egyptian influence had waned during Akhenaten's reign.

Tutankhamen died in about 1325 BC, having reigned for approximately nine years. He was scarcely out of his teens. The death seems to have been sudden, but its cause has never been satisfactorily established. Because of its unexpectedness, a proper royal tomb had not been completed, and a relatively small tomb of non-royal plan was hastily prepared for the dead king. A few years later, when Ay himself died, he was buried in the West Valley of the Kings in a tomb which may have been planned originally to receive the burial of Tutankhamen.

The Burial Chamber showing the position of the great quartzite sarcophagus, centrally placed; on the left the view looks east, with the entrance to the Treasury lying behind the sarcophagus. Four goddesses protect the contents with outstretched wings: centrally, as shown, Nephthys, to the left Isis, to the right Selkis, with Neith at the fourth corner. The view on the right shows the outer coffin of the king resting in the sarcophagus: it still contains the remains of Tutankhamen's mummy.

LEGEND

1	16 STEPS DOWN TO THE FIRST BLOCKED ENTRANCE
2	THE DESCENDING CORRIDOR
3	BLOCKED ENTRANCE TO BURIAL CHAMBER
4	THE ANTECHAMBER
5	HOLE FOR BEAM USED TO MOVE HEAVY OBJECTS
6	THE ANNEXE
7	THE BURIAL CHAMBER
8	MAGICAL BRICK RECESS
9	THE TREASURY

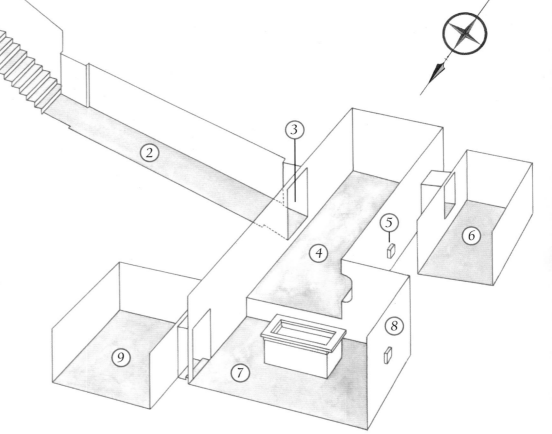

Paintings from the Burial Chamber: left the night bark
of Khepri sails above 6 night hours with their baboon
deities; right the king's mummy in a garlanded bier
on its way to burial.

151-153

Ay opens the mouth of the royal mummy;
Nut greets the king; Osiris welcomes the king
and his ka (spirit).

154

Pectoral scene of the king, supported by
Atum and Iusaas, is offered a long reign
by Amen-Ra.

The Tomb of Tutankhamen

155

The modest sepulcher which became Tutankhamen's last resting place was situated not far from the entrance to the main Valley of the Kings, in an area unexploited for royal burials up to that time, apart from the deposit of grave-goods known as KV 55, containing funerary material of the Amarna Period, possibly brought to Thebes during the reign of Tutankhamen. KV 55, like KV 62 (Tutankhamen's tomb) was not planned as a royal tomb in the conventional form of the 18th Dynasty. The simple original plan of KV 62 was probably adapted, in so far as time allowed, to accomodate a royal burial set out in some semblance of what was thought to be necessary for a king at that time. There is much evidence from the way in which the tomb's equipment was disposed in the four rooms to suggest that the burial was hasty and to some extent prepared without the great care which

might have been expected for a king. There is, however, some need to be cautious in drawing conclusions from the conditions in the tomb of a king who died unexpectedly, and which represents the closest that may ever be discovered to a complete royal burial of the New Kingdom. Even so, what was discovered by Howard Carter in 1922 did itself not fully represent the original disposition of the grave-goods. Tutankhamen's tomb was entered by robbers on at least two occasions after the funeral; after the first robbery materials connected with the embalming of the body and the final rites at the time of inhumation were removed officially from the descending corridor, to be buried in the cache discovered by Theodore Davis in 1907—a discovery which indicated that the tomb of Tutankhamen probably lay in the vicinity.

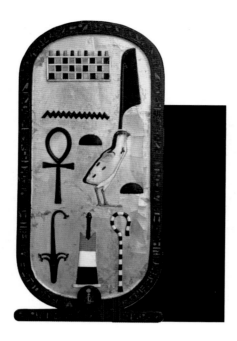

The site of the tomb had certainly been lost soon after its final closure, and it remained buried deep below the floor of the Valley of the Kings until it was discovered by Howard Carter on 4 November 1922. The dramatic events of that day formed the climax of his campaign of exploration in the Valley which had seriously begun in 1917. Tutankhamen was undoubtedly among the few kings whose tombs were still to be found, and Carter may by 1922 have concluded that the young king's burial was at the top of the list for discovery in that part of the Valley. Still, he did not know that the tomb was almost intact, containing in particular the actual burial and its attendant equipment in almost pristine condition. In spite of difficulties and setbacks Carter pursued the clearance of the tomb with exemplary care and dedication. The task was completed in 1932, almost ten years after the discovery. The significant dates in the process of excavation and clearance were as follows: 24 November, 1922, opening of the first sealed entrance; 27 November, 1922, opening of the second sealed entrance into the Antechamber; 16 February, 1923, formal entrance into Burial Chamber; 12 January 1924, opening

of the sarcophagus; 11 November, 1925, opening of the innermost coffin and the start of the examination of the mummy; 24 October, 1926, clearance of the Treasury begins; November-December, 1927, clearance of the Annexe; 27 February, 1932, removal of last parts of the shrines after consolidation, work in tomb completed.

The physical plan of the tomb, as already mentioned, was not that of a conventional royal tomb of the 18th Dynasty. It is not, however, possible to discover what precisely its design was before it was modified to receive the burial of a king. It is likely that the Burial Chamber, with its floor set lower that that of the Antechamber, was enlarged so as to

reproduce to some extent that part of a conventional royal tomb in which the burial area was lower that the pillared hall from which it was approached. The room must have been tailored in order to accomodate the great shrines which were to be brought into the Burial Chamber. Nothing could have been easy for the officials in charge of the burial, and it is probable that workmen had to be at hand up to the last moment to make modifications as the great components of the burial equipment were brought into the tomb. A very careful order of installation must have been prepared in advance; for example, the stocking of the Treasury had to be completed first, and its contents were to include some of

the most important items in the burial. Even so, there were objects in the Antechamber and the Annexe which should ideally have been placed in the Burial Chamber of the Treasury.

The tomb was dug deep into the bed-rock floor of the Valley of the Kings. Sixteen steps cut into the limestone led down to the descending passage. The six lowest steps were cut away in antiquity, no doubt at the time of the burial, to allow the movement into the tomb of some of the largest pieces of the funerary equipment, such as the canopic shrine, the sarcophagus, and the walls of the shrines, enclosing the sarcophagus. These cut-away steps were remodelled in stone and plaster before the

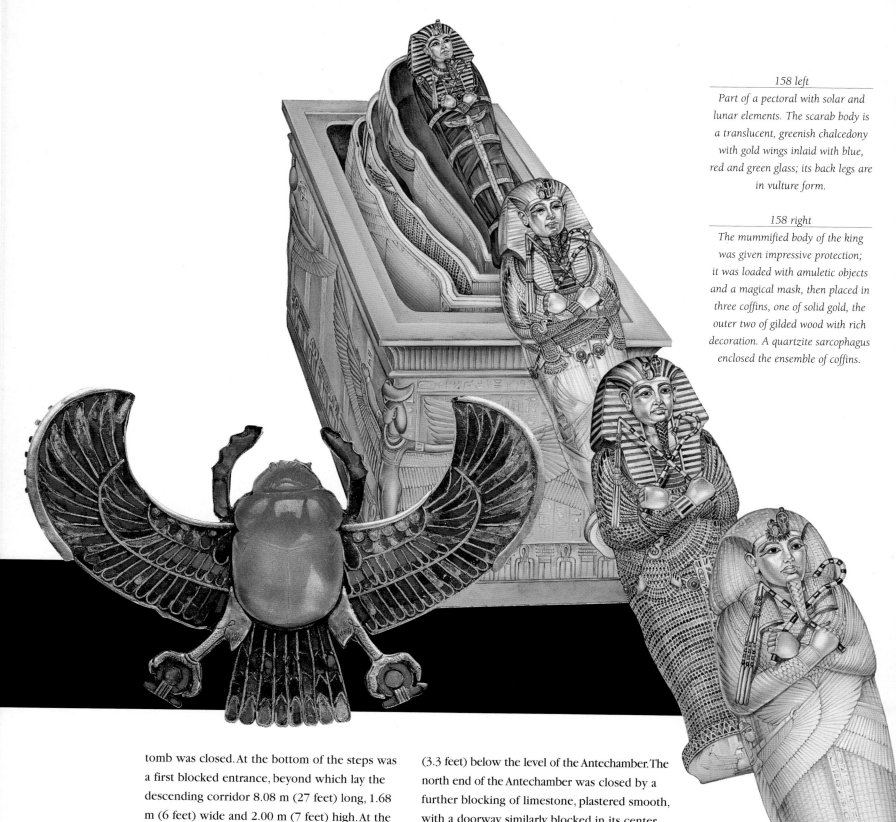

158 left

Part of a pectoral with solar and
lunar elements. The scarab body is
a translucent, greenish chalcedony
with gold wings inlaid with blue,
red and green glass; its back legs are
in vulture form.

158 right

The mummified body of the king
was given impressive protection;
it was loaded with amuletic objects
and a magical mask, then placed in
three coffins, one of solid gold, the
outer two of gilded wood with rich
decoration. A quartzite sarcophagus
enclosed the ensemble of coffins.

tomb was closed. At the bottom of the steps was
a first blocked entrance, beyond which lay the
descending corridor 8.08 m (27 feet) long, 1.68
m (6 feet) wide and 2.00 m (7 feet) high. At the
moment of the discovery this corridor was filled
with rubble, but originally it contained the
materials found in the cache excavated in 1907.
At the west end of the corridor lay the entrance
to the tomb, blocked by limestone and plaster
and sealed, like the entrance at the east end at
the bottom of the steps. The four rooms of the
tomb are still generally designated by the names
given them by Carter after the initial discovery.
The Antechamber, entered directly from the
descending corridor, is 7.85 m (26 feet) by 3.55
m (12 feet) with a roof-height of 2.68 m (10 feet).
The walls are rough cut, unplastered and
undecorated. At the south end of the west wall a
blocked doorway, scarcely one-metre (3 feet)
high and just over a metre (3.5 feet) wide, gave
access to the Annexe, a small chamber measuring
4.35 m (14 feet) by 2.60 m (9 feet), with a height
of 2.55 m (8 feet), its floor lying about one metre

(3.3 feet) below the level of the Antechamber. The
north end of the Antechamber was closed by a
further blocking of limestone, plastered smooth,
with a doorway similarly blocked in its center.
Beyond lay the Burial Chamber, the equivalent
of what is often called the burial crypt in royal
tombs of the more conventional design. It is
6.37 m (21 feet) by 4.02 m (13 feet), with a
height of about 3.65 m (12 feet). The floor level
is 0.94 m below that of the Antechamber. It is
the only room in the tomb with plastered and
decorated walls. Four niches, one in each wall,
contained the magical bricks which provided
extra protection for the precious remains of the
dead king. An open doorway in the eastern wall
of the Burial Chamber led into the Treasury,
which measured 4.75 m (16 feet) by 3.8 m (12
feet), with a height of 2.33 m (8 feet).

This bare description gives little idea
of what was actually found in this almost intact
royal burial. The most important part of the
tomb lay beyond the blocking which closed up
the north end of the Antechamber. It held the

159

Upper part of the innermost coffin
of solid gold. Tutankhamen is shown
wearing the nemes-headdress, the
protective vulture head and cobra
on his brow, and he holds in his
hands the crook and flail of divine
royalty. At the neck are strings of
gold and glass disk beads.

protected body of the king and those elements of the burial equipment essential for the posthumous well-being of the pharaoh. The royal body was placed in a nest of three coffins (the innermost of solid gold), set on a low, gilded, wooden bier within a quartzite sarcophagus. This protective group was itself installed within a series of four shrines which practically filled the whole of the chamber. Various objects of magical power were disposed around the outside of the shrines and in the narrow space between the two outermost shrines. The most important protective objects were placed on the body itself,

a remarkable 150 pieces—amulets, jewelry and other accoutrements—all invested with magical powers, designed ultimately to ensure the royal destiny in the Afterworld. In a conventional royal tomb, wall decorations were used to accomodate the texts and representations needed to help the dead king in his journey through the dark regions to achieve his appointed place beside the god Ra in the heavens. In Tutankhamen's tomb the paintings on the walls of the Burial Chamber mostly show simple episodes in the burial procedures, apart from those on the west wall—a representation of the hours of the night through

which the dead king would pass. Important texts concerning this nocturnal progress, and others concerning the fate of the king after death are contained on the gilded walls of the shrines.

From careful examinations it has become clear that many pieces in the burial equipment were originally made for other members of the Egyptian royal family, and adapted with changed inscriptions for Tutankhamen, for example, the middle coffin and the stone sarcophagus itself. Similar evidence from intimate material placed in the Treasury, confirms the modification of existing burial

160-161

Detail of the scene on the golden throne. Ankhesenamen anoints Tutankhamen with ointment from the vessel in her left hand. Sun rays, some holding the sign of life, come down on the royal couple – typical of the Amarna period when the throne was surely made.

161 bottom

The golden throne, the most remarkable piece of ancient Egyptian furniture. Made of wood it is covered with sheet gold inlaid with semi-precious stones, glass and faience. The dress of the queen and the kilt of the king are of sheet silver.

162 left

The canopic shrine. It and its
surrounding canopy are of gilded
wood, both with cornices and friezes
of uraei inlaid with colored glass.
On each side is placed the figure of
a protective goddess; here Isis and
Selkis are shown.

162-163

Alabaster royal heads, emerging
from the canopic chest. They are
stoppers of two of the depressions
holding the canopic coffins. Careful
portraits, they clearly do not
represent Tutankhamen, but
possibly his predecessor,
Nefernefruaten.

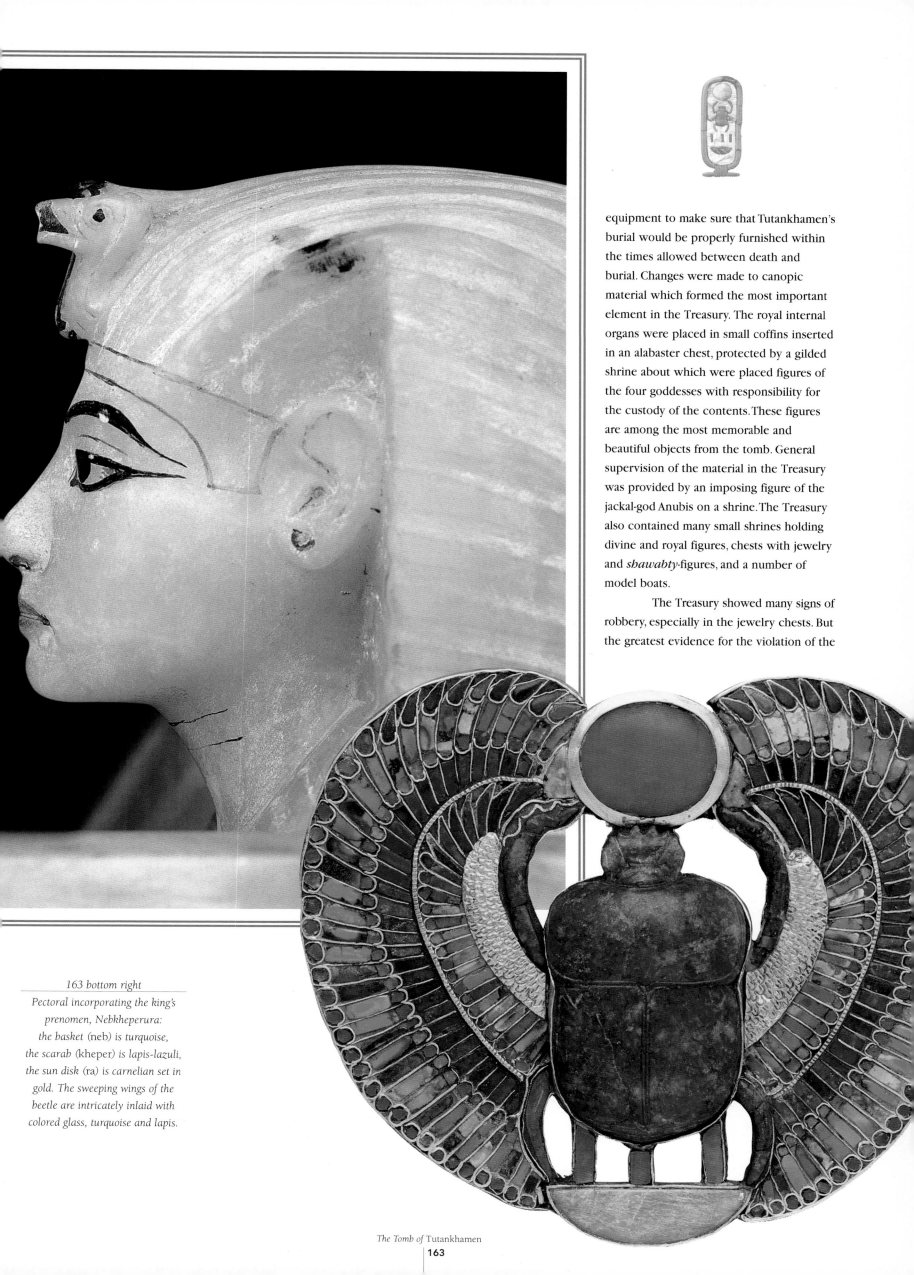

equipment to make sure that Tutankhamen's burial would be properly furnished within the times allowed between death and burial. Changes were made to canopic material which formed the most important element in the Treasury. The royal internal organs were placed in small coffins inserted in an alabaster chest, protected by a gilded shrine about which were placed figures of the four goddesses with responsibility for the custody of the contents. These figures are among the most memorable and beautiful objects from the tomb. General supervision of the material in the Treasury was provided by an imposing figure of the jackal-god Anubis on a shrine. The Treasury also contained many small shrines holding divine and royal figures, chests with jewelry and *shawabty*-figures, and a number of model boats.

The Treasury showed many signs of robbery, especially in the jewelry chests. But the greatest evidence for the violation of the

163 bottom right
Pectoral incorporating the king's prenomen, Nebkheperura: the basket (neb) is turquoise, the scarab (kheper) is lapis-lazuli, the sun disk (ra) is carnelian set in gold. The sweeping wings of the beetle are intricately inlaid with colored glass, turquoise and lapis.

The Tomb of Tutankhamen

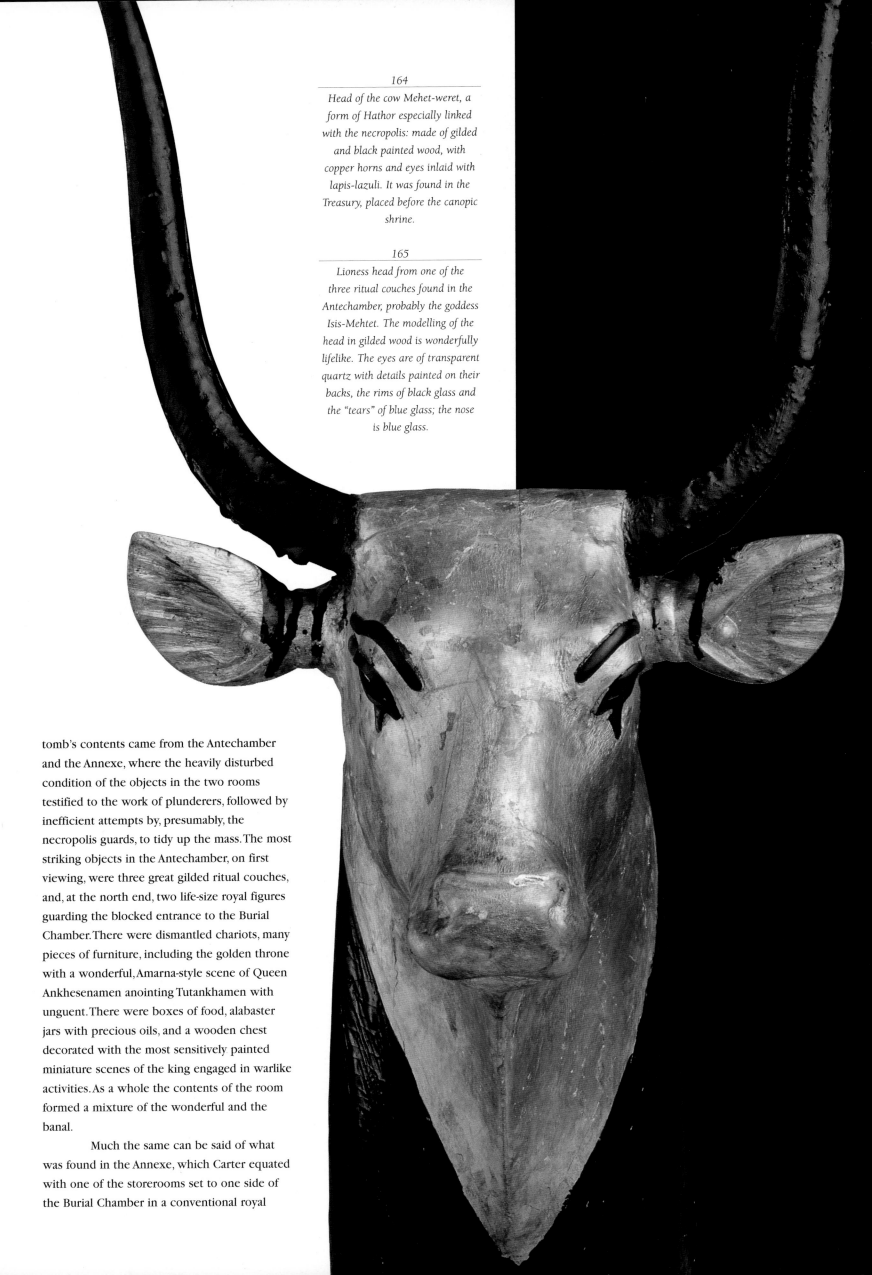

164

Head of the cow Mehet-weret, a form of Hathor especially linked with the necropolis: made of gilded and black painted wood, with copper horns and eyes inlaid with lapis-lazuli. It was found in the Treasury, placed before the canopic shrine.

165

Lioness head from one of the three ritual couches found in the Antechamber, probably the goddess Isis-Mehtet. The modelling of the head in gilded wood is wonderfully lifelike. The eyes are of transparent quartz with details painted on their backs, the rims of black glass and the "tears" of blue glass; the nose is blue glass.

tomb's contents came from the Antechamber and the Annexe, where the heavily disturbed condition of the objects in the two rooms testified to the work of plunderers, followed by inefficient attempts by, presumably, the necropolis guards, to tidy up the mass. The most striking objects in the Antechamber, on first viewing, were three great gilded ritual couches, and, at the north end, two life-size royal figures guarding the blocked entrance to the Burial Chamber. There were dismantled chariots, many pieces of furniture, including the golden throne with a wonderful, Amarna-style scene of Queen Ankhesenamen anointing Tutankhamen with unguent. There were boxes of food, alabaster jars with precious oils, and a wooden chest decorated with the most sensitively painted miniature scenes of the king engaged in warlike activities. As a whole the contents of the room formed a mixture of the wonderful and the banal.

Much the same can be said of what was found in the Annexe, which Carter equated with one of the storerooms set to one side of the Burial Chamber in a conventional royal

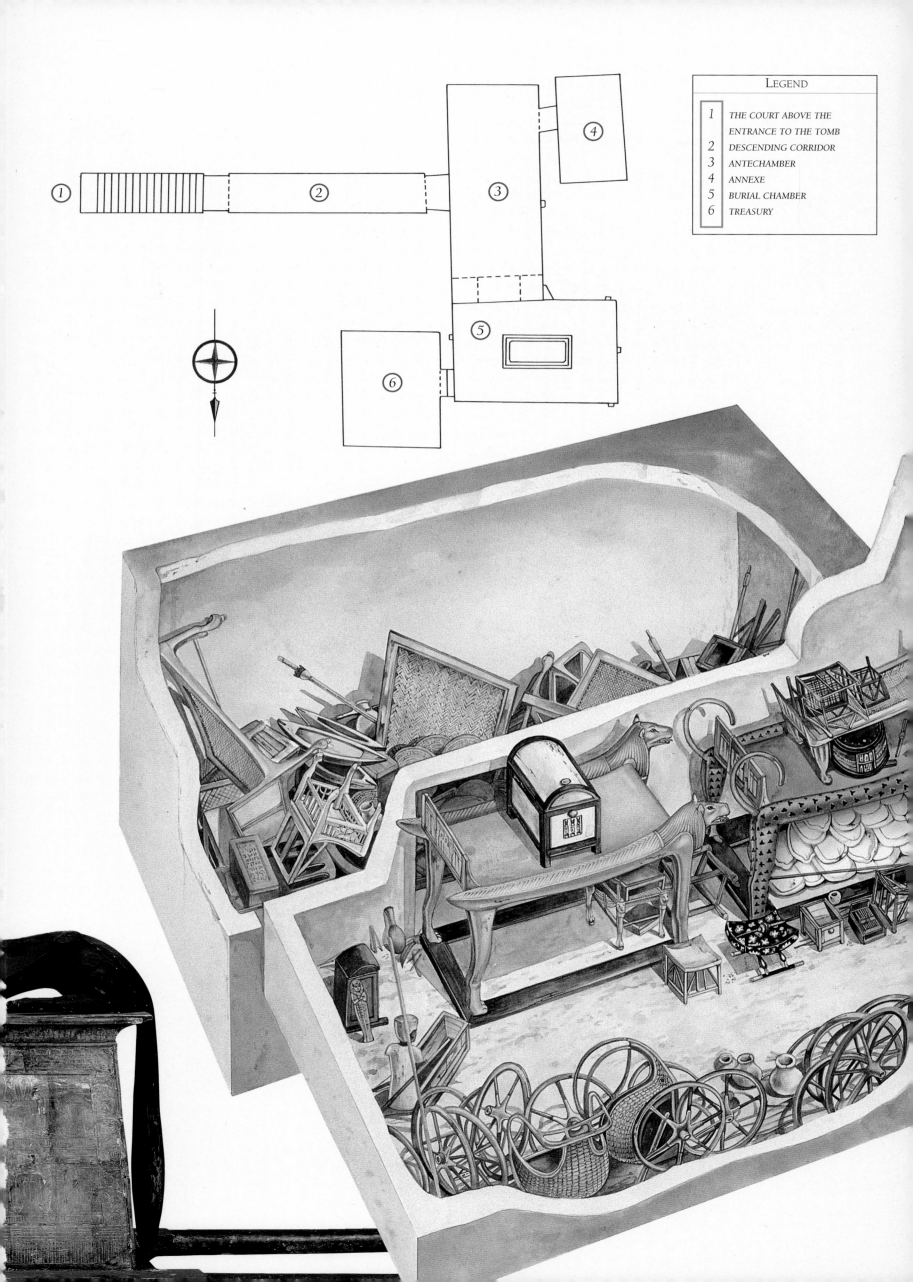

tomb. It had been intended to contain
principally materials to feed, refresh and restore
the dead king—jars of wine, alabaster vessels of
unguents and oils, boxes of food and baskets of
fruit. There was a kind of order in the lowest
layers in the room, but an impression of
haphzard stacking of other materials including
beds and other furniture such as the so-called
ecclesiastical throne, chests of *shawabty*-figures
and of clothing and jewelry. Much of the
disarray was undoubtedly due to the hasty
tidying of the tomb after the ancient robberies,
but it seems likely that the room was used as a
dump for what could not be stored elsewhere.
One may even wander whether some degree of
clutter or untidiness might not have been
common in all royal tombs at the moment of
closing and sealing of the sepulcher.

Such then was the tomb of a modest
burial for an unimportant monarch. So it had
always been considered; but perhaps the scale
and quality of its contents may not have been so
modest in comparison with what was consigned
to the tombs of earlier kings of the 18th
Dynasty. By any standard, Tutankhamen was not
meanly treated in death.

166

*Limestone statue, almost life-size,
of Amen, the god proscribed by
Akhenaten, but rehabilitated under
Tutankhamen, whose features this
sculpture portrays. It was found in
Karnak.*

171

*Head end of the quartzite
sarcophagus showing the upper part
of the figure of Isis in protective role.
Tutankhamen's name is clearly
carved, but there are traces of an
earlier inscription.*

167 left

Figure of Ptah, great god of Memphis,
always shown mummiform.
The head has a cap of blue faience;
the eyes are outlined in blue glass;
his beard and the amuletic staff
are bronze with gold.

167 top right

One of the gilded wooden figures found
in the Treasury. It is named on its base
Mamu, a little-known god, here shown
as a mummy with an Osiris beard,
and with post Amarna features.

167 bottom right

The impressive figure of Anubis on a
shrine, which guarded the sacred
canopic equipment. Many items
of jewelry, amulets and implements
were stored in compartments
in the shrine.

168-170

A cut-away reconstruction of the
tomb of Tutankhamen, showing the
disposition of many of the principal
objects in the tomb equipment. From
the entrance one steps into the
Antechamber, confronted by the
ritual couches with animal heads,
many pieces of furniture, and to the
left, dismantled chariots.
The Annexe, entered behind the
hippopotamus couch is roughly
stacked with furniture and boxes.
Behind the guardian statues in
the Antechamber lies the Burial
Chamber with its nest of coffins,
sarcophagus and four protective
shrines. At the bottom to the left is
the Treasury, with Anubis guarding
the canopic shrine, boxes of deities,
shawabtis and jewelry, and many
model boats.

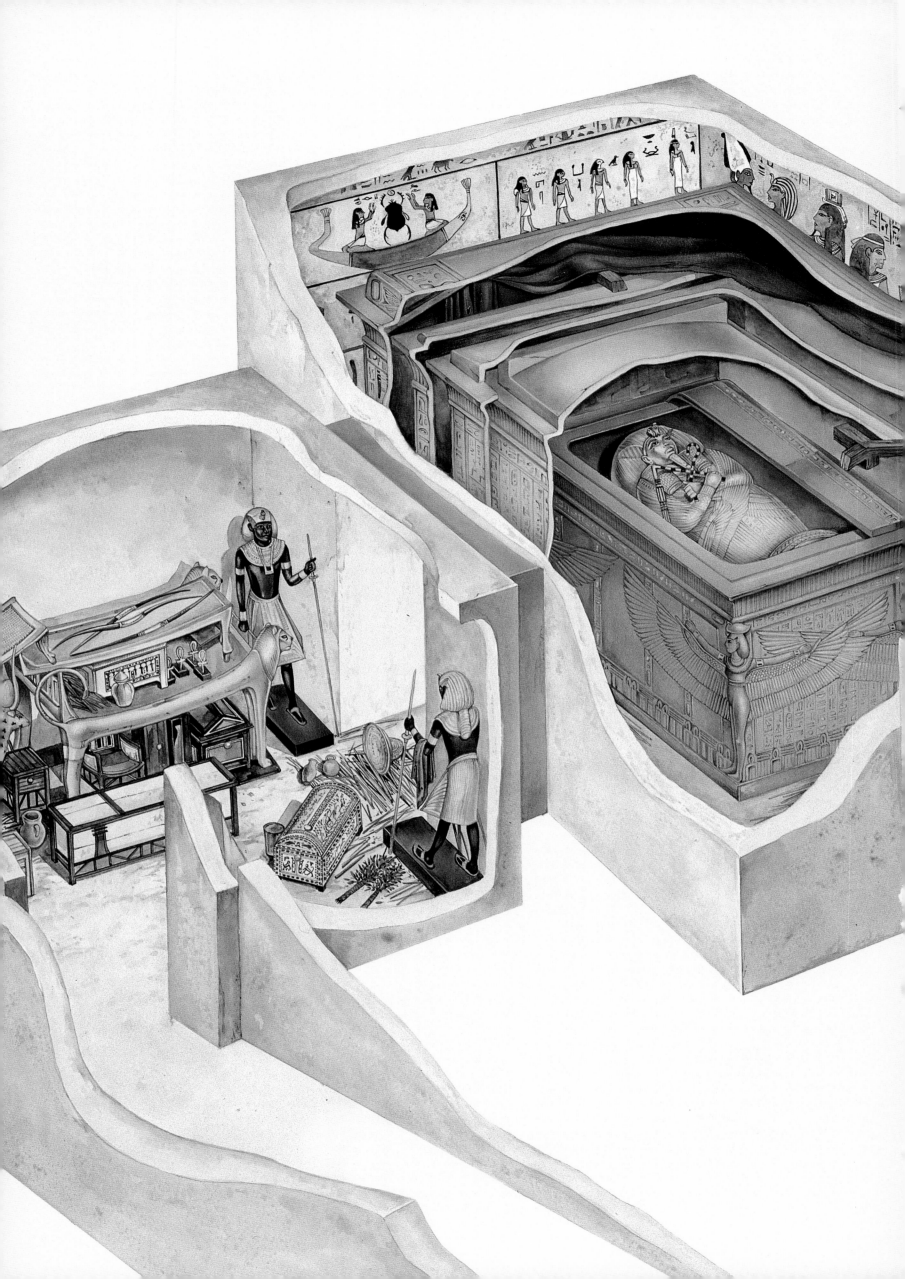

THE TOMB OF AY

by T.G.H. James

KHEPERKHEPERURA AY SUPERVISED THE burial of Tutankhamen, and succeeded him as pharaoh. He was not of the royal line of the 18th Dynasty, but had acted as regent for Tutankhamen during that young king's reign. He seems to have secured a claim to legitimacy by marrying his predecessor's widow, Ankhesenamen. He was already an old man at the time of his accession, and his reign was brief and undistinguished. With the support of Horemheb, his collaborator in securing the regime of Tutankhamen, he continued the process of restoring Egypt to a state of security and religious stability after the unhappy destabilization of the Amarna Period. His contribution to this process of national rehabilitation did not, however, save him from the *dammatio memoriae* with which the so-called Amarna kings were afflicted subsequently.

For his own burial, Ay prepared a tomb in the West Valley of the Kings, which may originally have been designed for Tutankhamen; it lies not far from the tomb of Amenhotep III. No foundation deposits have been found which would establish the identity of the royal person for whom the tomb was planned. It was discovered by Giovanni Battista Belzoni in 1816 during his first exploration of the royal valleys. He had visited the tomb of Amenhotep III, which had been found by members of the Napoleonic expedition, and he came across Ay's tomb by chance as he explored deeper in the valley. With the aid of a few workmen, but greatly hampered by ophthalmia, Belzoni was able to make a superficial exploration of the tomb. His general assessment of the discovery was reasonable; "from its extent, and part of a sarcophagus remaining in the

172-173

The burial chamber with the reconstructed sarcophagus. Painting on the left shows Ay, sometimes with his ka, receiving gifts from Nut, and embraced by Osiris. On the right, the first stage of the Book of Amduat, with the baboon deities of the hours of the night.

173 bottom

View over the sarcophagus to the decorated south wall of the burial chamber. At the top, two boats with Nephthys standing between them; the left one contains two falcon standards, the right the divine Ennead, the company of nine gods. Below are spells from the Book of the Dead.

Two vignettes from the scenes in the burial chamber: on the left, decoy ducks held in the royal hand, from the fowling scene on the east wall; on the right, one of the sacred baboons marking the hours of the night, on the north wall.

174 center

Part of the top register of the decoration on the west wall of the burial chamber: the goddess Nephthys stands behind the boat containing the company of nine gods who make up the Great Ennead. Re-Horakhty is followed by Atum, Shu, Tefnut, Geb, Nut, Osiris, Isis and Horus.

175

The east wall carries a double scene rare in royal tombs, showing Ay and his first wife Teye, engaged in the ritual hunts of hippopotamus and fowl. Here is part of the papyrus thicket with a flight of ducks – a very stiff composition, wholly unaffected by the grace of Amarna marsh scenes.

center of a large chamber I have reason to suppose that it was the burial-place of some person of distinction." Many years later the greatly damaged sarcophagus was removed to the Cairo Museum, but was reinstalled in the burial-chamber after the tomb was systematically cleared by Otto Schaden of the University of Minnesota in 1972.

The plan of the tomb is simple, and has been compared with that of Akhenaten at El-Amarna. Its axis runs approximately north-south; two corridors lead to a chamber which may have been intended for the well or sump found in earlier Theban royal tombs of the 18th Dynasty. There is no pillared hall, but a sarcophagus chamber with one small room opening off it, to hold the canopic equipment—the mummified internal organs with accompanying shrine and associated material—the equivalent of the "Treasury" in Tutankhamen's tomb. The burial-chamber alone has painted decoration, a simple scheme in which the king is depicted with various deities, and in a scene of hunting in the marshes. There is much ancient defacement. One wall only carries part of the composition "What is in the Underworld."

LEGEND	
A	ENTRANCE TO THE TOMB
B	FIRST CORRIDOR
C	STEPS DOWN FROM FIRST CORRIDOR
D	SECOND CORRIDOR
E	CHAMBER INTENDED FOR WELL
J	BURIAL-CHAMBER WITH SARCOPHAGUS
JA	CANOPIC CHAMBER

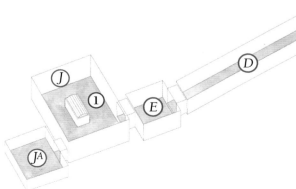

MAIN SCENES	
1	Birds hunting scenes, Book of Amduat and scenes with gods

176-177

Upper part of a low relief figure of
Horemheb offering two bowls of
wine to Hathor, Lady of the Two
Lands, goddess of the West. The top
of the was-scepter of power, held
out to the king by the goddess,
cuts across his left hand.

177

Statue-group of a kneeling
Horemheb making an offering of
wine or milk in bowls to a seated
figure of the great god of Heliopolis,
Atum, the creator deity, shown as a
king wearing the double crown of
Upper and Lower Egypt. The sides

of the royal throne carry scenes of
the symbolic uniting of the two lands
by Nile deities. The figure of Atum is
approximately life-size. Both figures
are separately carved and set into a
single rectangular base. The group
was found in a sculpture cache
in Luxor Temple in 1989.

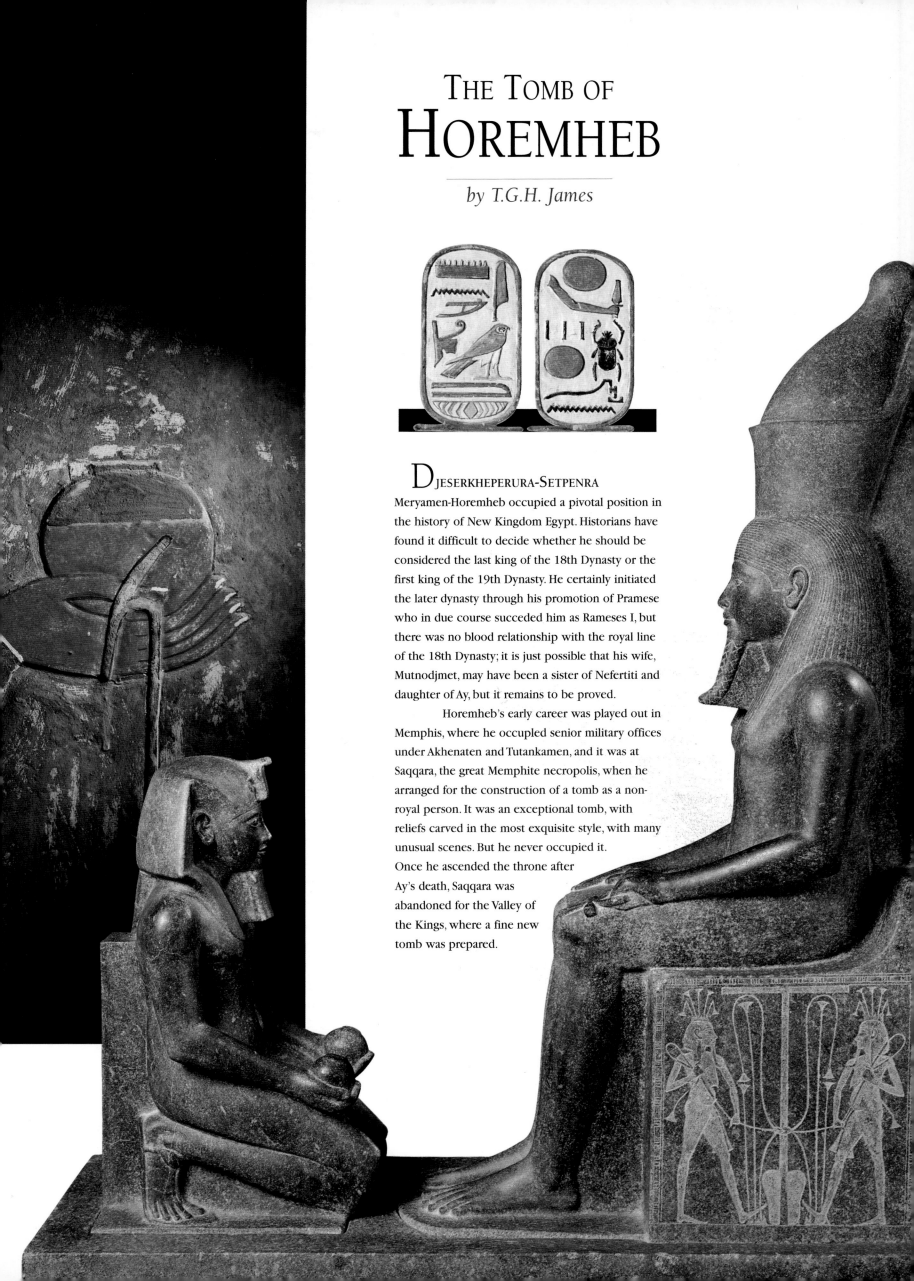

THE TOMB OF
HOREMHEB

by T.G.H. James

DJESERKHEPERURA-SETPENRA
Meryamen-Horemheb occupied a pivotal position in
the history of New Kingdom Egypt. Historians have
found it difficult to decide whether he should be
considered the last king of the 18th Dynasty or the
first king of the 19th Dynasty. He certainly initiated
the later dynasty through his promotion of Pramese
who in due course succeeded him as Rameses I, but
there was no blood relationship with the royal line
of the 18th Dynasty; it is just possible that his wife,
Mutnodjmet, may have been a sister of Nefertiti and
daughter of Ay, but it remains to be proved.

Horemheb's early career was played out in
Memphis, where he occupied senior military offices
under Akhenaten and Tutankamen, and it was at
Saqqara, the great Memphite necropolis, when he
arranged for the construction of a tomb as a non-
royal person. It was an exceptional tomb, with
reliefs carved in the most exquisite style, with many
unusual scenes. But he never occupied it.
Once he ascended the throne after
Ay's death, Saqqara was
abandoned for the Valley of
the Kings, where a fine new
tomb was prepared.

179 top

View of the well or sump room, crossed by a modern bridge, looking in the direction of the burial chamber. The upper walls are decorated with figures of the king offering to, and receiving presentations from, a series of deities. The ceiling is painted to represent the starry sky.

179 bottom

Three deities attend Horemheb (not shown) in the well room, to the right of the doorway leading to the first pillared hall. Osiris, shown mummiform, is seated, followed by jackal-headed Anubis and falcon-headed Horus-son-of-Isis (Harsiesis).

During his substantial reign of about thirty years Horemheb completed the social, religious and military rehabilitation of Egypt begun under Tutankhamen. He undertook building works at Karnak and Luxor, continuing and even usurping monuments started in the reigns of Amenhotep III and Tutankhamen. Many sculptures of the latter king were reinscribed with Horemheb's name, as if needed to expunge the memory of his predecessor through usurpation. He also dismantled the atonist temples built by Akhenaten and Nefertiti at Karnak, and used the material to pack the interiors of the pylons he constructed in his extension of the temple of Amun-Ra.

In planning his tomb Horemheb chose to return to the main Valley of the Kings. A site was selected a few hundred meters (feet) deeper in the valley, beyond Tutankhamen's tomb. In modern times, the tomb was discovered in 1908 by Edward Ayrton working for the American, Theodore Davis. The steep passages and stairs leading down as far as the well were checked with debris, mostly storm deposits. Beyond the well there were remains of intended blocking, but the inner parts of the tomb were not so encumbered. They were, however, deeply littered with archaeological debris, including the damaged remains of mummies, wooden figures of deities and underworld genii, and other funerary equipment. It was clear that the tomb

178

Head and shoulders of a figure of Hathor, Chief of the West, Lady of Heaven and Mistress of all the Gods. She wears a heavy, stepped wig of unusual design, topped by cow-horns enclosing the sun-disk. She receives an offering of wine from the king.

180-181

From the west wall of the antechamber: Horemheb "justified" before Osiris makes a presentation of wine to Harsiesis, the Great God, King of the Gods, Lord of Heaven. To the right stands Isis, the Great One, Mother of the God, Lady of Heaven, Mistress of the Gods.

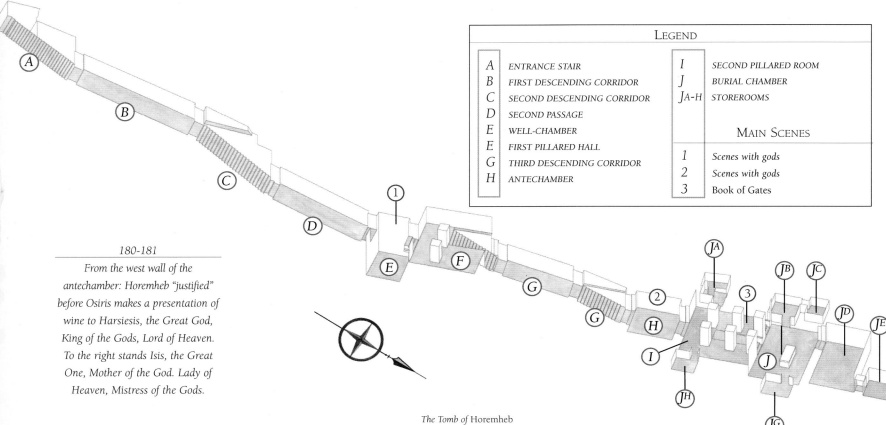

LEGEND			
A	ENTRANCE STAIR	I	SECOND PILLARED ROOM
B	FIRST DESCENDING CORRIDOR	J	BURIAL CHAMBER
C	SECOND DESCENDING CORRIDOR	JA-H	STOREROOMS
D	SECOND PASSAGE		
E	WELL-CHAMBER		MAIN SCENES
E	FIRST PILLARED HALL		
G	THIRD DESCENDING CORRIDOR	1	Scenes with gods
H	ANTECHAMBER	2	Scenes with gods
		3	Book of Gates

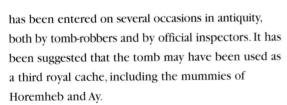

181 top

View along the axis of the tomb from the antechamber into the burial chamber and the crypt where the royal sarcophagus can be seen. The painted reliefs on both sides of the antechamber show Horemheb with gods, including Ptah, Anubis, Nefertum, and those shown opposite and below.

181 bottom

Horemheb, himself described as "the Osiris," makes a presentation of two bowls of wine to the Osiris, the Great God, Lord of the West, Lord of Eternity, who is shown as a mummy standing on a plinth, holding the royal flail and crook. The green of the god's flesh represents rejuvenation.

has been entered on several occasions in antiquity, both by tomb-robbers and by official inspectors. It has been suggested that the tomb may have been used as a third royal cache, including the mummies of Horemheb and Ay.

The plan of the tomb is considered to be the first of the transitional style which was common during the 19th and early 20th Dynasties. Earlier tombs in the Valley had a bent axis, in which the entrance axis was turned through about 90° to lead on to the burial complex. Later tombs had a single straight axis from entrance to burial chamber. Horemheb's tomb has what is called a jogged axis, in which the axis continues straight from the entrance to the first pillared hall, then jogs to the left and preceeds in the same direction to the burial chamber. In the tradition of earlier 18th-Dynasty tombs it is deep cut, with a succession of steep stairs and long corridors with sharp downword slopes. There is no decoration in the corridors and stairs until the well chamber is reached, and these initial stages of

182

Horemheb, shown as a living king, is embraced by the goddess Hathor, Foremost in Thebes; she wears on the head a standard with a falcon perched on it, the symbol of the West. On the adjacent wall of this antechamber the king is shown with deities, better seen overleaf.

187

The god Nefertum, divine son of Ptah and Sekhmet, and member of the Menphite triad of deities. He is shown here as a man with a divine beard, bearing on his head a lotus flower, source of the perfume endowing life at the time of creation.

183-186

The complete decoration on the west wall of the antechamber: jackal-headed Anubis greets the king; the king offers wine to Isis, Mistress of the Two Lands: falcon-headed Harsiesis offers the king appearance in the sky; the king offers wine to Hathor; he stands before Osiris.

the tomb are not smoothly finished, but roughly hewn through the limestone. The plausible suggestion has been made that the plan of the royal tomb may reflect to same extent the actual path of the nocturnal journey to be undertaken by the dead king. So may be explained changes in direction, the condition of the cutting, and, rather later in the New Kingdom, the character of the decoration in the corridors and the chambers.

The first decoration to be met in Horemheb's tomb is on the upper walls of the room in which the well or sump was cut. Here are relief representations of the king with various deities, executed in a style which harks back to the fine work of the reign of Amenhotep III. Colors are particularly strong, and the backgrounds of the scene are painted a striking greyish-blue. The overall effect, however, is rich but somewhat sombre. Similar scenes of the king with deities decorate the walls of the antechamber, the room before the pillared burial chamber. The decoration of this important room consists of a section of the *Book of Gates*, one of the major compositions found in the royal tombs of the New Kingdom, designed to enable the dead king to negotiate his way though the underworld. A fine red granite sarcophagus still stands in the burial crypt; at the time of discovery it contained the skull and bones of more than one individual, none seemingly belonging to the body of Horemheb. His mummy is probably one that will never be found.

188

Figure in sunk relief on the royal sarcophagus; it is Imsety, the human-headed son of Horus, one of the canopie deities who had particular responsibility for the deceased's liver. His body here is cut across by the outstretched wing of one of the protective goddesses.

189 top

The red granite sarcophagus of Horemheb in its proper position in the crypt of the tomb. Its sides bear representations of the four sons of Horus and of other deities, and the corners carry figures of the four protective goddesses with outstretched wings, Isis, Nephthys, Neith and Selkis.

189 bottom

Two sunk relief figures from the sides of Horemheb's sarcophagus, the falcon-headed Qebhsenuef, one of the sons of Horus, responsible for the royal intestines, and here protected by the outstretched wing of a goddess; and the jackal-headed Anubis who had general responsibilities for the process of mummification.

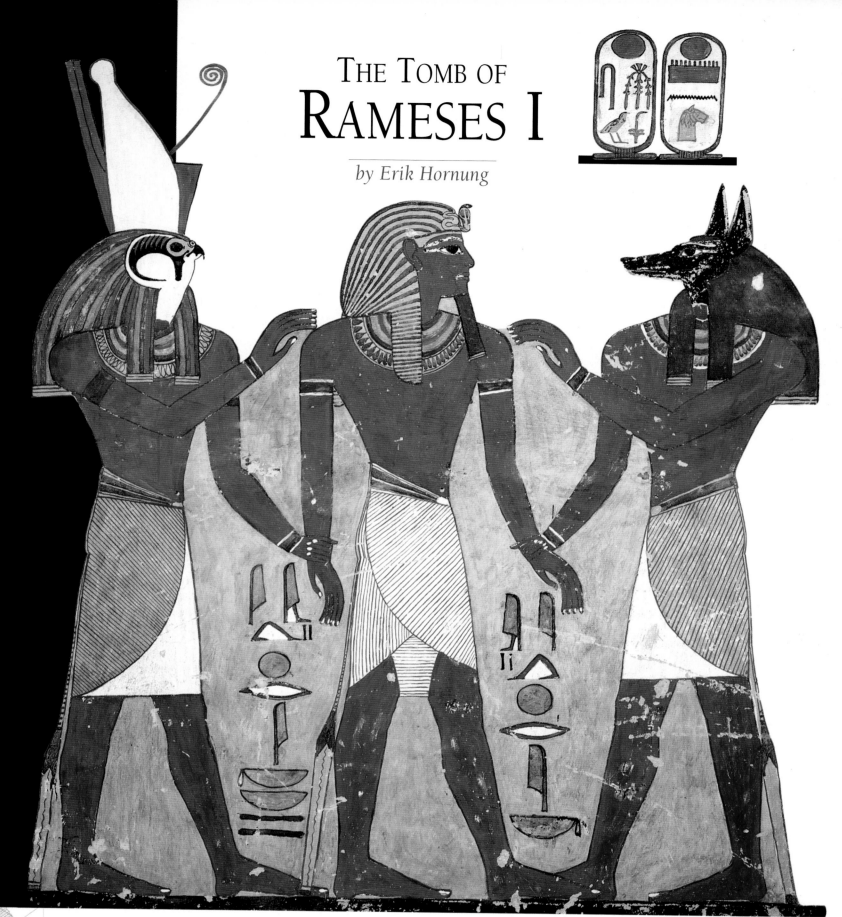

THE TOMB OF
RAMESES I

by Erik Hornung

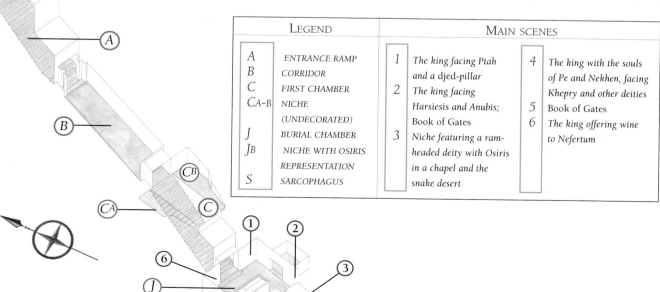

190

Rameses I between the gods Horus-son-of-Isis (on the left: with falcon head and double-crown), and Anubis with a jackal head. Each says to him: "I come to you [as protector and helper]."

191

Scene from the third hour of the Book of Gates shows the bark with the ram-headed sun god (surrounded by the snake Mehen), and with the gods Sia and Heqa. Below, the god Atum stands in front of the snake Apophis, which is threatening the course of the sun.

The Tomb of Rameses I

193 bottom
*Rameses I, fourth hour of the Book
of Gates. It begins (middle register)
with a gate, guarded by a snake.
The solar bark passes a series of
shrines with mummies, then follows
the time-snake and the twelve hours
of the night .*

192-193
*The back wall of the burial chamber
of Rameses I. On the throne are the
gods Khepri and Osiris; the thrones
sit on a mat and a base in the shape
of the hieroglyph of Maat. At right,
the king is being led in; on the left
he makes a sacrifice and rejoices
between two godlike beings.*

192 center
*View of the burial chamber of Rameses
I with the king's sarcophagus in the*

*center; at the head is a winged figure of
the goddess Nephthys. All walls have a
blue background; the pedestal is
painted in black.*

192 bottom
*Osiris standing on a snake, in a
shrine between the ram-headed
Anubis, and an uraeus-serpent. This
scene fills the niche in the back wall.
It belongs to the fourth hour of the
Book of Gates, dealing with the
protection of Osiris.*

THIS FOUNDER OF THE 19TH DYNASTY reached the throne at a great age and could not count on a long-lasting reign. Indeed, he ruled for only one year and four months. The planners of his tomb (KV 16) took this into account from the beginning, reducing dimensions and decoration to a minimum. After one stairway, one corridor, and a second stairway, we find the small burial chamber. Its walls are painted, but there are no reliefs. The granite sarcophagus of the king, too, is only decorated with paintings. The *Amduat* is missing in the wall scenes, replaced, as in the case of KV 57 (Horemheb), by part of the *Book of Gates*. On the side of the room, we see night hours from the *Book of Gates,* the third hour on the right, the fourth on the left. Both lack the upper register, because the low ceilings did not leave room for it. In the third hour, the solar bark is being pulled through an oblong structure, which ends on both sides with a bull's head. It is called Bark of the Earth and represents the underworld through which the sun god moves in his ram-headed night form. His voyage is repeatedly being threatened by the Apophis snake, shown under the bark. The snake is being overwhelmed by Atum and a group of nine gods. In the fourth hour, the sun god's bark passes a series of shrines with mummies painted in black. They lie in their death sleep, awaiting a call from the god that will wake them. He will then give them a new body which will no longer have the mummy shape. Below is a symbolic depiction of time. It is shown as a twisted snake body from which the individual hours are being born and into which they disappear again. The twelve night hours are represented by the twelve goddesses standing on triangular structures, painted half in black (darkness) and half with water

lines, symbolizing the way through the dark underworld, filled with primordial water. On the left, there was room for one more scene. It shows the king between Horus-son-of-Isis, and Anubis. The two long walls of the rectangular chamber are also painted with scenes that contain gods. On both sides of the entrance, Maat receives the king as he enters the room. She represents law, truth, and order, important values in the realm of the dead as well as the living. Behind her, Rameses prays or makes a sacrifice; he stands with Ptah on the left (in front of a large *djed*-amulet) and Nefertum on the right (with a *tit*-amulet), who carries a lotus flower on his head. In the center of the rear wall, Khepri (with a scarab beetle instead of a head) and Osiris stand back to back, overlooking the scene. Khepri is the rejuvenated morning shape of the sun god, while

Osiris in the New Kingdom is considered in his nightly form. In front of Osiris, dressed in a leopard skin, we see an Iunmutef-priest, considered to be the ideal son of Osiris. From right to left, Horus, son of Isis, Atum, and the goddess Neith lead the king in front of the god, holding each other's hands. On the left, Rameses, above four chests of cloth, makes sacrifices in front of Khepri. At the side, he appears between a soul from Nekhen (Hierakonpolis), with a falcon head, and a soul from Pe (Buto), with a jackal head. These are godlike powers, who together with the king conduct a ritual. Below this scene is a niche in which we see Osiris standing on a snake, protected by a *uraeus*-serpent, and cared for by Anubis, shown here with a ram's head (instead of a jackal's). Other wall niches are undecorated. All walls have a blue background, as in the tombs of Amenhotep III and Horemheb.

THE TOMB OF
SETI I

by Erik Hornung

WHEN GIOVANNI BATTISTA BELZONI from Padua discovered KV 17, the tomb of Seti I, in 1817, the world paid attention. Public interest grew even more when Belzoni published a detailed report about his discoveries and displayed a copy of some of the rooms of the tomb in an exhibition held in London in 1821. The exhibition was also shown in Paris.

Belzoni and all the early visitors of the tomb were impressed by the beauty of its colors, which were as fresh as if the painters had just finished their work. This included the colors of the hieroglyphs, each of which was drawn in a particular tone. The English consul Henry Salt, who financed Belzoni's works, painted a series of water colors that showed the intensity of the colors. But as early as 1829, Champollion, who had worked on the tomb with Rosellini, complained about its deterioration. Mechanical wear and tear, dust, and humidity have since then continued to erode its original beauty. After 1900, Howard Carter tried to renovate the tomb, but modern mass tourism continues to be a threat. Between 1921 and 1928, Harry Burton, who had photographed the entire treasure of Tutankhamen for Carter, photographed all of this tomb too, providing us with documentation of its condition at the time.

194

Head of Seti I on a pillar in the burial chamber (before the god Djeb). He wears the nemes-crown with the uraeus-serpent on the forehead, and an attached ceremonial beard. Around the neck, he has a wide collar of faience.

---

195 left

The goddess Isis, protecting the king with spread wings. She kneels beneath the astronomical ceiling of the burial chamber, on the left wall. The foot end of the king's sarcophagus lay toward this wall.

---

195 right

Alabaster head of a statue of Seti I, found in the cachette of the temple of Karnak. It is composed of six parts is in the Cairo Museum. Eyes and eyebrows of precious materials were added.

Seti I was the first important king of the Ramesside period. He initiated some of the most beautiful temple constructions in Egypt, especially at Karnak. It was also in Karnak that he immortalized his successful battles in Syria, in which the Egyptians had overcome the Hittites. He also worked to restore the images of gods that had been destroyed by Akhenaten and to reactivate the ancient cults. The high quality painted reliefs in his temples and in his tomb forms one of the highlights of Egypt's art history.

The design of this tomb was fundamentally new. Until the reign of Rameses III, it would be copied with only slight modifications. It not only introduced an architectural extension with its additional rooms, and a clear division into an upper and a lower section, but it is also new in that, for the first time a king's tomb was entirely decorated, from entrance to sarcophagus.

196
This pillar in the burial chamber shows the king and the sun god Ra-Horakhty, characterized by a falcon-head and a red sun disk. His other hand is holding an ankh-sign.

197 top
Head of the god Shu, from a pillar in the burial chamber. On his wig, he wears a high head ornament made from ostrich feathers; he also wears the gods' ceremonial beard. Shu is the god who every morning lifts the sun up into the skies.

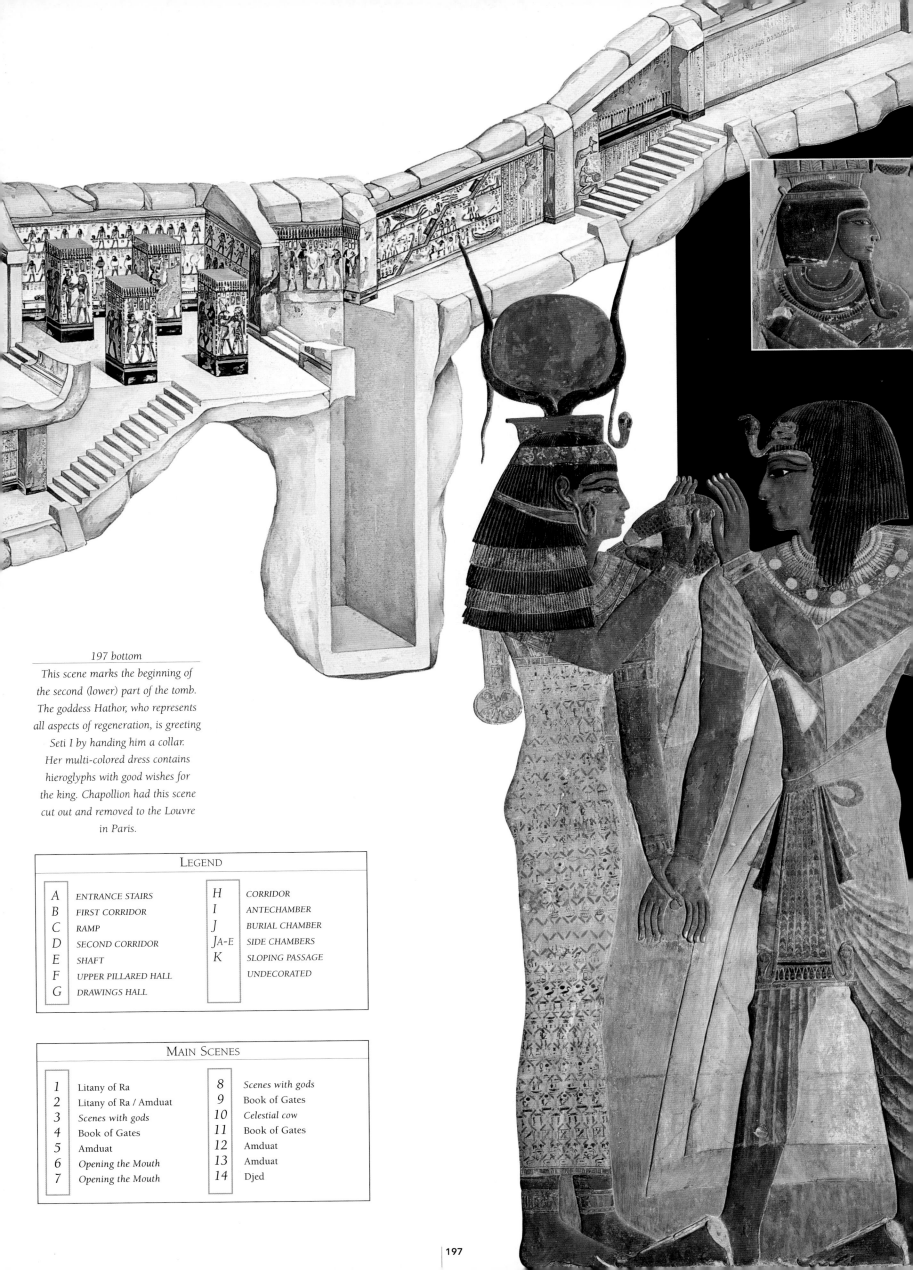

197 bottom

This scene marks the beginning of the second (lower) part of the tomb. The goddess Hathor, who represents all aspects of regeneration, is greeting Seti I by handing him a collar. Her multi-colored dress contains hieroglyphs with good wishes for the king. Chapollion had this scene cut out and removed to the Louvre in Paris.

LEGEND			
A	ENTRANCE STAIRS	H	CORRIDOR
B	FIRST CORRIDOR	I	ANTECHAMBER
C	RAMP	J	BURIAL CHAMBER
D	SECOND CORRIDOR	JA-E	SIDE CHAMBERS
E	SHAFT	K	SLOPING PASSAGE
F	UPPER PILLARED HALL		UNDECORATED
G	DRAWINGS HALL		

MAIN SCENES			
1	Litany of Ra	8	Scenes with gods
2	Litany of Ra / Amduat	9	Book of Gates
3	Scenes with gods	10	Celestial cow
4	Book of Gates	11	Book of Gates
5	Amduat	12	Amduat
6	Opening the Mouth	13	Amduat
7	Opening the Mouth	14	Djed

198 top

In the sixth hour of the Book of Gates, on the right side of the upper hall, we see a scene that deals with the unification of ba-soul and body, which is essential for a new life. In the lower register, mummies on a snake-shaped bier wait for this unification.

198 bottom

View of the upper pillared hall, with two of its four pillars. The walls are decorated with the Book of Gates, the pillars with scenes of the king in front of deities.

198-199

The uppered pillar hall, with a view into the following side room. This constitutes the end of the upper half of the tomb. The walls have a white background; only the scene of the king before Osiris, on the posterior wall, is highlighted with a yellow background, like the walls in the burial chamber.

Previously, only a few rooms of particular importance had been decorated. Except for a few unfinished pieces, all the decoration was done in painted reliefs. The background is mostly white, the shaft is blue, the burial chamber and some other important spots are yellow (or gold).

Beyond the entrance of the tomb, there is a scene on the left that shows the king praying in front of the sun god Ra in his falcon-headed day shape, with the sun disk. Then follows the title image of the *Litany of Ra*, with the sun disk in the middle. On the disk, a scarab beetle and a ram-headed god represent the morning and evening forms of the sun god. Animals (crocodile, snake, gazelle) represent enemy forces which are being overpowered again and again by the sun. The text of the *Litany of Ra* covers the rest of the first corridor; its purpose is to integrate the

king into the nightly course of the sun. On the left wall, 75 invocations constitute the first Great Litany highlighted again and again with "Praise to you, Ra, with superior power." On the right wall, cartouches with the king's name are dominant. The ceiling of the first corridor is painted with winged beings, taking the shapes of vulture-heads and snake-heads.

The second corridor has a stairway and two niches. In the upper part, we see figures that belong to the great Litany to the Sun. They represent various aspects of the god's nightly activities in the underworld. Below, on both sides, simply sketched, is the final text of the third hour of *Amduat*. At the end of the corridor, Isis and Nephthys kneel down, their hands resting on the protective *shen*-amulet. Above, on both sides, the god Anubis lies in the form of a jackal with a

collar and a red ribbon around his neck. There are references to Chapter 151 of the *Book of the Dead* (to which the four Sons of Horus also belong). Traces can also be seen in the passage to the next corridor. Above this passage, the goddess Maat is depicted in three shapes, each with wings. To the side are the cartouches of the king.

The third corridor shows the fourth nightly hour of *Amduat* on the right, the fifth on the left. Both hours deal with the voyage of the solar bark through a desert region called the realm of the god Sokar, "He who is on his sand." This in reality is the old god of the dead from Memphis, who in the New Kingdom is considered one with Osiris. The walls here are today severely damaged, but Belzoni managed to copy them completely.

Now follows a shaft, decorated with

199 bottom left

The goddess Hathor and the king, standing in front of her, his arm crossing her body. On her blue wig, Hathor is wearing cow horns with the sun disk, from which a uraeus-serpent hangs down. Traditionally in Egyptian art, women are depicted with yellow skin, men with red.

199 right

View from the lower side chamber into the upper hall with its four pillars. On both sides of the entrance we can see the solar bark of the Amduat, *on the left in the eleventh, on the right in the ninth night hour.*

scenes that are distributed almost symmetrically between the two longitudinal walls. They show the king in front of Isis, Hathor and Osiris. At the beginning, Horus-son-of-Isis is his guardian. On the back wall was a statue of the king, which has now disappeared before the trinity Osiris, Anubis and Horus. To the side, the passage to the upper pillar hall was originally closed and painted, to suggest that the tomb ended here.

200-201

The right wall of the antechamber, which Belzoni called "Hall of Beauties," because of its particularly beautiful reliefs. The ugly stains are from moulds that were made of the reliefs during the 19th century. The king appears (from right to left) in front of Anubis, Isis, Horus-son-of-Isis, Hathor, and Osiris.

The upper pillared hall now has four pillars decorated with additional scenes with gods. In the middle of the rear wall, a scene is highlighted by its yellow background. In it, Horus leads Seti in front of Osiris, who is on the throne; behind, Hathor stands as goddess of the west. The ceiling of this room is painted as a sky with stars. The walls are reserved for the *Book of Gates*, with the fifth night hour on the left and the sixth on the right. The sixth hour contains the highlight of the nightly sun journey, the unification of the sun god with his corpse, which in the *Book of Gates* remains invisible. Analogous to this scene, the *ba*-souls of the dead unite with their mummies, which lie in the lower register on a long bier in the shape of a snake (the symbol of rejuvenation). Each hour starts with a richly decorated gate, guarded by snakes.

In the fifth hour, one scene in the lower register received special attention by early visitors. It was often copied, but today is partially destroyed. It shows four representatives of each of the four races of mankind known to the Egyptians: Egyptians, Asians, Nubians, and Libyans. They are characterized by their typical clothing

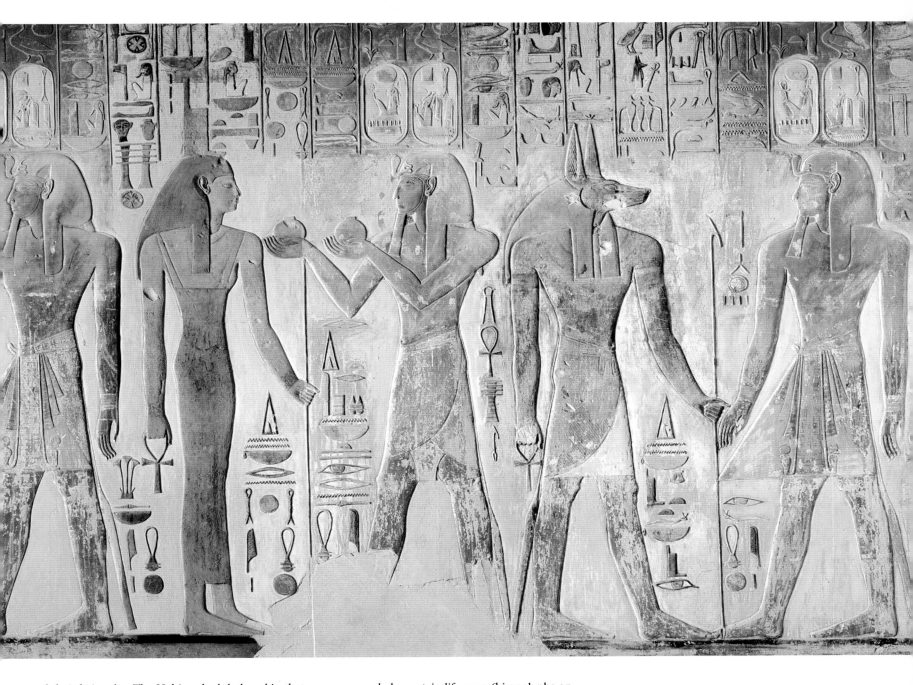

and their hairstyles. The Nubians had darker skin that the Egyptians, the Libyans lighter skin. It is unusual that the foreign peoples here do not appear as despised enemies, but are represented on the same level as the Egyptians. In a similar way, Akhenaten, in his Great Hymn to the Sun, stressed the care of his god Aten for all peoples; under Rameses II the Egyptians were fraternizing with the Hittites, who had previously been their enemies. Behind this scene, time appears as a snake on whose body all humans

are accorded a certain life span (hieroglyphs on the snake) in this world and the next. Analogous to this, gods appear in the upper register equipped with measuring sticks used to measure and delineate fields in the other world for all people. In between, Apophis is being subdued in its shape as a long snake.

Continuing along the existing axis of the tomb, we come to a side room with two pillars. It is a dead end but someone must have been looking

200 bottom

For a sacrifice being carried out during the Opening the Mouth ceremony, a cow is tied down and slaughtered. On the left, a priest dressed in a leopard skin supervises the scene.

201 bottom

The Iunmutef-priest, reaching out towards the king in front of the sacrificial altar. He is a symbol of the Osiris-son Horus; he wears a youth's sidelock, and with it a leopard skin, which is the traditional outfit of priests.

202 top
Seti in front of Ptah-Sokar, on a
pillar in the burial chamber.
The god, who is often considered
identical to Osiris, wears the
Osiris-crown on his falcon-head.
Above the king, the two
cartouches with his name are
highlighted by a white
background.

202 bottom
On a pillar in the burial chamber,
Thoth, a god with an ibis-head,
embraces the king. He is the protector
of religious writings and wears the sash
of a priest who reads to others. The
king's apron is different from the god's.

202-203
View from the lower part of the
burial chamber into the upper part
with its pillars. On the left, we see the
third hour of the Amduat; above the
pillars are texts from the book's short
version, above we see the astronomical
ceiling with constellations. The walls
in the upper part are decorated with
the Book of Gates.

for a continuation, as the destruction on the back wall shows. Decorations here are only sketched; they consist of three nightly hours from the *Amduat*, the ninth to eleventh. The oarsmen on the left wall (ninth hour) and the individuals who are swimming in the water in various positions (tenth hour) dominate. They represent deceased persons who did not receive a proper funeral (e.g., those who drowned in the Nile river), but who participate in the blessed fate nevertheless and who receive all that is necessary in the Netherworld. In the lower register of the eleventh hour, on the entrance wall, we see the punishment of those who were sentenced by the court of the dead. On the sides of the pillars, there are additional scenes with gods, again only as sketches.

The tomb continues with a stairway situated slightly to the left of the previous main axis. The walls are undecorated, but in the passage to the next corridor there was a particularly beautiful scene on a yellow background, showing Seti hand in hand with the goddess Hathor, who is wearing a richly crafted wig and above it cow horns and a sun disk. Her dress contains wishes for the king. Champollion and Rosellini, during their joint expedition, cut out both scenes, so that the left one can now be seen in Florence's archaeological museum, the right one in the Louvre in Paris.

203 top right

On a back wall of a side chamber is an image of the celestial cow, on which the sun god, after a rebellion by humans, departed earth. The texts at the side explain this image in detail.

203 bottom

The left wall in the upper part of the burial chamber. The bound "enemies" and the other figures belong to the Book of Gates' second hour. In the side chamber, whose entrance we see, the fourth hour follows. In the burial chamber, the walls have a yellow background, which represents gold.

The following two corridors provide an incomplete version of the ritual of the Opening the Mouth. This ritual's primary purpose was to bring to life a newly made statue in order to make it a living image of the deceased. In front of the scene showing the ritual, we see Seti on his throne next to an altar with loaves of bread, to which he reaches out with one hand. The other hand holds a scepter. In front of him, the Iunmutef-priest celebrates a rite dressed in a leopard skin. Each passage of the ritual is accompanied by illustrations, showing various cult actions by the king in front of a statue. The statue is placed on a sand hill and is cleaned by priests, then decorated and surrounded by offerings. At the end is a detailed list of sacrifices.

The figure of Seti on this throne has been severely damaged, but in old reproductions it was intact. The damage inflicted on the scenes of the Opening the Mouth took place after their modern rediscovery. Particularly damaged are the cartouches with the name of the king, because visitors cut out pieces of them as souvenirs. Today, fragments from the tomb's decoration can be seen in museums all over the world. Many details, however, have been lost and can only be seen in the old reproductions made by Belzoni, Alessandro Ricci, Henry Salt, Robert Hay and others soon after the discovery of the tomb. Fortunately, Belzoni carried out detailed and systematic documentation of the entire tomb, which he needed for the planned exhibition in London.

In the antechamber, which is adjacent to the two corridors with the Opening the Mouth, we find another kind of destruction. In the 19th century, before the development of photography, reliefs were often copied by making wet moulds. This destroyed or removed the colors of painted reliefs and ugly stains remained on the walls; consequently, little remains of the splendid colors of what Belzoni had called the "Hall of Beauties." Here again, Seti is shown sacrificing and praying before Anubis, Isis, Horus-son-of-Isis, Hathor and Osiris; on the back wall he is depicted in front of Ptah (left) and Nefertum (right, with a lotus flower on his head and a large Isis-blood amulet on his back). Both figures were severely damaged. Old reproductions show that in the entrance and the passageway to the burial chamber there were figures of the goddess Maat on each side

204 and 205
In front of the scenes of the Opening the Mouth, we see two images of the Iunmutef-priests in a leopard skin. One of them turns towards the king, in front of the sacrificial altar. The other one initiates the ritual of the Opening the Mouth.

which have now disappeared. A large fragment of one of these figures is in Florence. The ceiling of the antechamber is painted as a sky with stars, just like the ceiling in the front part of the burial chamber.

The real burial chamber is still divided into two parts, as it has been since the times of Amenhotep II. First, you enter a room with six pillars, then you walk past some stairs to a lower part, in which the king's sarcophagus was originally located. As a new element, we find a vaulted astronomical ceiling above this lower part, painted with lists of Dekan stars and with stellar constellations. The idea was that the soul of the deceased king could move directly from the sarcophagus to heaven, arched above him.

Of the six pillars, one is entirely destroyed; the others show serious damage. Some sides of the pillars, which are almost entirely intact, can be found in museums in Berlin; they are decorated with scenes with

gods, dominated by Osiris, entirely without goddesses. On all six sides that face the central axis, we see the jackal-headed (left) and falcon-headed (right) "Souls" of Buto and Hierakonpolis, old religious powers who are beating their chests with their fists to acclaim the king. On the first pair of pillars, we again see a Iunmutef-priest in a leopard skin, whom we already met in the ritual of the Opening the Mouth.

The upper parts of the walls were decorated with the *Book of Gates*, the lower parts with the *Amduat*. Each has three hour-segments. In addition, the king's sarcophagus, made from alabaster, contained a full copy of the *Books of Gates* and a number of quotations from the *Book of the Dead*. Belzoni removed this sarcophagus from the tomb; since 1824 it has been in Sir John Soane's Museum in London. The lid, with a figure representing the king, had previously been broken into many pieces.

On the right hand side, we see in the third hour

The Hippopotamus Constellation, in the astronomical ceiling of the burial chamber, belongs to the stars of the northern sky, but a precise identification is not possible.

206 bottom

The left wall of the burial chamber, with the entrance to the side chamber with its two pillars. After a depiction of the king

before the sun god is the first hour of the Amduat. Above are texts from a short version of the book, and Isis, shown as a winged goddess of protection.

207 top

The lower part of the burial chamber; in its center stood the king's sarcophagus. On the left, we see the second hour of the Amduat, in the center, the third hour.

Above, is Nephthys, depicted as a winged goddess of protection, and the vaulted astronomical ceiling. On the right, in the upper part, is the end of the "Lake of Fire."

207 bottom

In the third night hour, the solar bark is accompanied by other boats. Here we see the lion-headed goddess Pachet's bark (on the left) and the Baboon' Bark (right).

of the *Book of Gates* the "Lake of Fire," painted in red. Its water, as the accompanying text points out, is a cool refreshment for Osiris and the blessed dead; for other dead it constitutes a fiery heat. At the beginning of this hour, the solar bark passes a number of shrines with mummies that are standing upright; in the lower register, Atum appears in front of the Apophis snake.

The hours of *Amduat* begin on the left wall in the lower part, after a scene that once again shows Seti before a falcon-headed Ra-Horakhty. Towards the end of this wall, a large niche was cut, in which Anubis is shown at the Opening the Mouth before Osiris, together with the four Sons of Horus. Above the long version of

208-209 top	208 bottom	208-209 bottom
The entire middle register of the third hour of the Amduat shows barks with animal heads accompanying the solar bark (left) ona river in the underworld. Each bark has two oars and carries different aspects of the sun god, who from his bark turns towards Osiris.	*Three deities from the middle register of the Amduat's first night hour. Osiris, the lion-headed goddess Sekhmet are accompanied by a ram-headed figure representing the sun god as "The Great Illuminated One."*	*The beginning of the upper register in the Amduat's third hour. In sequence from left to right, we see Anubis; the crocodile-headed god "with terrible voice," a pair of gods who look after the pupils of the god's eyes; and a ram with knife, "who is slaughtering his enemies."*

the *Amduat*, we find the text of the short version, or as much as the available space permitted.

Each half of the burial chamber has two side rooms, which are integrated into the overall decoration design. In the front half, the left chamber is decorated with another hour (the fourth) of the *Book of Gates*. Here we find the mummies that are lying in a death-like sleep, as well as a depiction of time as a snake, together with the twelve goddesses of the night hours. The walls of the right chamber were reserved for an entire copy of the *Book of the Celestial Cow*, which had been found for the first time on one of Tutankhamen's gilded shrines.

In the beginning, the text contains the well-known "Myth of the Destruction of Mankind," the Egyptian version of the story of the great Flood. After an ancient paradise, during which gods and humans cohabitated on earth and daylight was eternal due to the sun's permanent presence, humans rebelled against the ageing sun god Ra. Ra discussed the issue with the other gods and sent the goddess Hathor as "his eye" (cobra snake) to punish the rebels. Some of them were destroyed by fire, but the rest were saved because Ra felt sorry for them and deceived the goddess by using blood-tainted beer. After this episode, Ra rearranged heaven and the underworld and left earth on the back of the celestial cow. In the

center of the back wall, we see a picture and description of this celestial cow, supported by Shu and other gods. In the future, the gods lived in heaven and in the underworld; humans remained alone on earth; they were able to imagine the presence of the gods only through the cult images in the temples.

The right chamber in the back was called the "Chamber of *Djed*" (a symbol of Osiris). In the entrance, it shows traces of a personified *djed*-pillar; beyond that it is undecorated. On the left, the chamber is particularly large, equipped with two pillars, and entirely decorated. On the pillar sides, Osiris in various shapes is the main theme. One of the depictions shows the king as

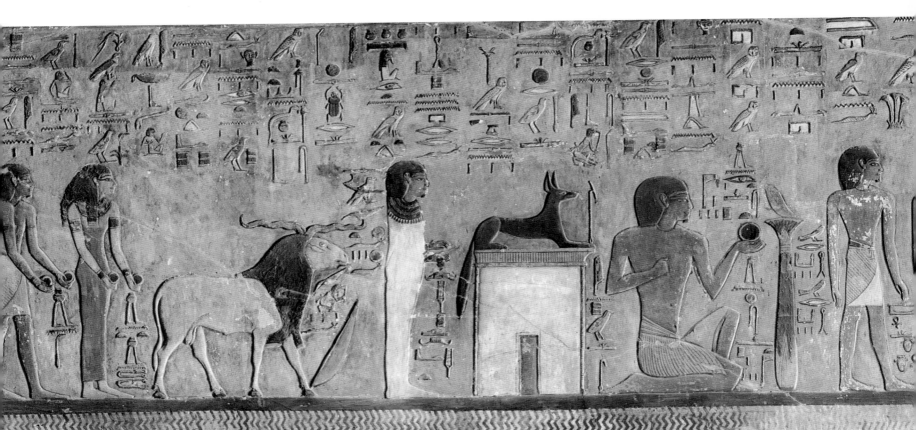

210 top

The side chamber with pillars, to the left of the burial chamber. On a pillar, we see Osiris between two imiut-symbols, and an image of the king on the throne, shown as Osiris; in the background, the Amduat's seventh hour.

210 bottom

The "Bull with the Thundering Voice" in the upper register of the Amduat's sixth hour. Bull and lion are interchangeable as royal animals; Osiris' title as "Bull of the Underworld" means that he is the ruler over the dead. Since next to this scene we see Isis, it is probable that this figure refers to some aspect of Osiris.

211

On one of the side chamber's pillars, Seti embraces an unusual representation of Osiris as Res-udja ("He who awakens intact"). The cap on his head normally belongs to the god Ptah. His green skin color indicates the renewal of his life. There is a clear difference in ceremonial beards: the king's is straight, the god's curved.

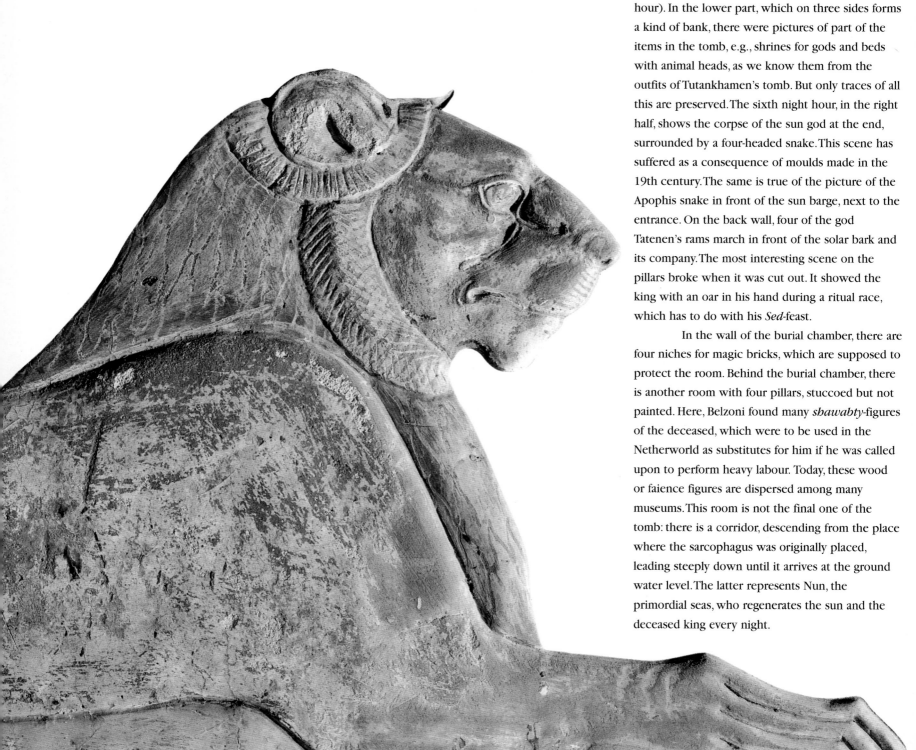

Osiris. In the upper part, the walls are decorated with scenes from the *Amduat* (sixth to eighth hour). In the lower part, which on three sides forms a kind of bank, there were pictures of part of the items in the tomb, e.g., shrines for gods and beds with animal heads, as we know them from the outfits of Tutankhamen's tomb. But only traces of all this are preserved. The sixth night hour, in the right half, shows the corpse of the sun god at the end, surrounded by a four-headed snake. This scene has suffered as a consequence of moulds made in the 19th century. The same is true of the picture of the Apophis snake in front of the sun barge, next to the entrance. On the back wall, four of the god Tatenen's rams march in front of the solar bark and its company. The most interesting scene on the pillars broke when it was cut out. It showed the king with an oar in his hand during a ritual race, which has to do with his *Sed*-feast.

In the wall of the burial chamber, there are four niches for magic bricks, which are supposed to protect the room. Behind the burial chamber, there is another room with four pillars, stuccoed but not painted. Here, Belzoni found many *shawabty*-figures of the deceased, which were to be used in the Netherworld as substitutes for him if he was called upon to perform heavy labour. Today, these wood or faience figures are dispersed among many museums. This room is not the final one of the tomb: there is a corridor, descending from the place where the sarcophagus was originally placed, leading steeply down until it arrives at the ground water level. The latter represents Nun, the primordial seas, who regenerates the sun and the deceased king every night.

THE TOMB OF
RAMESES II

by Christian Leblanc

THE TOMB OF RAMESES II (KV 7) IS located in the Valley of the Kings at the foot of the northern side of the main valley, about 40 m (132 feet) ahead of the tomb of Tutankhamen (KV 62). The vast tomb develops on two axes. Long corridors lead to an antechamber that opens on to the "golden chamber," in turn surrounded by several annexes.

Graffiti by visitors on the walls of the first corridors as well as traces of fireplaces on the ground of the deepest rooms, indicate that the tomb was still accessible in Roman times, although it was later blocked off for many centuries by debris deposited by torrential rains. The entrance of the tomb must have been visible at the time of the Expedition of Egypt, but it was only in 1817 that it was partially cleared, at the behest of the British Consul H. Salt. Work on the tomb was however suspended and it wasn't until much later, in 1913-1914, that new sporadic excavations were carried out by Th. Davis and H. Burton. In the intervening period, it attracted the curiosity of J.-F. Champollion and R. Lepsius who

carried out the earliest scientific examination of the site. Between 1917 and 1921, H. Carter who succeeded Th. Davis in the Valley of the Kings, cleaned up the entrance to the tomb and started excavations inside. Although Ch. Maystre visited the tomb in 1938-1939 to copy the text of the *Book of the Heavenly Cow* off the walls of a small chamber to the south of the main burial chamber, it was not until 1993 that works commenced for the systematic cleaning of the tomb, under the aegis of the Laboratory of Theban History and Archaeology of the Louvre Museum, as part of a study of funerary monuments of Rameses II in West Thebes. Because of the heavy damage inflicted on the tomb over the centuries, however, the project could not progress until large scale preliminary works were undertaken during the course of the excavations, thanks to the expertise of the French Central Laboratory of Bridges and Roads and funding from the French oil company, Elf-Acquitaine. Today, the tomb of Rameses II is almost completely cleared of the debris brought in by floods, although a great deal

of cataloguing, stabilizing and restoration work still needs to be completed before the tomb can be opened to the public.

A potsherd uncovered by E. Baraize in the Ramesseum in 1912 suggests that construction on the royal tomb commenced in the 2nd year of Rameses II's reign, "in the second month of the *peret* (germination) season, on the thirteenth day." This is confirmed in the first corridor where, in the *Litanies of Ra*, the king's coronation name appears in a form used before the end of the second year of his reign. Evidence uncovered during recent excavations indicates that the tomb was fully completed in just about twelve years. In the end room [J⁸], remnants of relief sculptures on pillars still bear traces of painting.

Unlike other royal tombs that, starting from the reign of Amenhotep IV/Akhenaten, were dug along a single axis, the ground plan of the tomb of Rameses II develops along two axes, in an arrangement typical of pre-Amarna tombs. It remains uncertain whether this choice of design was inspired by religious considerations, since the

flooring of the antechamber [I] of the tomb features contact between the calcareous bedrock of Thebes and marl known as Esna marl, that may have taken the ancient architects by surprise. The appearance of marl at this point could have led them to believe that by continuing digging downwards, they would be faced with a very unstable geological layer. Perhaps in order to avoid this major drawback that could have entailed abandoning the works, they may have decided to turn towards the right (east), where the calcareous layer seemed more stable. This option, no doubt the wiser decision in light of how far the works had already progressed, could explain the atypical dual-axis arrangement.

The tomb of Rameses II is the last royal tomb that still features decoration entirely in true relief, whether it be on limestone, or, in the case where the stone is not hard enough, using plaster. For reasons not yet fully understood, after this long reign, craftsmen gradually changed their technique. While true relief can be found side by side with sculpture in the round, in the tomb of

212 top

The entrance to tomb KV 7. This gives access to a succession of corridors leading to the Hall of Maat (antechamber) and the House of Gold (sarcophagus room). On the walls, several of the great royal burial reliefs have been delicately sculpted..

212 bottom

In the texts of the Litanies of Ra occupying the walls of the first corridor, the coronation name of Rameses II appears once again in its first version: Usermaatra.

212-213

Southern half of the sarcophagus room (J), before the archaeological excavation. In the course of the centuries, torrential sediment has entered the area and caused significant damage to the architecture.

213 top

Rameses II, armed with an axe, holds three foreign enemies by the hair (Nubian, Syrian and Libyan). Neutralizing forces hostile to Egypt or warding off evil is a favourite theme in the official paintings. Painted limestone relief, from Memphis. Cairo Museum.

213 bottom

Among the items of burial goods are several types of shawabtis. One of the finest of these shows the king in the form of a mummy, with the features of his face and the outline of his headgear emphasised in black. Blue anhydrite.

214

Bust of a statue of Rameses II from Tanis. The king, whose face still shows the features of a young man, is wearing a pleated ceremonial costume and a broad necklace. He is holding a heqa-scepter, one of the symbols of royalty. Quartz diorite. Cairo Museum.

214-215

Southern half of the sarcophagus room (J) after the archaeological excavation. In the central part, in the vaulted ceiling, the sarcophagus of Rameses formerly lay, protected by a group of chapels. To the rear, in the niche of the room (J¹), is a statue of Osiris in high relief.

215 bottom

Liturgical vases in situla form with the cartridges of Rameses II, decorated with lotus flowers at the base. Purchased in Egypt by G. Bénédite at the start of the 20th century, it is not impossible that these vessels belonged to the funeral goods of Rameses II. Blue earthenware. Louvre.

Legend		Main Scenes	
A	RAMP	*1*	Litany of Ra - First corridor (B)
B	FIRST CORRIDOR		
C	SECOND CORRIDOR	*2*	Book of Amduat - Third corridor (D)
D	THIRD CORRIDOR	*3*	Ritual of Opening the Mouth - Fourth and fifth corridors (G-H)
E	WELL OR 'PLACE OF REST AND WAITING'		
F	'CHARIOT ROOM' AND ANNEX (F¹ AND F²)	*4*	Book of the Dead, chapter 125 - Antechamber (I)
G	FOURTH CORRIDOR	*5*	Book of the Celestial Cow - Annex (J²)
H	FIFTH CORRIDOR	*6*	Book of the Gates and Book of Amduat - Sarcophagus room (J)
I	ANTECHAMBER OR 'ROOM OF MAAT'		
J	SARCOPHAGUS ROOM OR 'GOLDEN DOMAIN'	*7*	Book of Amduat - Annex (J³)
		8	Book of the Gates and Book of Amduat - Annex (J⁶)
J¹, J², J³, J⁴ J⁵, J⁶, J⁷ AND J⁸	ANNEXES ANNEX ROOMS OR 'THE RESIDENCES OF THE GODS'	*9*	Canopic jars - Annex (J⁷)
		10	Book of the Dead, chapter 110 - Annex (J⁸)

other royal tombs in the Valley of the Kings, did not escape pillage in ancient times. An early attempt at profanation is reported in the Strike Manuscript in Turin, dating back to the 28th year of the reign of Rameses III:

"(...) Now, see, Userhat, with Pentauret, removed the stones in front of the tomb of Osiris-King Usermaatra Setepenra, life-health-strength, the great god. Furthermore, he stole a bull bearing the brand of the Temple of Ousermaatra Setepenra (the Ramesseum): it can now be found in his stable. (...).

"(...) And Kenna, son of Ruta acted identically with regard to the seal of the tomb of the royal children of Osiris-King Usermaatra Setepenra, life-health-strength, the great god. (...)."

Intense tomb robbery in the Valley of the Kings towards the end of the Ramesside period, required the remains of famous pharaohs to be shifted to a safer location. The mummy of Rameses II, first deposited in the tomb of his

Merenptah (KV 8) and a few other kings, scenes and texts in the last Ramesside tombs were sculpted using exclusively the second technique.

The clearance work carried out in recent years has uncovered the themes of the iconographic decoration of the tomb of Rameses II. Besides the large classical compositions with scenes of welcome followed by depictions of offerings to various divinities, the tomb also features accounts from funerary epics, most of which are heavily damaged. The walls of the corridors bear the *Litanies of Re*, as well as scenes from the *Book of Amduat* which is in the Underworld and of the ritual of the "Opening of the Mouth." While the decoration in the chariot room [F¹] and its annexe [F²], still clogged by debris, remains to be unearthed, excavations have revealed that the walls of the vertical shaft [E], at least 6 m (20 feet) in depth, bear sculptural decorations depicting the 12th division of the *Book of Amduat*, a feature not repeated in any other tomb in the Valley of the Kings. The antechamber [I] of the tomb is decorated with depictions from chapter 125 of the *Book of the Dead*, together

with the scene of the weighing of the heart, that cover a part of the walls, while the great epics, such as the *Book of Amduat* and the *Book of Gates*, re-appear in the golden chamber [J] and in several annexes, especially rooms [J³], [J⁴], [J⁵], [J¹] et [j⁶].

The little room [J²] that opens on to the burial chamber from the south was covered with the text of the *Book of the Heavenly Cow*, that also adorned the wall panelling of hammered gold over wood in the largest of the shrines in the tomb of Tutankhamen, and, a little later, in the tomb of Seti I. The walls of the chamber [J⁷] feature four containers for canopic jars, guarded by the goddesses Isis and Nephthys who flank the doorway. The last chamber [J⁸] is decorated with chapter 110 of the *Book of the Dead*, with vignettes that, as in a papyrus, develop over one register, above large, deep niche benches.

The tomb of Rameses II, like almost all

father (KV 17), was later removed by high priests, to the cache at Deir el-Bahari, where it was rediscovered in 1881 by H. Brugsch and G. Maspero. Three inscriptions on the cover of the replacement coffin in which the venerable king was re-buried, bear witness to these tribulations. The first text, in hieratic characters like the others, lies above the knees. It reports that the first prophet of Amen-Ra, Herihor, was entrusted in "the sixth year of the era of renewal, in the third month of the *akhet* (flood) season, on the fifteenth day" to with the transfer of the mummy of Rameses II, re-swaddled and covered in garlands of flowers. The second inscription, covering the first and dated to the 10th year of the reign on Siamen, states that on "the seventeenth day of the fourth month of the *peret*

The sarcophagus of Rameses II was
originally laid on a burial bed. Or
at least, so it would appear from
the remains recently found, among
which there are two superb
limestone heads of a lioness, in the
image of the goddess Isis Mehtet,
sculpted in the round and painted
yellow. The frame of this bed,
made up of a great slab,
undoubtedly bore the body of this
animal in relief on its profiles.

(germination) season," a group of priests removed the mummy from the tomb of Seti I and carried it to the tomb of Queen Inhapi at Deir el-Bahari, where the remains of Amenhotep I had already been deposited. The third inscription on the coffin lies at the top of its head and indicates that this task was carried out three days later "on the 20th day of the fourth month of the *peret* season in year 10."

Although most of Rameses II's funerary equipment has been sacked or lost, recent excavations have unearthed some remaining objects. Over 450 calcite fragments uncovered in the debris clogging the corridors and rooms, revealed that the king's remains were placed in a sarcophagus, quite like the one used for Seti I, decorated both on its inner and outer surfaces with scenes from the *Book of Gates*. Originally, the sarcophagus rested on a bed, as suggested by the two superb limestone lion heads, sculpted in the round and painted in golden yellow. The bed frame, made up of a large slab, almost certainly evoked the shape of a lion in relief. A similar bed, but cut into a large block of calcite, can still be seen in the tomb of Merenptah (KV 8).

A small pit dug into the floor of the "gestation crypt" in the southern half of the burial chamber, was uncovered in 1995. In shape and location, it is very similar to similar small pits found in the tombs of Thutmosis I (KV 38) and Amenhotep III (WV 22). The pit was probably used to house the calcite canopic chest, fragments of which have been found inside the pit. In this tomb, the pit was covered at mid-depth by a limestone trap-door, the edges of which rested on a small ledge. If the upper half contained the canopic chest, protected at surface level by a shrine, it is probable that other objects occupied the lower section, hidden by the trap-door. The available space is sufficient to accommodate, for example, the four magnificent blue situla-shaped vases (in the Louvre Museum since the beginning of the century) that contained remnants of the materials used in the mummification of the king

as well as organic remains. It is highly probable that these vases in faience, used in embalming the king, were previously used for a completely different purpose, and may have played a part in religious rituals at the temple of Amen, for instance. Surviving fragments of the canopic chest suggest that it was hewn from a single block of calcite, as shown in its modern reconstruction. The chest included four cylindrical cavities that probably held the golden canopic jars containing the royal viscera. The general outline of the chest is comparable to the canopic chests of Amenhotep II and Tutankhamen, currently in the Egyptian Museum in Cairo.

There are several examples of *shawabty* of Rameses II, in wood, limestone or even copper, in collections of ancient Egyptian artefacts around the world. These have been mainly uncovered during official or illegal past excavations in the Valley of the Kings, or purchased from previous collections, but none rivals the fragmentary *shawabty* unearthed during our research. The figurine, found in the burial chamber is truly exceptional. Carved in bluish anhydrite, it depicts Rameses II in the form

of a mummy, at the height of his youth, wearing the *uraeus* headdress. Facial features and hair are highlighted in black. The folded legs, found separately, were attached to the rest of the statuette by mortice and tenon type joints.

A large number of potsherds were found on the flooring of the various chambers: pieces of stone containers, the calcite or limestone covers of which bore the royal cartouche (the pharaoh's name in hieroglyphs framed by an oval) or were decorated with a lotus with petals outlined in black. Other fragments include remnants of containers in faience and especially pottery, bearing labels of their contents, generally wine or fresh fat, in hieratic characters. Revealing in their shape and consistency, these potsherds are perfectly consistent with the historical periods the tomb has been through: the Ramesside period (funerary furniture), the Third Intermediate Period (utility vessels from the period coinciding with the transfer of the king's mummy), and lastly the Roman and Copt periods (break-ins and visits of the tomb). Large stoppers in limon or plaster, some of which bear a seal with the king's names, complete the rich archaeological material recovered from the tomb.

217

Sought for some time, the stone sarcophagus of Rameses II reappears today in the form of fragments in the tomb, as the archaeological excavation goes ahead. In limestone in the shape of a mummy, it was decorated with the Book of the Gates *in the inside and on the outside.*

THE TOMB OF
MERENPTAH

by Edwin C. Brock

MERENPTAH HAD HIS TOMB CONSTRUCTED
in a hillside at the confluence of two
watercourses, well above the main valley floor in
the second branch wadi to the west. Greek and
Latin graffiti show that the upper chambers were
accessible since antiquity as far as the first pillared
hall. Flood debris encumbered the lower corridors
and burial chamber, however, until cleared by
Howard Carter in the 1903-1904 winter
excavation season. The tomb was planned in part
by Pococke, the Napoleonic scholars and Burton.
Although scenes from the tomb were recorded in
the first half of the 19th century by Champollion,
Lepsius, Burton and Hay, the decoration has never
been fully published.

218 left
*This granodiorite bust of
Merenptah now in the Egyptian
Museum, Cairo (JE 31414, CG
607) was discovered by Petrie
in the ruins of that king's
mortuary temple in 1891.*

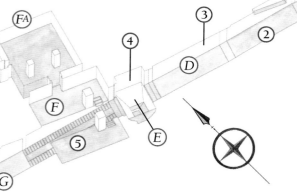

219
*Merenptah addresses his prayer to
Ra-Horakhty as he enters the tomb.
This scene at the entrance to the first
corridor of the king's tomb is
followed by the opening scene of the
Litany of Ra with its introductory
text appearing in the text column
to the right.*

LEGEND AND MAIN SCENES

A	ENTRANCE	I	FIFTH CORRIDOR	1	King and Ra-Horakhty, Litany of Ra
B	FIRST CORRIDOR	J	BURIAL CHAMBER	2	Litany of Ra
C	SECOND CORRIDOR	JA-D	SIDE CHAMBERS	3	Amduat
D	THIRD CORRIDOR	s1	OUTER	4	Gods
E	WELL CHAMBER		SARCOPHAGUS LID	5	Book of Gates, King and Gods
F	FIRST PILLARED HALL	s2	SECOND	6	Opening the mouth
FA	SIDE ROOM		SARCOPHAGUS LID	7	King and Gods, Book of the Dead
G	FOURTH CORRIDOR	K	REAR CHAMBER	8	Opening of the mouth
H	ROOM	KA-C	SIDE CHAMBERS	9	Book of Gates, Book of the Earth, King and Gods, Astronomical figures (on ceiling)

220

The burial chamber of Merenptah's tomb has a vaulted ceiling and sunken floor in the center, flanked by four pillars on each side. The lid of the second granite sarcophagus rests on a modern base of limestone blocks. The cartouche shape of the lid encloses the figure of the king. In the background, remains of a scene showing a large ram-headed bird representing the soul of Ra is surmounted by the final scene from the Book of Caverns depicting the emergence of the revitalized sun god.

221 top

This view to the rear of the first pillared hall shows the central descent flanked by a pair of pillars. The expected second pair of pillars were cut away by the tomb builders. The center of the rear wall is taken up with a double scene of the king offering to Osiris. The theme of the king offering to Osiris is repeated on the sides of the two pillars facing us but survives only on the left pillar. The loss of decoration on lower parts of the walls and pillars indicates the height of the deposit of flood debris in this tomb.

221 bottom

This detail of the scene from the wall is an adaptation from the final scene of the Book of Caverns. Human-headed birds representing souls, together with bent fans symbolic of shadows represent different aspects of the dead in the next world.

The entry stairway, now covered by modern steps, descended to the first gate followed by a sloping corridor (B), a stairwell with recesses at the top (C), and another sloping corridor (D). Progress was interrupted by a vertical shaft cut into the floor of the next chamber (E), with a pillared hall (F) beyond. A side room (Fa) with two pillars opened off the north side of this hall and a central descent ramp cut into the floor of the hall lead to another sloping corridor (G), a square chamber (H) and second sloping corridor (I) that gave access to the burial chamber (J). This chamber is divided into three sections, consisting of two lateral platforms, each with four pillars, flanking a central hall with vaulted ceiling and a lower floor. A small room is located at each end of the platforms and a rectangular passage (K) to the rear has three rooms opening off its sides and ends. None of the side rooms off J or the lateral rooms off K has yet been cleared.

Four stone sarcophagi were provided for the king's burial, three of red granite and an innermost calcite one of mummiform shape, placed one inside the other. They rested on a base of calcite blocks set into a pit in the burial chamber floor. The jambs in the gates above room H were cut back in order to make room for the passage of the massive outer sarcophagus. Five pairs of holes were cut for the temporary insertion of wooden beams across the corridors. Ropes passing around these beams were let out to control the descent of the sarcophagus boxes to which they were attached.

The *Litany of Ra* decorates the walls of the first two corridors, followed by the fourth and fifth hours of the *Amduat* in the third corridor and the fourth, fifth and sixth divisions of the *Book of Gates* in the first pillared hall. Traces of the Opening the Mouth ritual remain on the walls of corridor G and *Book of the Dead* spell 125, together with images of the king and gods decorate room H. The burial chamber displays new decorative themes, including extracts from a composition now called the *Book of the Earth*.

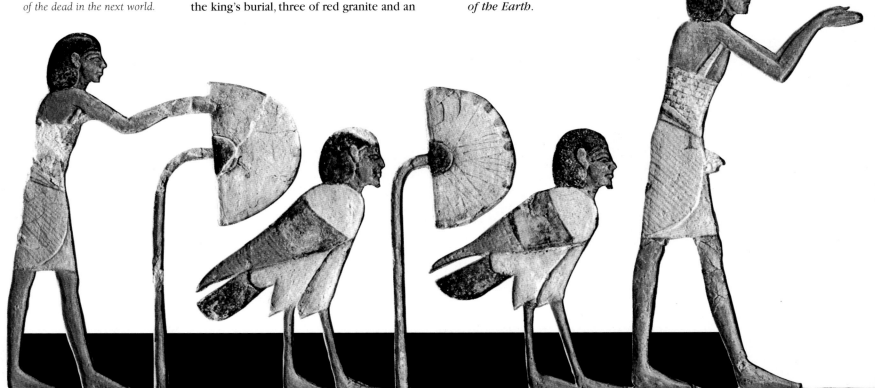

THE TOMB OF
TAUSERT AND SETNAKHT

by Hartwig Altenmüller

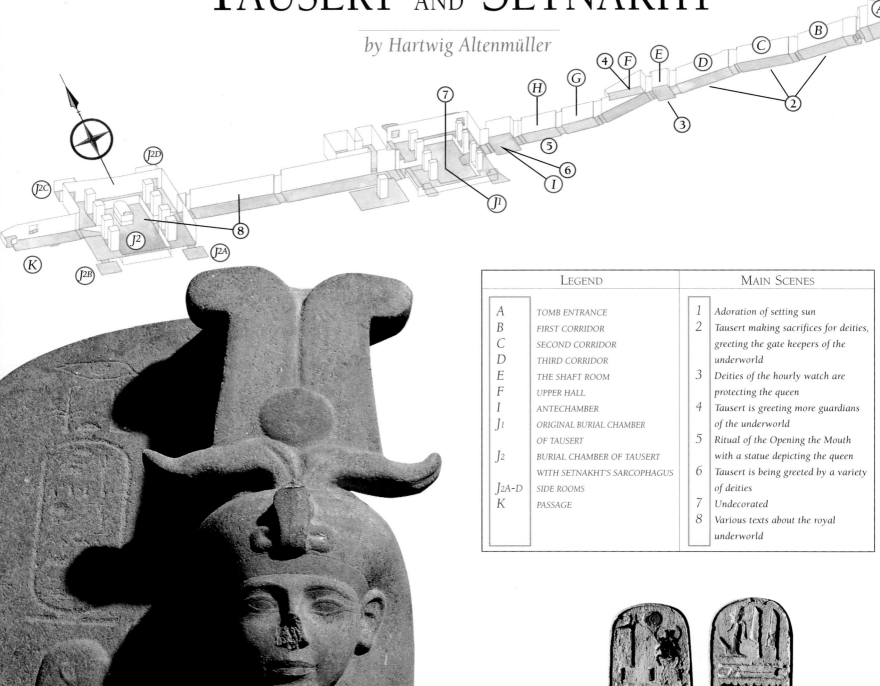

LEGEND		MAIN SCENES	
A	TOMB ENTRANCE	1	Adoration of setting sun
B	FIRST CORRIDOR	2	Tausert making sacrifices for deities,
C	SECOND CORRIDOR		greeting the gate keepers of the
D	THIRD CORRIDOR		underworld
E	THE SHAFT ROOM	3	Deities of the hourly watch are
F	UPPER HALL		protecting the queen
I	ANTECHAMBER	4	Tausert is greeting more guardians
J1	ORIGINAL BURIAL CHAMBER		of the underworld
	OF TAUSERT	5	Ritual of the Opening the Mouth
J2	BURIAL CHAMBER OF TAUSERT		with a statue depicting the queen
	WITH SETNAKHT'S SARCOPHAGUS	6	Tausert is being greeted by a variety
J2A-D	SIDE ROOMS		of deities
K	PASSAGE	7	Undecorated
		8	Various texts about the royal
			underworld

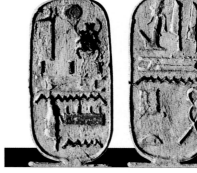

222 left

Inside the large sarcophagus hall ordered by Tausert, at the end of the tomb, we find Setnakht's granite sarcophagus. On its cover, there is an image of the king in the mummified shape of Osiris holding the royal scepter and the whip of Osiris.

222 right

The name of Setnakht, written on the sarcophagus, consists of two parts: the coronation name 'Userhaura-Setepenra-Meriamen" (Userhaura, chosen by Ra, chosen and beloved by

Amen), and the birth name "Setnakht Mererimen Merira" (Setnakht, permanently beloved by Amen, and beloved by Ra).

223

The sarcophagus hall of the 'Great Royal Wife' Tausert was decorated with texts and images from royal underworld books during her joint reign with king Siptah. Some images are from the New Kingdom's Book of Gates. The pillars show images of protective deities. One of them is Horus-son-of-Isis (Harsiesis), with his double-crown.

224 left

Queen Tausert's voyage into the other world leads her past a number of pictures that show gates of the underworld and their guardians armed with knives. The final destination of the voyage is Osiris. When the tomb was usurped, the queen's image was replaced by cartouches of Setnakht.

IN THE MIDDLE OF MAY 1182 BC, at the beginning of the 4th month of the *shemu*-season, in his first year in power, pharaoh Rameses III accompanied the mummy of his father Setnakht to a grave at the western end of the Valley of the Kings.

The funeral procession moved towards a tomb that shortly before had been prepared for the king. It was not the burial site that had originally been chosen for Setnakht, who had died during the 3rd year of his reign, but the grave of a queen who had reigned until the middle of March of 1186 BC. She had been the last ruler of the 19th Dynasty, going back to Rameses II, one of the few women on the pharaoh's throne. With her death the 19th Dynasty came to an end.

The reasons for this rather unusual choice of a burial site that had already been occupied by another ruler are clouded by mystery. Setnakht was to have been buried in grave number 11 in the Valley of the Kings, which he had begun to construct immediately after his ascension to the throne as the 20th Dynasty's first ruler. Building work was already advanced when Setnakht died on 7 March 1183 BC. During the 70-day period needed for his embalming and mummification, there would have been enough time to complete grave number 11, and turn it into a regular ruler's grave.

224 right

Isis and Nephthys are protecting Osiris, the ruler of the underworld, sitting on his throne. The two sisters are wearing the typical outfits of grieving women; on their heads we can see the hieroglyphs indicating their names. Isis, who can be seen in the front row, is raising her hand as a protective gesture. Her beautifully painted face could be a portrait of queen Tausert.

224-225

The 'Great Royal Wife' Tausert is received by a group of gods when she enters the tomb. One of the gods is Horakthy, the sun god, ruler of heaven, who is accompanied by the goddess Maat (decorated with a feather).

225 bottom left

The Memphis god Ptah, standing in a shrine, is one of the protective deities of the other world. He has the shape of a mummy; his two hands are sticking out from the shroud and hold the so-called Ptah-scepter. Behind him, we see the goddess Maat with her arms represented as wings.

225 bottom right

Osiris is shown as master of the underworld. He is holding a scepter and a whip in his hands; on his head, the so-called atef-crown. On the side, his throne is decorated with little feathers, colored in the blue hue that characterizes the world of the gods.

However, his successor Rameses III, decided differently. Grave number 11, which had been reserved for Setnakht, was not completed. (It was later to become the burial site for Rameses III). Queen Tausert's grave, number 14 in the Valley of the Kings—with its overall length of 112 meters (370 feet) one of the Valley's largest—was chosen as a substitute. The site that was already occupied by the remains of queen Tausert was hurriedly cleared for Setnakht. It was redecorated and new texts were applied, thus preparing it for its new occupant, King Setnakht.

In the early part of the 20th Dynasty, it was highly unusual to confiscate the royal tomb of a predecessor. Each king of that period, with the exception of Rameses III, was buried in the tomb that he had constructed for himself.

It is certain, therefore, that there were extraordinary circumstances that moved Rameses III not to bury Setnakht in his prepared tomb, but in another one. We must assume that the change of Setnakht's burial site from KV 11 in the central part of the Valley of Kings to the west of the valley did not correspond to Sethnakht's wishes in his last will, but was based on a fundamental and very personal decision by Rameses III.

The real reasons to abandon tomb KV 11 are open to speculation. What we know for sure is that once the decision was made to bury Setnakht in Queen Tausert's tomb (KV 14), this was carried out without further complications. Queen Tausert's tomb fulfilled all the necessary conditions for a regular royal tomb. Its architecture, the decoration of its walls,

and the outfitting of the burial chamber were those of a regular tomb of the Ramesside period.

In spite of its 'elitist' position within the Valley of the Kings in Thebes, the tomb Setnakht had usurped had originally not been planned as a burial site. It was Queen Tausert herself who had laid the foundations for the use of KV 14 as a royal tomb. The site's previous history, which consists of a number of phases, can be reconstructed when looking at the overall design and concept of the tomb. The tomb of Queen Tausert, which nowadays is usually (and without justification) called Setnakht's tomb, was constructed over a period of ten years. Its architecture reveals four distinct construction periods, all of which are connected to Tausert. An expert of Egyptian history who observes the tomb's architecture

226-227

The sarcophagus hall of Queen Tausert's tomb is designed like a king's tomb. The main difference from a king's tomb is the reduced dimensions of the room and the pillars. The wall decoration, too, resembles that of a king's tomb: the walls are decorated with scenes from the Book of Gates, normally only found in kings' tombs. The pillars show protective deities. In the lower part of the sarcophagus hall, we see pictures of royal burial offerings.

227

The pillars in the sarcophagus hall are decorated with various deities, who have assembled to protect queen Tausert. Among the gods we can see the moon god Thoth, wearing a crescent moon on his ibis-head. He represents the night. Then there is Hathor, with the sun disk between the cow horns, representing the day. Ptah-Sokar of Memphis has the shape of a mummy. With a double-scepter and a whip he is reigning over the underworld with Osiris, god of the dead.

and decoration in detail will recognize that Tausert's ascent to power is reflected in the different building phases. Construction was begun on the 8th day of the first month of the *peret*-season, during the second year of Seti II, i.e., in December 1199 BC. The construction was ordered by Seti II. He had decided to concede his Queen Tausert, his 'Great Royal Wife', the unusual privilege of a grave in the Valley of the Kings, an honor that not even Rameses II had planned for his queen, Nefertari.

The second building phase coincides with the reign of King Siptah, who ascended to the throne in 1194 BC. He generally maintained the plans approved by Seti II and authorized the continuation of work to create a 'queen's tomb'.

The building was 60 meters (200 feet) long and the sequence of its rooms made it into a miniature copy of a king's tomb. In the year 1190 BC, during the first half of Siptah's reign, Tausert's tomb consisted of an upper and a lower burial area, culminating in a large sarcophagus hall (which, however, was not identical to a king's sarcophagus hall).

The third phase of construction fell in the period when Tausert ruled the empire together with Siptah, probably in the year 1190 BC. In that year, Tausert accepted the royal regalia and began to make the first changes to the tomb's layout and décor. During this period, a second sarcophagus hall with the normal dimensions used for a king's was

constructed behind the existing 'smaller copy' of a chamber. The decoration of the tomb is enriched with 'royal themes'.

The fourth and final phase of construction saw the actual creation of a royal tomb. After she ascended to the throne in 1187 BC, Queen Tausert, now pharaoh, ordered the rearrangement of her tomb as a prestigious royal burial place, changing the entire décor to exclusively royal motifs. In addition to the first sarcophagus hall, a second, larger one was built for a pharaoh's coffin so large that all the corridors and entrances of the tomb had to be enlarged. The walls were now decorated with images and texts from underworld books, like a true royal tomb.

228-229

The eastern wall of the sarcophagus hall is decorated with scenes from the Book of Gates. The book describes the state of the underworld and enumerates twelve rooms, which are visited during the night by the sun god. The ninth hour of the Book of Gates is dominated by a rectangle of water with people who drowned, drifting in various positions within the primordial waters. They are being animated by the sun god. In the upper register, the blessed dead, in the shape of birds, receive food during the night. In the lower register, the damned are being devoured by a fire-spitting snake.

229 top

On the wall next to the door, between the third and fourth corridor, the goddess Maat sits on a basket and greets those who enter the room. On the northern wall, there is a depiction of the goddess, positioned on some papyrus plants, symbol of Lower Egypt. On the southern wall, we see her with lilies, the symbol plants of Upper Egypt.

229 bottom

In the Book of Gates' 10th night hour, the sun god is fighting against Apophis. A variety of beings, among them snakes, are participating in the punishment of the sun god's enemies.

230

The sarcophagus hall of Tausert's tomb, northern and southern section. At two ends of the sarcophagus hall there are depictions of additional underworld books. In scenes from the Book of Caverns, on the northern wall, there is the depiction of a being with wings; above it, the resurrection of the sun early in the morning, in three different shapes: as a sun disk, a scarab, and a child. Complementary to this, scenes from the Book of the Earth, on the southern wall, show the resuscitation of the sun god, depicted as a mummy, during the night.

To sum up, construction of this tomb had been initiated by Seti II for his 'Great Royal Wife'. After Tausert's ascent to the throne, the 'queen's tomb' was altered to become a real royal tomb. This is the tomb Rameses III took for his father Setnakht. The usurpation of the tomb did not require much effort. The only things that had to be changed were the images of a female pharaoh labelled with Tausert's name which were part of the tomb's decoration. The remainder of the decoration remained.

Within the period of 70 days required for the process of embalming and mummification between the death and funeral of the king, all images of the queen were covered with stucco. In the tomb's upper rooms and in the sarcophagus hall the image of the female pharaoh was covered, and the one of the male pharaoh Setnakht was painted. In addition, Setnakht's cartouches were added. In other places in the tomb there was not enough time to change the old imagery; all that could be done was to cover up the queen's images and replace them with giant Setnakht cartouches, executed in black ink.

Since only the images and writings of Queen Tausert were eliminated and replaced by Setnakht's pictures and cartouches in tomb KV 14, the overall design of Queen Tausert's tomb has been preserved almost completely. The decoration we see today goes back almost entirely to Tausert. It provides an unusually pure example of artistic works during the reign of pharaoh Siptah and Queen Tausert, between 1190 and 1185 BC.

230-231

On the southern wall, we see the complementary Book of the Earth. Here, too, we see a resuscitation of the sun god, particularly with the animation of the sun's corpse at the end of the night. The dead sun god is shown as a mummy lying down, surrounded by disks and stars. His living form is represented by a standing mummy.

231 bottom

In the sarcophagus hall of the female pharaoh, Tausert, we can now see the monumental sarcophagus of King Sethnakth. The sarcophagus, which was broken in ancient times by robbers, has now been renovated. Its lid shows the pharaoh in the shape of a mummy.

LEGEND			
A	ENTRANCE	F	PILLARED ROOM
B	FIRST CORRIDOR	FA	SIDE ROOM
BA	SIDE ROOM	G	FOURTH CORRIDOR
BB	SIDE ROOM	H	ANTECHAMBER
C	SECOND CORRIDOR	I	ANTECHAMBER
	WITH 8 SIDE ROOMS	J	BURIAL CHAMBER
D	THIRD CORRIDOR	K	REAR ROOMS
E	WELL CHAMBER	L	REAR ROOMS

THE TOMB OF
RAMESES III

By Edwin C. Brock

232-233

A detail from the east wall of the third corridor of Rameses III offering incense. The figure of the king actually represents his father Setnakht, whose cartouches were plastered over and re-inscribed for Rameses III. The elaborate headdress alludes to Ra and Osiris, as well as his own regal status.

233

This granodiorite statue of Rameses III in the Egyptian Museum, Cairo (JE 36682, CG 42150) was found by Legrain in the "Cour de la Cachette" at Karnak Temple in 1905. The king is shown carrying a processional standard topped with the head of a ram, a symbol of the god Amen.

MAIN SCENES			
1	*King and Ra-Horakty, Litany of Ra*	*12*	*Divine standards*
2	*Food preparation*	*13*	*King and gods*
3	*Boats for Abydos Pilgrimage*	*14*	*Amduat*
4	*Litany of Ra with form of Ra*	*15*	*Gods*
5	*Nile gods and agricultural deities*	*16*	*Book of Gates, Kings and Gods, Double Osiris*
6	*Nile gods and nome deities*	*17*	*King and Gods, Book of Gates*
7	*Bull and seven cows, sacred oars*	*18*	*Opening of the Mouth*
8	*Harpists before solar gods*	*19, 20*	*Gods*
9	*Images of Osiris*	*21*	*Book of Gates, Book of the Earth*
10	*Fields of Reeds*	*22, 23*	*Gods*
11	*Furniture and luxury goods*	*24*	*Gods, Book of Gates*

EXCAVATION OF THIS TOMB WAS BEGUN for Setnakht and carried out as far as the room formed by the westward extension of the third corridor (D) where traces of his names exist. Work was abandoned because it ran into KV 10. Rameses III apparently added side rooms off the first and second corridors, continued cutting the remainder of tomb, and added more decoration. Hieratic graffiti documenting inspections in the 21st Dynasty have been noted in the first pillared hall, side chambers off the first and second corridors, and burial chamber. Remains of the king's coffin were found in the KV 35 cache but his mummy itself was discovered in the Deir el-Bahari cache TT 320. Third Intermediate Period human remains were noted by the Napoleonic expedition and James Burton in a side room off the burial chamber. The tomb was accessible in upper chambers since Graeco-Roman times.

The tomb was known to European travelers since the 18th century as "Bruce's tomb" after the Scottish traveler James Bruce who visited the tomb in 1768. It was also called the "Tomb of the Harpers" because of the scene of two harp players published by Bruce. Richard Pococke visited in the late 1730s and made a partial plan of the upper chambers, showing the collision with KV 10, although the orientation of the two tombs is reversed. William Browne was able to gain access to the burial chamber and its side rooms in 1792, where he left his name. The scholars in Napoleon's "army of savants" recorded the tomb's plan as well as some of the scenes in its side chambers,

including a somewhat more accurate version of the harpers. Belzoni removed the sarcophagus and lid which are now in the Louvre and Fitzwilliam Museum in Cambridge respectively. Nineteenth century European explorers such as Lepsius, Champollion and Rosellini, published certain details of the tomb's decoration. A Polish mission fully documented the tomb in the 1970s but this material has yet to be published.

Several unusual architectural features occur in this tomb. The entryway (A), with a descending central ramp flanked by steps, has two pairs of pilasters cut at the south end, each topped with the

235 top right

These seated figures on the rear wall of the first east side room off the second corridor represent deities associated with grain and agricultural fertility. The poorly preserved figures below represented cobras dressed in robes again as personifications of food offerings.

236 left

Rameses III offers an image of the
goddess Maat to Osiris, seated
before a table of offerings.
The presentation of this symbol,
also an element in his own name,
indicates the royal responsibility
for establishing and maintaining
divine order.

236 bottom right

This detail from the north wall
of the enlargement of the third
corridor shows the king offering
incense and libations. The figure
originally represented Setnakht,
but the cartouches were plastered
over and re-carved for Rameses III.
He pours the libation from an
unusual triple vessel.

237

This detail of the east face of the
southeast pillar in the first
pillared hall depicts Rameses III
offering incense. The style differs
from the royal representations
found in the first three corridors
and dates to the time when the
tomb was decorated for
Rameses III.

236 top right

The king offers a libation from a
vessel capped with a ram's head, a
symbol of the god Amen-Ra. In his
other hand he holds a cup with
burning incense. These two
purification offerings are presented
to the "Noble of Hermopolis."

head of an antelope. Two decorated rooms were cut
into the east and west walls of the first corridor (B)
and four pairs of small rooms were cut into the walls
of the second corridor (C). In previous New Kingdom
royal tombs, the second corridor had developed from
a room with a descent cut into the floor to a
stairwell with trapezoidal niches at the top. With
KV 11, the niches became a pair of rectangular
recesses set high in the walls at the beginning of
the corridor. The alteration of the third corridor
(D¹ᴬ) into a room (D¹) resulted from the collision
with KV 10 as an attempt to shift the axis of the
corridor to the west. The continuation of this
corridor (D²) through the south wall of D¹ was
carried out to avoid the other tomb and, to further
ensure this, the floor rises rather than being level or
sloping down. The well shaft (E), the last example of
such an excavation, is partly filled with debris from
flooding and from filling-in to allow the removal of
the sarcophagus by Belzoni. The first pillared hall
(F) beyond has a large side room (Fᴬ) and a central
ramp descent leading to a lower corridor (G), two
antechambers (H, I) and the burial chamber (J). This
tomb is the last to have a fully cut burial chamber
with subsidiary rooms at the corners, after the
pattern established in the 19th Dynasty by

238

The head end of the red granite sarcophagus of Rameses III shows the goddess Nephthys kneeling on the symbol for gold. Her out-spread arms are provided with wings, an allusion to her personification as one of the two kites or mourners of Osiris.

239 left

The sarcophagus box of Rameses III was acquired by the Louvre from the collection of Henry Salt while the lid was acquired by the Fitzwilliam Museum in Cambridge from Belzoni. The right side of the sarcophagus is decorated with the seventh hour of the Amduat.

239 top right

This view of the burial chamber illustrates the damage from the flooding of the tomb after the well shaft was filed. Pressure from the expansion of the stone in contact with the wet debris has caused pillars to shatter and parts of the vaulted ceiling to collapse.

239 bottom right

This unusual group statue from Medinet Habu shows the king being crowned by Horus and Seth. It is now in the Egyptian Museum, Cairo (JE 31628 CG 629) and has been exensively restored. The figure of Seth is hypothetical and Thoth, also depicted in coronation scenes, could have been here instead.

Merenptah. The floor of the chamber is lower in the center and surrounded on the north and south by two platforms with four pillars on each. The central area of the ceiling is vaulted, but flat between the pillars and the walls. The large granite sarcophagus that once rested in the center of the floor was aligned along the main axis of the tomb contrary to previous sarcophagus installations. There are three chambers (K^1, K^2, L) on axis to the rear of J, the third (L) having long low recesses on the sides and a vaulted ceiling.

The decoration in painted sunk relief is well preserved as far as the first pillared hall and includes the *Litany of Ra*, extracts from the *Amduat* and *Book of Gates*. Other themes included depictions of the offering to various gods. The decoration in the lower corridors and burial chamber are poorly preserved as a result of the effects of past floods that entered the tomb. Remains of scenes from the *Book of Caverns* and the *Book of the Earth* can be found in the burial chamber. Stylistic differences between the decoration of the first three corridors and the remainder of the tomb reflect the different periods of work under Setnakht and Rameses III. Decorative innovations in the tomb are primarily in the subject matter of the side rooms off the first and second corridors. These include food preparation, offerings from different parts of the realm, and funerary equipment.

THE TOMB OF
RAMESES IV

by Erik Hornung

AFTER THE ASSASSINATION of Rameses III, his son Rameses IV managed to stop the conspiracy begun in the harem and punished those who were found guilty. To re-establish public order, which had been disturbed, the new king confirmed (in the Harris Papyrus) all the donations that his father had made to the temples. He also added his own foundations. He then concentrated on building a temple for the dead, which was planned to be enormous in size but remained incomplete.

It took a long time until a location was chosen for the new royal tomb. One reason was the use of a new planning concept. Previously, from one government to the next, royal tombs had been ever larger and more richly decorated; each king wanted to outdo his predecessor. Now, in a time of economic difficulty, this came to an end. Rameses IV reduced the overall size and the amount of decor, deleted pillars, stairways, side chambers, and images of the king with the gods. In return, he increased the tomb's basic dimensions, so that it was much larger than the ones before—a palace-tomb with corridors over three meters (10 feet) wide and four meters (15 feet) high.

In the 19th century, it was used as a "hotel" for many expeditions that worked in the Valley of the Kings, including Champollion and Rosellini (1829), and Robert Hay, Furst Puckler, Theodore Davis, and many others. Many Greek and Coptic graffiti were written on the tomb's walls and the sargophagus—which still lies in the tomb—indicate that there were also many visitors and residents during antiquity. The tomb's facade was richly decorated with scenes of the coronation of the king and with a scene in which Isis and Nephthys venerate the sun disk. On the disk are images of the sun god in his morning and night shape, as a scarab and as a ram-headed god. The corridors no longer lead steeply downwards, as in former tombs, but are almost horizontal. The first two corridors are still reserved for the text and the

240 top

The coronation name of the king, sealed in a cartouche: Heqamaatra setepenimen, "Ruler of Maat is Ra, chosen by Amen." On the left, the royal title "Son of Ra."

240 bottom

A scene from the fourth hour of the Book of Gates. Time is shown as a meandering snake, from which the night hours are being born as goddesses. After their journey, they are swallowed again by the snake. The blue triangles represent the water in the underworld.

241

View through the burial chamber with the sarcophagus decorated with scenes from the sun god's nightly voyage. On the walls, parts of the Book of Gates; on the ceiling two images of the goddess Nut with a red sun disk, which she swallows in the evening, and gives birth to in the morning.

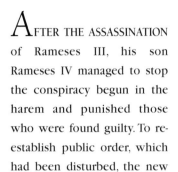

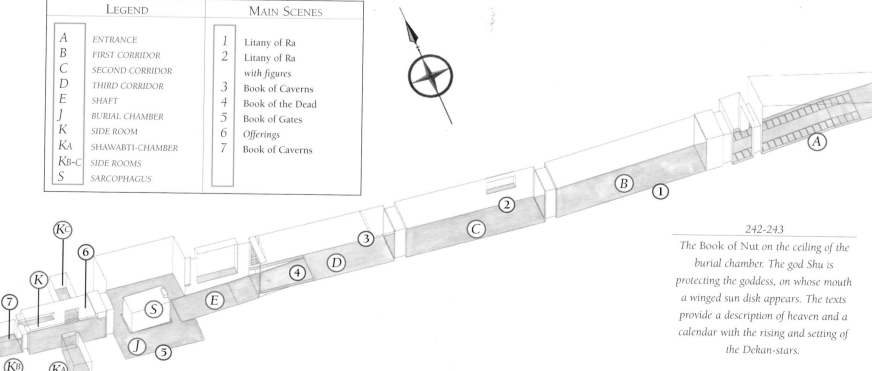

LEGEND

A	ENTRANCE
B	FIRST CORRIDOR
C	SECOND CORRIDOR
D	THIRD CORRIDOR
E	SHAFT
J	BURIAL CHAMBER
K	SIDE ROOM
KA	SHAWABTI-CHAMBER
KB-C	SIDE ROOMS
S	SARCOPHAGUS

MAIN SCENES

1	Litany of Ra
2	Litany of Ra with figures
3	Book of Caverns
4	Book of the Dead
5	Book of Gates
6	Offerings
7	Book of Caverns

242-243

The Book of Nut on the ceiling of the burial chamber. The god Shu is protecting the goddess, on whose mouth a winged sun disk appears. The texts provide a description of heaven and a calendar with the rising and setting of the Dekan-stars.

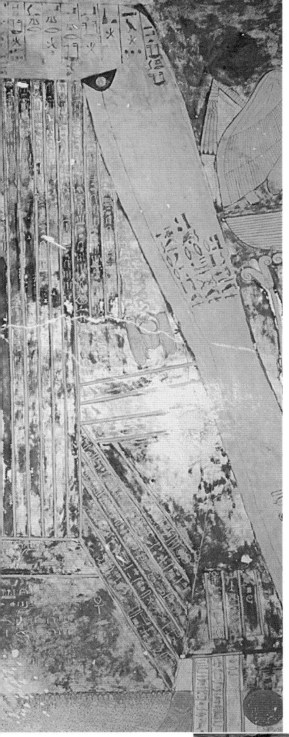

figures from the *Litany of Ra*, after the usual initial scene that shows the king before the falcon-headed sun god Ra-Horakhthy. The great litany, on the left wall and on the end of the right wall, can easily be identified by the stereotypical beginning of its 75 lines. On the ceiling, birds protectively spread their wings. There are vultures, falcons, and winged scarabs. The second corridor has niches on both sides decorated with figures from the solar litany. Other figures follow, some painted on the ceiling. Below, there are texts from the solar litany. The final texts from the *Amduat*, normally found at this place in a tomb, are missing.

In the third corridor, the *Amduat* has been replaced by a more recent book about the underworld: the *Book of Caverns* (first and second part). The many ovals in the depictions represent sarcophagi, in which there are gods or deceased people who are blessed. In the lowest register, the punishment of enemies is shown: they are tied down and some of them have already been decapitated. The ceiling, at first, is straight and decorated with stars; later, it becomes vaulted, with detailed royal regalia in the center. From the middle of the room, an oblique ramp leads to the burial chamber. It crosses the antechamber, which is decorated with texts from the *Book of the Dead*, above all with Chapter 125, dealing with the judgement of the dead. Highlighted in yellow within the texts are numerous cartouches with the king's name. The burial chamber is nearly filled by the king's monumental granite sarcophagus.

Here, too, Rameses IV exceeded the measurements that had so far been customary (length 3.55 meters-12 feet-, height 3.32 meters-11 feet). On the walls, we can see the second, third, and fourth hours of the night from the *Book of Gates*. In each of these hours, the king kneels in the bark before the ram-headed sun god, sacrificing to him a figure of the goddess Maat. The predominant color is yellow, in spite of the texts' white background. This marks the burial chamber as "A House of Gold". The flat ceiling (no longer vaulted) is decorated in a novel way: instead of stellar constellations it contains two large figures representing Nut, the celestial goddess. She bends forward over earth, protected on the left by the god Shu. Within this framework, the *Book of Nut* was inserted on the left. It contains a description of heaven and its phenomena; on the right, there is part of the *Book of the Night*, in which the nightly voyage of the sun god through the goddess' body is described. Behind the burial chamber is another room, which is no longer decorated with reliefs but with paintings. The texts are from the first part of the *Book of Caverns*; in the niches, there are sacrificial offerings and various deities in shrines. This room leads to two narrow chambers, where the funerary figures (*shawabtis*) were kept; the walls are also decorated with *shawabty*-figures. There is another, final chamber, with paintings of burial offerings (beds, shrines, canopic jars). Above its entrance, a double-sphinx symbolizes the underworld, through which the solar bark, visible above, proceeds on its voyage.

243 top

Entry wall of the burial chamber, with a sequence from the second hour of the Book of Gates, showing the "Tired Ones" and "Bound Enemies" before the god Atum.

243 bottom

The Book of the Night on the ceiling of the burial chamber, surrounded by the celestial goddess Nut, who is leaning on the earth with her hands and feet. Instead of the underworld, the sun god here travels through her body, to be reborn the next morning.

This granodiorite statue of Rameses VI grasping a captive Libyan is in the Egyptian Museum, Cairo (JE 37173, CG 42152). A lion strides beside the king and a falcon's wings frames his crown. It was discovered in 1904 in a cache of statues buried north of the Seventh Pylon at Karnak.

The center of the rear wall of the first pillared hall, above the descent, has a double scene of Osiris seated in a shrine. Images of the king offering to various gods appear on the pillars and the goddess Nut frames the Books of Day and Night on the ceiling.

An ostracon showing two soldiers wrestling found in KV 9 in 1890 is now in the Egyptian Museum, Cairo (CG 25132). The text quotes one of the combatants: "See I'll weaken you and throw you down before Pharaoh." A similar scene appears in Medinet Habu below the window of appearaces.

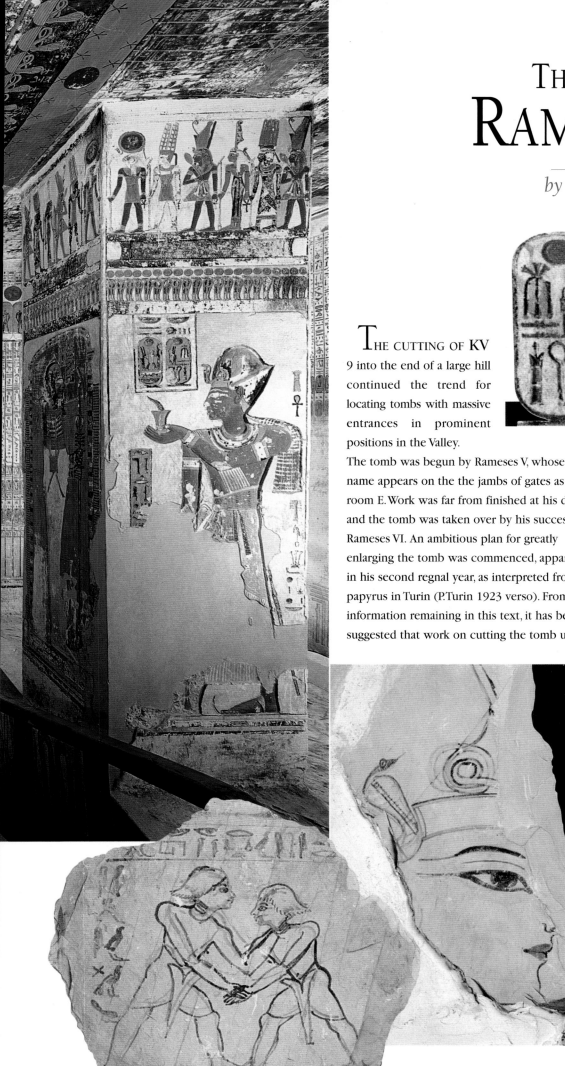

THE TOMB OF
RAMESES VI

by Edwin C. Brock

The cutting of KV 9 into the end of a large hill continued the trend for locating tombs with massive entrances in prominent positions in the Valley.

The tomb was begun by Rameses V, whose name appears on the the jambs of gates as far as room E. Work was far from finished at his death, and the tomb was taken over by his successor, Rameses VI. An ambitious plan for greatly enlarging the tomb was commenced, apparently in his second regnal year, as interpreted from a papyrus in Turin (P.Turin 1923 verso). From the information remaining in this text, it has been suggested that work on cutting the tomb under Rameses V had progressed as far as the second corridor below the first pillared hall.

An account of the theft of metal objects and cloth from the tomb at an uncertain date is found in Papyrus Mayer B. An inspection graffito of year 9 of Rameses IX in the burial chamber may post-date this event. The mummy of Rameses VI, discovered re-buried in KV 35, was found to have been severely damaged by tomb robbers, who appear to have hacked the mummy apart in their search for valuables. The stone sarcophagi that encased the king's coffin were subsequently broken up during an attempt to quarry some of the stone for other uses. The red granite outer sarcophagus box, with a floor a meter (3.3 feet) in thickness, was split in half laterally and its sides broken away. The green conglomerate inner mummiform sarcophagus was not desired for reuse and the box and lid were smashed up and thrown into the central pit in the floor of the burial chamber. The foot end of the outer sarcophagus box over-balanced and fell into the central pit, effectively blocking removal of either half, and the quarrying operation was abandoned.

The tomb was completely accessible from antiquity and was frequently visited in Graeco-Roman times, when it was known as the tomb of Memnon, as numerous graffiti in Greek and a few in Latin attest. This identification may have resulted from a similarity of the first cartouches of Rameses VI and of Amenhotep III, for whom the famous Colossi of Memnon was made. The many Coptic graffiti also found here show how it served as a refuge for early Christian hermit monks. It was reported on by early explorers in the 18th century and was known to the members of the Napoleonic Expedition as the "Tombe de la Métempsychose," influenced, no doubt, by the scene of the Judgment Hall of Osiris from the *Book of Gates* in the third corridor (D). Daressy cleared all of the tomb in 1888 except for the burial chamber pit. This latter feature was

245 bottom right

A detail of a limestone ostracon from KV 9 now in the Egyptian Museum (CG 25144) is a sketch of the head of a king. Although no representations in KV 9 depict the king wearing this type of headdress, a similar image in relief is in the tomb of Rameses III.

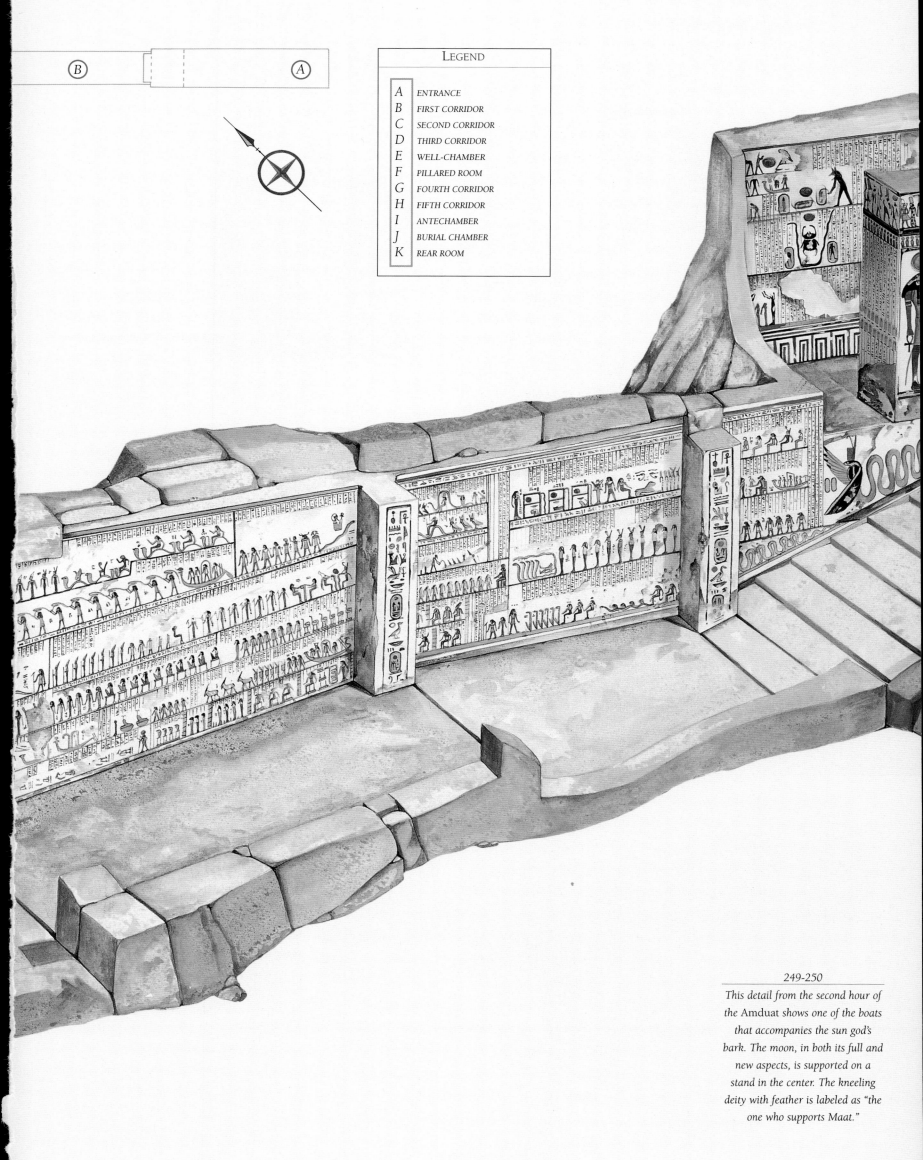

249-250

This detail from the second hour of the Amduat shows one of the boats that accompanies the sun god's bark. The moon, in both its full and new aspects, is supported on a stand in the center. The kneeling deity with feather is labeled as "the one who supports Maat."

LEGEND

A	ENTRANCE
B	FIRST CORRIDOR
C	SECOND CORRIDOR
D	THIRD CORRIDOR
E	WELL-CHAMBER
F	PILLARED ROOM
G	FOURTH CORRIDOR
H	FIFTH CORRIDOR
I	ANTECHAMBER
J	BURIAL CHAMBER
K	REAR ROOM

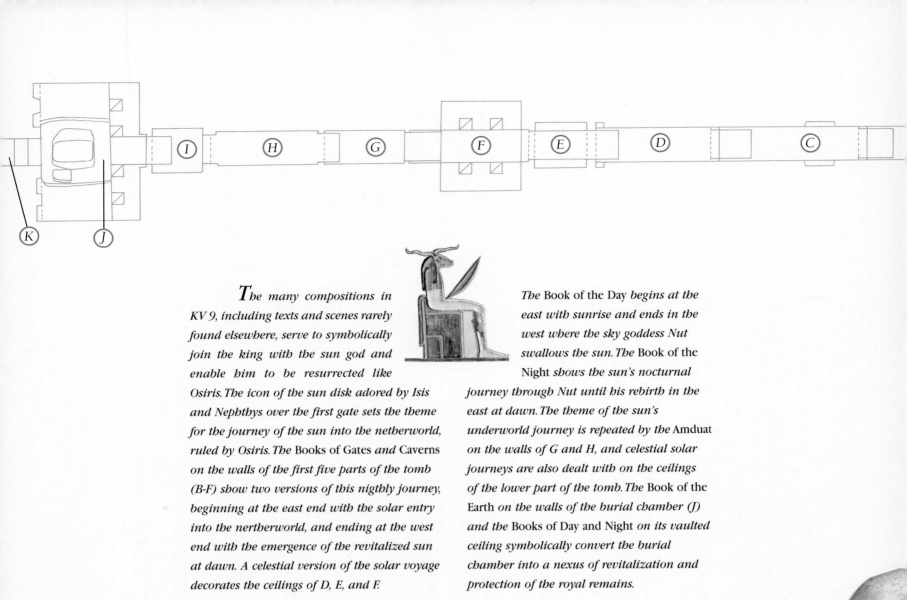

The many compositions in KV 9, including texts and scenes rarely found elsewhere, serve to symbolically join the king with the sun god and enable him to be resurrected like Osiris. The icon of the sun disk adored by Isis and Nephthys over the first gate sets the theme for the journey of the sun into the netherworld, ruled by Osiris. The Books of Gates *and* Caverns on the walls of the first five parts of the tomb (B-F) show two versions of this nightly journey, beginning at the east end with the solar entry into the nertherworld, and ending at the west end with the emergence of the revitalized sun at dawn. A celestial version of the solar voyage decorates the ceilings of D, E, and F.

The Book of the Day *begins at the east with sunrise and ends in the west where the sky goddess Nut swallows the sun. The* Book of the Night *shows the sun's nocturnal journey through Nut until his rebirth in the east at dawn. The theme of the sun's underworld journey is repeated by the* Amduat *on the walls of G and H, and celestial solar journeys are also dealt with on the ceilings of the lower part of the tomb. The* Book of the Earth *on the walls of the burial chamber (J) and the* Books of Day and Night *on its vaulted ceiling symbolically convert the burial chamber into a nexus of revitalization and protection of the royal remains.*

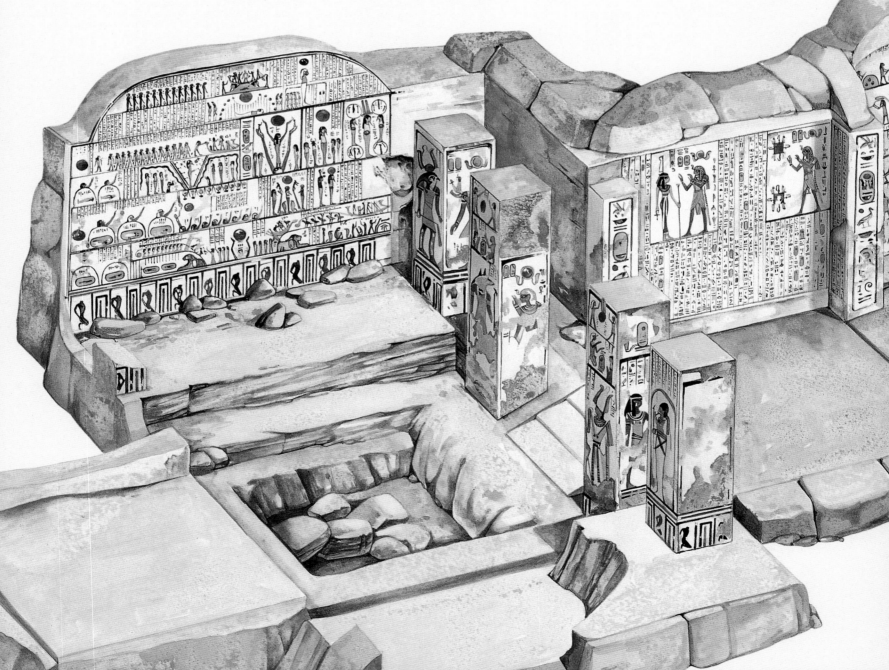

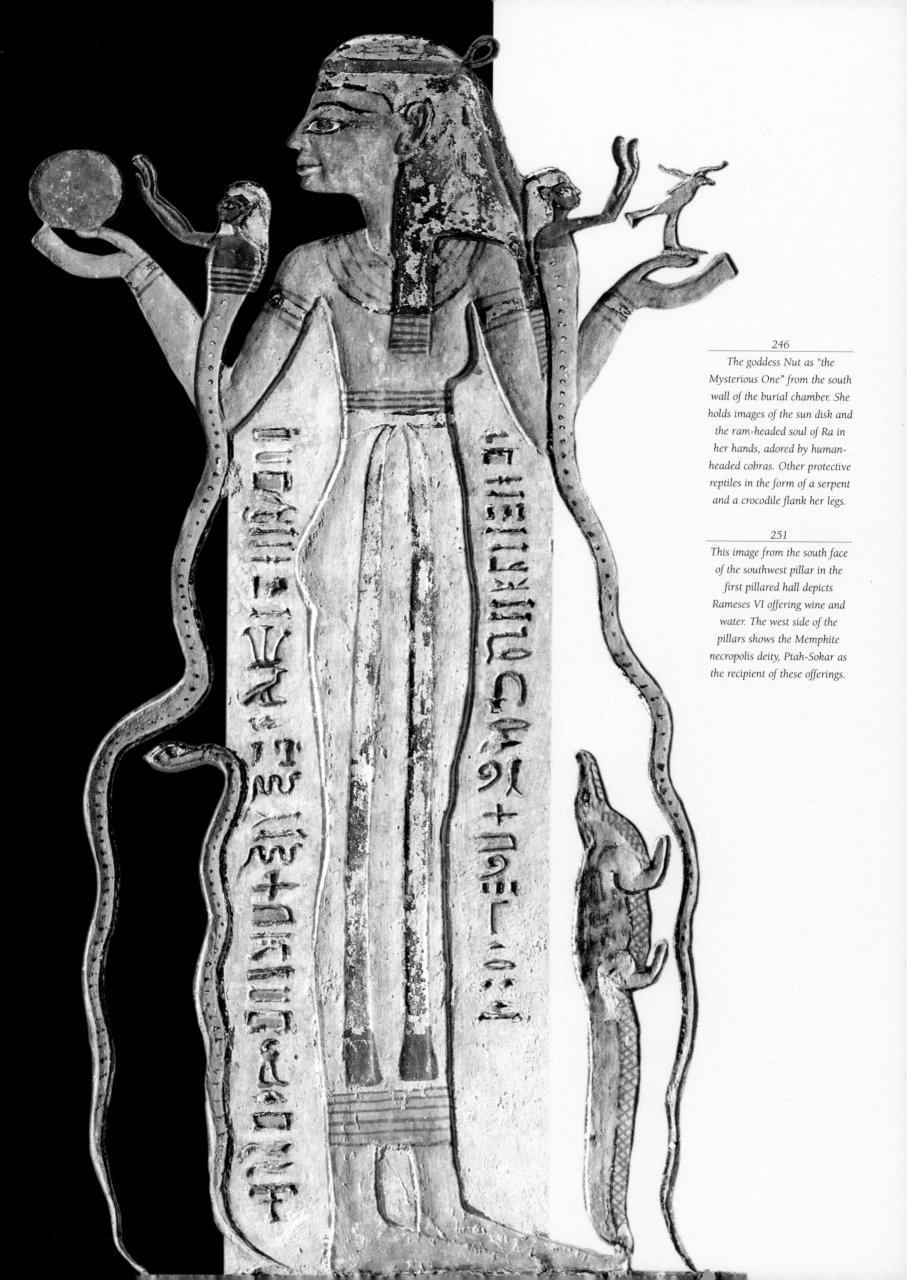

246

The goddess Nut as "the Mysterious One" from the south wall of the burial chamber. She holds images of the sun disk and the ram-headed soul of Ra in her hands, adored by human-headed cobras. Other protective reptiles in the form of a serpent and a crocodile flank her legs.

251

This image from the south face of the southwest pillar in the first pillared hall depicts Rameses VI offering wine and water. The west side of the pillars shows the Memphite necropolis deity, Ptah-Sokar as the recipient of these offerings.

not cleared until nearly 100 years later by Brock in 1985, when fragments of burial equipment still remaining in the debris, including *shawabtis*, and remains of the sarcophagi were uncovered.

In general, the plan of the tomb follows the design established in the 19th Dynasty, although the well shaft was never cut in room E and there is no room off the right side of the first pillared hall (F). Side rooms off the burial chamber or beyond it are also lacking, although the cutting of that chamber was never completed. The open-air entryway has no steps with a central ramp but slopes gently to the first gate and corridor (B), and the first three corridors have little appreciable slope. There are two rectangular horizontal niches high in the walls at the beginning of the second corridor (C) and a pair of vertical recesses near the floor at the end of the third corridor (D). While they were cutting the ceiling of the second lower corridor (H) beyond the first pillared hall (F), the tomb builders accidentally broke into the floor of one of the rear chambers of KV 12, now of unknown date and ownership. As a result of this collision, both the ceiling and floor levels of H were lowered in order to safely bypass KV 12. As noted above, the burial chamber was unfinished, with only two of the eastern set of four pillars completely freed from the bedrock. What would have been the western set of four pillars were cut only as piers, and the short chamber K remains from the west end of the axial cut of the burial chamber, extending to the intended rear wall. The two wide platforms to the north and south of the floor would have been cut back to the side walls, perhaps leaving projecting narrow ledges if completed.

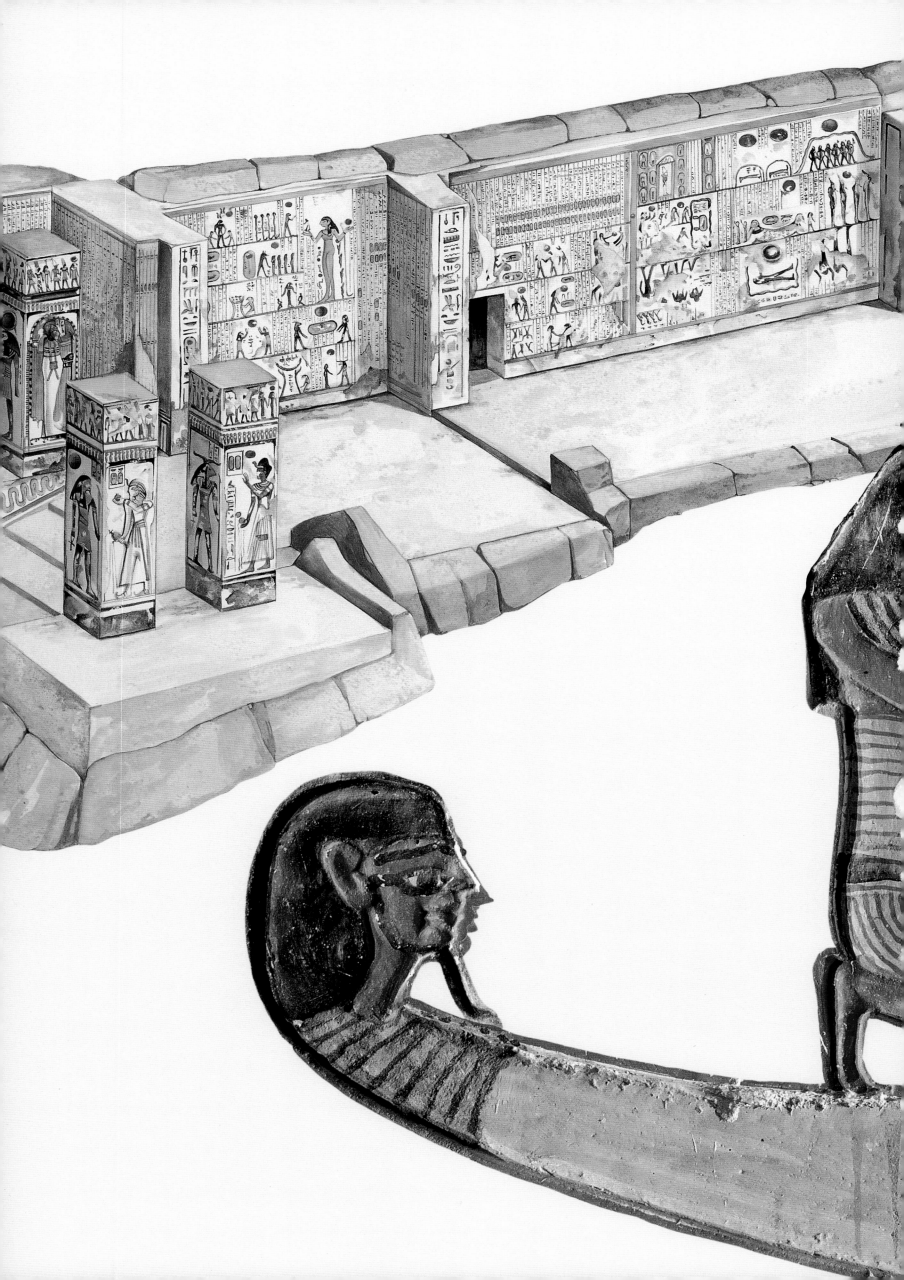

252 top

The figures in this detail from the top of one of the pillars in the first pillared hall are part of an elaborate writing of the prenomen of Rameses VI. The first two figures represent Ra and Amen, while the king holding a mace stands for the word neb, "lord."

252 center

This view into the first corridor shows the king offering incense to Ra and Osiris. The beginning of the Book of Caverns follows. The reliefs at the beginning of this corridor have suffered from the effects of nature and man and are less well preserved.

252 bottom

The fifth section of the Book of Caverns is characterized by the two large figures of the goddess Nut on the right and Osiris on the left. Nut holds images of the sun as a disk and a ram-headed man. The lower register deals with the destruction of the damned.

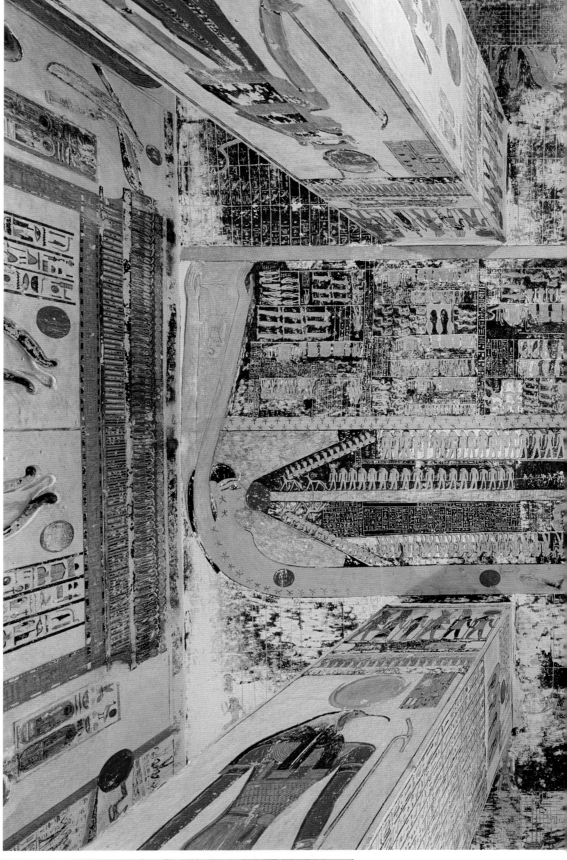

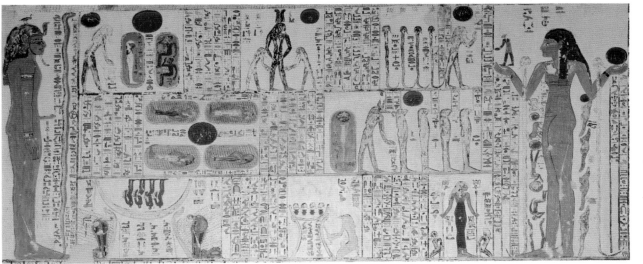

252-253

The ceiling of the first pillared hall (F) is dominated by the figure of Nut framing the Books of the Day and Night. These two compositions describe the sun-god's journey by day and night over and through the goddess of the sky. Representations of astronomical figures surround the central scene.

The Tomb of Rameses VI

An unusual feature is the pit hewn into the center of the floor. This apparently was cut in two phases, first as a narrow rectangular pit with straight sides. The upper portions of the sides were then roughly cut back to form a wider depression in order to accommodate the underside of the massive red granite box.

Contrary to some descriptions that tried to draw an analogy with the situation in the burial chamber of Rameses VII (KV 1), this box was not inverted over the pit as a cover, but rested over the pit in the normal manner, with opening facing up, to contain the mummiform inner sarcophagus. Copious remains of resinous material from some ritual anointing oil were poured over the mummiform sarcophagus, coating the exterior of both the lid and box of this inner sarcophagus, and pooled on the floor of the outer granite box. This situation would have been impossible if the granite box was inverted, and there are no traces of this resinous substance on the floor of the pit.

This tomb has one of the most varied decorative programs of any tomb in the Valley of the Kings. The most complete versions of many of the funerary compositions previously used in New Kingdom royal tombs, such as the *Amduat*, the *Book of Gates*, the *Book of Caverns*, the *Book of the Day*, the *Book of the Night*, and the *Book of the Earth* are found here. At the same time, the *Litany of Ra*, a constant element in Ramesside tombs since Seti I, is absent. Conversely, there are several new compositions found in this tomb, particularly on the ceilings. Admittedly, the damaged state of the lower chambers' ceilings in the equally large tomb of Rameses III might have provided antecedents for some of these compositions, but this can no longer be determined.

The decoration of the first corridor begins with a scene of the king offering to Ra-Horakhty, followed by Osiris, now shown on both

253 bottom

Three registers from the ninth division of the Book of Gates. *The human-headed birds at the top are the souls in the Island of Fire. Those who have drowned float in the the middle register. A large serpent spits fire at bound enemies of Osiris at the bottom.*

sides of the corridor. Instead of the usual presentation
of the *Litany of Ra*, the commencement of the *Book of
Gates* follows on south wall and the *Book of Caverns*
on the north. The ceiling of the first corrridor is
decorated with astronomical figures such as those first
encountered on the burial chamber ceiling of Seti I's
tomb. These images of constellations are continued
on the second corridor's ceiling and the continuation
of the *Book of Gates* and *Book of Caverns* are found
on its walls. The remainder of these two
compositions decorate the walls of the third
corridor (D) and chambers E and F.

The *Book of the Day* and the *Book of the
Night* are painted on the ceilings of these passages
and chambers (D, E, F), with a single elongated figure
of the sky goddes Nut framing both compositions.
The two books are arranged side by side, with the
Book of the Day occupying the north halves of the
ceilings and the *Book of the Night* the south halves.
The sequences of scenes for each of the hours are
arranged so that the beginning of the *Book of the
Day* is at the east end and its end at the west,
following the sun's daily course. The beginning of
the *Book of the Night* is at the west end and
terminates in the east coinciding with the sun's re-
appearance at dawn on the eastern horizon. In this
way the decorative scheme follows the apparent
movement of the sun in this world and the next.
Additional astonomical scenes, showing various
constellations, as well as star clocks, are also found
on the ceiling of F chamber. The king is shown
offering to various gods on the pillars in this

chamber and at the center of the rear wall there is a double scene of Osiris receiving the king's offering.

Large-scale images of two winged cobras reperesenting the goddesses of Upper and Lower Egypt undulate down the sides of the central descent. The walls of the two corridors beyond (G, H) are decorated with the *Amduat*, although there has been some crowding and mixing of registers from the latter half of the text on the north wall. The ceiling of corridor G is decorated with representations of the day and night barks of the sun god. These are shown in different views, both in plan and elevation, together with separate images of the sun god and his companions, including the great coiled serpent Mehen who protects him. These figures give the impression of being taken from a set of instructions for fashioning the image of the sun god's boats.

254 top

The ceiling of corridor G displays figures connected with the sun god's celestial journey. The left half show different aspects of the solar boats. At the center is the serpent that surrounds the sun god and the figures on beds on the right belong to the Book of the Night.

254-255 bottom

These two figures from the upper register of the second hour of the Amduat, *represent the gods Thoth and Khnum, each holding a large knife. They are part of a group of judges in the netherworld who act on behalf of the sun god.*

255 top

These two details from the seventh hour of the Amduat *show three birds with human heads wearing the crowns of united Egypt, and Osiris protected by the Mehen serpent. This hour deals with the destruction of the enemies of Osiris and the defeat of Apophis, enemy of the sun god.*

Figures on lion-shaped beds, similar to scenes in the *Book of the Night* decorate the remainder of the ceiling, together with processions of gods found both in the *Book of the Day* and the *Book of the Night.*

The ceiling of corridor H is decorated with enigmatic scenes unique to this tomb. On the longer flat portion of the ceiling three rows of figures are painted in yellow on a dark blue background. At the east end of the central row, a large sun disk with the head of a ram and a scarab emerging from it is followed by a strange boat with human heads and arms at the prow and stern, bearing the ram-headed form of the sun god. Seven gods with disks in place of heads adore the sun god and are followed by two pairs of gods with a disk topped by a human head between each pair. This central row of figures is flanked by squating figures with disks for heads in one row and with human heads topped with stars in the other, probably representing hours of day and night. At the east end of each of these two flanking rows is a panel containing a bull's head at each corner with a sun disk between its horns and two goddesses in the center facing outwards. Each of these panels is followed by three mounds enclosing strange mummiform figures. The sloping part of the ceiling at the west end of the corridor displays a large lunar disk and cresent flanked by four bowing gods and images of hearts. Below this register, the sun god with two ram's heads stands in a boat with human heads and arms at prow and stern. This image is flanked by pairs of gods bending over a prone

goddess with a disk surmounted by a head above. At the end of the corridor, above the gate to chamber I, is a representation of a solar disk from which four serpents emerge to spit flames at four figures of enemies. The smaller disk placed above with a crocodile's head and that below with a snake's head recall the figures accompanying the sun disk at the beginning of the *Litany of Ra*. Two large figures of gods with disks for heads and serpents for feet flank this central group. It is at this point that the tomb cutters accidentally broke through to KV 12 and this image has been interpreted as a protective device to avert any malign powers coming through this breach after it was sealed up. The south side of the scene is now damaged as a

258 top
A detail from the top register of the Book of the Earth *found on the south wall of the burial chamber. A large solar disk is embraced by two pairs of arms and flanked by goddesses who hold disks and stars representing the hours of day and night.*

258-259
This scene taken from the representation of the Book of the Earth *is also from the south wall of the burial chamber. A recurring theme in these compositions is the punishment and annhiliation of the enemies of the sun god and of Osiris, depicted here as red bound figures.*

258 bottom
Another detail from the Book of the Earth *on the south wall of the burial chamber. Two gods raise the soul of Osiris in the form of a human-headed bird wearing the Upper Egyptian crown.*

259 bottom
A large solar disk topped by the head of a goddess is flanked by two cobras, the Devourer and the Fiery One. Two gods representing Atum and the Seizer grasp a serpent that passes beneath the head of the goddess.

259 top

In this detail from the Book of the Earth, *again from the south wall of the burial chamber, the sun god appears as a ram-headed man. Four mummiform figures standing in yellow mounds represent the corpses of Geb Osiris, the One in the Coffin, and Shu.*

result of intruders breaking through the filling between the two tombs.

Chamber I is decorated with scenes and texts from the *Book of the Dead* ensuring the king's moral purity and providing him with the power to enter the realm of Osiris. The texts from spells 124 and 125, including the declaration of innocence from the final judgement, are inscribed on the walls on the south half of the chamber. These are accompanied by images of the king and a god representing magical power. The king adores two pools of fire surrounded by four baboons on the north wall, accompanied by *Book of the Dead* spell 126. He appears again on the same wall adoring Maat, the goddess personifying divine order and recites a prayer to this goddess. The remainder of the walls bears texts from *Book of the Dead* spells 129 and 127 which allow the

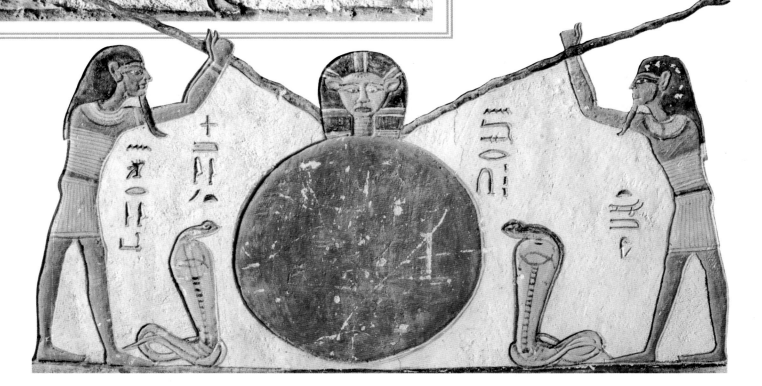

261 top
This large mummiform figure is unidentified. The smaller mummies flanking this figure depict Nun, Khepri, Tefnut and Shu. Nun personnifies the primeval waters of creation, Shu and Tefnut are the first offspring created and Khepri is the rising sun god.

260 top
A detail from the Book of the Earth *on the north wall of the burial chamber. A kneeling god named Iay, "the Adorer" bows between two cobras called the Flaming One and the Fiery One. To the left is a mummiform figure Waway, also a name associated with fire.*

260 bottom
This figure of a lion is one of a pair that represent Aker, the personification of the earth, guarding entry to the netherworld. The cobras with human-heads and arms who tow the sun god out of Aker at dawn are shown to the right.

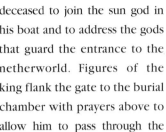

deceased to join the sun god in his boat and to address the gods that guard the entrance to the netherworld. Figures of the king flank the gate to the burial chamber with prayers above to allow him to pass through the gates of the netherworld and to declare his state of purity. The decoration of the ceiling of this chamber is divided into two parts. The eastern half shows the king twice in the day and night boats accompanying the sun god beneath the winged sun disk. The western half has the resurrection of Osiris as its theme. The god is shown lying on a bed in his sarcophagus, but raises his head to recieve the sign of life from his son Horus whose image has now been lost.

The burial chamber has a complex group of scenes decorating its walls. These have been grouped together by some scholars under the general title of the *Book of the Earth* or the *Book of Aker*. The ancient name is not known and it is not certain if these scenes and texts form part of a single composition or are an amalgamation. There is no apparent sequence of texts and images, no sense of opening and

closing sections, as in the books describing the solar journey. Some of the images appear in other compositions in this tomb, some were found in earlier tombs, and others occur in later ones, but many occur only in this chamber. The north and south walls are each divided into four major registers of scenes. On the north, the solar boat is shown associated with the double headed sphinx-like image of Aker, the so-called god of the earth, perhaps best understood as the personification of the netherworld or perhaps the guardian of the approach to it. The sun's rays revive various figures in mounds and mummiform guardians. On the south wall, the sun appears both as a ram-headed man and a great disk, often with figures emerging from it. Images of Osiris are also found and more gods in mounds. The destruction of enemies is repeatedly shown. Similar images adorn the rear wall flanking the central niche bearing the final scene from the *Book of Gates* of sun's dawning. The vaulted ceiling is decorated with the double image of Nut framing the *Books of the Day and the Night*.

262-264

The vaulted ceiling of the burial chamber is decorated with two compositions describing the sun god's journey through the day and night skies. The double image of the sky goddess Nut shown back-to-back along the center frames the Book of the Day *above and the* Book of the Night *below.*

265

A close-up of the head of Nut at the end of the Book of the Day *on the burial chamber ceiling. The goddess prepares to swallow the solar disk at dusk in preparation for the sun god's nightly journey through her body.*

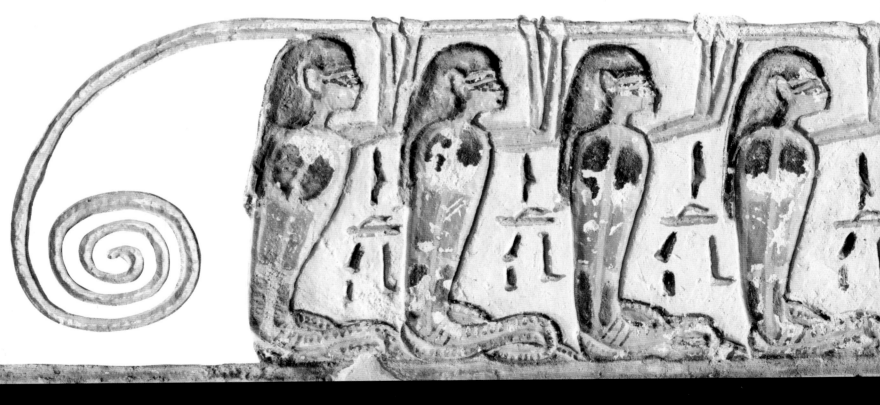

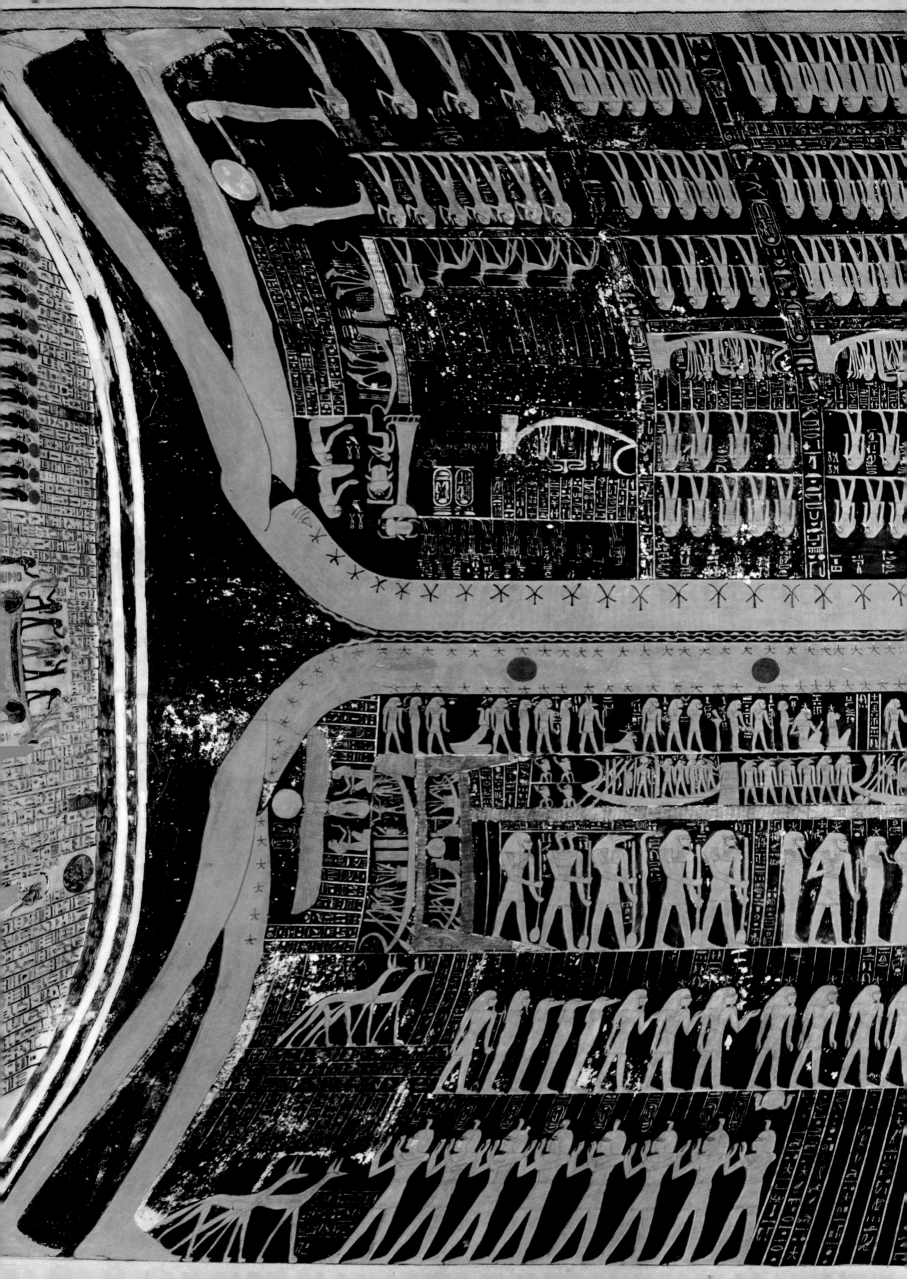

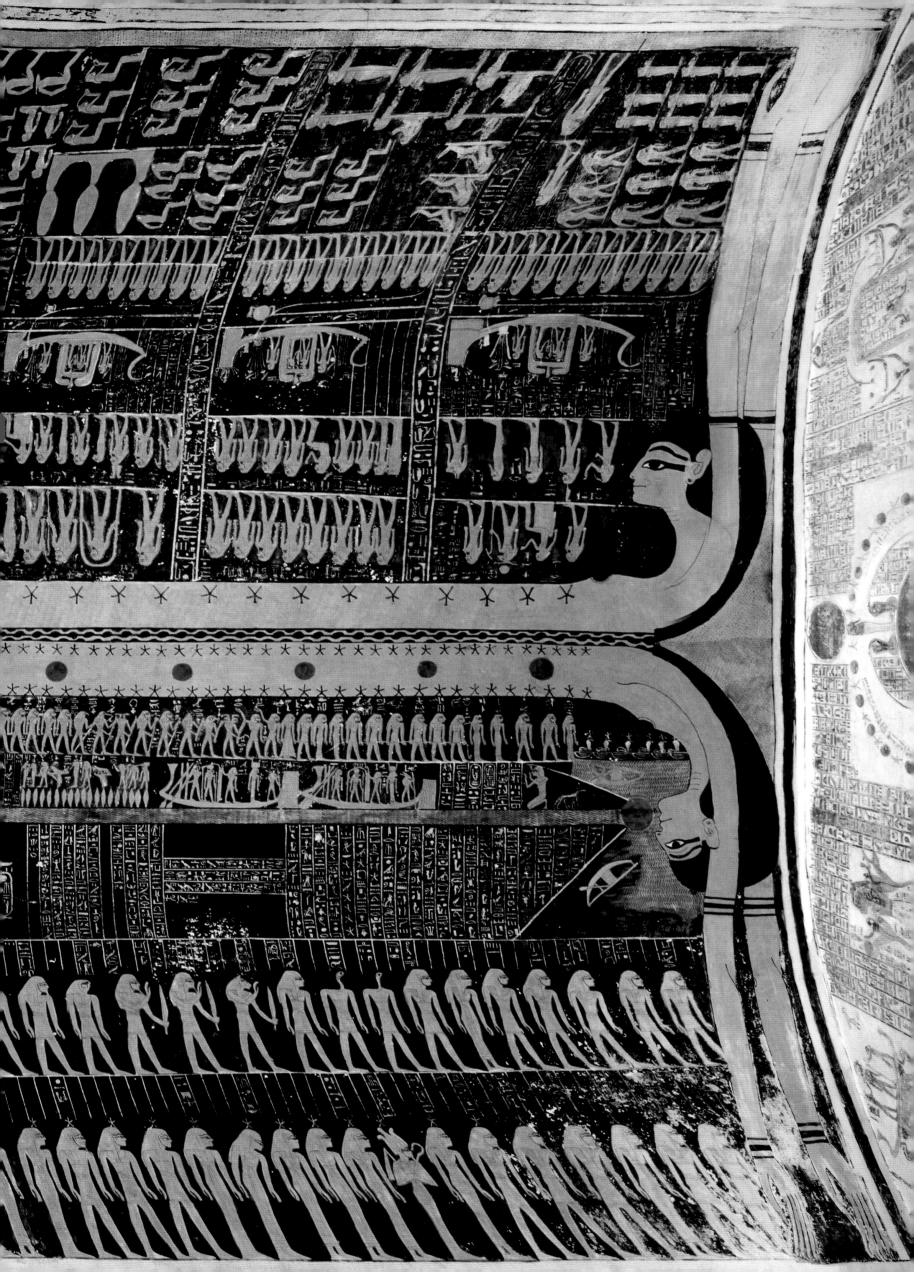

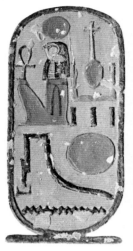
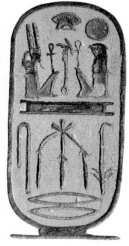

THE TOMB OF
RAMESES IX

by Edwin C. Brock

266 bottom left

This detail of a scene on the north wall of the third corridor depicts the king carrying a staff as he proceeds into the tomb. In spite of the elaborate costume the figure is reminiscent of the life size wooden figure of the king found in the tomb by Henry Salt and now in the British Museum.

266-267

This detail from the south wall of the second corridor illustrates part of the composition known as the Book of Caverns. Here part of the fourth section is shown, with a centrally placed figure of the sun-god as a ram-headed man. The figure of the king offering a libation is an unusual addition to the composition.

T HE TOMB OF RAMESES IX WITH ITS prominent entryway in the base of the hill left of the center of the Valley remained open through antiquity, after the king's mummy was moved to TT 320. It was noted by the Napoleonic Expedition, and explored in the 19th century by Salt, Champollion, and Lepsius. The tomb was thoroughly cleared in 1888 by Daressy who found numerous ostraca and a wooden figure of the king.

In at least two areas, the architecture of KV 6 appears to be influenced by KV 11, the tomb of Rameses III. Two pairs of pilasters were started at the end of the entry passage (A), although only the lower portions were partly cut from the rock. The two sets of side chambers on the north and south walls of the first corridor (B) are also reminiscent of the situation in KV 11 although here they are undecorated. Contrary to some opinions, the unfinished cutting of the first side chamber on the south is not likely to have been due to the builders having detected the burial chamber of KV 55 below, since approximately five meters (17 feet) of rock separate the tombs at this point. The floor and ceiling of the passages after the first corridor of the tomb

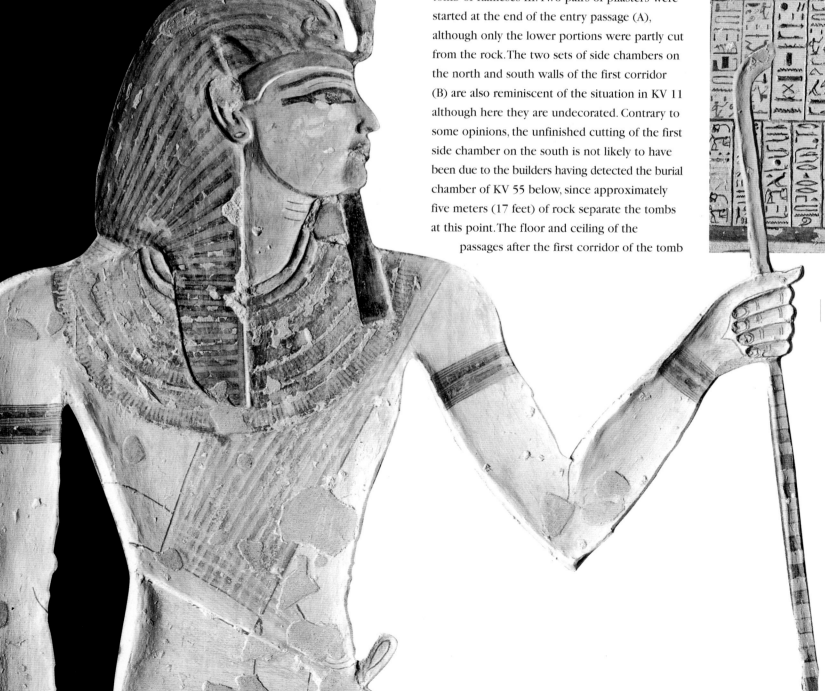

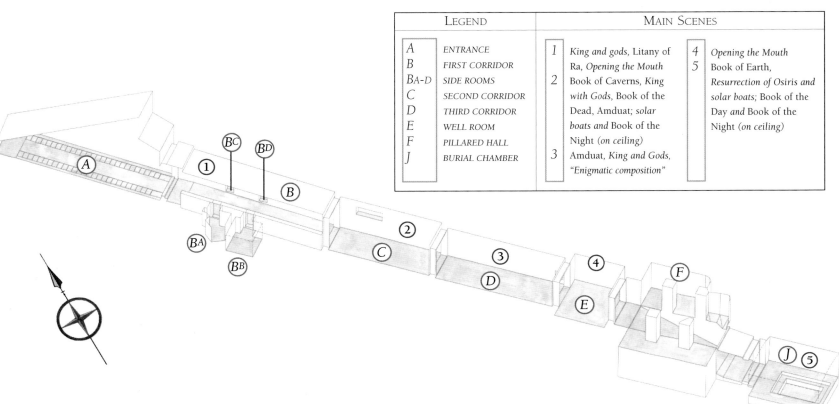

are nearly level as far as the first pillared hall (F). The cutting of this chamber was left unfinished with the two rear pillars and the walls beyond only partly freed from the bed rock. Instead of the usual set of two lower corridors and an antechamber the descent in F leads directly to the burial chamber (J). The burial chamber itself is

small and narrow with a low vaulted ceiling. Perhaps this had been intended originally as another corridor but had been changed to a burial chamber at the king's death. An unusual feature here is the two-tiered pit in the floor. No trace of any sarcophagus has been found as part of the burial equipment of Rameses IX and some suppose that a wooden shrine and coffin may have been accommodated in the shallow pit. Two crudely carved wood beams discovered by Daressy during clearance of the tomb may have served as runners for a sledge to move a large object like a shrine into the tomb.

The wall decoration in painted sunk relief appears to have been applied in different phases. Due perhaps as much to changes in concepts of the Afterlife as to lack of space, certain compositions such as the *Book of Gates* are lacking, while others such as the *Book of Caverns*, the *Amduat* and the *Books of the Day and the Night* are abbreviated.

The king's adoration of the sun disk, accompanied by Isis and Nephthys, is found on the lintel over the entrance. Variations on this theme are continued on the door lintels of second and third corridors. The beginning of the

first corridor (B) has scenes of the king offering to Ra-Horakhty and Osiris on the north wall and to a mummiform Amen-Ra with four ram heads, accompanied by the goddess Meretseger on the south wall. The *Litany of Ra*, minus its opening scene, continues the decoration of the north wall, ending with a priest purifying the king as Osiris. The first section of the *Book of Caverns* occupies the remainder of the south wall, while the second, third and fourth sections of this book are crowded onto the south wall of the second corridor (C). Large-scale figures of the king, accompanied by a goddess holding his names, and of the king worshiping Khonsu alternate with figures of the forms of Ra from the Litany and with texts and vignettes from the *Book of the Dead* on the opposite wall. The second hour of the *Amduat* appears on the north wall of the third corridor (D), together with excerpts from the third hour of the same composition. The south wall shows the king offering to Ptah and Maat, followed by an unusual scene of Osiris leaning against a sand hill protected by a serpent.

The composition in three registers which follows on the south wall of D is unique to this tomb and enigmatic both in the writing of its text and the meaning of the composition as a whole. While themes of solar resurrection and the triumph over enemies are easily inferred, there may be iconographic re-interpretations of elements of more traditional compositions such as the *Amduat* and *Book of Caverns*.

The figures of the two priests to either side of the door to the pillared hall are derived from the Opening the Mouth ritual as was the priest purifying the Osiride king in the first corridor. In the burial chamber, extracts from the *Book of Earth* are placed on the side walls while the revival of the king and his journey in the night and day boats of the sun take up the rear wall. Brief excerpts of the *Book of the Day and the Night*, framed by figures of the goddess Nut decorate the ceiling. Astronomical figures, star clocks and extracts from the *Book of the Night* are found on the ceilings of the second and third corridors.

268-269

This part of the ceiling from the third corridor illustrates some of the compositions dealing with the sun god's journey through the heavens. In the central register a large serpent, representing Mehen the "Encloser," surrounds the king's cartouche with its protective coils much as it surrounds the sun god in his journeys. The king is shown twice to the right as king of Lower Egypt and of Upper Egypt. Farther to the right, the figures on the beds and those in the upper and lower registers are taken from the Book of the Night.

268 bottom

A detail of the ceiling decoration in the second corridor shows figures at the top representing the constellations of stars that revolve around the pole star. A desirable goal of the deceased was to join with these circumpolar stars known to the Egyptians as the "Unweary Ones," representative of an undying condition in the Afterlife. *The large squatting figure below surrounded by a grid is part of a star clock, used to tell time at night according to the appearance of certain stars over different part of the target's body at certain hours.*

269 bottom

The lintel of the third gate presents the sun disk in the center, worshipped by the king, shown twice, kneeling with upraised hands. Within the disk the sun god as a kneeling ram-headed man faces the left eye of Horus, another solar symbol and is praised by the small figure of a baboon. *The four bowing male deities to the right represent the four generations of male offspring of the sun god, Shu, Geb, Osiris, and Horus. To the left, the goddesses Isis, Nephthys, Neit, Serqet and Hathor raise their hands in a gesture of adoration.*

The Tomb of Rameses IX

THE VALLEY
OF THE
QUEENS

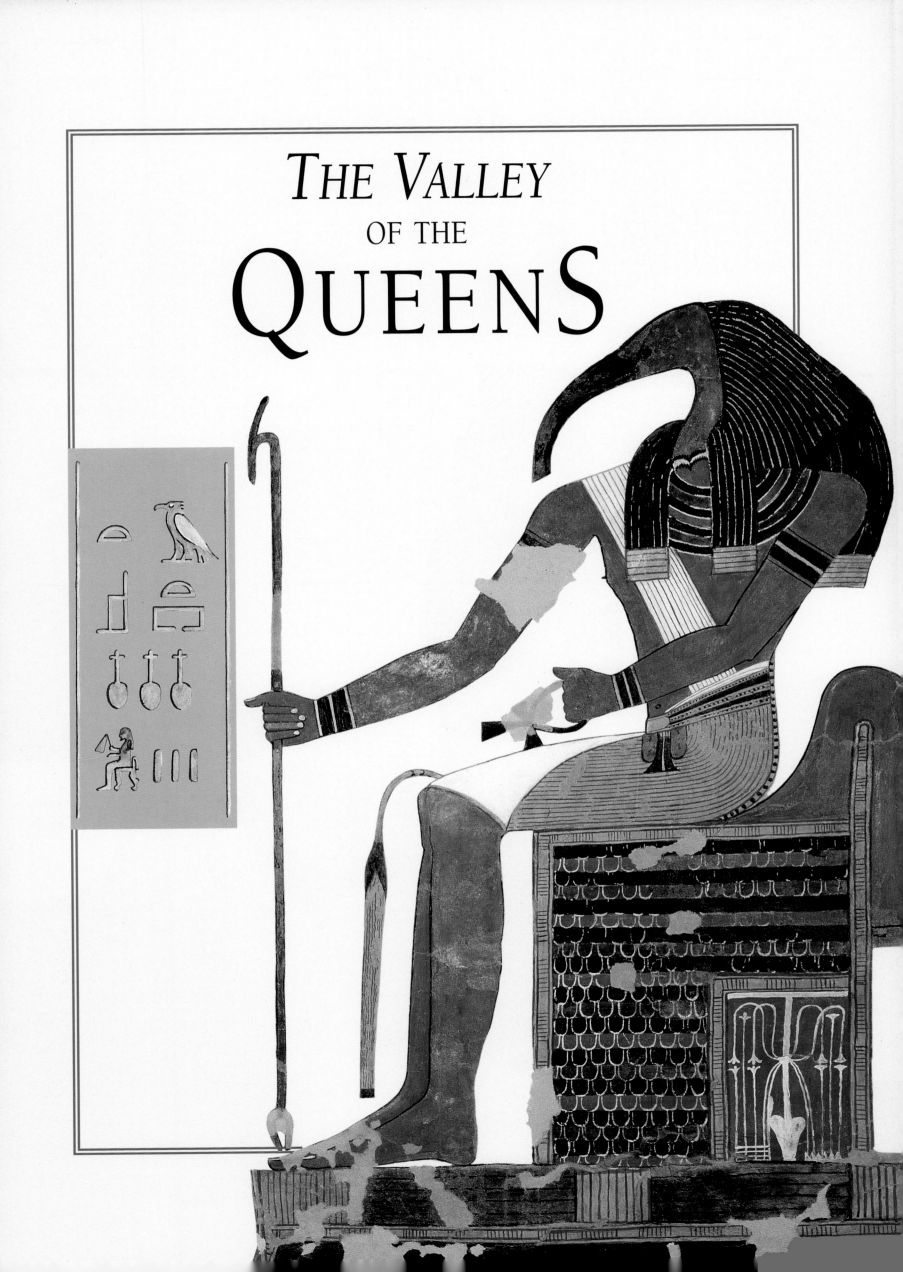

Western Thebes and the Queens of the Two Lands in the New Kingdom

by Christian Leblanc

THEBAN ARCHAEOLOGICAL documentation has preserved important evidence on the queens of the New Kingdom. Not only do we have abundant sources provided by the texts, but for some queens we also know the location of their tombs. The necropolis of the Valley of the Queens, located at the foot of the south side of the sacred western mountain, has revealed the tombs of the great royal wives of the Ramesside period.

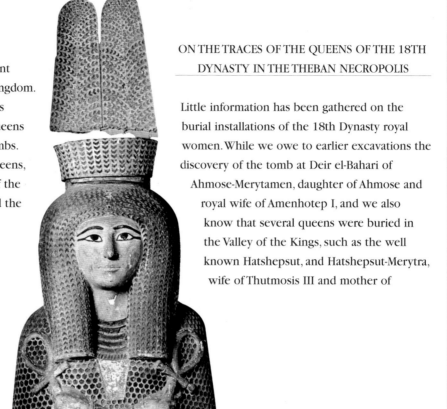

270

Nefertari, wife of Rameses II, shared the destiny of this king up to the 26th year of the reign. She was buried in a sumptuous tomb in the Valley of the Queens. QV 66: sarcophagus room (J). Detail of the south-east pillar.

271

Thoth with ibis head, the magician god who announces tomorrow and sees into the future. Tomb QV 66. Chamber (F), north wall.

272 left

Wooden, mummy-shaped sarcophagus of Queen Ahmose-Nefertari, mother of Amenhotep I and founder of the institution of the God's Wife. Together with the mummy of the queen in the tomb of Inhapi (TT 320), where it had been placed for protection during the 21st Dynasty, a number of royal remains from the New Kingdom were also found. Height 3.78 m. (13 feet) Cairo Museum.

272 right

Hatshepsut shown as a sphinx with the body of a lion. This painted limestone sculpture, in which we can see the feminine features of the delicate face of the queen, comes from the Temple of Millions of Years in Deir el-Bahari. Cairo Museum.

ON THE TRACES OF THE QUEENS OF THE 18TH DYNASTY IN THE THEBAN NECROPOLIS

Little information has been gathered on the burial installations of the 18th Dynasty royal women. While we owe to earlier excavations the discovery of the tomb at Deir el-Bahari of Ahmose-Merytamen, daughter of Ahmose and royal wife of Amenhotep I, and we also know that several queens were buried in the Valley of the Kings, such as the well known Hatshepsut, and Hatshepsut-Merytra, wife of Thutmosis III and mother of

Amenhotep II, a number of doubts and hypotheses remain, posed or suggested by various scholars, on the official marriages of the pharaohs of the New Kingdom. In this way, it has at times been presumed that Tiy, wife of Amenhotep III, and Tiy, the companion of the divine father Ay who became a king, may have shared the tombs of their wives, but in fact there is nothing that can confirm these suggestions. The idea is, however, far from being foreign to the conceptions of the Egyptians, as the case of common burial for Akhenaten and Nefertiti, at Tell el-Amarna, has already been put forward. In the Valley of the Kings, during the excavation of the tomb of Amenmesses from the 19th Dynasty (KV 10), elements have been discovered which

belong to the burial goods of a queen Takhat, identified by a number of scholars as the mother of the pharaoh, while others believe today that this was the royal wife of Rameses IX. Whatever the truth, it is precisely the absence of evidence within the context of the underground tombs of Amenhotep III and Ay that creates doubts on the notion of family burial. However, for the successor of Tutankhamen, it is interesting to note that in the course of the decoration of the royal tomb, queen Tiy occupied a dominant place in the iconic programme.

In the field, the lack of reliable indicators is even more problematic for the other queens of the 18th Dynasty who, if they were

272-273

At the extreme south of the Theban necropolis, the Valley of the Queens looks like a huge indentation in the Libyan plateau. Opening out broadly

over the plane, the main wadi is freely accessible. In ancient times, this would have made it easy to pillage the tombs out along its edges.

buried in Western Thebes, have still to this day not given up any trace of their tombs. Ahmose-Nefertari, the wife of the liberator Ahmose, had her residence of eternity in the Dra Abu el-Naga, but we must admit that a strange silence covers most of the eminent ladies of the crown, including Ahmose, sister and wife of Thutmosis I and mother of Hatshepsut, and Mutnofret, another royal wife and mother of prince Wadjmes, for whom a large chapel had been built on the edge of the desert, which was recently excavated. We have no idea where the tomb of Neferura is located. She was the oldest daughter of Hatshepsut and Thutmosis II, invested with the powers as sovereign of

the Two Lands and God's Wife. Some suggest that she could have been buried in Wadi Gabbanat El-Gurud, but there is no significant evidence to back this up. Although Thutmosis III caused some of his family to be represented in his sumptuous tomb in the Valley of the Kings, the tombs of his royal wives, Satiah and Nebetu, remain unknown, like that of Isis, the mother of the king, and Tya, the wife of Amenhotep II. It is true that in the cachette of tomb KV 35, discovered by Victor Loret in 1898, there are several female remains that were perhaps those of queens or princesses, but their identity has never been determined. We have absolutely no information on the

places where the burials might be of Iaret, Nefertari and Mutemuia, all three official wives of Thutmosis IV, might be.

With regard to the reign of Amenhotep III, no tombs have been confirmed in the Theban necropolis either for his daughter Satamen, with the title of great wife and married to the sovereign towards the end of his life, or for Henuttaunebu, Nebetah and Isis [II], princesses borne by Tiy who were given the position of royal wife. Finally, while the Amarna period seems particularly complex to analyze, due mainly to the transfer of burial goods and mummies to Thebes from the capital Akhetaten, we still have to ask ourselves

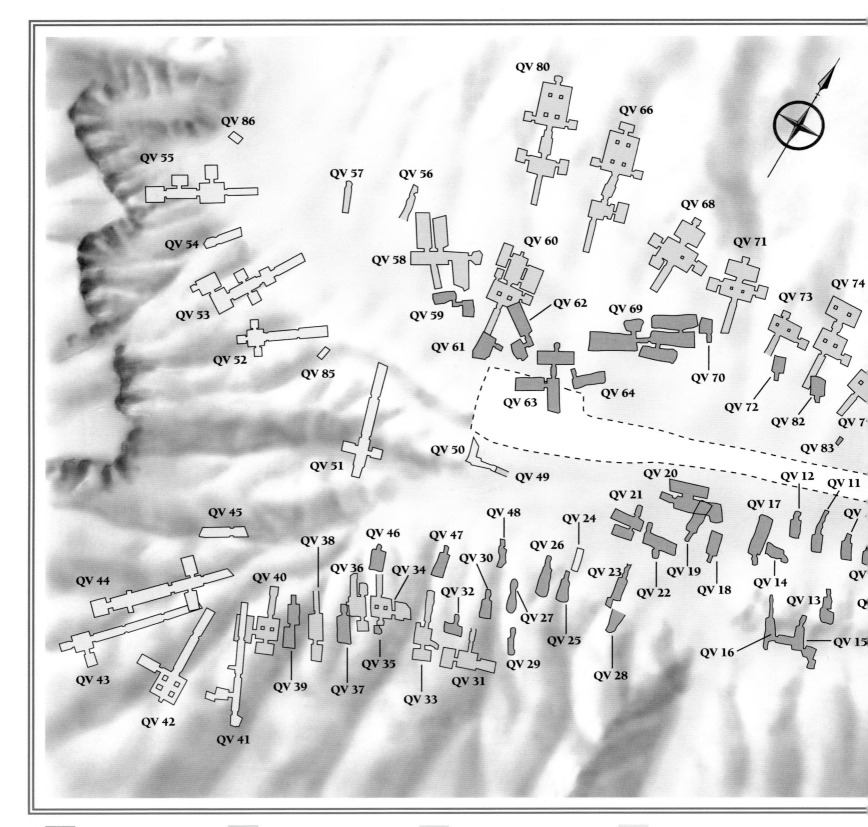

LEGEND

QV 1-7	ANONYMOUS TOMBS, 18TH DYNASTY.
QV 8	PRINCE HORI AND ANONYMOUS PRINCESS, 18TH DYNASTY.
QV 9-16	ANONYMOUS TOMBS, 18TH D.
QV 17	PRINCESSES MERYTRA (I) AND URMERUTES, 18TH DYNASTY.
QV 18-23	ANONYMOUS TOMBS, 18TH D.
QV 24	ANONYMOUS TOMBS, 20TH D.
QV 25-29	ANONYMOUS TOMBS, 18TH D.
QV 30	NEBIRY, 18TH DYNASTY.
QV 31	ANONYMOUS PRINCESS-QUEEN, EARLY 19TH DYNASTY.
QV 32	ANONYMOUS TOMB, 18TH D.
QV 33	PRINCESS-QUEEN TANEDJEMY, EARLY 19TH DYNASTY.
QV 34	ANONYMOUS PRINCESS-QUEEN, EARLY 19TH DYNASTY.
QV 35	ANONYMOUS TOMB, 18TH D.
QV 36	ANONYMOUS PRINCESS-QUEEN, EARLY 19TH DYNASTY.
QV 37	ANONYMOUS TOMB, 18TH D.
QV 38	QUEEN SATRA (GREAT ROYAL WIFE OF RAMESES I), EARLY 19TH DYNASTY.
QV 39	ANONYMOUS TOMB, 18TH D.
QV 40	ANONYMOUS PRINCESS-QUEEN, EARLY 19TH DYNASTY.
QV 41	UNFINISHED TOMB, 20TH D.
QV 42	PRINCE PAREHERUNEMEF AND MINEFER (SON OF RAMESES III AND WIFE OF RAMESES III), 20TH DYNASTY.
QV 43	PRINCE SETHHERKHEPSHEF (SON OF RAMESES III), 20TH D.

QV 44	PRINCE KHAEMWASET (SON OF RAMESES III), 20TH DYNASTY.
QV 45	UNFINISHED TOMB, 20TH D.
QV 46	IMHOTEP, VIZIR, 18TH DYNASTY (THUTMOSIS I).
QV 47	PRINCESS AHMOSE, 18TH D.
QV 48	ANONYMOUS TOMB, 18TH D.
QV 49-50	ANONYMOUS TOMBS, 19TH AND 20TH DYNASTIES.
QV 51	QUEEN ISIS-TA-HEMDJERET (GREAT ROYAL WIFE OF RAMESES III), 20TH DYNASTY.
QV 52	QUEEN TYTI (GREAT ROYAL WIFE OF RAMESES III), 20TH DYNASTY.
QV 53	PRINCE RAMESES-MERYAMEN (SON OF RAMESES III), 20TH D.
QV 54	UNFINISHED TOMB, 20TH D.
QV 55	PRINCE AMENHERKHEPSHEF (SON OF RAMESES III), 20TH D.
QV 56	UNFINISHED TOMB, 19TH D.
QV 57	UNFINISHED TOMB, 19TH D.
QV 58	ANONYMOUS TOMB, 19TH D.
QV 59	ANONYMOUS TOMB., 18TH D.
QV 60	QUEEN NEBETTAUY (DAUGHTER-WIFE OF RAMESES II), 19TH D.
QV 61	ANONYMOUS TOMB, 18TH D.
QV 62-65	ANONYMOUS TOMBS, 18TH D.
QV 66	QUEEN NEFERTARI (GREAT ROYAL WIFE OF RAMESES II), 19TH D.
QV 67	ANONYMOUS TOMB, 18TH D.
QV 68	QUEEN MERYTAMEN (DAUGHTER-WIFE OF RAMESES II), 19TH D.

QV 69	ANONYMOUS TOMB, 18TH D.
QV 70	NEHESY, 18TH DYNASTY.
QV 71	QUEEN BENTANAT (DAUGHTER-WIFE OF RAMESES II), 19TH D.
QV 72	PRINCE BAKI AND PRINCESS HATNEFERET, 18TH DYNASTY.
QV 73	PRINCESS HENUTTAUY (DAUGHTER-WIFE OF RAMESES II), 19TH DYNASTY.
QV 74	QUEEN DUATENTIPET (GREAT ROYAL WIFE OF RAMESES IV), 20TH DYNASTY.
QV 75	QUEEN HENUTMIRA (DAUGHTER-WIFE OF RAMESES II), 19TH D.
QV 76	PRINCESS MERYTRA (II), 18TH DYNASTY.
QV 77-79	ANONYMOUS TOMBS, 18TH D.
QV 80	QUEEN TUY (GREAT ROYAL WIFE OF SETI I), 19TH D.
QV 81	HEKA-(…), 18TH DYNASTY.
QV 82	PRINCE MINEMHAT AND AMENHOTEP, 18TH DYNASTY.
QV 83	ANONYMOUS TOMB, 18TH D.
QV 84-86	UNFINISHED TOMB, 20TH D.
QV 87	ANONYMOUS TOMB, 18TH D.
QV 88	PRINCE AHMOSE, 18TH D.
QV 89-94	ANONYMOUS TOMBS, 18TH DYNASTY.
QV 95	UNFINISHED TOMB, 20TH DYNASTY.

QV 76
QV 79
QV 78
QV 77
QV 7
QV 4
QV 5
QV 2
QV 3
QV 81
QV 1
QV 94

where the eternal resting places of several daughter-wives of Amenhotep IV or, more particularly, that of queen Ankhesenamen, the young widow of Tutankhamen, might be concealed. More systematic explorations, especially in the Western Valley, could enable us to solve the important archaeological questions related to the end of the 18th Dynasty.

THE LIVES AND DEATHS OF THE FOREIGN QUEENS AT THE COURT OF EGYPT

Among the Egyptian queens were a certain number of foreign princesses, wives of the king of Egypt in special circumstances. Peace treaties, or simply exchanges of gifts among the royal courts, could have been the reason for such matrimonial unions which reinforced good relations between Egypt and the countries on its borders. The annals of the New Kingdom are not lacking in information on the arrival of these noblewomen in the Valley of the Nile. For example, Thutmosis III, hero of seventeen military campaigns in Asia, married at least three Syrian princesses, after he had pacified this turbulent region.

A collective grave discovered in Western Thebes, in the Wadi Gabbanat El-Gurud, revealed up remarkable pieces of gilt work that belonged to young women named Mertet (Martha), Menway and Menhet, who arrived in the royal residence towards year 40 of the reign. Among the relics brought to light from their tombs are scarabs in dark green schist, and a version of chapter XXX B of the *Book of the Dead* on the bases, which included the identity of each of them and their position as royal wives.

In the reign of Thutmosis IV, it appears that around year 6 another foreign princess was received in Egypt. This was the daughter of Artatama I, king of Mitanni, who has at times been recognized, but with no satisfactory arguments to back this up, as Queen Mutemuia. There is in fact no indication among the Egyptian sources that enables us to be certain that this princess was raised to the rank of great royal wife, but we can imagine that she obtained at least a position identical to that of the Syrian wives of Thutmosis III. In a recent study, it was proposed that this Mitanian, after taking an Egyptian name, could be Henutempet, whose sarcophagus was transferred to the famous cachette of Deir el-Bahari after the pillaging at the end of the New Kingdom. If we accept this hypothesis, then the daughter of Artatama I was buried in the Theban necropolis, but in a tomb yet to be discovered.

Tiy, declared great royal wife at the start of the reign of Amenhotep III, is known to have been a woman with a strong personality, with great influence in the court. Although she played an undeniable political role, as we can see from the diplomatic correspondence she exchanged with the Mitanian sovereigns, Tushratta II in particular, we know that she was not the only wife of the king. The sources in the form of letters that have reached us for this period indicate that at least five foreign princesses married the pharaoh, and the first, the daughter of Shuttarna, prince of Naharina, bore the name of Gilukhepa. The marriage appears to have taken place around the year 10. An issue of scarabs commemorates the event and mentions above all the arrival at the palace of the noble lady, accompanied by three hundred and seventeen women chosen from among the most beautiful in the harem. Also in the first half of the reign, but without doubt of a much less exceptional nature, a marriage took place between Amenhotep III and the daughter of Kurigalzu, king of Babylon, a record of which has been kept in the form of the letters found in the archives of Tell el-Amarna. If we refer to other letters from the same site, the daughter of the king of Arzaua also joined the Egyptian court a little later. It was only towards the end of his life that Amenhotep III engaged in a final marriage with Tadukhepa, daughter of Tushratta II and niece of Gilukhepa. With the exception of a few allusions on their acquisition of official status, we know nothing of the day to day of these women in Egypt. Even though tradition has it that they joined the royal harems of Memphis, Miur (Faiyum), and Tell el-Amarna, where they had a number of duties, we quickly lose trace of them and we know next to nothing on the dates of their deaths. Only Tadukhepa appears to have escaped this obscurity, if we agree that she was married a second time to Amenhotep IV-Akhenaten, and, along with Nefertiti, took part in the religious renovation imposed by the king at Tell el-Amarna.

On this subject, it has been proposed that this foreign princess was the queen known by the Egyptian name of Kiya. If we accept this, we also have to accept that this noblewoman died at Akhetaten, and that the burial goods accompanying her mummy were transferred to Western Thebes after the abandonment of the Amarnan capital. This is at least what appears to have been revealed by the earlier discoveries in tomb KV 55 in the Valley of the Kings, where a fine coffin and beautiful calcite vases, first inscribed her name, then usurped by Merytaten were found. Egyptologists are far from being unanimous on the delicate question of the return of the mummies of the Armarnan family to Thebes, but it would be wrong not to take into consideration the data supplied by the new investigations. How can we not be surprised, for example, to note that many of the items of Tutankhamen's treasure bear the name of Ankhkheperura-Neferneferuaten? And what can we say if we agree on the notion of the identity being that of Neferneferuaten-Nefertiti? As Tutankhamen was buried with his burial goods in the Valley of the Kings, the hypothesis that the mummy of the great wife of Amenhotep IV was buried, together with her burial goods in the Valley of the Kings, can be accepted, as well as the hypothesis that part of the goods of Nefertiti was used to complete that of Tutankhamen. But once again, only the results of meticulous excavations in the Theban necropolis could, in the future, confirm or deny this fascinating opinion.

In the Ramesside period, diplomatic marriages continued to take place. Those that took place under the reign of Rameses II especially had beneficial consequences for the kingdom of Egypt, as well as for the Hittite empire. In the year 34, it was above all the marriage between the Egyptian sovereign and the oldest daughter of Hattusil III, which received the prominence in official propaganda. Maathorneferura, which was her Egyptian name, arrived in Pi-Ramesse accompanied by an important escort. She was honored with the prestigious title of Great Royal Wife, then some time later sent to the harem of Mi-wer, where we lose all trace of her. Did she remain for a long time in Egypt? Was she buried there after her death? These are questions to which we still have no answers. While what little evidence there is for her comes from the Delta, nothing has been found in Thebes regarding this foreign princess or those who preceded and followed her at the Egyptian court. The Valley of the Queens received the venerable remains of several wives and daughters of the great king, but has delivered up nothing on the possible presence of Maathorneferura, or of her daughter Neferur, born in the year following the marriage. To conclude that this necropolis was closed to foreigners would mean ignoring the case of one of the great royal wives of Rameses III, an Asiatic named Isis-ta-Hemdjeret, who gave birth to an heir to the throne of Egypt, and whose funeral was held under the reign of Rameses VI in *Set Neferu*. A tomb, numbered 51, had been prepared for this noblewoman, who became sovereign of the South and the North. Her mummy rested in an enormous pink granite sarcophagus, now broken, but still on site in the context of her vast eternal residence.

277

Tiy, wife of Amenhotep III and mother of Akhenaten, left behind the memory of an exceptional queen. She had a particularly eminent position at court. Involved in all the major events of the reign, she skilfully managed Egyptian diplomacy. Statuette discovered at Serabit el-Kadim, Sinai. Green soapstone. Cairo Museum.

THE VALLEY OF THE QUEENS AND THE ROYAL CHILDREN, OR THE REDISCOVERY OF *TA SET NEFERU*

South-west of the temple of Medinet Habu, in one of the natural basins created by water erosion millions of years ago, the ancient Egyptians established a royal necropolis known today as the Valley of the Queens. The base is marked by a cave and waterfall, preceded by an ancient dam. Today as in antiquity, this deep crevice with its peculiar shape receives waters from occasional torrential rains. It was impossible for this place to escape the notice of the priests and it became for them an admirable symbol of fertility, as confirmed by graffiti referring to the goddess Hathor, in both human and cow form, drawn in different parts of the cave.

During the New Kingdom, and especially from the Ramesside period onwards, the site was referred to by the name *Ta Set Neferu*, as we can see from a certain number of documents, including stelae, papyri and ostraca. This name has long been translated as "Place of Beauty," "Place of Splendors" or "Place of the Lotus," but as the result of discoveries made in the necropolis around twenty years ago, it was possible to propose a different meaning. While the archaeological excavations were able to demonstrate that the Valley of the Queens was a royal cemetery since the 18th Dynasty, they have also revealed that the place was used essentially, if not exclusively, for the burial of princes and princesses during this period. From this it was suggested that the *Nefru* were perhaps the royal children, and that the necropolis was the place where their eternal residences were prepared.

This hypothesis is further reinforced by the fact that this tradition remained even livelier during the 19th and 20th Dynasties, as not only the daughters of Rameses II, but also the sons of Rameses III were buried in this privileged place. However, it would appear that it was during this period that there was an innovation in the story of the necropolis, when its burial purpose was extended to the royal mothers and the great wives of the pharaoh.

Curiously, this development brought about the break-up of the organization that had prevailed up to that time. From the 19th Dynasty onwards, in fact, the Valley of the Royal Children and Queens no longer appeared to be the exclusive necropolis of the royal family at Western Thebes. From this point onwards, it shared this role with the Valley of the Kings. It

279 bottom
The village of Ta Set Neferu.
Remains of craftsmen's houses in the
heart of the necropolis. Installations
of this kind, mainly of modest
dimensions, have also been found in
different areas of the Valley of the Kings.

is undoubtedly this that explains that in this other royal cemetery tombs had been prepared for the sons of Rameses II (KV 5), a son of Rameses III (KV 3), a son of Rameses IX (KV 19), and even for Queen Tausert (KV 14) even before she became pharaoh. In addition, recent excavations carried out in the Valley of the Kings have confirmed that at least two other Rameses princes (Amenherkhepshef, son of Rameses III, and Montuherkhepshef, son of Rameses VI) found refuge in the tomb of the chancellor Bay (KV 13), where two enormous pink granite sarcophagi were found inscribed with their names.

In the Arab period, several place names were used for the Valley of the Queens, including *Biban el-Hagg Ahmed* (the "Gates of the Pilgrim Ahmed"), *Biban el-Sultanat* (the "Gates of the Sultans"), *Biban el-Banat* (the "Gates of the Daughters"), *Biban el-Harim* (the "Gates of the Women"), and *Biban el-Melekat* or *Wadi el-Melekat* (the "Gates of the Queens" or the "Valley of the Queens"). This latter name has been kept up to today.

Beyond the main valley and the south west branch, in which around ninety tombs were counted, some of them unfinished, the necropolis of the queens contains a number of lateral depressions. To the north, the site is bounded by the Valley of the Dolmen, where we find a rock sanctuary consecrated by the craftsmen of the tomb (Deir el-Medina) to Ptah and Meretseger, then by the Valley of the Three Wells, in which several tombs were prepared during the time of Thutmosis, and finally by the Valley of the Cord. Near this latter, against a rocky spur, the ruins of Deir er-Rumi still remain. This was a small monastery from the Byzantine period (6th-7th centuries AD), installed in the place of a Roman sanctuary from Antonine's time. To the south, the heart of the necropolis is simply flanked by the Valley of Prince Ahmose, the foothills of which contain a number of burial pits from the start of the New Kingdom while, at the top of the cliff there are the remains of several cells of anchorites and hermits.

278-279
To the north, erosion has undermined the Libyan plateau, creating three valleys that converge toward the main wadi: Valley of the Cord, Valley of the Three Wells, and Valley of the Dolmen, which lead to the craftsmen's village along an ancient path.

279 top left
A place of popular worship, this rock sanctuary is at the entrance to the Valley of the Queens. It was dedicated to Ptah, the creator-god of Memphis and patron of craftsmen, and Meretseger, "She who Loves Silence," the divinity who protected the holy peak of Thebes and the dead.

279 top right
The southern branch of the main wadi, bordered by the entrances to a number of tombs from the Ramesside period.

280 top

Among the items of burial equipment found in tomb QV 72 is this fine offering vase with its globular form, vertical handles and cylindrical neck. The hieratic inscription on the shoulder mentions the position and name of its dead owner, "the son of the king, Baki." Polished and painted terracotta. 18th Dynasty. Inspectorate of Qurna.

280 bottom

Stopper of a jar in the form of a human head representing a princess. Her title and name, "daughter of the king, Urmerutes," are engraved on the body. Found during the excavation of tomb QV 17. Painted limestone. 18th Dynasty. Inspectorate of Qurna.

TYPE A-AB-B - VALLEY OF THE QUEENS.
TYPOLOGY OF THE TOMBS OF THE 18TH DYNASTY.

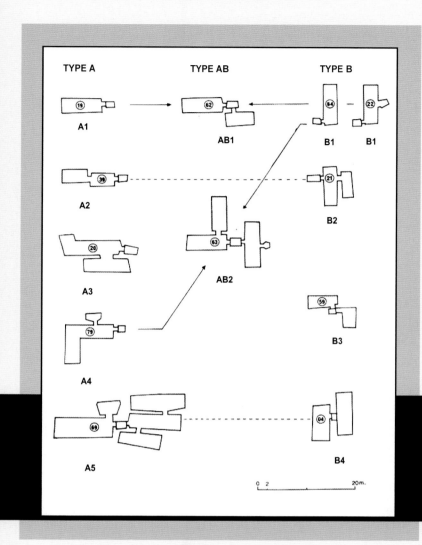

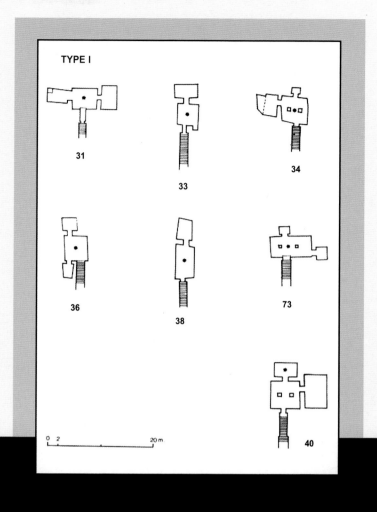

The Valley of the Queens was occupied from the 18th Dynasty onward. The reigns of Thutmosis I, Thutmosis II, Hatshepsut, Thutmosis III, Amenhotep II, Amenhotep III and Amenhotep IV are represented by burial pits, consisting of a vertical shaft dug out of the mountain, opening out onto one or more cellars with straightened but undecorated walls. The lack of any trace of superstructure suggests that these tombs did not include funeral chapels. For this period, only the discovery of remains of burial goods (jars, *shawabtis,* parts of games, ceramic vessels, papyrus and mummification fabric, etc) has enabled us to identify some of the dead buried in the necropolis, including such princes as Ahmose, Minemhat, Baki and Menkheperra, princesses such as Hatneferet, Ahmose, Urmerutes, Merytra [I], Merytra [II] and Tya, dignitaries or functionaries such as Nebiri, Nehesy, Imhotep, Nebamen and Kari, and finally a certain number of *khekerout nesout* that is people associated by some scholars with the royal nursery.

From the start of the 19th Dynasty, *Ta Set Neferu* was opened to the great royal wives and formed the true counterpart to the Valley of the Kings. The sites were entrusted to the craftsmen of *Set Maat* (Deir el-Medina). Unlike the princely tombs of the 18th Dynasty, the tombs of the queens from the Ramesside period, designed as true burial apartments, are decorated in line with an iconic repertoire in which the texts take their essential inspiration from the *Book of the Dead.* But as with tombs of the royal children, the superstructure contains no places of worship, although in the necropolis of the Theban nobles these do exist. Could this absence be explained by the fact that the members of the royal family were associated with the cult of the pharaoh in the Temples of Millions of Years? This would not be impossible. It was for Satra, great wife of Rameses I, that the first queen's tomb in this necropolis was prepared. In the reign of Seti I, it appears that several other tombs were prepared but, curiously, these were never inscribed with names. For this reason, we will probably never know the owners of tombs QV 31 (prepared for a great royal wife), QV 34 (probably destined for a queen), QV 36 (for a princess) and QV 40 (whose owner had to have the rank of princess or great royal wife). On the other hand, tomb QV 33 was given a name at a later date, as a cartouche, originally blank, was inscribed with the name Tanedjemy, a lady of the crown who held the titles of princess and wife of the king.

All these tombs, similar in plan, contain a ramp, antechamber and burial hall, and are grouped in the same sector of the necropolis, along the southern side branch of the main wadi.

282

This bust of Merytamen, daughter and royal wife of Rameses II, was found in 1896 by Flinders Petrie, in a monument situated at the northern outskirts of the Ramesseum. The seductive queen is wearing a wig of fine locks, a double headband with the two royal serpents at the front, and a hat surrounded by a frieze of round uraei. She holds the menat-necklace, an attribute of Hathor, in her left hand. Recent excavations on the site have brought to light a number of other fragments of this sculpture, which originally showed the queen standing in a walking posture. Painted limestone. Cairo Museum.

TYPE II - VALLEY OF THE QUEENS.
TYPOLOGY OF THE TOMBS OF THE RAMESSIDE PERIOD.
KINGDOM OF RAMESES II. 19TH DYNASTY.

Rameses II chose a different area for the tombs of the women in his court, at the foot of the northern side of the main wadi where the eternal residences built during his reign are located. This is where the tombs for his mother, Queen Tuy (QV 80), his great wife Nefertari (QV 66), and several of his daughter-wives, including Nebettauy (QV 60), Merytamen (QV 68), Bentanat (QV 71), Henuttauy (QV 73) and Henutmire (QV 75) are dug. Also prepared for one of his daughters, tomb QV 74 was only occupied later by Queen Duatentipet, great wife of Rameses IV.

From the architectural viewpoint, it is interesting to note that their plan underwent a number of developments. Annexes were added to the main chambers and at times, as with the cells of Tuy (QV 80) and Nefertari (QV 66), the infrastructure is over two levels connected by a ramp.

In the Ramesside period, a hamlet (*whjt*) grew up at the heart of the Valley of the Queens, in the part situated between the tomb of Tuy (QV 80) and the cave-waterfall. With an area estimated as in the region of 700 m2, this little settlement was made up of houses built in dry stone, with three to five rooms and an opening towards the north. In these houses—whose ruins have been excavated and restored—lived some of the craftsmen of Deir el-Medina who worked on the tombs of the queens and princes. They produced a number of fine *ostraca* with decorations, which came to light during the clearing of the site. Towards the Roman period, some of these modest houses were dismantled, while others, after being modified in the Coptic period, were undoubtedly reoccupied for residential or religious purposes.

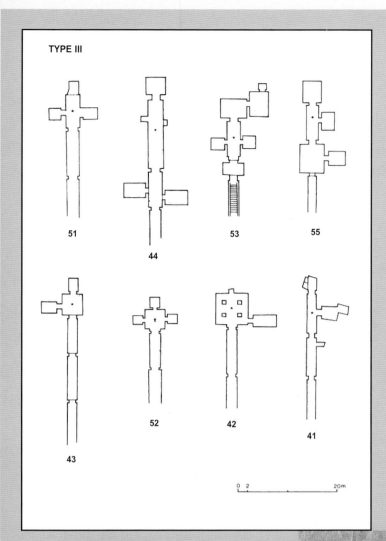

TYPE III

51   53   55

44

52   42

41

43

0 2   20m

283 left

Ostracon showing a seated noble, smelling a lotus blossom, with a priest kneeling to the front. Sketched in red with black outline. Valley of the Queens (1991). Ramesside period. Limestone. 18 x 25 cm (7 x 10 inches). Inspectorate of Qurna.

283 right

Statuette of the royal wife Ahmose-Nefertari, wearing a plaited wig which partially covers the vulture's skin. She holds a floral scepter in her left hand. This remarkable deified queen was honored by a cult which continued to the Third Intermediate Period. Painted wood. Louvre. From Deir el-Medina. Reign of Rameses II.

TYPE III - VALLEY OF THE QUEENS.
TYPOLOGY OF THE TOMBS OF THE RAMESSIDE PERIOD.
KINGDOM OF RAMESES III. 20TH DYNASTY.

In the reign of Rameses III, new sites were begun on the south west side of the main wadi. The programme included the digging and decoration of tombs for princes, starting from that of Rameses-Meryamen (QV 53) and Amenherkhepshef (QV 55). In this sector, the craftsmen also prepared the tombs of queens, those destined for the great wives of the king, Tyti (QV 52) and Isis (QV 51).

At the end of the southern side branch, Rameses III ordered other work to be carried out for at least three of his older sons. These included the eternal residences of Khaemwaset (QV 44), Sethherkhepshef (QV 43) and Pareherunemef (QV 42, in which the mother of the prince, Queen Minefer, also appears to have been buried). Two other tombs were also begun during this reign, but remained unfinished: QV 41 and QV 45. Compared to the 19th Dynasty tombs, the plan underwent modifications, as by now the arrangement of the rooms resembles a suite

of corridors recalling the underground tombs in the Valley of the Kings.

The Papyrus of Turin (cat. 1923, v 17) refers to activity in the Valley of the Queens during the reign of Rameses VI. Six tombs were built, of which no trace has so far been found. But the cartouches of this sovereign on the door of the sarcophagus chamber of Queen Isis and indicates that it was in this period that tomb QV 51 was built to contain the remains of the great wife of Rameses III.

During the 20th Dynasty, and more precisely towards the end of the reign of Rameses III, economic disorder and social problems were rife in Western Thebes. These events led to strikes, then, a little later, to the profanation of the royal tombs and the Temples of Millions of Years. The Valley of the Queens did not escape this sacrilege, and several commissions of inquiry were appointed. Certain documents (the Abbott Papyrus, the Meyer A Papyrus, the Ambras Papyrus, the Journal of the Necropolis of Thebes) speak of the administrative and legal action of the period by the royal functionaries to ascertain the violation and pillage of the tombs.

In the Abbott Papyrus, for example, several lines regard the profanation of the tomb of Isis (QV 51) and the arrest of those presumed responsible. As was the case with the pharaohs, it is probable that after these tragic events the mummies of queens and royal children from the Ramesside period were also transferred by the priests to a site probably outside the necropolis. This at least could explain why no remains of figures buried in the Valley of the Queens during the 19th and 20th Dynasties have been found in past or recent archaeological excavations.

The Third Intermediate Period saw a transition in the story of the necropolis. Starting from the 22nd Dynasty, the majority of the tombs that had been pillaged were reused for the first time. Brought to light not only by the rough conversions carried out in the pits of the 18th Dynasty or the tombs from the Ramesside period, but also by the discovery of a large amount of archaeological materials, this reoccupation is known to have continued to the Saite-Persian period. The evolution that took place suggests that the burial activities by the Theban priests had been resumed, which led to the redistribution of the tombs in the form of concessions to families. The beneficiaries were minor functionaries, priests, and people working on the land, as surveyors or farmers, cultivators of flowers and gardeners, and even perfume makers. As far as women were concerned, we know of a few called "Mistress of the house," or, in rare cases, "Singer of Amen."

The funeral goods found in most of the tombs also provided interesting observations. From the Third Intermediate Period, we can see that in the Valley of the Queens that the rich pottery, furniture, games and weapons, basketry and even the jewelery virtually disappeared from the tombs. We can also note that the strict ceremonies of death had evolved, with a multiplication of sarcophagi and *shawabtis*. Although they were still used, canopic jars no longer play more than a symbolic role. Sometimes they were replaced by miniature coffins. The risk of pillaging and even the state of extreme poverty into which the country fell at this time does not offer a satisfactory explanation of this fact. Everything leads us to believe that the origin of this phenomenon was a spectacular change in funerary customs: earthly goods no longer had a place in the other world.

In the Roman Period the Valley of the Queens underwent intensive reuse. Transformed into a popular cemetery and used as such from the start of the Roman Empire until the middle of the 4th century AD, it now found itself linked, both territorially and administratively, to Memnonia. In other words, it operated like other necropolis complexes on the west bank, in accordance with other systems put in place for a highly extended burial function, dealing with all the aspects connected with the mummification of the dead, the manufacture and sale of goods for eternity, the distribution of concessions, the organization of funerals and all the after-death operations and transactions in general. Modelled, as might have been expected, on what had existed during the times of the pharaohs, this full undertaking service developed into what now became a lucrative industry.

The pharaonic tombs on the site underwent general reuse. To make space for the new occupants and meet growing demand, quite often those in charge of the necropolis expanded the tombs. In the burial chambers of the 18th Dynasty, underground networks made it possible for several tombs to communicate with each other. Tunnels, sometimes dug deep, led to the secondary chambers. In the eternal residences of the Ramesside period, it was necessary to dig trenches to give access to the more or less spacious rooms into which the dead were packed. Inside these tombs, there were dozens of mummies, and in some cases more than a hundred (QV 15-16, QV 34, QV 39).

Due to the constraints imposed by the overcrowding of the dead and the increasing lack of burial space, the principle of concessions to families disappeared and was replaced by a grouping of the dead in accordance with the areas of the village they came from. Whether these came from Western Thebes or from nearby towns, in virtually every case these were people from modest origins. Sometimes mummified animals found a place within these tombs, especially falcons and ibises, as we learned from the excavations in tombs QV 3-4, QV 9-10, QV 11-12 and QV 53.

While burial traditions continued, they were significantly simplified. Although much less attention was paid to it than in earlier periods, mummification remained the most widely used ritual practice. Reinforced as necessary by palm ribs or a board, the bodies were wrapped in a series of shrouds. A plate or shroud painted with mythological scenes in most cases completed the burial ritual. Increasingly, however, the dead were laid in a wooden or terracotta sarcophagus. Simply put, burial goods now consisted of nothing more than a pottery vessel and, much more rarely, imitation jars and *shawabtis*.

The sacred nature of the Theban mountain, as well as the presence of later sanctuaries under the rule of Antonius in the Valley of the Queens and in Medinet Habu, could explain the recovery of burial activity in the necropolis at the time.

Towards the second half of the 4th century AD, *Ta Set Neferu* became a refuge and place of meditation for anchorites and hermits. Tombs, cells and natural shelters were quickly prepared and inhabited. Emerging Christianity progressively became more structured and the first monasteries appeared. On the sides and in the folds of the western mountain of Thebes, there were at least a dozen of these, among which Deir el-Rumi formed the central element of the *laura* (heremit's cells) established in the Valley of the Queens in the 6th-8th centuries.

THE ICONIC CHARACTERISTICS OF THE TOMBS OF THE VALLEY OF THE QUEENS IN THE RAMESSIDE PERIOD

Together with the dead, whether a queen, princess, or prince, gods and genies were the leading players who emerged in the great mural compositions of these tombs. As in the temples, these developed over two axes, one royal but also nocturnal, directed towards the interior of the tomb, the other, divine but also solar, directed towards the outside (the religious east). As a general rule, the image retraces, as in the sequences of a film, the travels of the "glorified one" in his or her new domain. We see the dead welcomed in the other world, then their travels through the lower regions, where a number of obstacles are encountered and many transformations undergone. There is movement upwards into the kingdom of the elected of Osiris, a prelude to regeneration. The gods and goddesses encountered protect and assist the

dead in overcoming the tests, where necessary whispering the magic formulas to pacify malevolent genies that could block the path, and intervene in favour of the dead. Finally, having reached the end of the journey, the dead, now not only "justified" but also "transformed," becomes identified with Ra himself. Inspired directly by the *Book of the Dead*, this iconic system, although at times condensed due to the space available, is found in all the tombs in the Valley of the Queens dating to the Ramesside period.

Of high quality, the style of the images is no less formal. Due to the hieratic nature of the attitudes, these paintings contrast with the decoration of the private burial

chapels of the time. On the other hand, the artists were particularly concerned with detail, both in the painting of the faces—the exceptional series of portraits of Queen Nefertari are a good example of this—and in the costumes and finery, which give a significant idea of the richness and variety of the royal and princely wardrobe in the 19th and 20th Dynasties. From a more technical viewpoint, we should emphazise that while the sculptors, due to the fragile surface on which they worked, could only express their art in an imperfect manner, the painters, using a palette of sparkling colors, were able to correct these imperfections in a remarkable manner.

The iconic programme sometimes remained unfinished in certain tombs in the necropolis. For example, the funeral chamber of Queen Satra (QV 38) has only preliminary sketches, and the sculptors had no time to model the scenes traced out on the walls by the

draughtsmen. In five other tombs (QV 36, 42, 43, 44, 55), it is the painters who failed to finish their work, leaving a number of figures in relief with no color. Finally, during the preparatory work, the craftsmen could express their skills on the walls whose surface still had received no decoration. This is certainly the case in at least two tombs in the necropolis, where we can see sketches of a king (QV 55) and a princess (QV 36) traced out in black or red ink.

In traditional scenes of welcome, consecration, adoration, libation and fumigation, the iconic repertoire is organized primarily around paintings of offerings of food (braziers, *meret*-boxes, cones of perfumed fat, fabrics, bouquets of papyrus, jars of ointment, bread or wine, as in the symbolic effigy or Maat). Paintings of the queen seated before a table loaded with delicacies, or playing the *sistrum* to entertain a god, are already becoming less frequent, and the evocation of the dead alone, playing *senet* (QV 66), became exceptional.

286-287
The royal wife of Rameses II, Nefertari "Beloved-of-Mut," with the kherep-*scepter, the offering of food for the god Atum. Wearing a fine robe of transparent pleats and a number of jewels, the queen wears the vulture skin beneath a hat to which two feathers are attached. Tomb of Nefertari (QV 66). Detail of the scene on the rear wall (right hand side) of the hall (F).*

THE TOMBS OF THE QUEENS

In their "eternal residences," queens and princesses pose in attitudes that vary only slightly. They are most frequently standing, sometimes seated before a table of offerings or, even more rarely, kneeling. The wives or daughters of the king are frequently dressed in a long, flowing robe of fine pleated white material, tied at the waist with a belt that falls forward in two or four embossed sections. In most cases, they wear the traditional vulture skin on their heads, over a simple cap or one adorned with cobras (*uraei*). Over this headdress, there are sometimes two long straight feathers, at the bottom of which is the disc of the sun.

288-289
Nefertari, in ceremonial costume, presents jars of wine to the goddesses Hathor, Serket and Maat. Between the royal wife and the goddesses is a table piled with offerings such as cakes, loaves fruit and vegetables. Tomb of Nefertari. Inner ramp (register above the banquet, right hand wall).

288 bottom
Two of the four sons of Horus, Hapy, with the head of a baboon, and the falcon-headed Duamutef.

289 bottom

Anubis in the form of a jackal, lying on the roof of a chapel. Protector of graves and patron of embalmer priests, his task is to lead the dead queen to the gates of the kingdom of Osiris.

These feathers, as some examples show, could be replaced by lotus fruits whose flexible stalks spring out of the cap. In the tomb of Isis (QV 51), we see another variant on this theme in at least two places.

The queen's headdress is surmounted by a kind of diadem made up of rearing and circling snakes. Interesting for their originality, two other designs show the sovereign with a *modius* on which there are two circling cobras and a vulture wearing an *atef*-crown (QV 52), and two rearing snakes protected by the wings of a falcon or vulture (QV 42, 51, 52).

Pectoral or necklaces with several rows of beads, bracelets, armlets are the essential items in the jewelry shown in the paintings of queens and princesses in these tombs. Sometimes they also wear earrings. Most models take the form of small floral motifs, rings, studs, rosettes or, most frequently, snakes, as in the tombs of Nefertari (QV 66), Merytamen (QV 68)

and Nebettauy (QV 60). It is also be of interest to note the more unusual items worn by these eminent ladies.

In the tomb of Nefertari, on the north-east wall of the western side room of the sarcophagus room, the queen appears in the form of Osiris. This is the only confirmed (or at least preserved) example of this. Standing, the sovereign is wound in a shroud from which there emerges only the head, wearing a classical three part wig covered in the vulture skin and cap. By way of finery, the wife of Rameses II wears a pectoral with a series of bands falling to the level of her breasts.

Also in this tomb, on the south-west wall of the antechamber, is the only image of the queen in the form of a bird spirit. Perched on a niche that is a simplified reproduction of the tomb, the bird is shown with a human head, that of Nefertari, wearing the vulture skin and cap.

Hatshepsut and Tiy are shown in the

form of sphinxes, and this notion was not abandoned with the queens of the Ramesside period. This is confirmed by an image of Tuy on the north-west wall of an annexe chamber of her tomb (QV 80). The great wife of Seti I here takes the form of a lion with human head, wearing the vulture skin surmounted by a cap and two long, straight feathers. The sovereign offers balsam to a god whose face has disappeared. In the tomb of Bentanat (QV 71), two similar sphinxes adorn the northern and southern openings of the door that gives access to the eastern side room of the antechamber. Lying on a chapel with a door, the oldest daughter of Rameses II is also shown with a human head, but this time she wears a wig in long sections which partially conceal the vulture skin on which is laid a cap without feathers. These original paintings of Bentanat are placed on a high frieze made up of two *djed*-pillars and a knot of Isis.

In several places in the tomb of Tiy (QV 52), the great wife of the king takes on the features of a young girl, while in certain other places she is shown as an adult woman. Wearing a flowing, pleated robe which the artist has painted with skill and clarity, and wearing fine sandals with up-turned toes, the princess-queen wears a short wig with a cobra on the front which fits onto the head. The typical plait of childhood falls to the longer side, at the back. In two cases, the headdress is dominated by a cap with two tall feathers, in front of which is the solar disc. The theme of the queen in the company of her daughter is exceptional, as it only appears in one tomb in this necropolis, that of Bentanat (QV 71). It appears on the east wall of the sarcophagus room. Standing behind her mother in a pose of adoration, "the daughter of the king, engendered by him," is quite clearly distinguished from Bentanat by her youthful

appearance, the youthful curl falling over her shoulder, and a lotus flower whose umbel falls slightly to her forehead. She wears a ring in her ear which partly conceals the wig. Unique in a burial situation like this one, this painting also confirms that the marriage of the king with his daughter, in this case Bentanat, the oldest daughter of Rameses II and Isis-Nofret, who later became a great royal wife, really was consummated. The anonymous princess shown in the tomb is clearly shown to be the result of this special union, and the idea that these sacred marriages between father and daughter were merely symbolic now has to be abandoned. Another painting of this young girl can also be seen, showing her before the goddess Nephthys, on the west wall of the same chamber. The general appearance is similar to the one in the previous scene, but in this case she has a straight plait that falls to the side of the face.

290-291
Nekhbet, in the form of a cobra, protects the cartouche of Nefertari, laid on the golden symbol and surmonted by the sun disc. Lower ramp (register above the banquet, left hand wall).

292-293
The goddess Hathor, "She who Presides in Thebes," the "Lady of the Sky," welcomes the royal wife Nefertari. Sarcophagus room. South west pillar (western face).

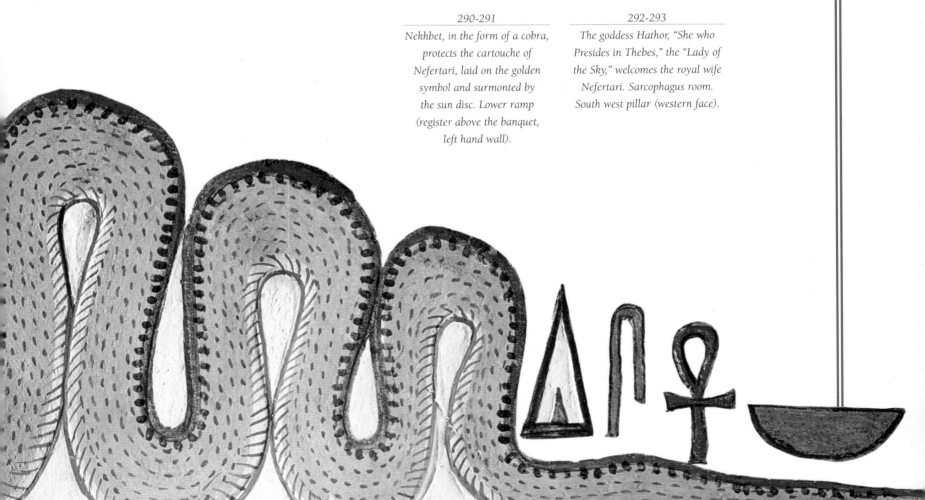

During her journey towards the other world, Nefertari has to give offerings to the gods she meets. Here, the royal wife and Lady of the Two Lands presents jars of wine to the goddess Isis, who promises her in exchange eternal life like Ra, the sun. Lower ramp, upper register, left hand wall.

The cartouche of the queen, Nefertari ("The most beautiful"), Meretenmut ("the Beloved-of-Mut") with the protective shen-symbol resting against it.

THE TOMB OF
NEFERTARI

by Christian Leblanc

THE GREAT ROYAL WIFE OF RAMESES II, Nefertari, mother of Prince Amenherkhepshef, the eldest son of the sovereign, occupied a dominant place during the first three decades of the reign. Her memory was immortalized by a number of monuments, especially in the south of Egypt. In West Bank monuments at Thebes, she is often seen by the side of her husband. Her appearance in the region as from year 1 is also confirmed by a fine relief of the tomb of Nebunenef, a figure to whom Rameses gave the prestigious role of first priest of Amen. She was present at the ceremony of investiture which took place at Abydos, and is shown by the side of Rameses, appearing at the window of the palace. In the Ramesseum, we know that she shared the little monument adjoining the main temple, on the northern side, with her mother-in-law. It is perhaps to this mammisi that reference is made on a stela in the Berlin museum, which we know by the name of Superintendent of the Domain of the Castle of the Great Royal Wife Nefertari, beloved of Mut, a certain Iuy. During solemn festivals, such as that of Min, god of the harvest, the queen took part in the ritual. On the western face of the northern post of the second pylon, we see her in the upper register performing a dance in honor of the god of fertility. She was without doubt shown in other scenes, but the dismantling of most of the walls after the abandonment of the official cult has deprived us of a precious documentary source. While in the tomb of Rameses II (KV 7) the titles and name of Nefertari are engraved on the opening of a door to a corridor, it is above all in the temple he had built in Abu Simbel, then the tomb prepared in the Valley of the Queens,

Vignettes from Chapter 17 of the Book of the Dead. (1) Image of a bird similar to a phoenix, but which in fact is a grey heron. Originating in Heliopolis, this is one of the tangible manifestations of the god Ra. Also incarnated in him is the soul of Osiris (a latent form of the sun). These two facets, solar and chthonian, opposites but complementary, make this divine bird the symbol of the periodic return of the instant of creation. (2) Isis and Nephthys, in the form of female kites, watch over the mummy of Nefertari stretched out on a funeral bed in the form of a lion's body in the ritual tent. (3) Genie of the Nile, with black skin, shown with a wig and loincloth made simply of strips. He holds a palm frond in his right hand, a symbol of the millions of years or, more precisely, the indefinite renewal of life on the earth. Antechamber (C), west wall, upper register.

The double lion, Ruty. In this image (here incomplete), we see Shu and Tefnut, guardians of the horizon, a mythical place comparable to the threshold of the Other World, but which was also the lair in which the god Ra was regenerated. Antechamber (C), west wall, upper register.

Evocation of the queen in the form of the ba-bird (her soul) on the roof of a building which is simply the stylized reproduction of her tomb. Antechamber (C), south wall, west side, upper register.

where the sovereign pays the most vibrant homage to the woman who shared the destiny of the kingdom by his side for so many years. For his beloved queen, who died around year 26 of the reign, Rameses had prepared a sumptuous eternal residence, one of the jewels of Western Thebes. A milestone in official pictorial art, this tomb, with its refined decoration and the great delicacy of the reliefs, pays tribute to the formidable skill of the craftsmen of the time. Designed with two levels and adorned with paintings that tell of the journey of the queen towards the Domain of Osiris, then her return to the light of Ra, the tomb of Nefertari, in terms of its architecture and its decoration, shows an admirable summary of the destinies awaiting the royal dead in the other world.

It was discovered in 1904 by Ernesto Schiaparelli of the Italian Mission of the Museum of Turin, then restored between 1988 and 1992 by the J. Paul Getty Institute of Conservation, within the context of a joint project with the Supreme Council of Antiquities of Egypt. The tomb is once again accessible to tourists, but only in limited numbers.

The antechamber (C) which marks the first stage in the route towards the west, is also the room in which the dead sovereign makes her journey by night. From the outset, welcomed by Osiris and Anubis on the walls of the right half of the room, the wife of Rameses II goes towards the inner ramp (H) of the tomb. On the opposite side, on the walls in the left half of this room, there is a long reverse text arranged in columns, referring to

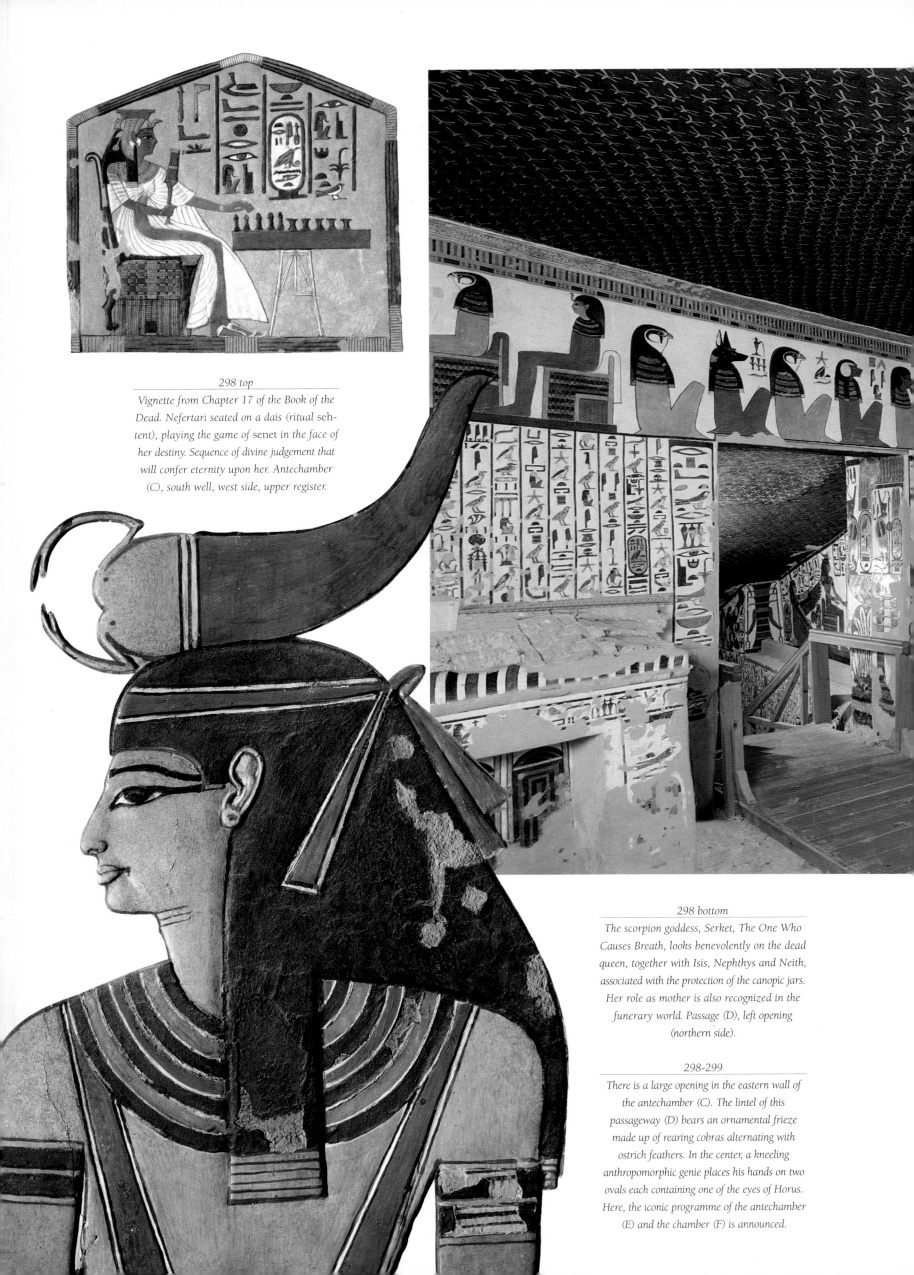

298 top

Vignette from Chapter 17 of the Book of the
Dead. Nefertari seated on a dais (ritual seh-
tent), playing the game of senet in the face of
her destiny. Sequence of divine judgement that
will confer eternity upon her. Antechamber
(C), south well, west side, upper register.

298 bottom

The scorpion goddess, Serket, The One Who
Causes Breath, looks benevolently on the dead
queen, together with Isis, Nephthys and Neith,
associated with the protection of the canopic jars.
Her role as mother is also recognized in the
funerary world. Passage (D), left opening
(northern side).

298-299

There is a large opening in the eastern wall of
the antechamber (C). The lintel of this
passageway (D) bears an ornamental frieze
made up of rearing cobras alternating with
ostrich feathers. In the center, a kneeling
anthropomorphic genie places his hands on two
ovals each containing one of the eyes of Horus.
Here, the iconic programme of the antechamber
(E) and the chamber (F) is announced.

her exit into day. This is Chapter 17 of the *Book of the Dead*, with some references to Chapters 71 and 175, with the vignettes reproduced one after another in the upper register of the three walls. Here we see the invocations that would protect the dead, enabling him to play *senet* in the Beautiful West, as well as leave the empire of the dead when he wished. The scenes adorning the walls of the vestibule (E) and chamber (F) form two coherent iconic groups, but to understand their religious meaning we have to go to the axis of the two rooms and consider that the all decoration on the left half corresponds to the chthonian (nocturnal) world and that on the right refers to the solar (daytime) world. In this way, the first image we

see is that of Serket at the left opening of the passageway (D). This protector goddess, whose name takes a scorpion as its ideogram, opens the way to Nefertari, as will be done again, a little further on, by Maat, shown at the openings of the door of the chamber (F). Entering the antechamber, the sovereign is guided by Isis to the incarnation of the eternal future, the god Khepri with the black scarab head. On the opposite side, we find Neith at the right opening of the passageway (D) This goddess plays a very specific role in the solarization of the dead. It is she who is responsible for regenerating Osiris, feeding him and uniting him with Atum. Like Serket, Neith opens the way to Nefertari who, reaching

the antechamber (E), is led forward by Harsiesis—whose cosmic and solar nature is yet another source of protection along the route—towards Ra-Horakhty, personification of eternal day, accompanied by his daughter-wife, Hathor-Imentet. Goddess-mother par excellence, this latter has the privilege of helping the child, in this case the dead queen, back into the world, seated on her mystical lap, and here she incarnates the western mountain of Thebes. After passing through the door of the chamber (F), the dead queen continues her journey alone into the beyond, and the first thing she meets is the effigy of Ptah, enclosed in a gilded *naos* resting against a *djed*-pillar.

LEGEND

A	RAMP OR ACCESS STAIR TO THE TOMB	G	DOOR
B	DOOR	H	INNER RAMP
C	ANTECHAMBER	I	DOOR
D	PASSAGEWAY TOWARDS THE ANTECHAMBER	J	SARCOPHAGUS ROOM OR "GOLDEN RESIDENCE"
E	ANTECHAMBER	K	WESTERN SIDE ANNEXE
F	SIDE CHAMBER	L	EASTRERN SIDE ANNEXE
		M	ACCESS TO THE "RESIDENCE OF OSIRIS"

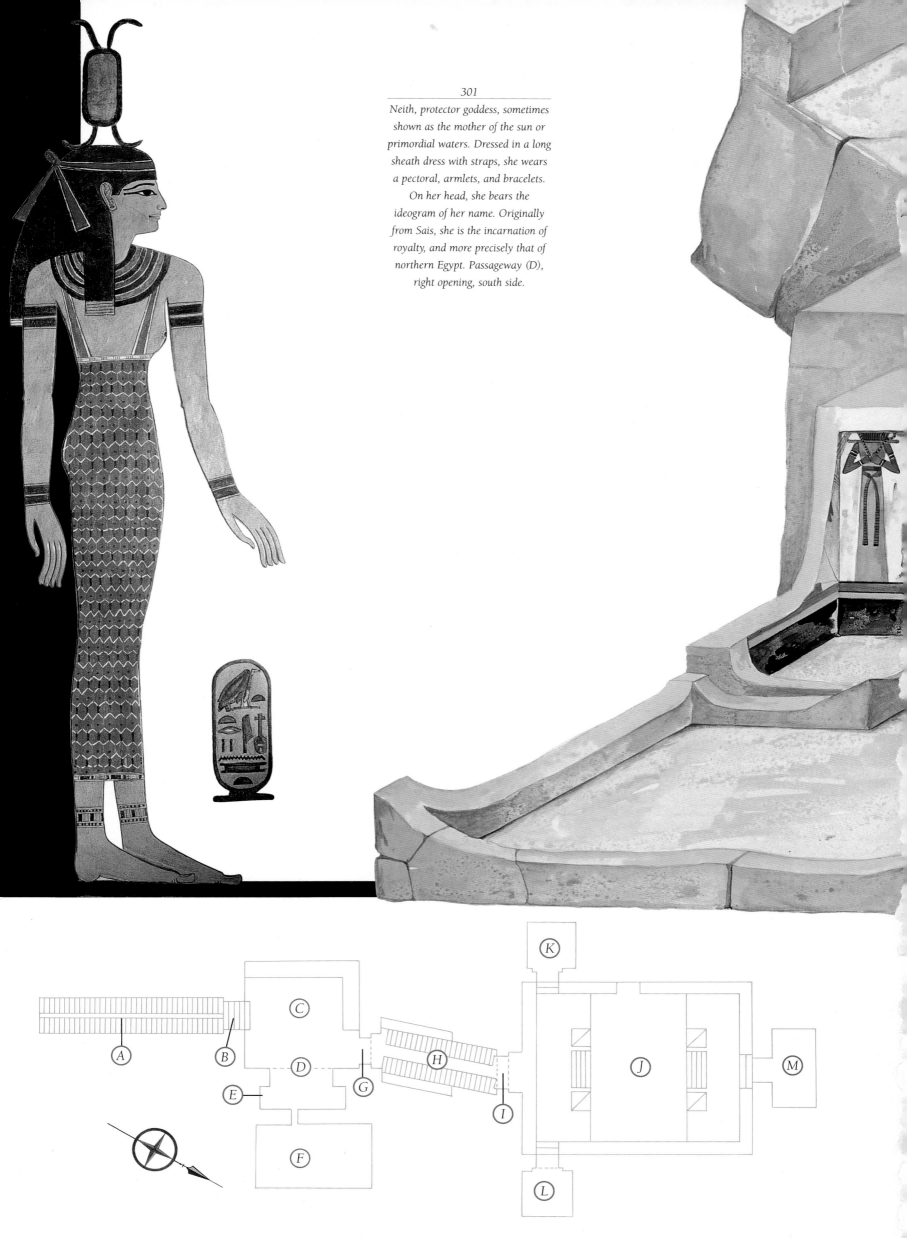

301

Neith, protector goddess, sometimes
shown as the mother of the sun or
primordial waters. Dressed in a long
sheath dress with straps, she wears
a pectoral, armlets, and bracelets.
On her head, she bears the
ideogram of her name. Originally
from Sais, she is the incarnation of
royalty, and more precisely that of
northern Egypt. Passageway (D),
right opening, south side.

The Tomb of Nefertari

300

Isis, the "Lady of Heaven," with a pair of horns that surround the sun, gives the breath of divine life to Nefertari, who wears the vulture skin, a typical feature of royal mothers. Sarcophagus room, southeast pillar (east face).

305

Portrait of Nefertari on the south wall of the antechamber (E) of the tomb. Wearing make-up and jewelry, this extremely elegant queen was the mother of several children of Rameses II, including the princes Amenherkhepshef, Pareherunemef, Meryra and Meryatum.

304 top

Kneeling winged Maat. Daughter
of Ra, always shown as an
anthropomorphic figure with a
feather on her head, this goddess
represents justice, balance, and
social and cosmic order. Together
with Osiris and Thoth, she takes
part in the judgement of the dead,
at the moment when the heart is
weighed. Lintel of the door (I)
leading to the "Golden Residence."

The Tomb of Nefertari

By taking possession of her eternal abode, Nefertari sets forth on a long odyssey that will lead her, stage by stage, to the Kingdom of Osiris. The gods Anubis and Osiris, depicted on the walls to the right side of the antechamber (C) receive the dead queen in her new domain. Under the protection of Anubis, Nephthys and Isis, represented at the sides of the inner stairwell (H), she gradually proceeds towards the Kingdom of the Dead. Upon reaching the Golden Residence (J), where her mortal remains assume their place, the queen goes through doors and porches passing by fierce guards. After having successfully overcome these obstacles, she is acknowledged as triumphant by Osiris, Hathor of the West and Anubis, and is entitled to enter the sanctuary (M) that leads to the kingdom of the god of the dead. Her return to light takes place in the opposite direction. In the vestibule (E) and the chamber (F), just before her regeneration and transfiguration, Nefertari is presented before several divinities. It is here that she goes through an essential metamorphosis, through her passage from the kingdom of Osiris to that of Ra, still in her cocoon. Finally, the climax of this route takes place in the antechamber (C) where the glorified queen emerges into the light and is represented as the sun rising above the horizon, an image so well depicted on the soffit of the door (B).

Before the venerable image of the creator god of
Memphis, she makes the offering of fabrics, then
presents herself before the ibis-headed Thoth,
seated on a backed throne. At this point in the
journey, the queen has to recite Chapter 94 of
the *Book of the Dead*, the formula inscribed
behind her over several columns, whose content
will procure her the pot and palette of a scribe,
objects possessing magical powers conferred
upon them by Thoth, the incarnation of the Word
of Creation. After overcoming this test, Nefertari
finishes her nocturnal journey by making a great
offering of food to Osiris, in a scene that
occupies the left half of the rear wall. At this
point, the queen is able to embark on the route
leading to her solar rebirth, and this concept can
be no better expressed than in the painting to
the right on entering room (F). There, between
the goddesses Nephthys and Isis, Osiris-Ra,
united in the same body, is shown in the form of

a ram-headed mummy. This particular image,
which simply shows the absorption of Osiris by
Ra, represents the crucial stage that Nefertari has
to overcome. Leaving behind the outer skin of the
god in mutation, she is now freed of the chains of
death, and may prepare to reappear as a new sun
on the eastern horizon of the sky. In this sense,
Chapter 148 of the *Book of the Dead*, of which
only the vignette is reproduced, appears to be in
the right place, as this contains a formula that is
useful to the sovereign in obtaining provisions in
the afterlife, and is above all necessary for her
transfiguration in the heart of Ra and ensure that
she is strong before Atum. It is in fact toward this
god, personification of the creator, as well as the
victor over the forces of the night, that Nefertari

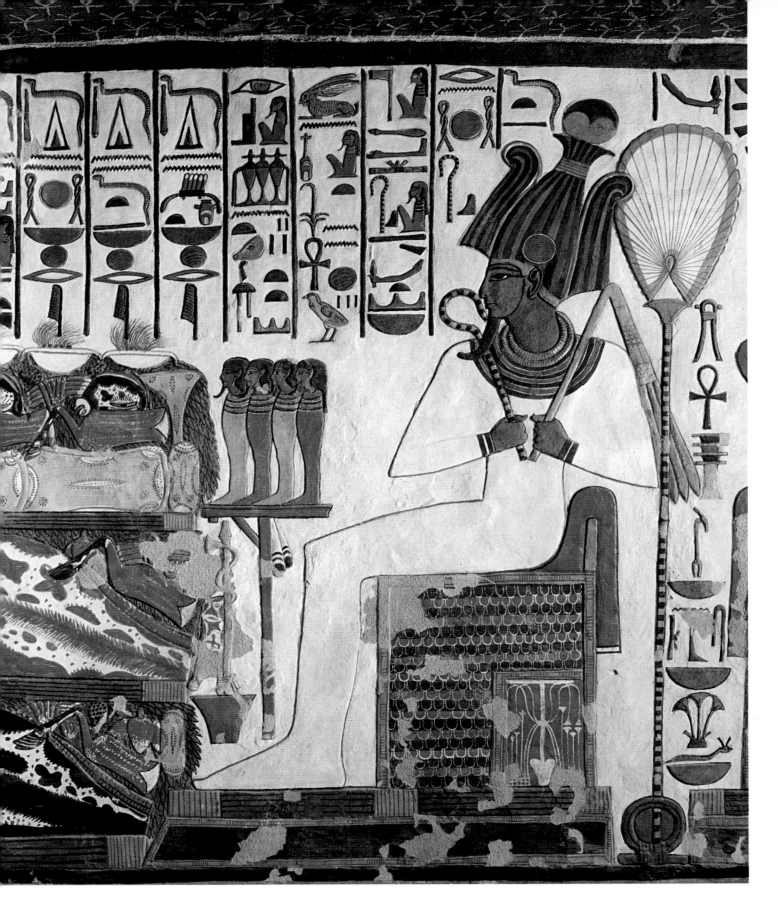

goes, regenerated, to make the great offering of food to him.

In this way, through their themes and their ritual positioning in the tomb, the paintings we describe refer on the one hand to the world of the night, synonym of the queen's past, and on the other the solar world, the universe in which she prepares for her future. Access to the lower level of the tomb is by way of the door (G), whose lintel is adorned with the four sons of Horus (Imsety, Hapy, Duamutef and Qebhsenuef) in the form of mummies, seated one behind the other. The jambs contain only the titles and the name of the dead queen. On the stairway, the decoration is organized over two registers. Above the bench, the theme is the offering of jars of

306-307

Consecration by Nefertari of the great offering of food before Osiris, who oversees in the west. On a stand, before the god, the four sons of Horus are shown. Chamber (F), east wall, northern half.

307 bottom

Detail of the vignette in Chapter 148 of the Book of the Dead. Three of the seven divine cows, accompanied by the bull known as "the Male of the Cattle, the superior who resides in the Red Castle." Chamber (F), south wall.

The Tomb of Nefertari

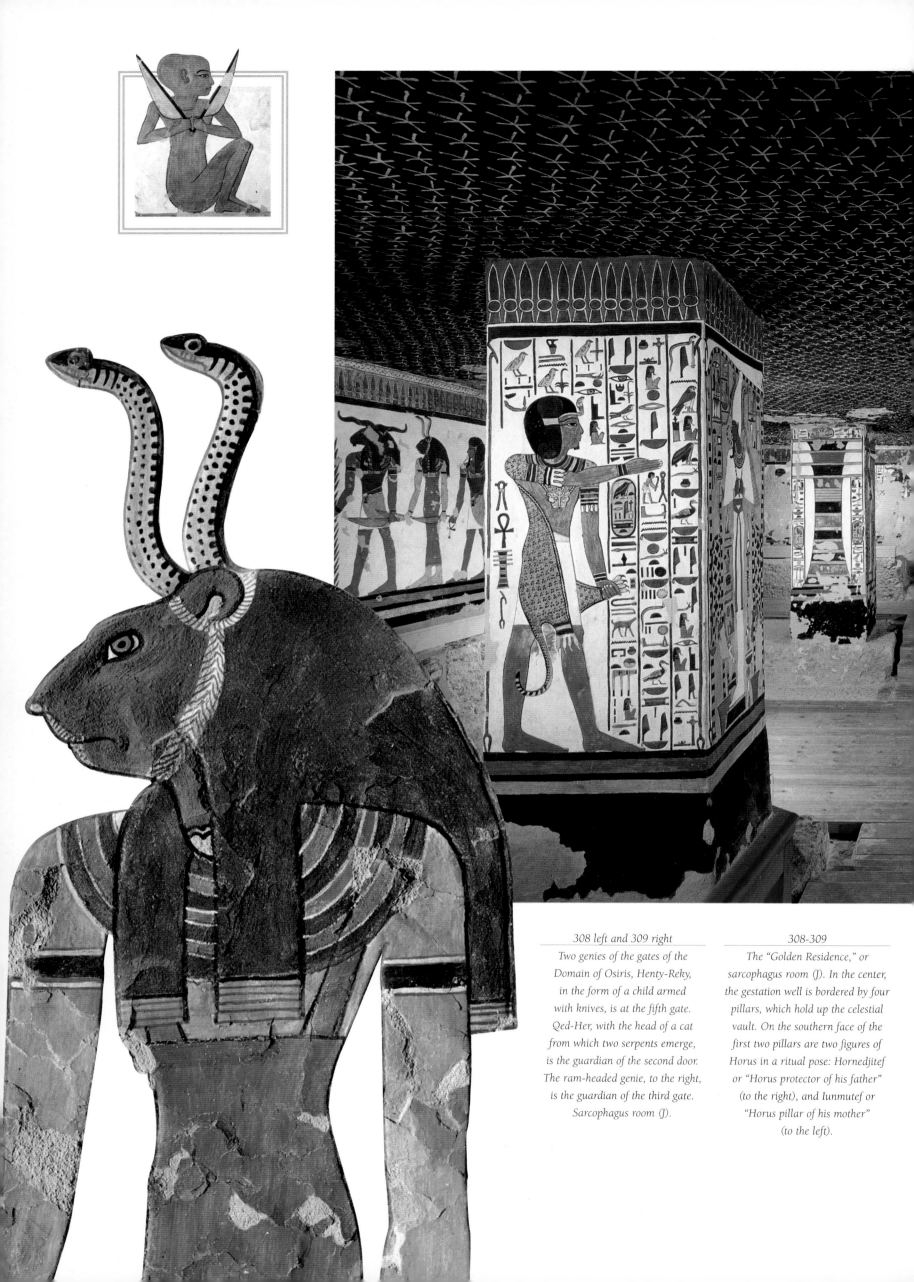

308 left and 309 right

Two genies of the gates of the
Domain of Osiris, Henty-Reky,
in the form of a child armed
with knives, is at the fifth gate.
Qed-Her, with the head of a cat
from which two serpents emerge,
is the guardian of the second door.
The ram-headed genie, to the right,
is the guardian of the third gate.
Sarcophagus room (J).

308-309

The "Golden Residence," or
sarcophagus room (J). In the center,
the gestation well is bordered by four
pillars, which hold up the celestial
vault. On the southern face of the
first two pillars are two figures of
Horus in a ritual pose: Hornedjitef
or "Horus protector of his father"
(to the right), and Iunmutef or
"Horus pillar of his mother"
(to the left).

On the other side, the vignettes and texts refer to Chapter 146 of the ritual. The formulae here are complementary to the previous ones, and it is with these that Nefertari overcomes these final stages in her wanderings to rejoin Osiris. At the end of this route full of obstacles, from which she emerges finally victorious, the great royal wife of Rameses II reappears, in adoration, before the triad of gods that preside over the destinies of those of the west—Osiris, Hathor-Imentet and Anubis, shown in the right half of the rear wall of the room (J).

Four pillars border the gestation well where, in the past, the pink granite sarcophagus of Nefertari lay. These correspond to the supports of the heavens, represented by the starry ceiling. Their faces are adorned by the images of the gods, some

wine, made by Nefertari to several gods. To the left is Isis, followed by Nephthys and Maat, to whom she presents small spherical vessels. To the right, the same drink is offered to Hathor, Serket and, once again, to the winged Maat. The lower register is almost entirely occupied by columns of text, welcoming addresses to the sovereign by Anubis (on both walls), Isis (on the left wall) and Nephthys (on the right), before she enters the realm of the dead.

As we go through the door (I), above which we see the effigy of the goddess Maat with outspread wings, we enter the sarcophagus room and approach the kingdom of Osiris in the Field of Reeds. However, to reach this, Nefertari has to

overcome a number of pitfalls and traps set by malevolent genies or the negative forces of the lower world. Formidable guardians of the gates and porches of the mysterious Duat await her, armed with knives. Before these strange figures, it is essential that the queen pronounce their names and those of the passageways where they await. Only knowledge of these can save her from annihilation and enable her to continue on her journey towards the domain of the god of the dead.

To the left, as we enter, this dangerous journey begins. Chapter 144 of the *Book of the Dead* has this as its exclusive theme, and occupies the walls of all this half of the room.

seen alone, such as Osiris, Iunmutef and Hornedjitef, or in the company of the queen, such as Hathor, Isis, Imentet and Anubis. The symbolic receptacle of the spinal column representing resurrection, the *djed*-pillar also appears in these supports in four places, always facing each other, as do the images of Osiris.

The *shawabtis* of Nefertari, arranged in their boxes and the canopic jars were laid in the sarcophagus room (J). The latter were in a cavity of square section cut into the bench running along the left hand wall. The faces are adorned with the image of the sons of Horus and the goddess Nut. On the rear wall of the annexe (K), we can see that these canopic jars had been

shown under the protection of the sons of Horus. These genies, as well as the goddesses Nephthys and Isis, protectors of mummified organs, are shown on the side walls of this small room, while Nefertari, in the form of a standing mummy, adorns the inner face of the left door jamb. In annexe (L), under the benevolent gaze of the goddess of Maat, who occupies the rear wall, are two scenes of adoration. In one, the dead sovereign pays hommage to the cow Hathor emerging from the folds of the western mountain, and in the other this rite of veneration is addressed to Anubis and Isis, both of whom are seen seated. The particularly derelict condition of small annexe (M) makes it impossible to reconstruct its decoration, of which there remain only small traces. Nevertheless, this chamber, as in the other tombs from the Ramesside period in the Valley of the Queens, appears to correspond to the passageway that gives access to the Domain of Osiris.

A monumental *Book of the Dead*, where the walls replace papyrus and painted reliefs replace vignettes, the sumptuous eternal residence of Nefertari admirably sums up by the distribution of the iconic themes the major stages in the journey through the Empire of the Dead. But the greatest conclusion to this journey is undoubtedly to be found in the soffit of the entry door (B), where, emerging from the eastern horizon, the queen regenerated and assimilated with the sun, forever immortal in her victory over the world of darkness.

310	311
Inside a naos-chapel, Osiris-Unennefer with the green skin is shown with the attributes of royalty. Dressed in a white girdle and wearing the atef-crown, he is flanked by two animal skins in which the divine fluids are kept. Sarcophagus room (J), detail of the northern face of the north west pillar.	*In an extremely delicate gesture, Hathor the Western goddess holds the hand of the dead queen. Around her arms, Nefertari wears a piece of jewelry made up of beads and the udjat-eye, symbol of restored wholeness. Sarcophagus room (J), detail of the northern face of the north west pillar.*

The Tombs of the Sons of Rameses III

by Christian Leblanc

THE TOMBS OF THE OLDEST SONS OF Rameses III, Pareherunemef, Sethherkhepshef and Khaemwaset, lay at the upper extreme of the southern branch of the main Valley of the Queens wadi. The tombs of two other princes, for the younger sons of Queen Tyti (QV 52), Amenherkhepshef (QV 55) and Rameses-Meryamen (QV 53), lay nearby. We are tempted to believe that for the maternal line of Tyti the excavation and decoration program for the tombs in this necropolis was as follows, in chronological order: the craftsmen first began on tomb QV 53 of Rameses-Meryamen (in which the decoration of the walls of the sarcophagus room ought to refer to the first four portals of the Domain of Osiris from Chapters 145 and 146 of the *Book of the Dead*); then tomb QV 55 of Amenherkhepshef (where we have portals 5 to 8 inclusive of the Domain of Osiris); then tomb QV 44 of Khaemwaset (portals 9 to 16 inclusive of the Domain of Osiris). A fourth, unfinished, tomb should have received the illustration of the last five portals.

THE TOMBS OF THE PRINCES

It is believed that the theme of the king presenting his son to the gods of the other world was an innovation ordered by Rameses III for the decoration of princely tombs in the Valley of the Queens. But in most of the scenes in the tombs of Amenherkhepshef (QV 55), Khaemwaset (QV 44), Sethherkhepshef (QV 43) and Paraherunemef (QV 42)—all sons of Rameses III, the father accompanies the son and guides him towards the Domain of Osiris. Therefore, we have to realize that these original sequences date back at least to the reign of Rameses II. In fact, it is in tomb KV 5 of the Valley of the Kings, prepared for several sons of the great pharaoh, that in the first antechamber such paintings show the king followed by his elder sons for the first time. This subject, appearing in the 19th Dynasty onwards, was then returned to by Rameses III in the Valley of the Queens, as well as in the Valley of the Kings: princely tomb KV 3, though unfinished, still has paintings of this kind in the first corridor. This feature was abandoned at a

later date, and in tomb KV 19 of the Valley of the Kings, attributed to Montuherkhepshef, son of Rameses IX, only the prince appears on the walls, in the company of the gods.

In the Valley of the Queens, the wall paintings are well preserved in only four princely tombs. Still of a surprising freshness, the colors used in two of these tombs (QV 44, 55) show a rich palette, very skilfully used by the artist, especially to depict the splendid finery worn by both the royal and divine figures. In these scenes, the sovereign and his son are always shown standing, Rameses III always goes before the prince and intercedes on his behalf with the gods. While the queen, mother of the royal child, has no place here, we should note that in the burial chamber of the tomb of Prince Paraherunemef (QV 42) a wife of Rameses III was later added to the decoration. We see her before Osiris. This later composition undoubtedly has to be seen in relation to the burial of the mother of Paraherunemef in her son's tomb. As a general rule, Rameses III is dressed in a long, baggy,

312

Rameses III, son of Setnakht, the founder of the 20th Dynasty, had a number of tombs prepared for his children in the Valley of the Queens. Those of the princes Amenherkhepshef and Khaemwaset are the most interesting, due to the freshness of their colors. Their decoration shows the avatars to which the royal children have to submit as the move through the Other World, before reaching the Domain of Osiris.

313

Rameses III in ceremonial costume, accompanied by his son Khaemwaset, passes through the ninth gate of the Domain of Osiris, guarded by Dendeni, The Furious. The genie with the head of the green bubalus antelope is armed with two knives. Tomb QV 44. Sarcophagus room (E), north wall.

pleated linen loincloth, fixed at the waist by a belt, from the back of which hangs the ceremonial animal tail. From this garment, there normally hangs an apron bordered with ribbons, trapezoid in shape, with the head of a cat at the top. Vertical bands made up of chevron motifs decorate the visible face of this piece of gilt, which ends in a large horizontal plate showing six or seven coiled cobras. The starched costume of the king is sometimes fronted by a short, triangular loincloth, a feature common in the 19th Dynasty. Most frequently, the king is naked from the waist up, his chest protected by a liturgical sash which disappears when the upper body is concealed by a broad sleeved blouse which partly covers a pleated linen mantel knotted over the right breast. Another

falcon which protects the nape of the king's neck with its wings, the blue headdress that encloses the skull, and a highly elaborate *atef*-crown with horizontally twisted ram's horns. To all this, we have to add the solar *hemhem*-crown, fixed within a cap, which was placed on the *nemes*, a number of headdresses such as the winged model, made up of links of different lengths falling to one side, or the short wig (*ibes*) made up of a rectangular mesh, circled by a *seched*-diadem around which twines the body of a cobra. Behind these royal headdresses there nearly always hang one or two ribbons, a holdover from the Amarna period. Behind his father, or

costume, seen much more rarely—appears only twice in the antechamber of the tomb of Amenherkheshef (QV 55)—completes this royal wardrobe. Made up of three parts, a tunic of fine transparent fabric whose sleeves, bordered with beads, form a flounce, is worn underneath. Over this tunic, a corselet adorned by two embroidered falcons on the flaps, clings to the upper part of the chest and the shoulders of the sovereign. Finally, a loincloth at the front, with the classic apron over it, is the final item in this exceptional ceremonial costume.

Wearing sandals and adorned with necklaces, armlets and bracelets, Rameses III also wears a large variety of crowns and headgear, no less than twenty different models of which have been catalogued. Among those are the *khepresh*, the red or white crown, the *pschent* or double crown, the *nemes*, one example of which is adorned with a falcon dominating the solar disc, the white *khayt*, at the back of which there is sometimes a golden

314

Rameses III, wearing the ibes headdress with streamers and wearing a luxurious corselet costume, carries out the rites of praise and libation before Geb, "the father of the divine forms." Tomb of Khaemwaset (QV 44). Northern wall of the antechamber (B) or entrance room.

314-315

Shown in an attitude of adoration, Rameses III wears the khepresh-crown and a long white loincloth with gilding. Behind him, his son Khaemwaset is shown with the typical plait of childhood and wears a loincloth similar to that of his father, with a transparent pleated blouse. In his hands, the prince holds a multicolored behet-fan with papyrus shaped handle. Tomb QV 44. North wall of the sarcophagus room (E).

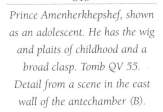

315

Prince Amenherkhepshef, shown as an adolescent. He has the wig and plaits of childhood and a broad clasp. Tomb QV 55. Detail from a scene in the east wall of the antechamber (B).

shown alone in the presence of the gods, the prince is regularly shown as a young boy with an elongated, shaven head, with the plait of youth falling to one side of his head, hiding his ear. Some paintings show him with a wig, but always with this plait held in place with a clasp. The costume in which he most frequently appears is a long linen loincloth tied at the waste by a broad embroidered belt. From this there hang three or four cords with pompons, at times with long, embossed ribbons. When he is not naked from the waist up, the prince sometimes wears a fine, almost transparent blouse, with broad, pleated sleeves, which stop at the elbows. While the blouse is virtually always the same, the loincloth may plunge down at the back and puff out at the front, or, as we can see from at least one example (QV, sarcophagus room), rise up at the back, with a triangular codpiece partly covered by a scalloped apron. In most cases, the son of Rameses III holds the flabellum-*khou* in one hand, at times together with a *heka*-scepter. In other scenes, the prince holds the crook and a long sash or the shaft of a splendid fan of ostrich feathers (*behet*). He is also at times found without these items, simply raising his arms in a gesture of adoration. Wearing necklaces and bracelets, he has fine sandals with up-turned toes on his feet, like his father. While Prince Montuherkhepshef is shown in the Valley of the Kings (KV 19) as a young man whose physical features are already those of an adult, in spite of having all the typical characteristics of a royal son, we can see that in the Valley of the Queens the heirs of Rameses III all appeared as young adolescents. This interesting difference does not necessarily reflect reality, as we know that several of the sons of Rameses III died when they were already adults.

THE TOMB OF
AMENHERKHEPSHEF

by Christian Leblanc

AMENHERKHEPSHEF, SON OF RAMESES III, was brought into the world by the God's Wife, God's Mother and Great Royal Wife, as stated in one of the inscriptions in his tomb in the Valley of the Queens. The proximity of the tomb of Tyti, as we can see from the repetition of these titles in the inscriptions regarding the queen, provides a significant indication of the maternal descent of the prince. Apparently dying around year 30 of the reign, Amenherkhepshef was not one of the elder sons of the king. On the basis of the princely relief in Medinet Habu or the relief of the festival of Min in the temple-altar of repose of Rameses III in Karnak, we know that he performed a number of functions, including that of fan bearer to the right of the king, royal scribe and cavalry commander. He also had the title of Superior of the Two Lands, which was undoubtedly a post in the management of the administrative affairs of the kingdom. In the Valley of the Dolmen, a partial stela in his image was found in the sanctuary of Ptah and Meretseger. This must have been an ex-voto

	LEGEND
A	RAMP
B	ANTECHAMBER OR ENTRANCE HALL
C	WESTERN SIDE CHAMBER
D	SARCOPHAGUS ROOM
E	UNFINISHED WESTERN SIDE ANNEXE
F	ACCESS TO THE DOMAIN OF OSIRIS. CHAMBER UNFINISHED OF TRANSFIGURATION AND REBIRTH. THE INITIAL SITE OF THE SARCOPHAGUS WAS IN ROOM D

316

Rameses III and Amenherkhepshef are received and escorted by Isis the "Sovereign of the West." The king, wearing a sumptuous loincloth adorned with feathers and completed with an embroidered corselet, is accompanied by the prince brought into the world by the royal wife, who holds the ostrich feather khu-fan in his right hand. South-east wall of the antechamber (B).

316-317

Rameses III wearing make-up, wearing the nemes with the uraeus at the front and a false beard. Husband to at least four official queens, he was the father of several children. Amenherkhepshef, who was royal scribe and commander of the cavalry, was one of the sons of Tyti, a sovereign who was buried in tomb QV 52.

317

The two cartouches with the names of Rameses III: Usermatra Meryamen, "Powerful is the universal order of the god Ra, The Beloved of Amen" (right); Rameses Heqaiunu, "Ra engendered him" "Sovereign of Heliopolis" (left). The word "glorified" added here is necessary as the king is accompanying his son to the Other World.

Main Scenes

1-2 Rameses III accompanied by the prince presents himself before several gods: scenes of welcome	**4-5** Rameses III and Amenherkhepshef present themselves to the guardian genies of the gates preceding access to the Domain of Osiris
3 The decoration of this room is unfinished. It consists only of an image of the king wearing a pshent	

318-319

After fumigation for the god Ptah of Memphis, Rameses III intercedes for his son with Ptah-Tatenen and two genies: Duamutef (with the head of a black dog) and Imsety (with a human head), sons of Horus and protectors of the canopic jars. In each picture, the crowns and royal headgear are different. East wall of the antechamber (B).

318 bottom left

Portrait of the venerable Isis, divine mother. Wearing a blue three part wig and the vulture skin, the goddess also has a headdress adorned with six uraei. North-east wall of the antechamber.

produced in homage to the dead prince by the craftsmen who worked on the construction of his eternal residence. From Deir el-Medina, comes another incomplete stela on which he is seen in the company of one of his brothers, but the name of this latter has unfortunately been lost.

In tomb QV 55 the decoration features only Amenherkhepshef and his father, even though one of the inscriptions tells us that it was produced at the request of Rameses III for "the great royal children." This could mean that the tomb was also used for other princes (which however was not the case). Inside the final chamber, a sarcophagus that was initially to be placed in the pit of the burial room, remained unfinished. Prepared for the prince, in the end it was abandoned. From recent research, in fact, we have learned that Amenherkhepshef was never buried in *Ta Set Neferu*, as another sarcophagus, originally sculpted for Queen Tausert, then removed and altered for this son of Rameses III, was discovered in the tomb of the chancellor Bay (KV 13). The change of place for the funeral of Amenherkhepshef remains unexplained, unless it was the case that the social disturbances that were already rife in the Theban necropolis towards the end of the reign of Rameses III were the reasons. At this time, in fact, we know that the craftsmen of *Set Maat* were demonstrating in the Valley of the Queens and that, with a view to finding a solution to the crisis the vizier had to go in person to the sites where the strikes were taking place.

318 bottom right
Adorned with the winged disc of the sun, the lintel of the door leading to the chamber (F) represents the goddesses Wadjet and Nekhbet who, in the form of cobras, protect the royal cartouches. In the background, the unfinished prince's sarcophagus. This was originally located in the symbolic pit of rebirth (today filled in) of the room (D).

319 bottom
Hathor, "Sovereign of the West," receives Rameses III and prince Amenherkhepshef. By way of welcome, the goddess wishes the king "an eternity of jubilees and an eternity of life and strength." South-west wall of the antechamber (B).

320 top
Behet-*fan made up of painted ostrich feathers. This superb object was generally used by senior officials who occupied the honorary role of "fan bearer to the right of the king." Princes Amenherkhepshef and Khaemwaset were themselves holders of this position.*

THE TOMB OF
KHAEMWASET

by Christian Leblanc

320 bottom
The guardian of the eleventh gate of the Domain of Osiris, Pefesakhuef, "The one who inflames his brazier." Tomb QV 44. Sarcophagus room (E), north wall.

320-321
Rameses III accompanied by Prince Khaemwaset, who had among his most important roles that of priest of Ptah in Memphis. One of the oldest sons of the king, he was the issue of the same maternal line as that of his younger brother Amenherkhepshef. Here, his father presents him to divinities from the Other World, including the god Shu-Ra, on whose wig an ostrich feather is attached, the ideogram of his name. North wall of the antechamber (B).

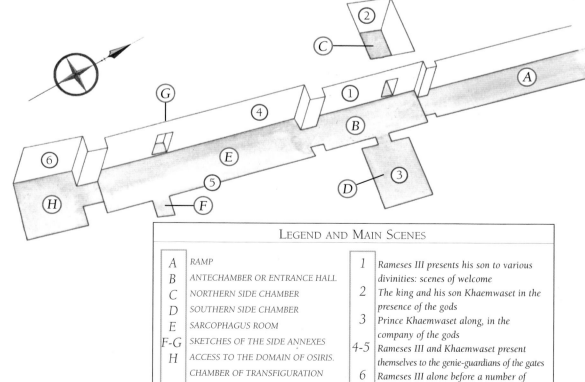

Fan-bearer to the right of the king and *sem*-priest are the two titles of Khaemwaset, another son of Rameses III, in the relief in the temple of Medinet Habu. For this prince, tomb QV 44 was prepared in the Valley of the Queens, and here, on at least two walls, we learn that he was also the eldest son, therefore presumably heir to the crown. This information is important, as it brings to light the fact that he was born of a great royal wife, rather than the presumed mothers of the princes Sethherkhepshef and Pareherunemef. According to the latest studies on the family of Rameses III, it was Queen Tyti who was the mother of Khaemwaset.

At one point in the reign, he performed the prestigious role of high priest of Ptah in Memphis, but we have to abandon the idea that he was buried in the religious

LEGEND AND MAIN SCENES

A	RAMP	1	Rameses III presents his son to various divinities: scenes of welcome
B	ANTECHAMBER OR ENTRANCE HALL	2	The king and his son Khaemwaset in the presence of the gods
C	NORTHERN SIDE CHAMBER		
D	SOUTHERN SIDE CHAMBER	3	Prince Khaemwaset along, in the company of the gods
E	SARCOPHAGUS ROOM		
F-G	SKETCHES OF THE SIDE ANNEXES	4-5	Rameses III and Khaemwaset present themselves to the genie-guardians of the gates
H	ACCESS TO THE DOMAIN OF OSIRIS.		
	CHAMBER OF TRANSFIGURATION	6	Rameses III alone before a number of divinities
	AND REBIRTH		

The Tomb of Khaemwaset

322 top

Heir to his father Osiris, the god Harsaisis, "Horus, Son of Isis," is shown in falcon-headed form, wearing the atef-crown. Behind him, Rameses III makes a gesture of adoration. South wall of the room (H).

322 bottom

The knife-wielding genie Nebneryu ("Lord of Fear"), shown with the head of a lion. His role is to protect the emergence into day of Prince Khaemwaset, who takes on the form of the young genie Herymaat, ("He who rules over harmony"), shown naked. East wall, northern half of the room (H).

322-323

At the back of the room (H), Osiris with green skin, on two sides, faces Neith (left) and Nephthys (right). Emerging from a blue lotus flower, coming to life on the feet of the god and climbing up his legs are four small figures representing the sons of Horus (Imsety, Duamutef, Qebhsenuef and Hapy).

the earth to receive the sarcophagi that we find in several tombs.

This cavity also exists in the tomb of Khaemwaset, but it has been filled in since it was discovered.

Finally, it is in the room that extends the burial chamber that the prince appears to be regenerated. Assimilated to Osiris with the green skin, that is, "He Who Triumphs over Darkness," Khaemwaset, transfigured, emerges into day, guided by the stars painted on the ceiling and directed towards the religious east, with which he merges.

capital of the north, where no evidence of a burial in his name has been found. The cover of a princely sarcophagus discovered earlier in tomb QV 44 by the Italian mission from the Egyptian Museum in Turin appears to confirm that Khaemwaset was buried in *Ta Set Neferu*.

Without doubt he was buried during the reign of Rameses IV as there is an inscription to this pharaoh around the monument.

In the prince's tomb, Khaemwaset, preceded by his father declared glorified (*maa-kheru*), we enter the underworld from the entrance hall. In two annexes to the side of this room the dead prince is shown alone among the gods. In the places where Rameses III does not appear, the transformations of death are already in operation. As in the tomb of Nefertari, the "golden room" symbolizes above all the outposts of the Domain of Osiris. Formidable hybrid genies armed with knives guard the gates, as in the theme of Chapters 145 and 146 of the *Book of the Dead*. On the southern wall, the king presents his son to Sekhenur ("The Great Tightener"), My ("The Cat"), Saupen ("The Protector") and "He Who Imposes Abasement, Who Provokes Weakness and Emerges as Death" (*Di-kesu-uden-bega-per-*

em-mut). On the opposite wall, other figures such as Dendeni ("The Furious"), Pefesakhuef ("He Who Inflames His Brazier"), Hedjiaua and Nehes-her-per-em-duat ("Vigilant Face Emerging from Duat") open the way to the prince, who timidly moves forward towards the last stage in his nocturnal journey. This is the place of gestation, reminiscent of the large pit dug out of

323 bottom left
Rameses III offers jars of wine to the ibis headed Thoth. As reward for this gift, the god promises him "a life as long (as that of) Ra and as many years (as those) of Atum, Lord of the Two Lands, in Heliopolis." South wall of the room (H).

323 right
Anubis and a lion at rest watch over the prince's tomb reproduced on one side of the chapel with grooved cornice and a door. East wall, south side of the room (H).

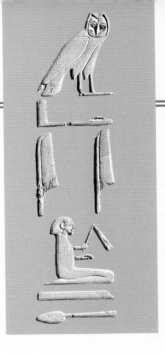

THE TOMBS
OF THE
NOBLES

Deir el-Medina a Village of Craftsmen at the Heart of the Theban Necropolis

by Mohamed A. el-Bialy

324

The animated udjat-eye, holding a lamp from which two flaming streaks emerge. This protective symbol shows Pashedu, kneeling in a pose of adoration. The background shows images of the sacred western mountain. Deir el-Medina. Tomb of Pashedu (TT 3).

325

Procession of bearers of offerings in the tomb of Menna (necropolis of Sheikh Abd el-Qurna, TT 69). The first of these figures grasps the wings of a number of ducks while his companions bear two fishes from the Nile, lotus flowers and bunches of grapes.

326-327

View of the village and necropolis of Deir el-Medina. The houses, grouped within a surrounding wall, are divided into two sections by a main road. Between the temple of Hathor-Maat and the residential area are the ruins of a number of cult shrines, while further to the north a crater marks the location of a well dug during the New Kingdom.

327 bottom

Detail from the tomb of Sennedjem (TT 1).

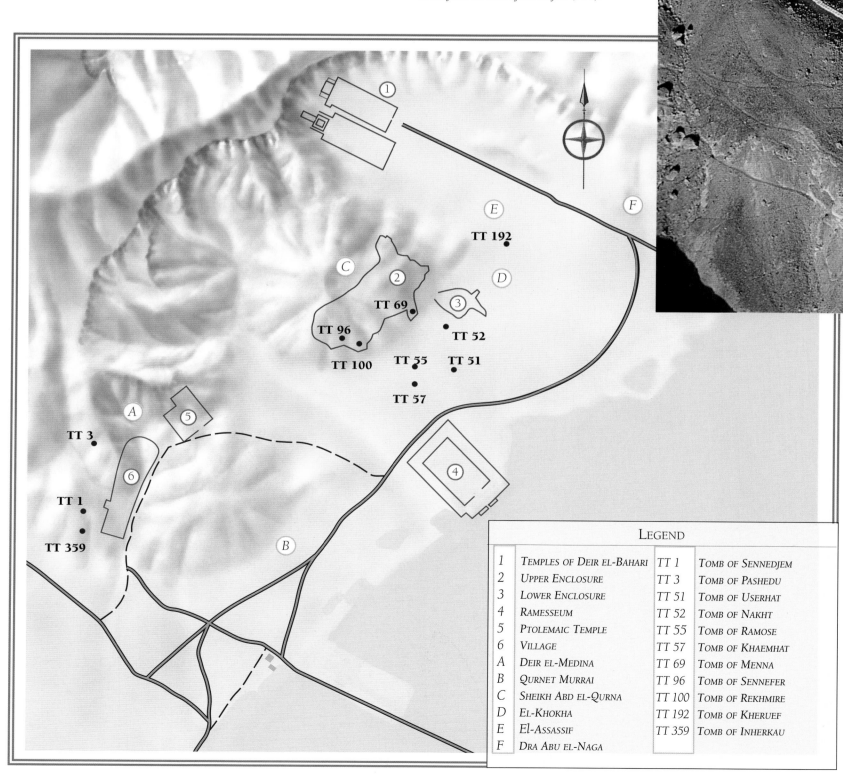

LEGEND			
1	TEMPLES OF DEIR EL-BAHARI	TT 1	TOMB OF SENNEDJEM
2	UPPER ENCLOSURE	TT 3	TOMB OF PASHEDU
3	LOWER ENCLOSURE	TT 51	TOMB OF USERHAT
4	RAMESSEUM	TT 52	TOMB OF NAKHT
5	PTOLEMAIC TEMPLE	TT 55	TOMB OF RAMOSE
6	VILLAGE	TT 57	TOMB OF KHAEMHAT
A	DEIR EL-MEDINA	TT 69	TOMB OF MENNA
B	QURNET MURRAI	TT 96	TOMB OF SENNEFER
C	SHEIKH ABD EL-QURNA	TT 100	TOMB OF REKHMIRE
D	EL-KHOKHA	TT 192	TOMB OF KHERUEF
E	EL-ASSASSIF	TT 359	TOMB OF INHERKAU
F	DRA ABU EL-NAGA		

CRADLED IN A LITTLE VALLEY, BETWEEN the imposing heights of the Theban mountains and the hills of Qurnet Murrai, the village of Deir el-Medina owes its current name to a small monastery founded there, not far from the Ptolemaic temple dedicated to Hathor-Maat. The site, dominated by the famous peak at whose foothills the pharaohs of the New Kingdom were buried, is known to have housed a community of workmen involved in the construction of the royal tombs. In ancient times, it was known as *Ta Set Maat* or The Place of Truth although some texts refer to it under other names: *Pa-Kher* (The Tomb), *Pa-Demi* (The Town), *Set-Aat* (The Large Square), and even "The marvellous Place of the powerful King" according to 18th-Dynasty accounts.

THE VILLAGE

Founded at the beginning of the New Kingdom, the village was a fully-fledged official institution placed under the authority of the vizier, and almost certainly dates back to king Amenhotep I, as suggested by the special cult to him and his mother Ahmose-Nefertari, practised by the inhabitants of *Set Maat*. In fact, up to the end of Ramesside period, both of them were considered the patrons of the community and were depicted in the decorations in the village burial ground as divinities venerated under specific aspects. Statues of Amenhotep of the Village and of his mother, the Lady of the Village, were carried in procession during popular and official festivals. At least one sanctuary was dedicated to them, staffed mainly by *wab* priests.

While similar villages no doubt existed close to royal construction sites since the Old Kingdom, the settlement at Deir el-Medina is not only the best preserved but also the most renowned, thanks mainly to the wealth of information about its functioning and development over time, uncovered during excavations, especially by B. Bruyère, between 1922 and 1951. Although recent research conducted on the Giza plateau has revealed a complex housing workers who helped construct the pyramids and a nearby burial ground; at Faiyum, another village, also dating back to the Middle Kingdom was founded at the el-Lahun site; a town set up by Akhenaten at Tell el-Amarna included a whole town district for royal craftsmen; but most of these urban settlements, built in mud brick, did not survive the ravages of time and pillage, and are today nothing more than desolate ruins, if not totally razed to the ground as at Akhetaten.

Scholars have no clue as to the size of *Set Maat* at the time it was founded by Amenhotep I,

since the earliest limits of the settlement date to the reign of Thutmosis I who built a wall around the village using bricks bearing his seal. Under the reign of the general-pharaoh Horemheb, the settlement was extended to the south and west. It covered 5,600 square meters (61,000 square feet) in this phase, but it was expanded even further by Rameses II, who added several residential units and cult chapels. In its final stage, the village was reduced to fewer than 70 houses, built in staggered stones and unbaked mud brick. The rather fragile building materials, most probably used in the beginning, were gradually replaced by more stable stone structures capable of resisting the torrential rains. A large number of inscriptions in fact refer to often devastating floods. For instance, under Ahmose I, a violent storm hit the region and destroyed a royal necropolis at Dra Abu el-Naga, probably housing the tombs of the kings of the 17th Dynasty. This event, perceived at the time as a fully-fledged disaster, is recorded on a stela found in the temple of Karnak.

Enclosed by a defensive wall with guarded gates, the village of Deir el-Medina seems a distant forebear of medieval fortified cities, albeit on a much smaller scale. Within the walls, the houses, built side by side along the main street and smaller side streets, feature a mean surface area of about 70 square meters (755 square feet) and an almost identical ground plan. Houses were made up of three or four rooms, with a terrace or a basement in certain cases, and typically included an entrance room with a large structure in brick against the rear wall accessible by a small staircase. This room may have served a dual purpose, as a bedroom by night and the family chapel by day, especially since it housed the family's commemorative stelae and even the busts of ancestors. The kitchen, open to the sky, was fitted with various amenities including dough troughs and basins, although few families seemed to have possessed an oven for bread, the basic staple at the time. While there may have been ovens that have now disappeared, it is far more

probable that the large number of breads, flat cakes and cakes were baked directly in temple kitchens and then distributed to the craftsmen, together with other commodities and products, as part of their salary in kind.

Water was supposed to be provided from a very deep well dug outside the walls to the north, but the well was never completed and some other means was used to keep the village supplied with water, probably using donkeys in a system that still used today to supply the Qurna settlements on the slopes of the Theban mountains. Used as a landfill, the well of *Set Maat* was eventually filled with debris that provided archaeologists with a rich treasure of information on the lives and times of the craftsmen living in the village.

The craftsmen of *Sat Maat* owned their homes and also enjoyed a funerary concession for themselves and their families. These boons, that fell under royal privilege, were granted them in exchange for their work at the construction

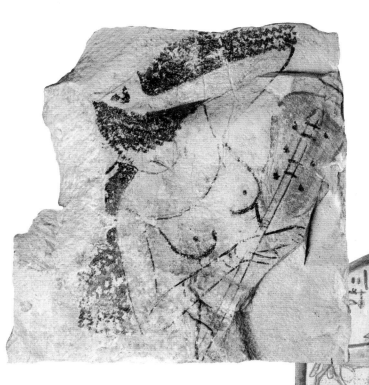

site they were assigned to. Their work consisted exclusively in preparing royal and princely tombs in the two main official necropolises of West Thebes: the Valley of the Kings (*Ta Sekhet Aat*) and the Valley of the Queens (*Ta Set Neferu*).

The village included a tribunal (*kenbet*) that judged disputes between craftsmen, mainly based on alleged dishonesty. More serious offences, such as theft, adultery and murder, were also tried by the village tribunal. Foremen, scribes and craftsmen could be called as witnesses or to serve as jurors, depending on the seriousness of the offences. Sentences and punishments were meted out after consulting the oracle of the deified Amenhotep I.

Nearby constructions include the sanctuaries and chapels devoted to the cult of various divinities including Amen, the Hidden One, Hathor, Amenhotep I and his mother. There were also other buildings dedicated to rituals, such as the chapel used for the rites for the Feast of Opet. Built outside the village walls, these religious monuments lay mainly to the north of the settlement, at the foot of a ridge closing the little valley. To the south west, halfway between the village and the Valley of the Queens, was a rock hewn sanctuary to Ptah, the patron of craftsmen and to Meretseger, She who loves silence, the goddess, often depicted in the form of a cobra, placed in charge of protecting the necropolis at Thebes.

THE PEOPLE

The inhabitants of the village were free and surviving census records show that the settlement was not heavily populated. Census lists that only took men into account suggest, for instance, that 48 craftsmen lived in the village at the beginning of the reign of Rameses II. This number fell to 40 under Rameses III, then reached 120 in the time of Rameses IV.

Curiously, the craftsmen were all placed under the heading of "those who answer the call," a term that is sometimes translated as the "auditors (of the Tomb)." They made up a sort of "crew" that was divided into two halves; the right side and the left side. While B. Bruyère once suggested that this division was made on the basis of the two large royal construction sites, with one of the teams working in the Valley of the Kings and the other in the Valley of the Queens, greater credence is now given to another idea put forward by Christian Leblanc, who noted that two texts inscribed on the pillars of two benches in the tomb of Nefertari mention that a consignment of plaster had to be equally divided between the two sides of the work team.

According to their training, the craftsmen were stone cutters, plasterers, draftsmen, sculptors or color-painters. Other trades included carpenters, goldsmiths and craftsmen specializing in funerary equipment. Their work consisted in digging and decorating

the tombs in the royal and princely necropolises. These men were placed under the authority of two foremen, one for the right side and the other for the left, who were also treated as elders within the community. These foremen acted as liaison officers between the village inhabitants and higher authorities, especially the vizier and the Director of the Treasury. Together with scribes and the delegates, they were in charge of local administration, warehouse management and the distribution of material and salaries. Although the post was not strictly hereditary, foremen were often succeeded by their sons.

The craftsmen received their pay every ten days. This salary in kind, paid through the royal treasury and local temples, consisted of several commodities: wheat, barley, leavened and flat bread, vegetables, fruit, firewood. Depending on the circumstances, these basic commodities were sometimes augmented by wine, honey, milk, fish, meat, even clothing. The Strike Papyrus of Turin, a document dating from the reign of Rameses III, tells of some of the difficulties that the craftsmen living in *Set Maat* had to face. The men working on the sites went on strike and took to the streets at the doors of the temples to demand outstanding wages. The papyrus gives the impression that some of the men already played a role as social leaders in the labor conflict, defending the interests of the community. At one point, a craftsman by the name of Nakhtamen, calls his companions to

strike with the words: "It has been twenty days since the beginning of the month and we have not yet received our rations!" All the men then follow him to protest in front of the warehouse of the temple of Horemheb where they finally receive their salaries, including 46 sacks of wheat.

Women were entrusted with a variety of mainly domestic tasks. Their role included seeing to the education of children. Certain wealthy families employed maids. The community had no school, but there must have been some sort of apprenticeship through which at least the more talented children were taught the basic rudiments of art, allowing them to aspire later to follow in their fathers footsteps later.

Besides the population that lived within the walls of the village, there were also people living outside the community. These outsiders maintained close relationships with the inhabitants of *Set Maat*. Guards were placed at outposts to ensure the security of the inhabitants. Blacksmiths set up workshops close to the village and fashioned or repaired the tools used by the work teams. Cobblers as well as the local physician also lived outside the village. Lastly, unskilled laborers were a specific category of workman and were employed for more or less long periods, following the needs of the work sites: they worked as water carriers or removed rubble and debris when tombs were dug.

Unskilled labor was also used for the supervision of the lighting of the worksites and in the preparation of plaster for walls. These laborers may also have been hired for various jobs within the community itself.

Work days were followed by leave for rest and feasts. These periods of celebration were shared by all the inhabitants of the village. Besides the main religious events such as the Feast of Opet or the Beautiful Feast of the Valley, the craftsmen of the village also joined in other regional or local festivities such as the feast days dedicated to Hathor, Renenutet or Bastet. Periods of leave were also used to prepare the craftsmen's own eternal abodes in the necropolis adjacent to the village.

330 and 331
Tomb of Rekhmire (TT 100). A high ranking functionary of Thutmosis III who acted as mayor and vizier, Rekhmire had a magnificent burial shrine built in the necropolis of Sheikh Abd el-Qurna. On one of the walls, are the different work activities, in the form of a satire of crafts.

Sculptors, tailors, brick makers and carpenters are shown engaging in their crafts. The carpenters were a particularly sought after corporation. There were those who produced the door frames and doors of houses and tombs, but their skills were mainly used in the preparation of part of the burial goods. Coffins,

beds, tables, statues, amulets, caskets and shrines were some of the items produced in their workshops. This profession was also made use of by the specialists, such as the gilders, who applied gold leaf to the most precious items of furniture, or the scribes and engravers, who sculpted the sacred formulae in the material.

332 top

Tomb of Pashedu (TT 3). A figure living during the reign of Rameses II, Pashedu also had a fine tomb built in

Deir el-Medina. In one of its rooms, the deceased, accompanied by his very young daughter, presents himself in adoration before the god Ra-Horakhty.

332 bottom

Tomb of Sennedjem (TT 1). In Egypt, the sun god appeared in different forms. He could be depicted as a falcon-headed figure, as the sun itself or as a ram-headed figure,

holding a stick. This latter image was that of the setting sun. The white-skinned calf with black spots in the burial chamber of Sennedjem is an image of the sun re-emerging at dawn.

THE NECROPOLIS OF DEIR EL-MEDINA

"Embellish your eternal abode! Enrich your place in the West!" such was the wise counsel that the ancient Egyptians heeded to ensure the dignity of their continuing life after death. At Deir el-Medina, at the end of the valley, on the heights that overlook the village, one finds the tombs of Sennedjem (TT 1), the foreman Inerkhau (TT 299 and TT 359) and of Pashedu (TT 3), Nakhtamen (TT 218) and the sculptor Ipuy (TT 217), all artists of the Ramesside period, famous for their beautiful, picturesque decorations.

These tombs were generally divided into two parts: the burial chamber and the funerary chapel. In the beginning these were personal tombs that were gradually extended to receive the remains of other family members. This is why they sometimes cover several levels. The underground chamber was decorated with motifs taken from the *Book of the Dead*, but side by side with very conventional scenes, one also finds paintings featuring great expressive freedom, depicting the family of the deceased. The compositions are mainly polychromatic although in some tombs a monochromatic decoration prevails, with yellow and black dominating both characters and text. The tombs of Nebenmaat (TT 219) and Nakhtamen (TT 335) bear splendid witness to this.

The chapel was generally walled in and crowned with small pyramid. Access was through the door of a narrow pylon that opened on to a courtyard, with a stele or an altar for the funerary cult at the back. It was here that the deceased's family and friends gathered for commemorative ceremonies.

THE NECROPOLIS OF QURNET MURRAI

Located to the east of Deir el-Medina, this New Kingdom necropolis includes tombs dating to the 18th, 19th and 20th Dynasties. It was reserved mainly for royal officers, some of whom held high positions at the court.

Large areas of this part of the Theban mountain are as yet unexcavated although recent research has uncovered the tomb of an anonymous personage whose son, Nedjem was a ritual-priest in the service of the funerary domain of a certain Seneb, a so-far unknown royal son of Thutmosis II. Nothing remains of the funerary chapel but the burial chamber bears witness to rich wall decorations featuring, especially, a representation of the descendents of the deceased and his wife who is described as Singer of Hathor and Mistress of

332-333

*Tomb of Inherkhau (TT 359). In the
necropolis of Deir el-Medina, the
burial chamber of the servant
Inherkhau, overseer at the time of
Rameses III-Rameses IV, is undoubtedly
one of the most beautiful, due to the*

*refinement of its decoration. Here the
deceased, in a superb white linen
costume, performs an act of adoration
before the Souls of Pe, a mythical
town in Lower Egypt. The three genies
shown kneeling are incarnations of
Horus, Imsety and Hapy.*

the House. Other tombs have been
uncovered in this cemetery, such as the
unfortunately heavily damaged eternal abode
of the wise Amenhotep, son of Hapu, the
famous Overseer of works in the service of
Amenhotep III. This foreman who was raised
to the rank of vizier was honored, upon his
death, by a cult temple built a little to the
south west of the Amenophium, the mortuary
temple of Amenhotep III. It is also on this
part of the hill that one finds the tomb of
Huy (TT 40), royal son of Kush
and superintendent of the
southern provinces during the
reigns of Amenhotep IV and
Tutankhamen. Close by lie the
tombs of Amenemheb, Shepherd
of the Domain of Amen-Ra (TT
278) and a certain Imeneminet,
a lector-priest (TT 277).

333 bottom left

*Tomb of Neferrenpet known as Kenro
(TT 178). In the necropolis of
El-Khokha, Neferrenpet, scribe of the
Treasure in the Domain of Amen at the
time of Rameses II, had his tomb
prepared, and superbly decorated.
Among the sacred themes, we see the
dead functionary in adoration before
Osiris and Isis (divinities incarnating
the terrestrial world) and Ra-Horakhty
and Maat (divinities personifying the
celestial world).*

333 bottom right

*Tomb of Ipuy (TT 217). Sculptor at the
time of Rameses II, Ipuy was buried in
the necropolis of Deir el-Medina. His
burial chamber contains finely colored
scenes. The everyday and working life of
the deceased make up the main themes,
together with those showing his journey
towards eternal life.*

THE NECROPOLIS OF SHEIKH ABD EL-QURNA

This is the largest part of the Theban necropolis, bordered to the south by the cemetery of Qurnet Murrai and to the north by a few hills beyond which lies the Deir el-Bahari embayment. Dominated by the mausoleum of a Muslim saint, and marked by a scattering of Qurnawi dwellings set up on the hill several decades ago, this large hilly area features several hundred civil tombs, mainly dating to the 18th Dynasty, built on the upper reaches and in the piedmont plain of the mountain.

These more or less large tombs include a chapel-vestibule or an open air courtyard and an end room perpendicular to the first. In most cases, the burial chamber is never decorated at the beginning of the New Kingdom. Prepared for court officials, these tombs belonged to viziers, governors, mayors, administrators and other noble dignitaries. They also served as the eternal abodes of high-ranking military officers, such as lieutenants and troop commanders, as well as staff attached to the powerful clergy of Amen at Karnak. Priests and officiants, directors of the agricultural domains of the god,

superintendents and scribes of the economic offices of the great temple also enjoyed the benefit of a tomb to the west of Thebes. The oldest is undoubtedly the tomb of Anetfoker (TT 60) a vizier of Sesostris I. Middle Kingdom tombs, however, are rare at Sheikh Abd el-Qurna, although excavations currently undertaken at the extremity north of the Ramesseum by a French team of the CNRS research institute are shedding more light on this period. Several New Kingdom 18th-Dynasty tombs, decorated with painted plaster merit special attention, such as the tombs of Ineni, architect to Thutmosis I (TT 81), Rekhmire, vizier and governor under Thutmosis III and his son Amenhotep II (TT 100), Menna, land registrar during the reign of Thutmosis IV (TT 69) as well as Nakht, who, during the same period, served as an astronomer at temple of Amen (TT 52). However, the most splendid example of private pictorial art is most certainly the burial chamber of Sennefer, who under Amenhotep II served as mayor of Thebes, with its renowned ceiling decorated with vines and elegantly painted pillars and walls (TT 96). Some of these tombs feature highly delicate relief decorations. The most beautiful are

without doubt the tombs of Khaemhat (TT 57) who served as agriculture minister to Amenhotep III, Benia child of the *kap*, but also director of works (TT 343), Ramose (TT 55), vizier to Amenhotep IV. Although Ramose's tomb remained incomplete after he accompanied the pharaoh to his new city, it is still quite large and includes a hypostyle hall with fasciculated floral columns.

The site features several interesting Ramesside tombs, especially the tombs of functionaries of Seti I and Rameses II: Userhat, first prophet of the royal *ka* of Thutmosis I (TT 51), Nedjemger, director of the gardens of the Ramesseum (TT 348), Nakhtamen, in charge of the altars at the same temple (TT 341) or even Amenwahsu, who served as a scribe in the House of Life at the temple (TT 111).

The most remarkable tombs from the reign of Merenptah, include the tomb of Tchay, scribe of the Master of the Two Lands (TT 23), and from later periods, the tomb of Khonsumes, scribe of the treasury of the domain of Amen (TT 30) as well as that of Ramose (TT 132), a royal scribe who also served as superintendent of the treasury under Taharqa.

334-335

Panorama of the necropolis. In the foreground, the hills of Sheikh Abd el-Qurna and El-Khokha. In the background, in a cliff setting, is the Sublime of Sublimes, the famous temple of millions of years that Queen Hatshepsut had built here, today known as Deir el-Bahari.

335 top

Tomb of Menna (TT 69). Scribe of the fields of the king of the Two Lands, probably during the reign of Thutmosis IV, Menna was the owner of a magnificent tomb built in Sheikh Abd el-Qurna. In the shrine, significant episodes of the working life of this functionary are shown over several registers. We can also see religious scenes like this one,

where Menna, accompanied by his wife and two of his sons, pays homage to Osiris, whose divine image is shown inside the shrine.

335 center

Tomb of Rekhmire (TT 100). Bearers of amphorae containing products from the agricultural estates.

335 bottom left

Tomb of Kheruef (TT 192). The tomb that Kheruef, steward to the great royal wife Tiy, had built in El-Assassif, shows highly refined sculpted decorations. This large tomb is worthy of the prestigious role occupied by its owner. In the shrine are scenes showing the sequences of the royal jubilee. Amenhotep III in all the majesty of his position, his wife and several of their daughters are shown as they perform the rites.

336

Tomb of Kheruef (TT 192).
Two princesses, daughters of
Amenhotep III and Tiy, make
a libation of water during the
ceremonies involved in the royal
jubilee. These young girls,
unfortunately not named, were

sculpted in limestone with an
extraordinary delicacy, as we can
see in particular from the
treatment of the faces and hair.
As with many other tombs, the
tomb of Kheruef remained
unfinished, which explains why
several reliefs were not painted.

337 bottom

Aerial view of the necropolis of
Dra Abu el-Naga, highly extended
and appearing as a particularly
damaged site. Several
archaeological missions have been
working on the clearing and study
of the tombs for some years.

THE NECROPOLISES OF EL-ASSASIF AND EL-KHOKHA

In the plain and on the sides of the hills bordering the group of temples at Deir el-Bahari to the north, lie the necropolises of El-Assasif and El-Khokha, that extend the burial site at Sheikh Abd el-Qurna. The tombs at El-Assasif that are the eternal abode of certain Middle Kingdom, New Kingdom and Saite princes, lie on the lower reaches of the mountain and even extend into the plain. Their main feature is their imposing size. A monumental entrance way, followed by a large staircase, opened on to a courtyard housing a mud brick pylon that provides access to the underground parts. The oldest of these tombs including those of Kheruef, chamberlain to the royal consort Tiy (TT 192) and the scribe Samut, known as Kiki (TT 409) are still clearly identifiable, by their well developed ground plan, as falling within the New Kingdom tradition. The later tombs, on the other hand, feature a much more complex architectural layout. This can be observed in the tombs of Montuemhat (TT 34), fourth prophet of Amen and prince of the city during the reigns of Taharqa and Psamtik I, the tomb of Pabasa (TT 279), grand chamberlain to the Nitocris, God's Wife of Amen, as well as those of Ankh-Hor (TT 414), Aba (TT 36) and Harwa (TT 37), that date from the same period.

To the south east, access to the valley is barred by a small hill: this is the necropolis of El-Khokha that contains magnificent New Kingdom tombs. These include the tombs of Puiemra (TT 39), second prophet of Amen under Thutmosis III, Nebamen and Ipuky (TT 181), sculptors at the court of Amenhotep III and Amenhotep IV as well as the tomb of Neferrenpet known as Kenro (TT 178), scribe of the treasury of the domains of Amen-Ra under Rameses II, all of which still bear exceptional mural depictions of the day-to-day and professional lives of their illustrious owners.

THE NECROPOLIS OF DRA ABU EL-NAGA

Beyond the temple of Hatshepsut, towards the north, extending for about one kilometer (mile) into the foothills of the Libyan mountain chain, lies the necropolis of Dra Abu el-Naga featuring, most importantly the tombs of the 17th-Dynasty kings and princes, all of which are no longer accessible today. This burial site also houses several New Kingdom tombs, including that of Tetiky (TT 15), son of Ahmose, the first pharaoh of the 18th Dynasty. Although the necropolis was devastated by a violent storm during this period, necessitating restoration works on several damaged tombs, the site was not abandoned. Under the reigns of

Hatshepsut, Thutmosis III, Amenhotep II and Thutmosis IV, several royal functionaries had their tombs located here, including Tauty (TT 154), Nebamen (TT 17), Antef (TT 155), Djehuty (TT 11), Neferrenpet (TT 140), User (TT 260), Nehemauy (TT 165). During the Ramesside period, the burial site continued to be used, and the underground burial chambers of Shuroy (TT 13), Ramose (TT 166), Amenmes (TT 19), Panehesy (TT 16), Raya (TT 159), and Tjanefer (TT 158) date from this period. But Dra Abu el-Naga was also the site of one of the oldest private tombs in West Thebes: the tomb of a royal scribe of Sesostris I, Ruy (TT 255). This tomb was visited by J.-F. Champollion, during his expedition to Thebes in 1829.

THE NECROPOLIS OF EL-TARIF

El-Tarif is the name given to the northernmost and oldest of the necropolises of West Thebes. Located not far from the temple of Seti I, the necropolis is accessed by a turn-off northwards from the road. Today, the area is mostly taken up by houses that mask the main tombs. This sector, previously prospected by W. Flinders Petrie and more recently excavated by D. Arnold, was identified as the burial site of a line of 11th-Dynasty kings. A large tomb known as

Saff el-Dauaba is believed to be the eternal abode of Antef I, and the two tombs close by have been reserved for his successors. However, this attribution has never been confirmed by documents and C. Vandersleyen suggests that the first of these tombs was prepared for Mentuhotep I.

Later, during the New Kingdom, the necropolis was extended but lost its royal character, and was transformed into a public cemetery serving commoners in Thebes. In 1987, excavations undertaken by the Supreme Council of Antiquities of Egypt uncovered rectangular pits and even shafts, about two or three meters deep (7 or 10 feet), that communicated with undecorated burial chambers. In this graves, the bodies, reduced to skeletons, were not mummified. On the other hand, small tables with offerings and a large quantity of pottery found close to the burial chambers allowed for the precise dating of these inhumations.

Like all Theban necropoleis, the site of El-Tarif underwent transformations during the Third Intermediate Period. Funerary constructions became increasingly more rare on the West Bank, and public cemeteries gradually extended into the foothills and even into the main plain, where the Temples of Millions of Years are located. Large numbers of Middle and New Kingdom tombs were refurbished and re-used during this period.

338-339

Tomb of Ramose (TT 55). Governor of the town and vizier during the reign of Amenhotep IV, Ramose had a veritable palace of eternity built at the foot of the hills of Sheikh Abd el-Qurna. The beauty of the reliefs is thrilling,

as we can see from this detail in which the sculptor, showing exceptional talent, has given life to the faces. After leaving Thebes to follow his king to Tell el-Amarna, Ramose abandoned this tomb, which in the end remained unfinished.

The highly decorated outer coffin of Sennedjem vividly shows him in human form wearing an elaborate wig and jewelry, rather than the standardized Osiride form of other Egyptian coffins. This style is unique for the period and other coffins from the same cache show individuals dressed in normal human costume.

The Tomb of
Sennedjem

by Morris L. Bierbrier

It is extremely rare in the history of Egyptian archaeology for a tomb to be discovered intact with the bodies of the deceased and their grave goods undisturbed. The tomb of Tutankhamen is one such famous example. At Deir el-Medina the undecorated tomb of Kha from the 18th Dynasty was found unrobbed by Italian archaeologists, and its contents are now displayed in the Museo Egizio at Turin. The tomb of Sennedjem and its contents also survived unpillaged by ancient robbers but not by modern ones.

The most visible signs of the flourishing character of the community of Deir el-Medina during the 19th Dynasty are

340-341

Sennedjem and his wife Iineferti are depicted plowing, sowing, and reaping their crops in the Fields of Iaru, the Egyptian version of Paradise. The trees are heavily laden with a rich harvest to sustain them. The Egyptians believed that life in the Afterworld would be similar to that lived on earth.

341 bottom

The udjat-eye of Horus was regarded by the Egyptians as a symbol of good luck and protection. According to legend, it was ripped from the god during his struggle with the evil god Seth and replaced by the sun god Ra.

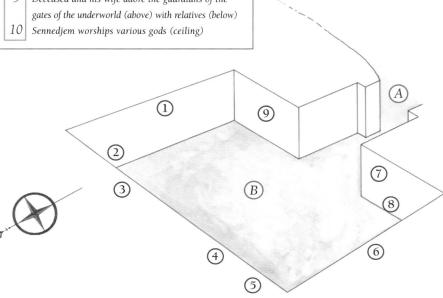

342

The tomb of Sennedjem was sealed by a great wooden door. One side (right) shows Sennedjem and his relations worshipping Osiris and Maat (upper) and Ptah-Sokar-Osiris and Isis (lower). On the reverse the deceased and his wife enjoy a game of senet before a pile of offerings.

342-343

The vaulted underground burial chamber of Sennedjem would have originally been filled with his burial equipment. The far wall shows the deceased and his wife adoring various deities. On either side, paintings depict the mummified corpse of the tomb owner, in one case being tended by Anubis, the god of mummification.

343 bottom
A son of Sennedjem performs the
Opening the Mouth ritual on the
mummified body of his father.

This ceremony was undertaken prior
to burial so the body would be
magically revived and serve as a
home for the spirit of the deceased.

344-345

Another view of the burial chamber shows the full view of Sennedjem in paradise at one end. Above the scene, baboons worship the sun god Ra in his solar barque. To the left the deceased is escorted by Anubis before piles of offerings.

344 bottom

This highly painted pottery vessel was one of the grave goods retrieved from the intact burial of Sennedjem. Most grave goods were prepared by the workmen themselves and, without precious materials, they often painted dummy jars of wood to resemble works in precious stones such as lapis-lazuli.

345 top

The god Osiris, Lord of the Underworld, in full regalia stands before an altar on which rests a water-pot cooled by lotus blossoms. He is flanked by two udjat-eyes at the top and two sacred fetishes in the lower part of the scene.

the tombs of the workmen which were built on the cliff face opposite the village. Most of the tombs appear to date to the first part of the reign of Rameses II (ca. 1270 BC).

No evidence survives regarding the construction of these tombs, but it must be presumed that they were built by the workmen themselves with materials supplied by the central government.

The plans of the tombs are similar. A mud-brick pylon leads to an enclosed open courtyard which sometimes has within it a large stela depicting the funerary rites. At the opposite end of the court an entry is located to a vaulted chapel which is decorated with wall paintings. The wall surface has been smoothed down, a thin layer of plaster has been applied, and the

surface was then painted. On the outside the chapel was topped by a mud-brick pyramid surmounted by a stone pyramidion dedicated to the sun god Ra-Horakhty. Sometimes a stela dedicated to the same god would be set in the side of the pyramid. A shaft either from the chapel or from the courtyard was cut leading to one or more underground chambers, either directly or reached by a short corridor, which would be decorated in whole or part and would have contained the bodies and goods of the deceased.

The workman Sennedjem must have flourished during the reign of Seti I and the very early part of the reign of Rameses II. He does not appear in the roster of year 40 of Rameses II, in which one of his sons is apparently mentioned.

345 bottom
Dressed in the leopard skin which denotes a priestly rank, a son of the deceased pours a water libation before his seated parents. Beside their chairs stand their young son and daughter shown as children with the side locks of youth.

It would seem that his tomb was built and decorated either at the end of Seti I's reign or very early in that of his successor. A shaft in the courtyard led via a short corridor to the burial chamber. Most of the tombs which were built at this time were destined to serve as family vaults for the descendants of the owner, but that of Sennedjem was only used for a very limited period for the burials of himself, his wife, and 18 other relations. Two of his more prominent sons in the community—Khons and Khabekhnet—built their own tombs, but it appears that they were later reburied in that of their father. His tomb was sealed at some point after year 40 of the reign of Rameses II and remained undetected and unrobbed.

On or about 1 February 1886 the tomb of Sennedjem was discovered at Deir el-Medina with its wooden door still in position. Unfortunately, no detailed account of the excavation was attempted, but notes were taken by a visiting Spaniard Eduardo Toda. Apart from the stunning painted decoration of the tomb chamber, the objects inside gave a vivid picture of the style of burial of a prosperous workman. While many of the objects remain in the Cairo Museum, others were dispersed throughout the world so the visual impact of this marvellous discovery has been lost and only the wall paintings remain to attest the craftsmanship of the workmen of Deir el-Medina.

346 left

This painted wooden statue depicts the workman Sennedjem dressed in his best linen garment. The statue, and most other tomb equipment, were made by the workmen themselves. It could serve as a house for the soul of the deceased if the body perished.

346-347

The wooden outer sarcophagus of Khons, son of Sennedjem, is painted with religious texts and scenes. The goddesses Selkis and Neith are shown on one side. In the centre of the long side the mummy of the deceased is being embalmed by Anubis and protected by the goddesses Isis and Nephthys.

347 bottom

This shawabty figure and coffin are inscribed with prayers on behalf of the workman Sennedjem. Shawabtis were believed to perform any manual labour which their owner was called on to perform in the Afterlife. The design of the one on the left with its white background and red lines is distinctive of Deir el-Medina.

347 top

This beautifully painted shawabty box belonged to the funeral equipment of the workman Khons, son of Sennedjem. Although Khons possessed his own tomb, his burial and those of his wives were presumably removed to that of his father where it was later discovered.

348-349

The painted vault of the underground burial chamber of Sennedjem shows the deceased, sometimes with his wife, worshipping various deities. Prominent in the barque of the sun god Ra-Horakhty is the benu-bird who gave rise to the Greek legend of the Phoenix.

THE TOMB OF
INHERKAU

by Morris L. Bierbrier

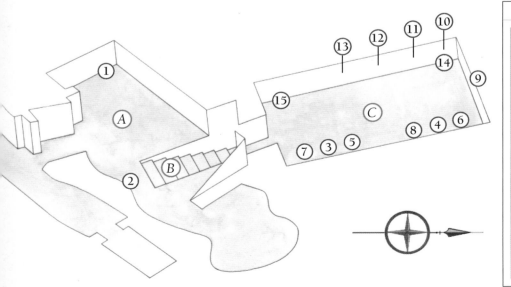

	LEGEND		
A	UPPER CHAMBER	7	The deceased and his family receive offerings from his relatives (lower register)
B	STAIRS	8	The deceased seated before relations, one of whom carries a snake rod (lower register)
C	BURIAL CHAMBER	9	The deceased and a son worship Ptah and Osiris in a double scene (end)
	MAIN SCENES	10	The cat slays the serpent (middle register)
1	Decorated ceiling of upper chamber	11	The deceased worships Horus (middle register)
2	The deceased and his wife offer to deceased kings and queens	12	Anubis and the mummy of the deceased (middle register)
3	The deceased worships a serpent (midle register)	13	The deceased worships the benu-bird (middle register)
4	The deceased worships four jackals (middle register)	14	The deceased and his wife listen to a harpist (lower register)
5	The deceased worships a ba (upper register)	15	Relatives offer libation to the deceased couple (lower register)
6	The deceased adores the horizon (upper register)		

THE MAJORITY OF THE TOMBS AT DEIR el-Medina were built during the early part of the 19th Dynasty. It would appear that only the most wealthy individuals in the community built their own tombs thereafter. The tomb of Inherkau is the sole surviving tomb from the 20th Dynasty (ca. 1140 BC), and its owner could certainly afford its construction since as foreman he was one of the principal men in the village.

The work gang was supervised by two foremen, one for the left side and one for the right side. It would seem that these foremen were first appointed by the vizier, who had overall charge of the workforce, for their ability but gradually the post became hereditary in certain families. The foremen were responsible not only for overseeing the construction work in the Valley of the Kings but also, with the scribe, for the distribution of materials for work and the payment of salaries to the workmen. The payments were made by the central government in kind, notably emmer wheat and barley. The foremen, of course, received a much higher proportion than the ordinary workmen. The foremen were also prominent in the local court which settled internal disputes within the community. Each foreman was assisted by a deputy who was usually a close relation.

350-351

These two scenes are located in the better preserved second burial chamber of the tomb. On the left Inherkau, dressed in his finest clothes and wig, kneels in worship of four jackals, while on the right he stands in adoration of a serpent.

350 bottom

This detail depicts a hawk pearched on the symbol for the West. Since in Egypt most cemeteries were located on the western bank of the Nile, as indeed were those of Deir el-Medina, the West signified the Land of the Dead to the ancient Egyptians.

351 bottom

This charming family group conveys the intimate feeling of some of the scenes from the tombs at Deir el-Medina. Inherkau and his wife receive offerings from two of their sons, while surrounded by four of their grandchildren. The young age of the children is indicated by their nakedness and side locks of youth.

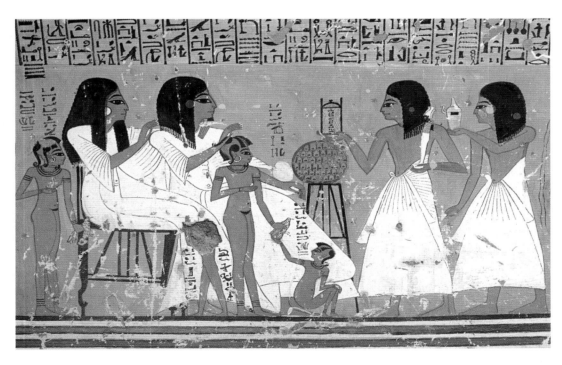

352 top

This view shows the front vaulted chamber of the tomb of Inherkau. This room has been severely damaged and many of the scenes have been hacked off the walls by early antiquities collectors, but enough remains to convey a stunning mural impact.

352 center and bottom

The ceiling of the first chamber of the tomb is not decorated with natural scenes like those in Sennedjem or in the second chamber of the same tomb. Instead the ceiling is composed of different highly-colored patterns of rosettes, spirals intertwined with the names of Inherkau and his wife Wabet, and intricate petal designs. The different patterns are separated by lines of text to set off the variations of design.

The family of Inherkau obtained the position of foreman of the left side early in the reign of Rameses II in the person of his great-grandfather Qaha who was the son of a chief craftsman in the community. His ancestors are known to his great-grandparents. Qaha was in office in the reign of Rameses II showing evidence also that the family was relatively well off then. Qaha had a large house in the village and both he and his son and successor possessed tools. His

grandson Hay held the position of foreman at the end of Dynasty 18 and served until year 21-22 of Ramesses III of Dynasty 20.

Inherkau joined the workforce at the end of the 19th Dynasty as an ordinary workman but not surprisingly was promoted to the rank of deputy to his father by year 17 of Rameses III and succeeded his father five years later. He was certainly in office under Rameses VI and possibly under Rameses VII, thus filling the post of foreman for over thirty years. He was influential enough to ensure that the office passed on to his son although the family may have temporarily lost control of the position in the tomb robbery scandals of the reign of Rameses IX.

Thus Inherkau certainly had the power and means to enable him to build his very impressive tomb with its fine painted wall scenes. Unlike the royal tombs of the Valley of the Kings,

353

This section of the decorated ceiling depicts the heads of cattle topped with a sun disk between yellow spirals. The design has been linked to the bull's heads of Crete of 200 years earlier but may instead be symbolic of the goddess Hathor.

the tombs of the workmen did not restrict the decorations to purely religious scenes and texts. The scenes often depict the funerary rites and associated family wake. There the family, friends and neighbors of the deceased are shown taking part in the funeral or seated as couples with their children. There are also more intimate scenes of family life for which the tomb of Inherkau is a good example. Of course, these scenes were painted during the lifetime of the owner so he was in a position to choose whom he wished at his funeral for all eternity rather than being a historical depiction of what actually took place. Unfortunately, Egyptian terms of relationship can be very vague so it is not always possible to determine whether all the "sons," "brothers," and "sisters" are actually so or more distant relations such as in-laws, uncles, aunts, nephews, and nieces. Thus many of the sons depicted in Inherkau's tomb may not be sons at all.

The tomb of Inherkau is reached via a shaft from his chapel and consists of two underground vaulted chambers, one at a slightly lower level than the other. They were decorated with scenes painted on a yellow background. This color is deliberately meant to suggest that of a papyrus roll. It is presumed that the workmen's grave goods would normally include a papyrus *Book of the Dead*, but in fact only two have ever been recovered from Deir el-Medina. The spells in the *Book of the Dead* would ensure the deceased's entry into the Afterlife, but, in default of a papyrus, the prayers and spells inscribed on the tomb walls might have a similar effect.

The first chamber of the tomb contains a very interesting scene in which the deceased and his wife Wabet offer incense to a row of deceased former kings and queens of Egypt from the 18th to the 20th Dynasty. Similar scenes appear in some

354-355
The superbly decorated second burial chamber of the tomb shows the deceased worshipping various deities in the upper registers or receiving homage from his relations in the lower registers. The design is completed by an intricate colored pattern at the bottom of the walls.

355 top
The deceased and his wife in their finery are seated in front of a harpist who entertains them with his song of praise which is inscribed for all eternity on the wall. It is unlikely that Inherkau could afford to command such a performance in his lifetime.

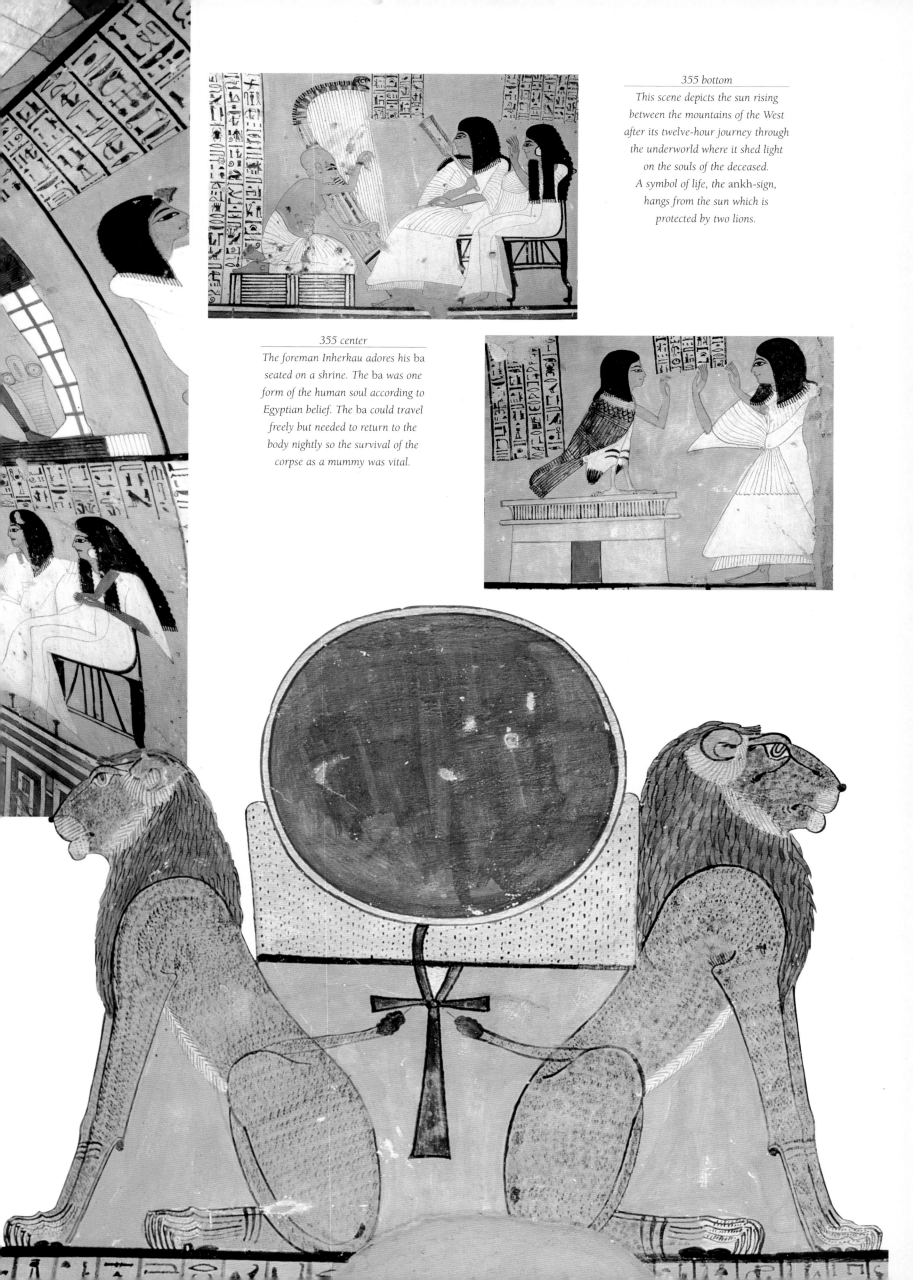

355 bottom
This scene depicts the sun rising
between the mountains of the West
after its twelve-hour journey through
the underworld where it shed light
on the souls of the deceased.
A symbol of life, the ankh-sign,
hangs from the sun which is
protected by two lions.

355 center
The foreman Inherkau adores his ba
seated on a shrine. The ba was one
form of the human soul according to
Egyptian belief. The ba could travel
freely but needed to return to the
body nightly so the survival of the
corpse as a mummy was vital.

356 top left

The tomb-owner Inherkau kneels in adoration of the god Horus in the form of a falcon. The plumage of the hawk and the pedestal on which he stands are delineated in fine detail, showing the skill of the ancient painter.

356 top right

The jackal-headed god Anubis offers a heart to the mummy of the deceased. The heart was believed by the Egyptians to be the seat of all intelligence and was retained in the body after mummification. On the left stands the standard of Osiris, lord of Abydos.

356 bottom

The foreman Inherkau stands before an altar with offerings in worship of the sacred benu-bird of Heliopolis. The bird wears the crown of the god Osiris to denote its connection with that god. It was believed to be the ba or spirit of both Osiris and Re.

357

The cat of Heliopolis, who is linked to the sun god Ra, slays the evil serpent Apophis beside a persea tree. In Egyptian mythology, the barque of the sun god was threatened daily as it passed through the underworld by this symbol of chaos which had to be ritually killed.

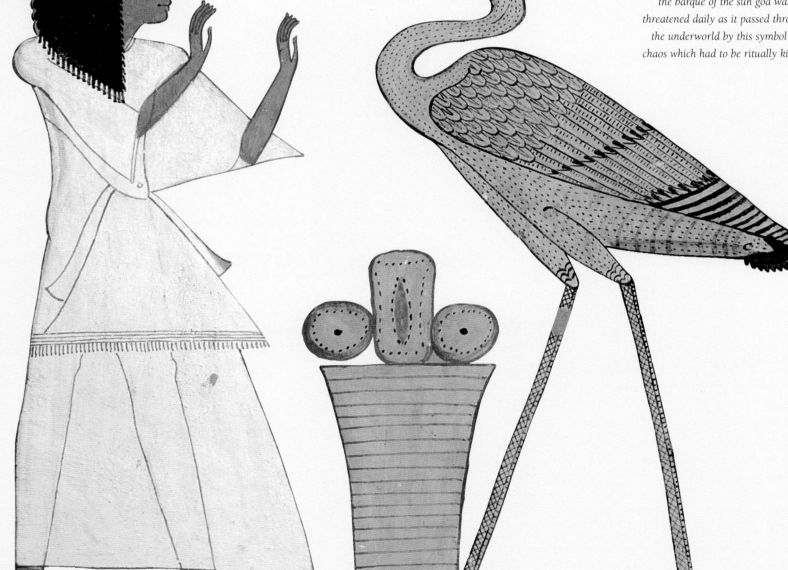

of the Deir el-Medina tombs from the early 19th Dynasty. The workmen seemed to be informed of some very obscure princes and princesses of the early 18th Dynasty, but that knowledge may be based on the cult of Amenhotep I and his mother Queen Ahmose-Nefertari. Thus the workmen's interest in royal history should be seen in a religious context rather than for purely historical interest. Still, the decision to include such scenes may not wholly rule out a sense of attachment to Egypt's past.

The village and tombs of Deir el-Medina were rediscovered about 1815 by clandestine excavators searching for antiquities for visiting travellers. Much of this material ended up in the major European museums such as the Museo Egizio in Turin and the British Museum.

No grave goods have survived from the tomb of Inherkau so it must be presumed that the tomb was robbed in antiquity. It was certainly open to visitors in the early part of the 19th century. Its fine reliefs attracted the attention of collectors, and several scenes, one of which was seen in the tomb in 1842, have been removed. It is indeed fortunate that so much of the tomb was spared to give a vivid impression of the artistic achievements of the Deir el-Medina craftsman in the 20th Dynasty.

358 top

This view of the vaulted burial chamber of the tomb of Pashedu shows the emplacement at the end of the chamber for his limestone sarcophagus which has now been destroyed except for a few fragments. The vault is decorated with rows of seated gods.

358 bottom

The deceased Pashedu and his wife Nedjembehdet are seated before an altar of offerings in a kiosk on board a boat. A young girl, presumably a daughter or granddaughter kneels at their feet. The boat is taking them to the West, the abode of the dead.

359

The vaulted entrance corridor to the main burial chamber is decorated on each side with a jackal seated on a shrine. Above the doorway of the main room a son of Pashedu worships the god Ptah-Sokar-Osiris in the form of a falcon. Three registers of relatives appear on the right.

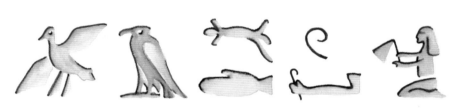

THE TOMB OF
PASHEDU

by Morris L. Bierbrier

THE TOMB OF PASHEDU IS FAMOUS for its brilliantly painted scenes, but little is known of the owner of the tomb apart from the inscriptions on its walls. The tomb is probably dated to the early years of Rameses II so Pashedu would have joined the workforce during the reign of Seti I. His father Menna was a workman for Amen which presumably indicates that he worked for the temple of Amen-Ra at Karnak. Thus Pashedu would have been the first member of his family to work for the community at Deir el-Medina.

The workmen specialized in various tasks during the construction of the tombs at the Valley of the Kings. Pashedu was a stonemason who helped to clear the passage through the limestone cliff. Other workmen were plasterers who smoothed the walls of the tomb, draughtsmen who painted the designs and inscriptions on the walls, and carvers who chiselled out the reliefs which were then painted.

Pashedu appears in his tomb with his wife Nedjembehdet and various sons who are not well attested in the village from other sources. However, a chapel is known of a foreman of the left side

Pashedu and his wife Nedjembehdet so it appears that the workman Pashedu was promoted to one of the two top positions in the community if only briefly. He must have held this position before year 38 of Rameses II when the post was filled by another man. He may have been intending to build a new tomb to reflect his enhanced status or simply settled for a new chapel instead.

A shaft from the courtyard of his original tomb enclosure leads down towards Pashedu's burial chamber. A corridor at the bottom of the shaft connects via a short vaulted gallery to an antechamber. Another short vaulted corridor leads into the richly decorated burial chamber. At one end of the chamber a painted limestone sarcophagus was built into the fabric to hold the remains of the deceased. This unusual feature has

been in only one other tomb at Deir el-Medina. It seems that other burials, like those in Sennedjem, were contained in loose wooden sarcophagi deposited on the floor of the burial chamber.

The tomb of Pashedu was rediscovered in 1834 by a band of Egyptian soldiers who were doubtless hunting for treasure. Most fortunately, the Scottish traveler and artist Robert Hay was in Thebes at the time and saw the tomb shortly after its discovery. It would seem that the tomb was robbed in antiquity as no grave goods are known apart from a possible fragment of a papyrus *Book of the Dead*. This is now in the British Museum but came from Hay's private collection so he may have picked it up on his visit to the tomb. Unfortunately, after the completion of his drawing, the stone sarcophagus was destroyed by antiquities hunters. Hay's drawing and the surviving fragments allow its general appearance to be reconstructed. The colors of the painted walls survive as vividly as the day they were painted.

360
Pashedu kneels down beside a dolm-palm beside a canal to drink the waters. The text, Chapter 12 of the Book of the Dead, *describes how the water will quench the fires of the underworld and so preserve the deceased from harm.*

---
361 top left
The sky goddess Nut emerges from the trunk of a sycamore-fig tree and pours a libation over the kneeling Pashedu whose hands are raised to catch the water.

His wife Nedjembehdet, stands, hands raised in adoration.

---
361 top right
Pashedu and his wife raise their hands in worship of Horus (not shown). His son and a granddaughter stand beside them. Nedjembehdet has a wax perfume cone on her head.

---
361 bottom
This fragment comes from the frieze of the deities which decorates the vault of the main burial chamber.

The goddess Hathor is shown first holding her Hathor-headed sistrum. Behind her sit the sun god Ra-Horakhty and the scorpion goddess Selkis, both holding ankh signs of life.

362-363
This scene depicts Osiris seated on a throne and wearing the royal nemes. A deity raises a burning brazier before him. Behind him lie the mountain of the West, an udjat-eye holding another brazier, and a falcon, while Pashedu kneels in adoration at the bottom.

THE TOMB OF
KHAEMHAT
by Lyla Pinch-Brock

364-365

Khaemhat, also called Mahu, wears a diaphanous tunic, and around his neck a beaded necklace and the shebyu-collar, a mark of esteem. He pours oil on a brazier for an offering of ducks. Khaemhat's tomb is one of the few non-royal sepulchers in the Theban necropolis decorated in relief. Sir Robert Mond, working for the Antiquities Service, tackled the cleaning of the blackened walls in 1903 "...by scrubbing with soap, water and elbow grease." In so doing he also may have inadvertently removed the last vestiges of paint.

The Tomb of Khaemhat

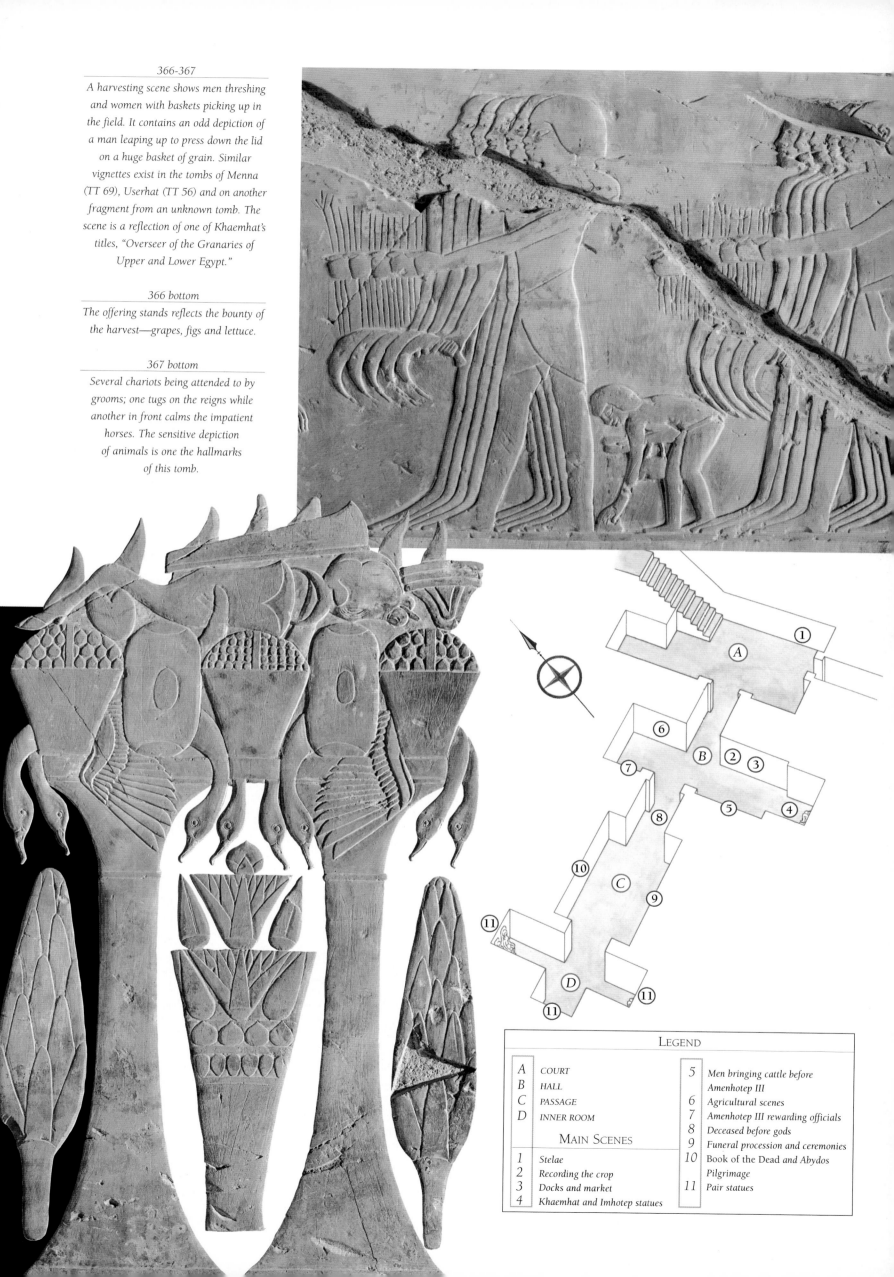

366-367

A harvesting scene shows men threshing and women with baskets picking up in the field. It contains an odd depiction of a man leaping up to press down the lid on a huge basket of grain. Similar vignettes exist in the tombs of Menna (TT 69), Userhat (TT 56) and on another fragment from an unknown tomb. The scene is a reflection of one of Khaemhat's titles, "Overseer of the Granaries of Upper and Lower Egypt."

366 bottom

The offering stands reflects the bounty of the harvest—grapes, figs and lettuce.

367 bottom

Several chariots being attended to by grooms; one tugs on the reigns while another in front calms the impatient horses. The sensitive depiction of animals is one the hallmarks of this tomb.

	LEGEND		
A	COURT	5	Men bringing cattle before
B	HALL		Amenhotep III
C	PASSAGE	6	Agricultural scenes
D	INNER ROOM	7	Amenhotep III rewarding officials
		8	Deceased before gods
	MAIN SCENES	9	Funeral procession and ceremonies
		10	Book of the Dead and Abydos
1	Stelae		Pilgrimage
2	Recording the crop	11	Pair statues
3	Docks and market		
4	Khaemhat and Imhotep statues		

THE TOMB OF KHAEMHAT (TT 57), IS one of a group (TT 126, TT 295, TT 102) clustered around a courtyard in the western end of the Sheikh Abd el-Qurna necropolis. It has been known since its discovery in 1842 by George Lloyd, a traveler, botanist, and amateur archaeologist, who excavated at Thebes with French Egyptologist Prisse d'Avennes. Shortly after making his discovery, Lloyd was killed by the accidental discharging of his gun, providing a rather inauspicious debut for the doomed tomb.

Prior to 1884, the year when Victor Loret, soon to become Director of the French Institute of Archaeology, wrote a description of the tomb, many impressions of the reliefs were made by softening newspaper with water and pressing it onto the wall.

These "squeezes" are probably partly responsible for the present condition of the tomb, which is now almost completely bereft of color, giving it a ghostly appearance. The impressions were given to the Egyptian Museum in Boulak, and in 1886 went to the Boston Museum of Fine Arts. Their subsequent examination by Associate Curator Dows Dunham revealed details missing from Loret's description, and they are now the only evidence we have of some missing texts (most were published by Lepsius). The Boston material includes a squeeze of a head of Khaemhat, taken when the relief was still in the tomb (the original is now in Berlin, replaced by a cast) and a number of copies of scenes and texts.

The decoration was ideal for making

squeezes because it is very fine-quality low relief cut into limestone. TT 57 is one of only four private tombs from the reign of Amenhotep III to be decorated in relief. The others are Ramose, (TT 55); Amenemhet called Surero, (TT 48); and Kheruef, (TT 192). It is also one of the few to include a precise date, Year 30 of Amenhotep III. All of these tombs were apparently cut late in the reign. The time and expense involved in their construction suggests the owners were quite distinguished. As proof of the king's favor, all the tombs have fine depictions of Amenhotep III; only twelve tombs from this period contain such portraits.

TT 57 was planned by Sir Robert Mond, wealthy businessman-chemist and sometime

<table>
<tr>
<td>

368-369

Khaemhat, holding his symbols of office, supervizes the counting of the harvest. In the lower register, an overseer gives the tally to a scribe while the one behind passes on the good news to Khaemhat.

</td>
<td>

369 top

The artist has turned a scene of harvesters separating the grain from the chaff into a graceful pattern of movement.

</td>
<td>

369 bottom

Tillers bend to their task while another man scatters wide the seed he carries in his basket. The hoe became part of the hieroglyphic word "to hoe, cultivate."

</td>
</tr>
</table>

Egyptologist, during his general clean-up of the whole necropolis, done chiefly at his own expense, from 1902 to 1925. He found the tomb "...thoroughly plundered and the contents destroyed by fire, which has blackened the whole interior of the tomb." He cleared away the debris and replaced some fragments of relief found on the floor. In the process some objects came to light, wood and stone *shawabtis*, a *shawabti*-box, a bronze spear-head and a Ptah-Sokar-Osiris figure. In the courtyard he found three rock stelae, one mentioning Khaemhat, and the coffins of Pedamen and Khonsuiuefankh. Indications are that the tomb was occupied with burials up until the Roman Period, and thereafter by hermits who topped off the destruction with their greasy cooking fires.

The plan is a variation on the usual T-shaped one of the period, consisting of a hall and an inner room connected by a passage. Steps from the hall lead to a court.

The tomb contains emplacements for four sets of statues, three in the Inner Room—one for Mahu (Khaemhat's other name) and his wife Tiyi, one for Khaemhat and the Royal Scribe Imhotep, and one for Khaemhat and another woman. At the north end of the Hall is a statue niche for Khaemhat and once again the favored Imhotep. A relief of Tiyi is tucked in between, almost as an afterthought.

The tomb has a sub-structure as well as a superstructure; a shallow set of steps leads from a short passage off the inner room into a sloping tunnel that circles clockwise. Halfway down is a set of small rooms, and, at the bottom, a larger room and an antechamber. The latter was probably for the burial of the owner, and the former for his funerary equipment. Almost none of this was found; the burial may have been rifled in antiquity.

Of Khaemhat's two titles, "Overseer of the Granaries," was probably the most important. Harvest scenes are rare in Egyptian tombs, yet two out of five scenes (in tombs TT 120 and TT 48) were painted during the latter part of Amenhotep III"s reign. Arielle Kozloff has suggested this might have marked a special harvest festival, perhaps taking place in Karnak Temple. Although there is no such scene in TT 57, the measuring of crops and the recording of grain, and the deceased inspecting men measuring the crop appear.

Khaemhat's other title, "Royal Scribe," was

inscribed on a statue of Mahu and also on a small fragment of a diorite statue of Khaemhat found by Mond during his clearance. Yet since "scribes" could also take on the roles of artists and draftsmen, Khaemhat must have been influential in the choice of artists and decorative scheme for his tomb. According to Kozloff, only a few artists were involved in decorating the approximately forty tombs constructed during the lifetime of Amenhotep III. She believes that a master artist, of what she calls the Ornate Style, was at work, and may have been connected with the burgeoning realism that came to characterize the paintings at Tell el-Amarna.

The reliefs in TT 57, although incomplete, devoid of color, damaged and daubed with smoke stains, are nevertheless often unique and charming. And although many of the scenes are pro-forma and borrow heavily from the decorative programs of the tombs of Nakht and Menna, there are glimpses of daily life that are vivid and personal. The people portrayed, far from being cardboard cut-outs, seem to be imbued with individual features and

370

Khaemhat and men of rank bring offerings of ducks on braziers, a sheaf with quails and a ducks and a vase of lotus before Renenutet, "Goddess of Harvests" (not shown). The sculptor responsible for this tomb may also have worked in Ramose (TT 55).

371

The artist has carefully "balanced" the load of the central figure by facing one of the ducks in the opposite direction, making their heads a platform to hold the objects above.

personalities. Animals, such as a herd of bulls, are never stiff or static, but full of life. Remarkable are nurses with their charges bewailing the deceased, a butchering scene where a chubby boy holds the bull's leg, a pair of perky horses attempting to steady themselves on a ship. The same ship is shown piled with a bed and a chariot, and another ship has a row of oars topped with heads of the king sporting two different types of wigs. While birds flap overhead, porters unload the goods from the ship onto a dock. Aside from these unusual scenes, the tomb has many of the expected type, the deceased

offering to Osiris, the portrait of Amenhotep III, and an offering formula with many vessels identified by their contents. With Mond's work, investigation of TT 57 was virtually finished, although Harry Burton, working for the Metropolitan Museum of Art, took photographs of the tomb in the 1930s. Most of the scenes mentioned above have been published many times over in a number of scholarly and popular works, yet the tomb has never been fully-recorded. A publication by the Center of Documentation promises to rectify this.

372 top
A sphinx with the head of the king is showing trampling a foreign enemy in a scene on the arm of Amenhotep III's throne.

372 bottom
Scribes responsible for the counting of cattle present their papyrus rolls to Amenhotep III.

373
This trio of courtiers, cones of ointment balanced precariously on their heads, are part of a retinue led by Khaemhat for reception by Amenhotep III.

*Statues of the deceased and his wife
Tiyi form the main decoration in this
part of the tomb, but unfortunately
have been damaged.*

*The inner room sustained extensive smoke
damage, probably from cooking-fires
during the Coptic period or later when
Theban tombs were used as dwellings.
The description of Sheikh Abd el-Qurna
in the late 1900s by traveler Edward
William Lane leaves no doubt why almost
nothing was left when the tombs were
rediscovered in modern times. Most were
occupied, the owners lived on the fruits of
illicit excavation; mummy cases were
used for firewood, if not furniture, while
cows, goats and sheep munched on the
mummy wrappings.*

*Here Tiyi takes a minor role between
Khaemhat and Imhotep, Royal Scribe,
on a statue of the pair. The reason for
the latter's presence in the tomb
is unknown.*

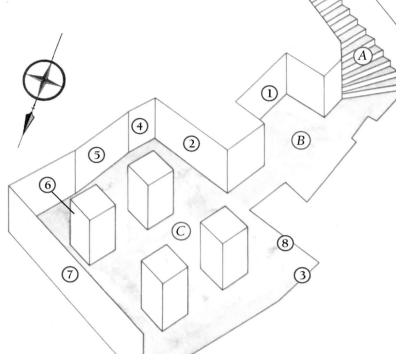

LEGEND

A	STAIRS	3	Sarcophagus and funerary goods brought to tomb
B	ANTECHAMBER	4	Purification ceremony
C	BURIAL CHAMBER	5	Scenes from the Book of the Dead
	MAIN SCENES	6	Priests offering before deceased
1	Mut-tuy and Sennefer funerary entourage	7	Pilgrimage to Abydos
2	Sennefer and Meryt	8	Meryt and Sennefer

376

On a pillar in the burial chamber, Sennefer with his wife, Meryt, sit beside the ished tree, symbol of eternal life. The abundant floral motifs reflect his title, "Superintendent of Amen's Gardens."

377

A portly Sennefer, his wife Senetnay and their daughter Mutnefert, appear on a statue in the Cairo Museum (JE 36574) found at Karnak.

THE TOMB OF
SENNEFER

by Lyla Pinch-Brock

T HE TOMB OF SENNEFER (TT 96) is one of the most popular on the West Bank, and with good reason; it is known as "the tomb of the vines," because of the gaily-decorated ceiling in the burial chamber.

The tomb has probably been open from at least the Graeco-Roman Period; the name "Alexander" on one of the hearts in the amulet Sennefer wears around his neck was doubtless written by a Greek visitor. Evidently the court was reused during the Coptic period since some installations typical of this period are built into the walls. Sir John Gardiner Wilkinson visited sometime after 1821, and in 1826 Robert Hay copied a few of the paintings, part of his notebooks in the British Museum Library. Finally, Howard Carter reported the tomb "reopened" by Sir Robert Mond in 1904.

378 left
Once badly damaged through robbery and rain, the tomb of Sennefer is now completely conserved with wooden floors and glass covering the paintings.

378 center
Sennefer stands upon a representation of the desert, the location of his tomb, in a vignette from the Opening the Mouth Ceremony. This would have taken place in front of the tomb.

378 top right
This scarab necklace in the Louvre Museum is similar to the one shown being presented to Sennefer on one of the pillars in the burial chamber.

Over the years there have been various attempts to rob paintings from the walls, and fallen fragments have disappeared. A funerary scene in the Florence Museum (no. 7637) is probably from the superstructure. A few other inscribed fragments were photographed during the work of the Metropolitan Museum of Art early last century. Large portions of the decoration are missing from the burial chamber, and blocks fallen from both sides of the hall were reinserted incorrectly. TT 96 also suffered some damage as a result of a storm and subsequent floods that devastated the West Bank in October, 1994. Since that time it has been completely conserved and glass installed to protect the paintings.

The tomb's large rectangular courtyard is enclosed by rough rock walls finished with plastered mud brick. The interior of the superstructure (called the funerary chapel) is very damaged and consists of a hall, passage and pillared inner hall. The east wall contains three statue-niches. Off this room is a smaller one with a single pillar. Since 1905 the funerary chapel has been used to store finds from other tombs, and later included Tutankhamen's. A later pit in the court communicates with the burial chamber and antechamber, both accessed through a steep stairway cut into the south-west side of the courtyard.

Sennefer was Chancellor to Amenhotep II and "Overseer of the Granaries of Amen," "Overseer of the

378 bottom right
A sem-priest purifies Sennefer and Meryt. The name "Alexander," a graffito from a Greek visitor, appears on the left heart scarab.

379
Although it hardly seems appropriate to characterize a burial chamber as "cheerful," this seems to be the general effect. Yellow predominates, as if the sun beamed down inside, and the owner and his family are shown smiling and content.

Fields of Amen," "High Priest of Amen in Menisut," "Superintendent of Amen's Gardens," "Mayor of the Southern City (Thebes)," during the reigns of Thutmosis III and Amenhotep II. As Mayor, Sennefer administered Thebes, the capitol of the country during most of the 18th Dynasty. He seems to have been particularly close to Amenhotep II. The king's name is written on one of the heart amulets he wears in a wall-paintings in the burial chamber, and one of Sennefer's wives, Senetnay, was the King's nurse. Her name, and those of his parents, Ahmose and Nub, are found only in the upper part of the tomb.

There is some debate as to whether Sentnefert, Senetnay (both Royal Nurses) Senetmi, Senetemiah and Meryt were all wives or names for

one and the same person. Senetnay, at least, seems firmly identified as his wife on a pair statue in the Cairo Museum (JE 36574) found at Karnak. Meryt is shown on several pillar-sides presenting her husband with gifts, and making the Pilgrimage to Abydos. Senetnay accompanies him offering to Amen, and performing other duties.

Sennefer had at least three daughters; Mut-tuy, seen in several scenes in the burial chamber; Mutnefert on the statue in the Cairo Museum, and Nefertiry on a statue in London (BM EA113). Aside from these statues, the only other attributable to Sennefer is a block statue in University College, London (UCL 14639), found by Flinders Petrie at Koptos.

The paintings in the funerary chapel are of an even higher quality than those below, and are presently being cleaned by Belgian conservators. They contain his biography, funerary banquet and harvesting scenes. The most important shows Amenhotep II blessing the harvest, the earliest of only five such scenes known.

Sennefer took the unusual step of having his burial chamber decorated, hence most of the scenes are funerary in content. His title, "Superintendent of Amen's Gardens" is reflected in two scenes with trees, and in the general character of the room. The antechamber opens up into a marvelous, bright "bower;" the ceiling, instead of being chiseled level, (purposefully, or perhaps

380 top and bottom

Meryt presents Sennefer with a necklace of amulets and a heart scarab. Compare these paintings with the one opposite to see the "hands" of two different artists.

380-381

An offering stand heaped with lotus, figs, grapes, bread and a haunch of beef vie for the eye with a scene of the owner and his wife making the "Pilgrimage to Abydos."

381 bottom

Meryt presents Sennefer with a lotus flower on the occasion of the Feast of the Valley. The figure beneath the chair is probably his daughter although she is not identified. The artist who painted this scene was less adept at delineating human proportions.

Aptly-named "the tomb of the vines,"
the ancient artist used the uneven
contours of the ceiling of the burial

chamber to wonderful effect,
painting it as a grape arbor, leaving
the vines to trail down the corners
of the room.

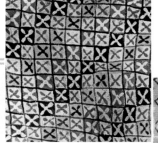

because the rock was too hard) was left in its undulating state, and the artist cleverly turned it into a grape arbor.

At least two painters seem to have been at work in the tomb, one less adept than the other at accurately rendering the proportions of the human body. The portraits of Sennefer show more character than is usual; he has large, distinctive features, his wigs or hair are elaborately arranged, and he sports a short beard. His large gold earring and "gold of honor" necklace, a mark of special favor, blaze brilliantly against his dark skin. Here he is shown as trim but stocky, but on his Cairo statue the folds of flesh on his belly emphasize his well-nourished state.

KV 42 has also been proposed, on the basis of canopic jars found inside by Howard Carter, to be the tomb of Sennefer and Senetnay. Whether the numerous jars remaining in the tomb up to its clearance in 2000 by the Luxor Inspectorate are inscribed with his name, is not known. If KV 42 was indeed a "boon from the king" then this would partially explain why no objects associated with Sennefer were ever found in his Theban tomb.

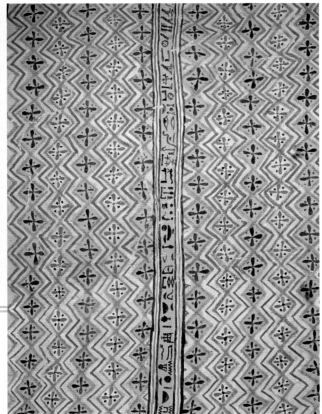

383
The geometric decoration on the ceiling of the burial chamber, probably an imitation of the colorful, woven matting that Egyptians used to decorate their houses, is known from the earliest times.

The Tomb of
Rekhmire

by Rita E. Freed

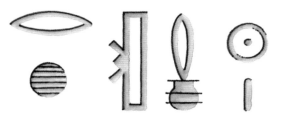

Rekhmire, vizier and mayor of Thebes, reached the apex of his career during the reigns of Thutmosis III and Amenhotep II, a time when Egypt's empire stretched to its farthest extent and her prosperity skyrocketed. He left behind a tomb that is not only one of the most beautiful in the entire necropolis, but also one of the most significant because of the light it sheds on political, religious, and technological practices of the time.

In all likelihood, Rekhmire's tomb was visited at least twice within a hundred years after his burial. Robbers emptied it of its contents and possibly also defaced the owner's image, and priests

of the heretic king and world's first monotheist, Akhenaten, erased both the names of individual gods wherever they appeared, and the word "gods."

Rekhmire's tomb was first revealed to the West by the French explorer of Egypt and Nubia, Frédéric Caillaud, who copied some of its scenes of daily life during his visit between 1819 and 1822 and published them in color in 1831 in his *Recherches sur les Arts et Métiers, les usages de la Vie Civile et Domestique des Anciens Peuples de l'Égypte, de la Nubie et de l'Éthiope*. A steady stream of early travelers followed, including Sir Gardiner Wilkinson (1825), Champollion and

Rossellini (1828), Bonomi (1832), and Hoskins (also 1832). Their drawings serve as an invaluable record of the tomb paintings, whose destruction was already noted by Hoskins during his second visit there in 1863. At that time Rekhmire's tomb served as home to an Egyptian family, including their livestock.

Except for a brief mention on an ostracon and a papyrus, all that is known about Rekhmire comes from his tomb. His most prestigious position was vizier, an office second in importance only to that of the king. As the king's deputy in charge of an area that extended from Aswan north to Assiut, his responsibilities included oversight of the land and

384 bottom

Gold and silver vessels are polished, incized, and hammered for the temple of Amen. Tongs for handling the molten metal and a blowpipe to maintain a hot fire are also shown. The gold probably came from Nubia and the silver from Sinai.

385 right

Rekhmire holds a scepter and walking stick and wears the high-waisted garment of the vizier, the most important official in the land underneath the king. He held this office from the reign of Thutmosis III until Amenhotep II.

384-385

Rekhmire's daughters (probably) present him with sistra and menats as he and his wife Meryet enjoy a great banquet in the Afterlife.

LEGEND

A	OUTER COURTYARD	7	Funeral procession
B	TRANSVERSE HALL	8	Hathor-Imentet, Anubis, and Osiris
C	PASSAGE	9	The deceased and his wife before the table of offerings
D	NICHE	10	False door, inscriptions and niche

MAIN SCENES

1	The deceased superintending the collecting of Upper Egypt taxes	11	Scenes of offerings and purification
2	Inscription	12	Scenes of life and of cultivation in a garden
3	Tributes of the foreign populations	13	Funeral banquet; scenes of musicians
4	Preparation and storing of the food	14	The deceased returns from a royal audience; ships
5	Artisans, smiths, and bricklayers at work	15	Hunting scenes in the desert
6	The deceased superintending the activities of craftsmen and workers	16	Grape harvest; preparation and storing of food
		17	Scenes of country life (damaged); the deceased superintends collection of Lower Egypt's taxes

The long passage of Rekhmire's tomb extends over 25 meters (82 feet) into the hill of Sheikh Abd el-Qurna. At the end, more than 6 meters (20 feet) above the floor is niche which once contained a statue of Rekhmire and his wife. Two shafts in the floor led to burial chambers, both of which were empty when they were excavated in 1894.

Two priests prepare a slaughtered and trussed ox as an offering to Osiris, god of the netherworld. While one pours a liquid libation into the severed neck, the other removes the right foreleg, the god's choicest morsel.

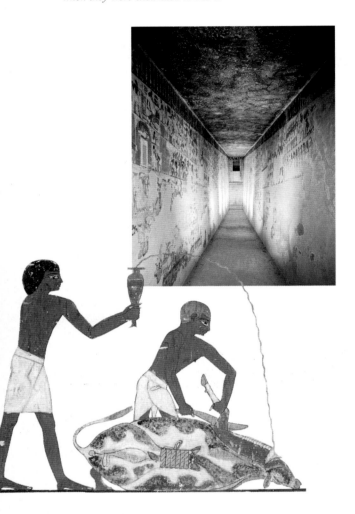

One of the duties of the vizier was to receive foreign tribute. Here Nubians, dressed in their traditional garb, bring products from their homeland, including ivory tusks, ebony, ostrich feathers, live animals and animal skins. Minoans with their tribute are depicted in the register above.

The 68 different episodes of Rekhmire's elaborate funerary procession are depicted on the west wall of his tomb, closest to his false door. Here, magical rites are performed in the upper register as his enshrined sarcophagus is dragged to its final resting place below. In the middle, attendants bring his household and personal effects.

maintenance of justice. (A second vizier held sway north of Assiut to the Delta.) The enumeration of his duties as vizier on his tomb wall is one of the most important administrative texts of the New Kingdom. Further information about Rekhmire's career is provided by the more than a hundred additional titles and epithets he lists in the rather self-laudatory autobiographical section of his tomb. Among his other key titles were Mayor of Thebes, and, in the religious sphere, Steward of the Temple of Amen.

The tomb also provides valuable genealogical information. Rekhmire rose to the vizierate through family ties. His great grandfather,

grandfather, and uncle all held the same office, which they had enjoyed without break since the reign of Thutmosis I. For reasons unknown, Rekhmire did not pass the position down to any of his children (at least five sons and three daughters).

The tomb is located on the southwestern face of Sheikh Abd el-Qurna, and it exhibits the simple T-shape common in the early years of 18th Dynasty. From a transverse hall of more than 20 meters (66 feet) in length, an east west passage over 25 meters (82 feet) long leads to an offering niche at its western end. Although narrow, the passage is made to appear larger through the height of its

ceiling, which soars from 3 meters (10 feet) at its entry to 8 meters (27 feet) at the niche end. Two 5 meter (17 feet) deep burial shafts opening into burial chambers for Rekhmire and his wife Bet were cut into the floor of the passage. Both were probably robbed long before they were opened in 1894. Based on the texts on the inner wall of the offering niche, it probably once contained a statue of the couple, no trace of which was ever found. Originally two granite false doors, one of which was taken by Champollion to the Louvre, sealed the niche.

The poor quality of the limestone in which it was cut dictated that Rekhmire's tomb be

388 top

A female harpist plays and sings at Rekhnmire's funerary banquet. The words of her song may be read in front of her. She is part of an all-female orchestra, which includes a lute player, a tambourine player, and two chironomists who clap to the beat of the music.

388 bottom

Artists took greater liberties in the depiction of servants, one of which is shown here in profile. As she bends to pour beer for her mistress, her hair, braided in cornrows, falls in front of her face. Behind her, another servant offers scented unguents in small vessels.

388-389

Among the many participants at Rekhmire's funerary banquet, only his mother, Bet, is seated on a chair.

A servant girl pours beer into her saucer. Behind, floral collars are tied around the neck of another female guest, who squats on a mat.

of the long passage, which also features the rituals of Rekhmire's funeral at its western end toward the niche. In a rare scene, bees are smoked out of their hives so that honey may be collected to sweeten bread or cakes.

Sculptors, carpenters, construction workers, metalworkers, jewelers, sandalmakers, and tanners practice their craft in exquisite detail, thereby providing valuable insights into the technologies of the time. The more-than-two-dozen different objects being prepared for Amen's temple, as well as the sumptuous foreign goods brought as tribute or diplomatic gifts remind the viewer of the tremendous wealth of Amen's temple during the Age of Empire.

The skill of Rekhmire's artists is nowhere better shown than at the meal which takes place at the vizier's funeral. Although the guests squat stiffly on mats as they partake of the banquet's treats, formality gives way to naturalism in the depiction of servants, one of whom coyly turns her back to the viewer as she serves her mistress. Her transparent dress reveals the outlines of her body beneath.

Despite damages wrought by tomb robbers, Aten's priests, bats, and livestock, Rekhmire's tomb remains one of the delights of the Theban necropolis.

plastered and painted, rather than carved. Artists covered every available surface of the walls and ceiling—in all a total of over 300 square meters (3,300 square feet)—with scenes and texts describing Rekhmire's life in this world and his transition to the next. The vizier's secular activities are depicted in the transverse hall. There he collects taxes that arrive as produce, livestock, and manufactured goods in the hands of local officials, holds court and dispenses legal verdicts, and scrutinizes temple provisions. He oversees planting, harvest, and the production of wine and foods. As the king's deputy he receives foreign dignitaries and their gifts. Men from Punt, Nubia, the Aegean, and Syria are depicted with the characteristic dress, hairstyle, and physiognomy of their region, and together they present a panoply of contemporary international culture. Some also bring their women and children so they might be raised in Pharaoh's court. In all, 57 different gifts are enumerated. Remains of hunting, fowling, and fishing scenes probably reflect both Rekhmire's leisure pursuits and his magical taming of malevolent forces.

Food is prepared and goods are manufactured for temple storerooms on the walls

389 bottom

Three women, shown en echelon smell or carry flowers and buds of the blue lotus. The lotus was a symbol of rebirth, because it closed at night but opened anew each day. It also may have served as a mild narcotic.

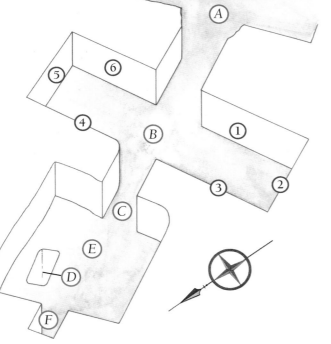

LEGEND	
A	COURTYARD
B	FRONT TRANSVERSE HALL
C	ENTRANCE TO INNER HALL
D	BURIAL SHAFT
E	INNER LONGITUDINAL HALL
F	RAISED STATUE NICHE
MAIN SCENES	
1	Burning offerings and agricultural activities
2	False door
3	Valley Festival banquet
4	Fishing, fowling, and wine-making
5	Burning offerings and offering bearer
6	Deceased and wife receive offerings

THE TOMB OF
NAKHT

by Melinda K. Hartwig

THE SMALL TOMB OF NAKHT (TT 52)
lies at the foot of the hill of Sheikh Abd el-Qurna, the
prestigious burial site for officials of the New Kingdom.
Local inhabitants of Qurna village appear to have
gained access to the tomb before it was cleared by the
Antiquities Service in 1889. Later, the English Egyptologist
Norman de Garis Davies and his wife Nina published
the tomb in 1917 under the auspices of The
Metropolitan Museum of Art which brought the tomb
of Nakht and its paintings to a worldwide audience.

All that is known about Nakht comes from
his tomb. Nakht was a scribe and an astronomer for the
temple of Amen-Ra at Karnak. In this capacity, Nakht
examined the location of the stars, sun and moon in

order to schedule festivals and cult ritual for the
temple. Nakht's scribal title signified that he was
both literate and part of the civil service of Egypt.
Nakht's wife, Tawy, was a musician of Amen,
indicating that she took part in music-making for the
god's cult. Tawy had one son, Amenemopet, who
may have been the issue of a previous marriage
since he is not described as Nakht's son explicitly.
Other sons and daughters doubtless appear in the
tomb, and were never inscribed.

No royal names occur with which to date
the tomb. The style of Nakht's chapel paintings are
very similar to other tombs such as Djeserkarasoneb
(TT 38) and Amenhotep-si-se (TT 75) and Nebseny

390-391

Accompanied by his wife and
children, Nakht stands on a reed skiff
grasping a throw stick and bird on the
left and on the right, his arms are
positioned to receive a harpoon that
was never painted. Green papyrus
stalks and umbels rise above a dense
thicket of reeds where the agitated
birds flutter, several whose necks are
broken by the boomerang. These
images operated on several levels
guaranteeing Nakht's provisioning,
and his rebirth and reproduction in
the hereafter.

On the top register from right to left, an elderly vintner and his assistant pick bunches of grapes. The grapes are then stamped by five men to produce juice. The vintner retrieves the juice that gushes forth from a spout in the side of the vat. The wine jars above symbolize the final product. Below, a fowler hidden in the reeds signals to his friends to pull shut the net. The trapped birds are then plucked and gutted. At the left end of both registers offering bearers bring food before a large offering pile.

392 top left

Detail of the east wing of the transverse hall showing Nakht and Tawy.

392 bottom left

An old farm hand leans into his plough pulled by two oxen. On the meandering ground line above, one kneeling laborer clears a wood indicated by the trees around him, which he fells with an axe. Another laborer tills the prepared earth with a hoe which is sprouting with crops.

392 bottom right

The hot and dusty work of winnowing is wonderfully captured here by young women tossing grain with wooden spoons to separate the wheat from the chaff. One girl stoops to refill her scoop while the other uses two small brooms to keep the pile tidy.

393 center

The west wing of the transverse hall is decorated with work in the field and images of Nakht and Tawy burning offerings on the front wall, and the celebration of the Valley Festival/funerary banquet on the back wall. The short wall contained the false door which served as a point of contact for the deceased between this world and the next.

393 bottom

The east wing of the transverse hall displays the deceased and wife burning offerings followed by offering bearers on the front wall, and images of fishing, fowling, wine-making and offering on the back wall. The wing ends with two registers of Nakht and Tawy seated, receiving offerings to ensure their eternal sustenance.

(TT 108) all of which are dated to the reign of Thutmosis IV on the basis of a royal cartouche in their chapels or other inscribed material. Another tomb chapel, that of Menna (TT 69), contains paintings which are stylistically similar to those in Nakht's and date to the transitional period between Thutmosis IV and his successor Amenhotep III. Figural details such as the plump, rounded proportions of the female figures,

elongated eyes with pupils that take up half of the upper eyelid, and plaits escaping from the wig indicate the decoration in Nakht was completed during the reign of Amenhotep III. As with so many tombs of this time period in the Theban necropolis, the short reign of Thutmosis IV points out that many tombs were actually completed in the reign of his successor.

Nakht's rock-cut tomb conforms to the usual inverted T-shape plan found in the private Theban necropolis. From an open courtyard, one enters into the chapel proper composed of a front transversal hall leading to a inner longitudinal hall that once held a statue group of Nakht and his wife in the raised back niche. Cut into the floor of the inner hall was the shaft which was filled with rubble after the burial to prevent access. The chapel, however, remained open for visitors to enact cult and admire the finely crafted paintings which, through the creative power of word and image, were intended to provide for Nakht and his family in the hereafter.

Only the front transversal hall is decorated. The inner longitudinal hall was plastered but never painted. As one enters the chapel, two figures of Nakht and Tawy flank the doorway, burning offerings to the gods. This action was associated with the celebrations of the Beautiful Festival of the Western Valley, a Theban necropolis festival that took place for two days around the new moon during the 10th month of the year. To the left, the next scene on this wall depicts agricultural activities and the harvest overseen by the deceased. To the right, Nakht and Tawy are followed by three registers of unfinished offering bearers. On the eastern back wall directly opposite the external doorway were scenes of hunting in the marshes, wine-making and fowling. The western back wall contained a scene of the banquet associated with Valley Festival which may also have doubled as the meal attended by family and friends during the

burial. The two short walls at either side of the front transversal hall held the false door on the west wall and an unfinished scene of offering bearers before the seated figures of Nakht and Tawy on the east.

The false door and the now-destroyed pair statue in the back niche were places of worship in the funerary cult of Nakht and his wife. The ancient Egyptians believed that the dead could pass through the false door and inhabit statues to receive funerary offerings. This idea is reinforced on the false door by six offering bearers who kneel bearing water, beer, wine, clothing, unguent, fruit and vegetables on either side of the door. Below, a pile of offerings is flanked by two female personifications of fecundity who magically guaranteed an abundance of funerary offerings.

The emphasis of scenes associated with the Beautiful Festival of the Valley in the chapel of Nakht is common in 18th-Dynasty Theban tombs. The Valley Festival was an annual family reunion when dead ancestors were reintegrated into the family unit. During the Valley Festival, the barks of the god Amen, his consort Mut, and their son Khonsu were carried from Karnak to the west bank to tour the royal mortuary temples and ended at the Hathor sanctuary at Deir el-Bahari. In the non-royal necropolis, the living and the dead hailed the procession. During this festival, offerings were burned for the sun god, animals were butchered, food offerings were made, and bouquets were presented. The culmination of the festival was an all-night vigil with banqueting,

music and drinking, the goal of which was to blur the limits between this world and the next so that the living could commune with the dead.

Understandably, many scenes in the chapel were concerned with Nakht's eternal nourishment. Images of hunting birds and spearing fish in the marshes, producing wine, preparing fowl, and farming certainly would provide the needed sustenance for the deceased's life in the hereafter. But these images also signified the cycle of seasons that Nakht, as an astronomer, tracked through the movement of the celestial bodies. The emphasis on the Valley Festival celebrations also linked Nakht to the cult of Amen-Ra, and commemorated his identity as a servant of that god.

395 bottom
A kneeling offering-bearer wearing a wig and short
wrap-around kilt presents three papyrus stalks
and a tray with baskets of grapes, bread
loaves and onions. A grapevine is held in his
outstretched hand.

394-395
A pile of offerings is presided over by
the Tree Goddess. The Tree Goddess
was a personification of fecundity,
and symbolized the wishes of the
ancient Egyptians to find
nourishment in the desert cemetery
that lay near the cultivation's edge.

396-397

A blind harpist sits cross-legged playing a harp and singing, evoking contemporary songs whose lyrics underscored the transitory nature of the world. Behind, a row of women squat on mats, sniffing or holding lotus flowers. Some playfully offer mandrake fruits to each other, while a servant girl leans over to adjust a lock of hair that has fallen loose from a woman's coiffure.

396 bottom

These three female musicians display the elegance of 18th-Dynasty Theban tomb painting. The first musician plays a standing harp, the second a lute, and the third a double-reed pipe. A sense of movement is relayed by the plucking of the strings and the innovative posture of the lutist who turns her head towards the piper while her upper torso faces frontally.

397 bottom

Nakht and Tawy face the entrance to the tomb and the outer world burning offerings to the gods, followed by three registers of offering bringers. The scene was drawn using a squared grid which aided the artist in the spacing and proportioning of the figures and texts.

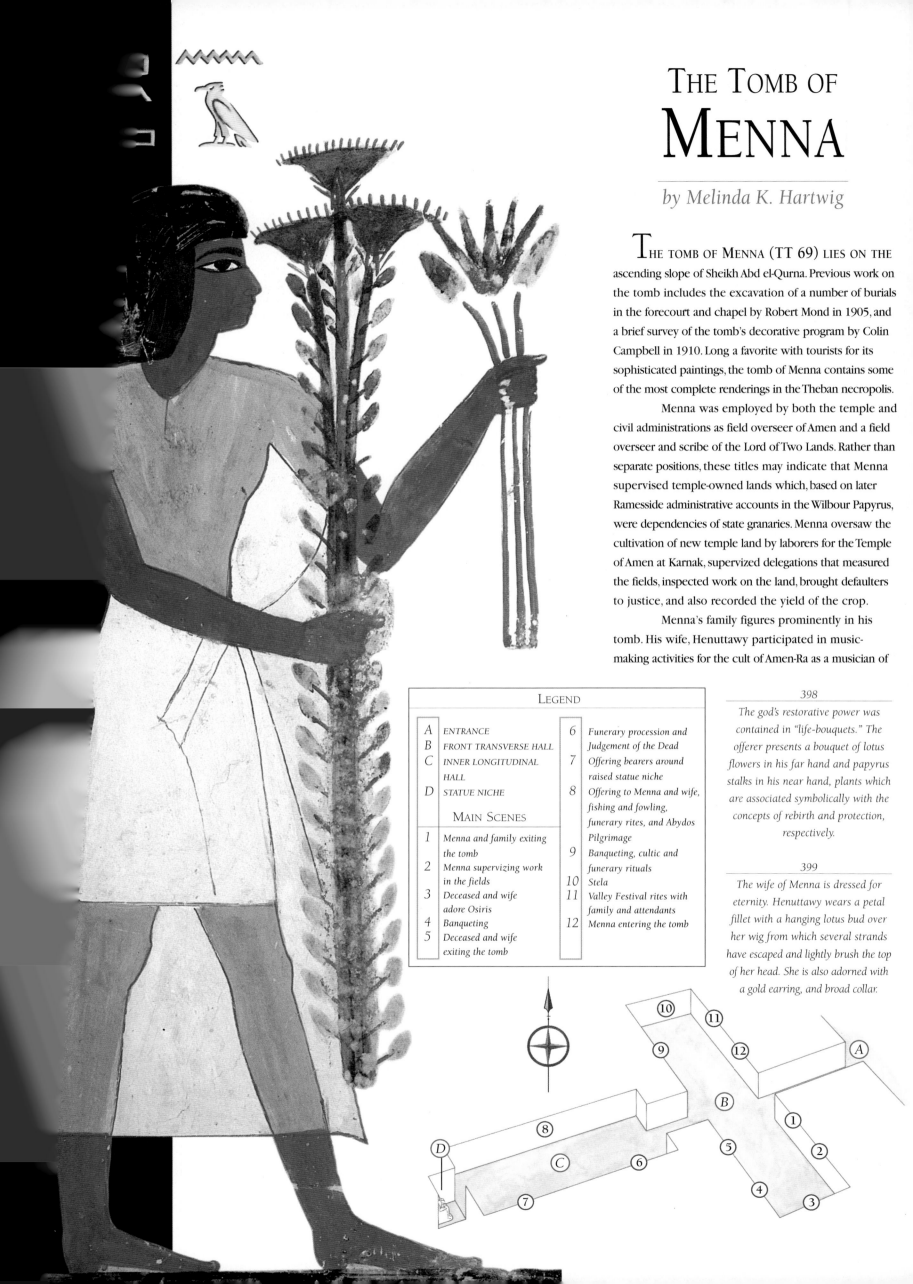

THE TOMB OF
MENNA

by Melinda K. Hartwig

THE TOMB OF MENNA (TT 69) LIES ON THE ascending slope of Sheikh Abd el-Qurna. Previous work on the tomb includes the excavation of a number of burials in the forecourt and chapel by Robert Mond in 1905, and a brief survey of the tomb's decorative program by Colin Campbell in 1910. Long a favorite with tourists for its sophisticated paintings, the tomb of Menna contains some of the most complete renderings in the Theban necropolis.

Menna was employed by both the temple and civil administrations as field overseer of Amen and a field overseer and scribe of the Lord of Two Lands. Rather than separate positions, these titles may indicate that Menna supervised temple-owned lands which, based on later Ramesside administrative accounts in the Wilbour Papyrus, were dependencies of state granaries. Menna oversaw the cultivation of new temple land by laborers for the Temple of Amen at Karnak, supervized delegations that measured the fields, inspected work on the land, brought defaulters to justice, and also recorded the yield of the crop.

Menna's family figures prominently in his tomb. His wife, Henuttawy participated in music-making activities for the cult of Amen-Ra as a musician of

LEGEND

A	ENTRANCE	6	Funerary procession and Judgement of the Dead
B	FRONT TRANSVERSE HALL	7	Offering bearers around raised statue niche
C	INNER LONGITUDINAL HALL	8	Offering to Menna and wife, fishing and fowling, funerary rites, and Abydos Pilgrimage
D	STATUE NICHE		
	MAIN SCENES	9	Banqueting, cultic and funerary rituals
1	Menna and family exiting the tomb	10	Stela
2	Menna supervizing work in the fields	11	Valley Festival rites with family and attendants
3	Deceased and wife adore Osiris	12	Menna entering the tomb
4	Banqueting		
5	Deceased and wife exiting the tomb		

398

The god's restorative power was contained in "life-bouquets." The offerer presents a bouquet of lotus flowers in his far hand and papyrus stalks in his near hand, plants which are associated symbolically with the concepts of rebirth and protection, respectively.

399

The wife of Menna is dressed for eternity. Henuttawy wears a petal fillet with a hanging lotus bud over her wig from which several strands have escaped and lightly brush the top of her head. She is also adorned with a gold earring, and broad collar.

Amen. She may also have been literate as indicated by a scribal palette that is depicted under her chair in several of the tomb scenes. Menna's daughter Amenemwaskhet held a high-status post as a lady-in-waiting in the court of the pharaoh. Menna also had two other daughters and several sons, one of whom followed his father into field administration.

The tomb of Menna dates to the transitional period between the reigns of Thutmosis IV and Amenhotep III. Thutmosis' short reign meant that many officials who served him completed their tombs during the reign of his son Amenhotep III, and the style of the decoration in a number of

Theban tombs bears this out. Figural proportions and facial details tend to be a stable measuring criteria because they represent the imprint of royal style on the private sphere. In the tomb chapel of Menna, female figures are rendered with the thinner proportions of the reign of Thutmosis IV as well as the more voluptuous curves of the reign of Amenhotep III. Their faces also exhibit open, oblique, elongated almond-shaped eyes with relatively round pupils that barely touch the lower lid and dishy profiles common in the reign of Thutmosis IV. Other female figures in the chapel also display the "closed," slanted, almond-shaped eyes with

pupils that touch almost half of the upper eyelid, a distinctive feature in the reign of Amenhotep III. A number of other stylistic, architectural, iconographical and inscriptional indicators support this transitional dating. The well-preserved state of the tomb chapel of Menna gives us a window into the ancient Egyptian's mortuary beliefs and how they were reflected in the architectural and decorative program. The tomb chapel of Menna is in the form of an inverted T-shape, typically used for rock-cut private tombs in the New Kingdom Theban necropolis. An entrance leads to a broad transverse hall bisected by a longitudinal inner hall with an elevated statue niche at the far end. The

painted images in the chapel of Menna were arranged
along these axes with scenes relating to the owner's
earthly and professional life in the front transverse
hall and those associated with his life in the beyond
in the inner longitudinal hall. In the ritual beliefs of the
ancient Egyptians, texts and images could be creatively
activated and act as substitutes in case offerings for the
tomb owner's cult were not forthcoming.

The left entrance wall of the chapel was
painted with the image of Menna, his daughter and
wife going out of the tomb towards the "east" and the
rising sun, accompanied by a hymn to the sun-god
Amen-Ra. This hymn records Menna's eternal desire to

see the god during the Beautiful Festival [of the
Valley], the annual royal and private ancestor festival
when the bark statues of the Theban triad (Amen,
Mut and Khonsu) traveled from Karnak on the east
bank to Deir el-Bahari on the west bank. Likewise on
the left side of the inner doorway between the
transverse and longitudinal hall, the deceased and
his wife are shown leaving the tomb to attend the
Valley Festival. On the right external doorway
thickness, the figure of Menna steps into the tomb
towards the "west" and the setting sun, the
metaphorical realm of the god of the underworld,
Osiris. Flanking the entrance on the right front wall,

402 top

Two men carry a basket filled with sheaves of wheat while below two girls fight. In the shade of a tree, one man nods off and another plays a flute beneath a hanging waterskin. Before them, an overseer supervizes men pitching wheat onto the threshing floor.

the figures of Menna and Henuttawy offer burnt offerings to the gods followed by their sons Sa, Kha, daughter Kasy, and other relatives and attendants. At the far end of the wall, the deceased couple sits receiving a bouquet from a man. These images refer to the celebrations that occurred during the Valley Festival when offerings were burnt for the gods and bouquets were presented to family ancestors. On the opposite wall to the left, Menna is seated on the upper register overlooking labor in the fields. Images of activities from the agricultural cycle decorate the wall, including ploughing, sowing, reaping, pulling flax, gleaning, threshing, winnowing, measuring the crops, and the recording of the grain measure. The artist has also included playful vignettes, from a thorn being

pulled from the foot of a girl by her companion, to defaulters brought to justice before the standing figure of Menna. Interspersed on 4 registers which are "read" from bottom to top, each vignette stood for a specific task and time period in the agricultural cycle that Menna oversaw. The fruits of all these labors are piled on a table in front of the seated Menna to nourish him eternally in the next world. On the two lowermost registers, another seated figure of Menna with his wife by his side receives his three daughters, two of whom are identified as ladies-in-waiting to the royal court. The two walls opposite the external doorway contained some of the most important scenes in the tomb. These walls were the first to be seen by visitors entering the tomb, and

402-403

On the right, four oxen tread the threshing floor while a man drives them around and around, flicking a branch to keep them moving. Two men stand on top of mounds of sheaves and fork them down onto the threshing floor. To the left, winnowers separate the grain from the chaff by tossing the ears into the air using wooden scoops. Beneath them, three winnowers stoop to gather grain.

403 top

The west wing of the transverse hall is decorated with images of work in the field on the front wall, banqueting on the back wall, and worship before Osiris on the short wall. Before the short wall, a burial shaft was cut into the floor, perhaps intended to link Osiris with the passage of the dead into the underworld.

403 center

Menna is seated on a folding stool with an animal skin cushion, overseeing the work in the fields. Before him are three registers of offerings, with a prostrate man reporting the results of the field measure above, and Menna's attendants and waiting chariot below.

stood at the point in the chapel's decorative program at which the earthly activities of the tomb owner depicted in the front transversal hall intersect with those in the hereafter in the inner longitudinal hall. The images revealed what the deceased most wanted to present about his life in this and the next world. Unfortunately, the banquet scene to the left is destroyed so the specific nature of the celebration is not known. Two seated images of Menna and Henuttawy remain at the far left of the wall, enjoying the festivities. The better preserved right back wall, however, shows Menna and Henuttawy seated on two registers with their backs to the door to the longitudinal room, receiving offerings or cult. Above, an unidentified man who is most likely their son, offers them a

floral bouquet often identified in ancient Egyptian by the term *ankh* or "life-bouquet." Although no texts accompany this scene, similar images of bouquet offering occur elsewhere, often accompanied by the phrase "For your *ka* (i.e. the soul of sustenance), an *ankh*-bouquet of the god, may he favor you, may he give you life". In this way, the act of offering the bouquet can be read as a conferral on Menna and Henuttawy of the god's strength and blessing for the eternal life. On the register below, the figure of a *sem* or mortuary priest (identified by his leopard skin garment), recites the now-faded offering list formula inscribed above the offering table. The list contained abbreviated guidelines for offering rituals that were creatively activated by the priest which would provide for the needs of the tomb owners in the next world. The four remaining registers were painted with images of offering, banqueting, cultic rituals and several funerary ceremonies connected with the Opening the Mouth. The left wall in the transverse hall contains an image of Menna

followed by his wife Henuttawy and two attendants praying to Osiris seated in a kiosk. In the hymn that accompanies the scene, Menna assures Osiris of his piety by saying "It is with truth foremost in my heart and with a heart without wrongdoing that I have come to you." In the register below, two men accompanied by offering-bearers set fire to a pile of offerings whose fragrance would appeal to the god. On the right wall is a painted stela divided into three registers. On the top, Anubis, the god of the dead stands before Osiris and the Western Goddess, the deity associated with the funerary realm in the west. On the right, the sun god Ra-Horakhty is seated before his daughter, the goddess Hathor. The middle register contains two couples seated back-to-back, and the lowermost register displays two antithetically placed images of the deceased and wife adoring, followed by a priest. Around the stela, men and women stand before offering tables with their arms raised in praise of the deceased. The scenes in the inner longitudinal hall emphasize Menna and Henuttawy's transition into the next world. Here images of the funeral procession, the funerary banquet, rites before

404 left

The inner hall of the chapel is painted with images of the funerary procession and the Judgement of the Dead on the southern wall, and scenes of rites before the mummy,

Pilgrimage to Abydos, fishing and fowling, and offering to the deceased couple on the northern wall. The end of the hall held a raised statue niche with an offering table before it.

The Tomb of Menna

404-405 top
The Western Goddess, also known as Imentet, stands holding an ankh-sign of life and a was-scepter, the emblem of Thebes, before two registers of offering bearers. Among the funerary gifts are cattle, a basket, a chest, and two mummiform statuettes.

404-405 bottom
Offering-bearers with funerary gifts that include stalks of papyrus, linen, a wooden box, a fan, wine and unguent jars, lotus blossoms, bread, fowl and tables heaped with various foodstuffs. Each man wears a wraparound kilt and a wig, and a few have shaven heads.

406-407

Menna is accompanied by his family in
the marshes, fishing with a harpoon and
fowling with a stick. Fish, geese, and a
crocodile frolic in the water, while, a cat
and ichneumon stalk a nest, left by the
birds who flutter caught by Menna.

407 center

Detail of the funerary procession
from the inner longitudinal wall.

406 bottom

The mummiform figures of Menna
and Henuttawy are seated under a
baldachin voyaging to Abydos. The
sails are unfurled on the tugboat
traveling upstream and rowers
propel the tugboat going
downstream. Every Egyptian aspired
to visit Abydos to associate
themselves eternally with the cult
of the funerary god Osiris.

the mummy, the pilgrimage to Abydos, fishing and fowling, offerings for the deceased, and the Judgement of the Dead predominate. At the far end of the hall was a raised niche that held the lower part of a seated statue group of Menna and Henuttawy surrounded by offering bringers bearing food, drink, and flowers. This group was the embodiment of the deceased and his wife, and was intended to receive offerings as indicated by the table set out on the ground before it. In contrast to the sophisticated and animated renderings in the transverse hall, the images in the longitudinal hall are uniform and static with a few lively exceptions. At the end of the southern long wall is an image of the Judgement of the Dead which is the earliest representation of its type in the Theban necropolis. Menna is depicted standing grasping his opposite shoulder in a gesture of respect before Osiris who

is seated in a kiosk. Before them, Menna's heart is weighed on a balance against a small figurine of Maat, the goddess of universal truth and harmony. Horus adjusts the balance while above, Thoth, the god of knowledge and writing, records the verdict. In ancient Egypt, the heart was believed to be the seat of thought, emotions and memory, and revealed the owner's character. Doubtless, Menna's heart balanced against Maat, ensuring his successful acceptance to the underworld. The image of fishing and fowling that appears in the middle of the northern longitudinal wall exhibits the luxurious painting and rich attention to detail that characterizes the decoration in the tomb chapel. While Menna's catch clearly provided for his and hixs family's eternal nourishment, this scene also operated on a religious/metaphorical level to guarantee Menna's reproduction and rebirth.

407 bottom
The ritual of the Opening the Mouth is being performed on the mummy of Menna to reanimate him. A priest touches an adze to the mouth of the deceased which would allow Menna to breath, eat, see, hear, and enjoy the provisions offered for his cult.

408-409

May, the king's superintendent of horses and messenger to foreign lands, and his wife Werel, who served the goddess Mut, are dressed in their finery for Ramose's funerary banquet. Artists have beautifully articulated the translucency of the garments, the curls of the hair, and the details of the jewelry.

THE TOMB OF RAMOSE

by Rita E. Freed

408 bottom

Guests at Ramose's funerary banquet are depicted on the east wall of the broad hall of his tomb. Shown here are his parents, his brother and sister-in-law, and others who were contemporaries of Ramose but not related to him. It appears Ramose had no children.

409 bottom

Had these elegant figures of Ramose's parents, Neby and Apuya, been finished, their painted decoration would have obscured the beauty of their carving. The relief decoration of the second half of the 18th Dynasty is unsurpassed in its delicacy and attention to detail.

Located in Sheikh Abd el-Qurna, the tomb of Ramose is one of the few on the West Bank at Thebes built during the early years of Egypt's heretic king Amenhotep IV/Akhenaten. Its interest lies not only in the delicacy of its carved and painted decoration, but also because it illustrates the transition to the dramatic new artistic style that accompanied that king's new religious ideology. Abandoned prior to completion, it also displays the different stages in the carving and decorating of a tomb.

Although seemingly of relatively humble and northern origins, Ramose rose to the rank of Vizier and Mayor of Thebes, probably during the reign of Amenhotep III, whose name is also mentioned in the tomb. He enjoyed judicial and priestly offices as well. His father Neby appears to have served in the north as superintendent of Amen's cattle and in the Delta as superintendent of Amen's granary. Ramose's wife Meryet-ptah is prominently featured in the tomb, which was most likely planned as her burial place as well.

Although other relatives and contemporaries of Ramose are depicted in the tomb, no offspring is mentioned. Accordingly it appears Ramose and his wife were childless.

Ramose's tomb was unknown to the western world until 1879, when Villiers Stewart cleared enough of the broad outer hall to recognize the iconography of Amenhotep IV/Akhenaten. Intrigued, he returned for more cleaning in 1882 and published his findings in 1879 in *Nile Gleanings*, a charming but unreliable work. Gaston Maspero, Director General of the Antiquities Service, continued the task, which was completed by Robert Mond working for the Metropolitan Museum of Art in 1924. It was this last expedition that restored the tomb to its present condition. The tomb consists of an outdoor forecourt leading to a broad hall, deep hall, and rear niche on the same east-west axis. Twenty-five steps with a central ramp for sliding a sarcophagus lead into the forecourt, whose asymmetrical shape was dictated, in all likelihood, by pre-existing tombs. The tombs presently cut into the sidewalls of the forecourt represent later additions. From the forecourt, four steps lead down into a

LEGEND	
A	STEPS WITH CENTRAL RAMP
B	FORECOURT
C	BROAD HALL
D	LONG HALL
E	INNER SHRINE

MAIN SCENES	
1	Funeral banquet
2	Funeral procession
3	The deceased makes an offering to Amenhotep IV and to the goddess Maat
4	The deceased before Amenhotep IV and Queen Nefertari followed by dignitaries
5	Ramose is hailed and receives foreign delegations and garlands of flowers from the temple
6	Priests before the deceased and his family and ritual list of offerings
7	Three maidens with sistra before the deceased and his wife. Purification of the statue of Ramose
8	The deceased, with his wife and bearers of offerings, burn incense

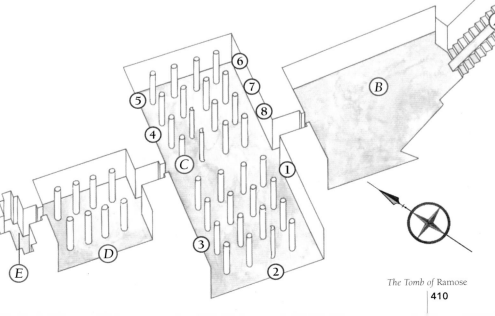

The Tomb of Ramose

large broad hall once occupied by four rows of four columns on each side of the longitudinal axis. When the tomb was usurped, six columns were completely cut away. The broad hall is the only area of the tomb that was decorated, although the walls of the next room, the deep hall, and the shrine following it were smoothed in preparation for decoration. In the deep hall, eight columns are arranged in rows of two. The innermost shrine, the focal point of the tomb features three niches intended for statues of the tomb owner and his family. Either they were never carved or have not been found.

From the southwest corner of the broad hall, a winding ramp and stair lead 51 feet down to Ramose's multi-room burial chamber. No trace of either human remains or burial equipment was found inside any of the chambers, and it is not clear that they were ever used. No visitor to Ramose's tomb can help but gasp at the beauty of its decoration. To the right and left of the entry into the broad hall Ramose, his wife, family members, and colleagues, take part in the vizier's funerary banquet as attendant prepare and bring offerings. Their raised relief representations are carved and modeled with exquisite detail. Every curl of a wig, bead of a necklace, and soft fold of a garment is rendered with unsurpassed skill and consummate precision. Complete, they would have been painted, but only the elongated eyes have been highlighted

412 top left

The north half of the west wall is the only part of Ramose's tomb executed in the revolutionary style of Amenhotep IV. Most of this section remains unfinished. The doorway leads to an undecorated long hall and statue shrine.

412 top right

View from the north in the broad (outer) hall of Ramose's tomb, with the entry on the left. The platform in the center was erected by a usurper. At the far end are scenes from Ramose's funeral, most of which was executed in paint only.

412-413

Attendants bring all the household and personal effects Ramose will need in the Afterlife as female mourners, young and old flamboyantly display their grief at his funeral. Unlike other walls of the tomb, what is shown here was only painted rather than carved.

413 top

Libyans, Nubians, and Syrians in their traditional dress, hairstyle and phsyiognomy raise their arms in homage to Amenhotep IV in these drawings, which represent Egyptian draughtsmanship at its best. These foreigners represent Egypt's traditional enemies.

in black. The relief style resembles some of the finest work executed during the reign of Amenhotep III, whose name is mentioned on this wall. Many gods are invoked; Amen's has been hacked out. In contrast to the east wall, the upper registers of the south wall were not carved at all but only painted. The most important scene from his tomb, namely his funerary procession, is located there. Accompanied by his colleagues, his sarcophagus, canopic chest, and the amorphous *tekenu* are brought to the tomb's entry (both literally and figuratively since the actual burial shaft descends from the same area), as male attendants transport food and household goods. In one of the most moving scenes, women and girls mourn Ramose's death. Although a professional group rather than, family, their tears seem real. In this funeral scene, neither iconography nor style betrays the hand of Amenhotep IV's artists. Continuing to the south side of the west wall, figures of Ramose approach representations of Amenhotep IV and the goddess of truth, Maat, enthroned under a baldachin. Their raised relief figures resemble the other raised reliefs in the tomb, although they lack their intricate detailing. This is consistent with the relief style seen at Karnak during the first years of Amenhotep IV's reign. North of the entrance to the deep hall, the style of decoration of the west wall changes dramatically. There, Ramose is awarded the gold of honor by Amenhotep IV and his wife Nefertiti, who are pictured at the window of appearance beneath Aten, the sun disk whose rays end in human hands which present life to the nostrils of the king and queen. This theme, as well as the style of the figures with their elongated heads, drooping chins, narrow upper torsos and voluptuous hips are characteristic of the Amarna style of Amenhotep IV, which also appears on his teletat blocks at Karnak. To the right of this scene, similarly styled figures were drawn in preparation for carving. The west wall is devoid of any decoration. The styles of Ramose's tomb decoration have given rise to much speculation. While art historians admire the decoration for its beauty and for its documentation of dramatic stylistic change brought about by Amenhotep IV, a number of historians view it as proof of a coregency between Amenhotep III and his son. For others, the different styles represent sequential, rather than contemporaneous work.

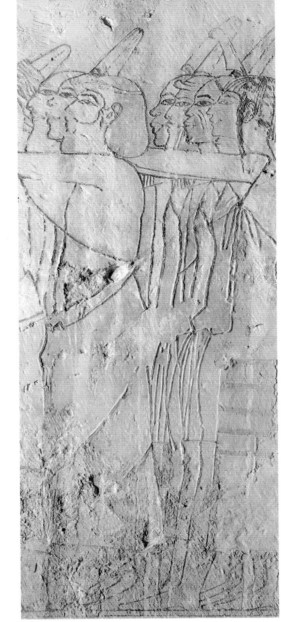

THE TOMB OF USERHAT

by Lyla Pinch-Brock

414-415

Userhat is seen leaving the palace (not shown) where he has received his rewards, jewelry that he wears and more set out on a table. He is greeted by a celebratory group of his wife and female relatives, playing drums or tamborines, their hair piled with flowers and cones of unguent.

414 center

Userhat has become one of the Westerners (the deceased) and is greeted by the Goddess of the West, whose gesture means "welcome."

The mounds represent the Western Desert, where he will be buried. The other gods adore Ra-Horakhty, who perches on the symbol of the west.

414 bottom

A lector reads the offering formula while a priest pours oil from a hs jar on an offering and censes the coffins of Userhat (note one is smaller than the other, so it could fit inside). On the left, mourners pour ashes on their heads to the extent that their bodies are streaked blue, as they bewail the passing of their patron.

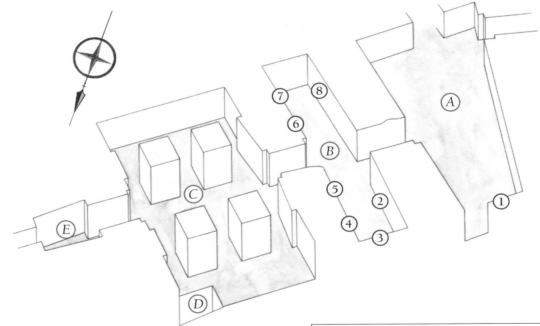

THE TOMB OF USERHAT (TT 51) WAS discovered by Sir Robert Mond on January 10, 1903. Mond seems not to have completely cleared the tomb, but he did find a large stone *shawabty* and a number of small terra-cotta *shawabty*, none naming the owner. The final clearance was left for Norman de Garis Davies to do, beginning in 1909, as part of his epigraphic work for the Metropolitan Museum of Art. Davies reported finding only one object—another *shawabty* figure, this time of charred wood. Davies did a complete copy of the paintings in outline, providing the groundwork for facsimiles of the paintings finished by his wife. Copies of the Tree Goddess scene are now in the Metropolitan Museum of Art and the Ashmolean Museum. The tomb was published by Norman Davies in 1927 in *Two Rammeside Tombs at Thebes*.

Robbery and destruction of the tombs were rife at this time, and Davies wrote in a letter, now in the MMA archives, "I wish very much to get the fine wall in Userhat's tomb finished, as—who knows—it might be destroyed before next year." His words were prophetic because in 1941, five pieces were cut out of the walls, and the eyes of most of the figures in the tomb chiseled-out. The Davies' copies are now the only complete ones of the tomb. Since that time some of the pieces have been replaced, the painting restored and protected by glass.

On the east jamb of the entrance, there was once an image of Usherhat with the inscription, "[he] shall take possession of his pyramidal tomb." Inside

Hathor, Goddess of the West, stands in front of a tomb with a small pyramid on top. These suggest TT 96 was originally equipped with this feature, not uncommon during this dynasty and the one preceding. Davies believed Mentuhotep's temple at Deir al-Bahari was the precursor.

The tomb consists of a small court, a hall, a pillared room and a burial chamber. The court is shared by the tombs of Neferhotep, Amenwahsu, and Khensmose, all from the first half of the 19th Dynasty. It contains two stele, one of stone and one of mud.

Because flooding is not unknown in the area, provision had been made to prevent water from entering Userhat's tomb—a depression in front of the door and a raised sill. The entrance was sealed by a wooden door set into sandstone doorjambs. The hall is almost completely decorated but the pillared hall was not decorated at all. Beyond it lies the antechamber and burial chamber, with emplacements for three coffins. Only the hall is presently accessible to tourists.

Userhat's title, "First Prophet of the royal *ka* of Thutmosis I," indicates he served in the cult of this deceased king during the reigns of Rameses I and Seti I. The cult center was probably in the Temple of Thutmosis I (called "the Mansion of the *Ka* of Aakheperkare"). Userhat is shown in the paintings with his wife and relatives offering to Thutmosis I and Ahmose-Nefertari, wife of King Ahmose. We know Userhat's parents were Khensem and Tausert, and his wife was called Shepset (Hatshepsut), but he also seems to have had two other wives whose names were obliterated, and a son and daughter.

The hall is replete with scenes that

416-417

Userhat, kneeling on a slab of ritually-pure alabaster, undergoes the purification ceremony four times, performed by eight priests using eight hs vases. Once purified, he greets a host of gods with gifts.

---
417 top

Userhat, in priestly garb and accompanied by his wife, son and sister, offers to Osiris. This scene is a wonderful example of the "ostentatious opulence" that characterized early 19th-Dynasty art, a time when heightened trade and commerce had made Egypt a wealthy empire.

---
416 top left

The painting at the end of the hall facing southeast, with the Tree Goddess with Userhat and his family, damaged in 1941, is the earliest example of the use of shading in Egyptian art.

---
416 top right

Priests pour oil on an offering for the deceased pair, a giant swag of onions, the top shaped like an ankh. Onions were associated with Osiris, god of the underworld, because of their strong properties associated with restoring the senses of the deceased. Art styles vary in this tomb, and the painting of the mourners in these two scenes is cursory.

are mostly funereal rather than reflections of daily life. The subject matter is the cult of the *ka* of Thutmosis I, Userhat's purification and judgement, and his rewards in life and death.

Although all the paintings are generally of superb quality, the Tree Goddess on the north wall of the hall is a masterwork. It also typifies what Arpeg Mekhtarian called, the "somewhat ostentatious opulence" characteristic of 19th-Dynasty art. Another example is the scene of Osiris under a baldachin attended by Hathor-Semyt, Maat and Anubis. Here, the artist has stuffed the interior space with every imaginable object, to the extent that it resembles a magician's dressing-room.

There are also some unusual depictions, like the row of dead birds (chickens?) piled on top of the offering-stands. Above the baldachin is a frieze of alternating Anubis figures and Hathor heads (guardian gods of the Necropolis), separated by *khekers*, also elaborately rendered. The offering table in front of the baldachin, stacked to staggering, is being prepared by Userhat dressed in priestly leopard skin. Yet even here, the artist was not content with the pelt's pattern, and embellished it with encircled stars and woven edging.

At least two artists seem to have been at work: the "master" responsible for the Tree Goddess painting and also the ladies' portraits on the east wall; another of less skill, although not inexperienced, seems to have been responsible for the priests and mourners shown on both registers on the east wall. The bulbous heads of the priests are a Ramesside characteristic, although it is not certain this shape was what was intended, since at least one head has been enlarged from its original artist's sketch. The hands are painted in a clumsy fashion and the incense-burner has been obscured by the floral swag, suggesting either the artist was forced to a speedy completion or had drunk too many jars of beer.

The hall appears complete, but was actually left unfinished; the *khekher* frieze and the ceiling decoration still bear the sketches of the "outline draftsmen" awaiting the brush of the master painter. The fact that most of the tomb was undecorated at the time of Userhat's death would suggest an early demise, except that the decoration of the hall was so elaborate that it must have taken a considerable length of time to complete.

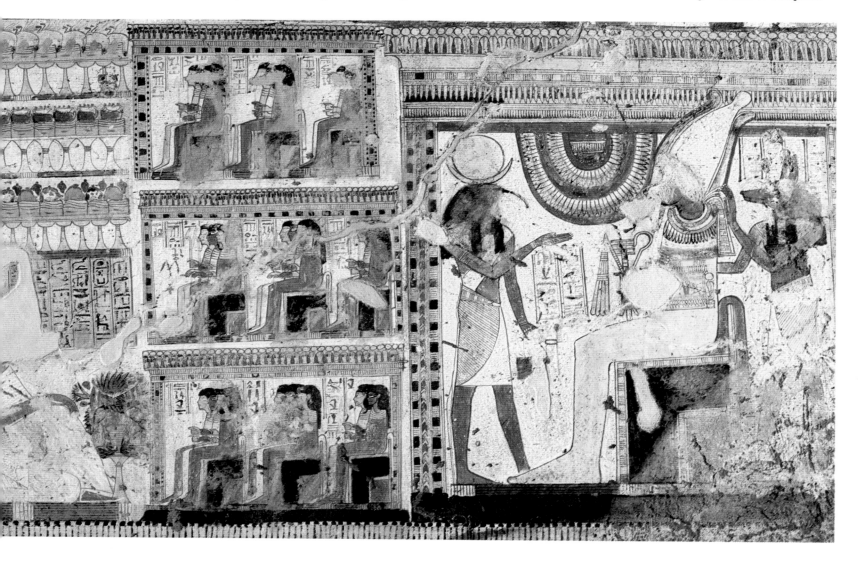

418-419
Offering-bearers bring tables laden with bread, beer, fruit, vegetables, fowl, flowers and djed-pillars. The offerings are for the soul of Ptah-Sokar, the pillar of Osiris.

419
Enthroned figures of Amenhotep III and Queen Tiy, observe the activities of the king's third jubilee festival in Year 37 of his reign. Here the traditionally male royal iconography of a sphinx trampling enemies, bound prisoners, and the unification symbol are part of the queens' throne.

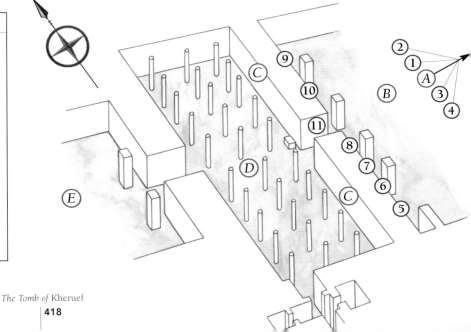

LEGEND		
A	ENTRANCE CORRIDOR	
B	GREAT COURT	
C	DECORATED WALL	
D	BROAD HALL	
E	LONG HALL	

MAIN SCENES

1 — Deceased adoring Ra
2 — Amenhotep IV with Tiy offers wine to Ra-Horakhty and Maat
3 — Amenhotep IV with Tiy offers censes before Atum and Hathor
4 — Amenhotep IV adores Ra-Horakty and libates before Amenhotep III and Tiy
5 — Amenhotep III and Tiy
6 — Eight princesses with vases
7 — Female dancers and musicians
8 — Deceased with officials before Amenhotep III, Hathor and Tiy
9 — Amenhotep III and Tiy followed by 16 princesses
10 — Deceased with Heb-Sed text of year 36
11 — Amenhotep IV and Tiy adore divinities

The Tomb of Kheruef

THE TOMB OF
KHERUEF

by Rita E. Freed

ALTHOUGH IT WAS NEVER FINISHED and has suffered greatly, the tomb of Kheruef stands out as one of the most important religious and historical documents in the Theban necropolis. It is likely its owner was a key figure in the organization of Amenhotep III's first and third jubilees, although representations of Amenhotep IV and his mother at the tomb's entry indicate he died early in the reign of the latter. The size of Kheruef's tomb—the largest private tomb at Thebes known to this day—bears testimony to his importance.

The first Westerner to enter Kheruef's tomb was the German Egyptologist Adolph Erman in 1885, and notes he made were published by Heinrich Brugsch in his *Thesaurus Inscriptionum Aegyptiacarum* of 1891. The famous philologist Sir Alan Gardiner worked there in 1911. Evidence of pillaging of the tomb in the early 1940s brought it to the attention of the Egyptian Department of Antiquities, who cleared, recorded and published it in 1980 in conjunction with the Epigraphic Survey of the University of Chicago.

The tomb is entered through a descending corridor, which opens out onto a large open court with pillared porticoes on the east and west sides. A door in the west wall of the court leads to a broad columned hall, followed by a long pillared hall and statue niche at the tomb's westernmost end. A burial shaft descends from the southwest corner of the broad hall and makes several right angle turns before ending in the second of two burial chambers. There is no evidence that Kheruef was ever buried there, although there were burials in many tombs which were cut into its walls from the Ramesside period on. The only areas of the tomb to receive relief decoration were the entrance corridor and the west wall of the pillared court. It is possible that the tomb was abandoned because the roof collapsed. Nevertheless, it was entered by enemies of Amen, Amenhotep IV, and Kheruef himself, and their names and images were defaced. Excavation of the broad hall yielded fragments of two statues of Kheruef in gray granite and quartzite.

Scenes carved on the west wall of the court are in the elegant and occasionally fussy raised relief style of Amenhotep III. The south side documents events during the king's first jubilee, which took place in Year 30 on the 27th day of the second month of the third season, according to an inscription in the tomb. In separate vignettes, Amenhotep III dressed in his jubilee garment enthroned beside Hathor and Queen Tiy awards Kheruef the Gold of Honor, the king and queen exit their palace, and Kheruef accompanies

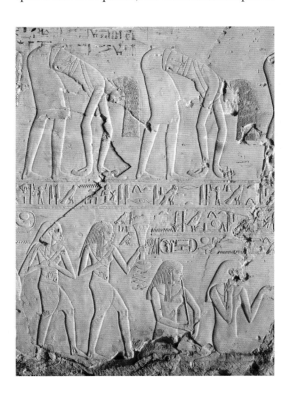

the king and queen as they are towed in a boat greeted by their daughters and a coterie of priests. Singers, dancers and musicians contribute to the festive atmosphere. The scene includes the first known representation of a tambourine.

The northern half of the wall, executed in the same style, celebrates Amenhotep III's third jubilee, which took place in Year 37. There the ceremony of the raising of the *djed*-pillar by the king and priests is featured. This symbol of stability was associated with Osiris, god of resurrection.

It is accompanied by singing, dancing, ritual combat, circumambulation of the wall of Memphis by cattle and donkeys, and preparation and transport of offerings. So important were these scenes, that more than a thousand years later priests surrounded them with a wall and continued to visit them.

Dancers, flutists, and singers take part in
Amenhotep III's first jubilee celebration.

420-421

Music and dancing formed an important part
of Amenhotep III's jubilee celebrations. It has
been suggested that the word hnn written above
these women clapping may be musical notation
for a humming sound they are making.

421 top

A monkey and a calf followed by a shrine are
at the head of the register of dancers.

421 center and bottom

According to the text, these dancers were
brought from the Western Desert oases to
participate in the erection of the djed-pillar.

422-423

Eight of the "Daughters of the Great Ones,"
who may been foreign princesses offer vessels of
to an enthroned Amenhotep III on the occasion
of his first jubilee festival. They wear the
diaphanous flowing garments of their time.

Egyptian Emotions

by Araldo De Luca

Intensely evocative: these are the words that describe the pale blue dawn over the Nile as the boat slid slowly down the river, the yellow of the desert that for millennia has hidden the incredible treasures that every morning I prepared myself to discover, but, above all, the strong, almost violent desire I felt to reveal the depths and colors as I switched on my carefully positioned lights against the background of a series of ancient buildings and

decorations that the weak light inside hardly disclosed.

Intensely evocative is the best way to summarize my photographic assignment in the Valley of the Kings, the Valley of the Queens and the Valley of the Nobles; if I pause to think, the memories and impressions flood back at an exponential rate.

The staff, for example; how could I possibly forget that friendly, efficient group who followed me during the three months of work. Everyone tried their hardest, often in conditions of great difficulty, so that every shot was as good as it could be despite the heat, the cramped spaces and the exhausting hours. Of everyone, I especially want to mention my assistant, Francesco Zanchi, and Gamal Safik, who handled public relations and reduced all problems to manageable proportions.

It was not at all simple to transport the huge amount of equipment down narrow corridors and into small rooms, nor was it easy to organize the hundreds of cables to light the interiors, nor was it straightforward to remove and replace the heavy glass plates that protect the elaborately decorated walls; yet everyone contributed their share, becoming, with me, the instigator of each shot.

The royal burial sites are a place of unequalled fascination, above all for those, like me, who discovered them after having had the extraordinary fortune to admire (and in my case touch and photograph) the incredible treasures found in the tombs that are today displayed in the Egyptian Museum in Cairo. On an earlier photographic assignment that lasted three months, I was privileged to photograph the most

425 top

A ventilation rig to pump fresh air into one of the tombs of the nobles. A 2 HP motor joined to a pipe 25 cm (10 inches) in diameter and up to 80 m (265 feet) long allowed work for days at a time to be performed in spaces measuring just a few square metres (square feet).

425 bottom

Khaemwaset tomb; Francesco Zanchi with the chromatic scale. This is a test to ensure an exact reproduction of the colour in the printed version.

valuable of these objects—the solid gold sarcophagi, the painted and gilded wooden statues, the pectorals made from colored stones and polychrome enamels—and on each occasion I entered a tomb, I tried to imagine them in their original location.

How many unexpected and different emotions I experienced! As I anxiously waited to enter Tutankhamen's tomb, it was impossible not to remember the dazzling golds and colored inlays of his grave goods, and when I entered, what a surprise it was to find just three small rooms! What, then, were the grave goods like that disappeared from the huge tombs containing multiple magnificently decorated rooms like that of Rameses VI? The five corridors, the room of

424 top

Araldo De Luca and Francesco Zanchi before their departure with 19 cases of equipment weighing 800 kilograms.

424 bottom

The tomb of Rameses VI; Egyptian workers remove the protective glass sheets from the frescoes to allow the photographs to be taken.

424-425

The tomb of Nefertari; Araldo De Luca during the shoot of a fresco along the stairs that lead to the lower room.

426 top
The tomb of Nefertari;
preparations for shooting the
lower room.

426 bottom left
The tomb of Nefertari; Araldo De
Luca looks at a Polaroid to check
the framing and the correct degree
of illumination required.

426 bottom right
The tomb of Merenptah,
sarcophagus room; Francesco
Zanchi reads the value of the
lights on the back wall while
three assistants position the 5
meter (17 feet) ladder made
especially by a local carpenter.

426-427
The tomb of Rameses VI;
preparations for shooting a side-
lit wall in the sarcophagus room.

pillars and the burial chamber filled with
crowded paintings that depict a huge collection
of magic and religious texts in complex,
sophisticated decorations. How was it possible
to forget the intense blue of the star-spangled
ceiling produced using ground lapis-lazuli and
decorated with chains of figures painted with
ocher and red pigments?

It is impossible, however, for a
photographer to disassociate any shot from the
technical environment it was taken in. The most
difficult problem was to illuminate the interiors
which were sometimes so vast or split into so
many sections that it took hours to set up the
lights and lay the cables, or so small or cluttered
with mirrors and barriers that it was difficult to
find suitable positions. In some cases I used the

open flash technique in which ten series of lamps comprising fourteen flashes each went off simultaneously. To capture the decorated walls I used a series of flashes positioned along one side only so as to highlight the reliefs.

Our flash equipment consisted of 12 x 1500 watt Bowens and 2 x 6000 watt Bowens giving a total of 30 kilowatts; then there were dozens of umbrella reflectors, diffusors, stands etc. to illuminate corners and hidden details.

For the photographs I used: a Silvestri 4 x 5 S with Schneider XL, 47, 58 and 75 Superangulon lenses—this is a versatile camera that I could position in the most restricted of spaces (where often I could not enter myself) yet still view the image on the polished glass. One of its advantages is its compactness yet it is

still able to mount a 120° viewing angle without creating distorsion or allowing micrometric decentralisation;

a Sinar P2 4 x 5 with thirteen different lenses to cover all possible requirements;

a Mamiya 6 x 7 with a range of lenses from 50 to 500 mm that I used to capture hundreds of details in difficult and precarious circumstances. This is an ideal handheld camera to use with a flash for all those shots taken on wood and rope ladders, sometimes over 5 meters (17 feet) high, to catch the most elusive of details.

I took 2500 f.to 4 x 5 plates and 800 rolls of f.to 120 Kodak EPR and EPP film. In the smallest tombs where the lack of oxygen and excess of dust made the air unbreathable, I

created a ventilation system from dozens of meters (40 feet) of 25 cm (10 inches) diameter pipes that made work possible despite the outside temperature on occasion reaching 50°C.

Most of the surfaces photographed were cleaned with gentle jets of compressed air, the dust of thousands of years on the floors was vacuumed up and the sarcophagi cleaned. We worked long hours: up at 5 and then in the tombs from 6am to 6pm. Between 7 and 8 pm we prepared the chassis used to unload and load the films and catalogued the photographs taken.

The equipment used on this unforgettable adventure was split into 19 cases weighing a total of 800 kilograms and I was assisted by 11 people.

GLOSSARY

Amun "The Hidden One," the principal god of New Kingdom Thebes, whose temple at Karnak was one of Egypt's largest. He was joined with the sun god as Amun-Ra and often referred to as "King of the Gods."

Ankh A hieroglyph, perhaps representing a sandal strap, that was the Egyptian word for "life."

Anubis God of the dead, represented as a seated or recumbent dog or jackal.

Atum A creator god, represented in human form.

Bark A model boat with a *naos* holding an image of a god, carried by priests in religious processions.

Books of the Netherworld Compositions of texts and figures describing the netherworld and the journeys of the sun god to and through it. There are several books, including the *Book of Amduat, Book of Gates, Book of Caverns, Book of the Earth, Book of Nut, Book of the Day and Night, Book of the Heavenly Cow, Book of the Dead*, and the *Litany of Ra*. They are found in royal tombs of the New Kingdom and are descended from earlier religious documents such as the *Pyramid Texts* and *Coffin Texts*.

Canopic jars Stone or pottery vessels in which mummified organs were stored in a tomb. The jar lids were often carved with the heads of the Four Sons of Horus: Amsety (whose jar held the liver); Hapy (lungs); Duamutef (stomach); and Qebehsenuef (intestines).

Cartouche An oval loop of rope enclosing the nomen and prenomen of a pharaoh. Its shape was also used for sarcophagi in some 18th and 19th Dynasty royal tombs (e.g., KV 8, Merenptah), and for the plan of the burial chamber (e.g., KV 34, Thutmosis III).

Co-regency The overlapping reigns of two rulers, thought to ensure a peaceful

transition. There is much discussion about how many co-regencies occurred in dynastic Egypt.

Ennead The nine deities described in the creation myth proclaimed by Heliopolitan priests.

False door An elaborately niched stele in a tomb or temple in front of which offerings might be placed and through which the *ka* of the deceased could move between the realms of the living and the dead.

Foundation deposits Ritual objects, especially model tools, buried at temples or tombs and intended magically to ensure the survival of the building for eternity.

Hathor A goddess represented both as a woman or a cow whose name means "House of Horus" and who was considered the mother of each of Egypt's pharaohs.

Heb-Sed Festival A royal jubilee, in theory (but rarely in fact) celebrated by a pharaoh in his 30th regnal year as an act of renewal and rejuvenation.

Hieroglyphs "Sacred carved letters" in Greek. Egyptian writing system, used primarily for religious and historical texts on tomb and temple walls. About 6,000 different signs are known but fewer than a thousand were regularly used.

Hieratic A script consisting of cursive, simplified forms of hieroglyphs, used primarily for writing on papyri and *ostraca*.

Horus Falcon god closely associated with kingship and the goddesses Isis and Hathor.

Hypostyle hall A large, roofed columned hall in an Egyptian temple. The term is Greek for "resting on pillars." The hall is thought to symbolize the swampy lands that surrounded a primeval mound on which creation took place.

Isis Sister and wife of Osiris, mother of Horus, mother of pharaoh, and a popular goddess of women, children, and health.

Ka With the *ba* and the *ankh*, the life-forces of a human being. After death, the *ka* moved between this life and the next and partook of offerings provided for its continued existence.

Kiosk A small, roofless temple with pillars, often used to temporarily house statues of deities during religious processions.

Maat Goddess associated with truth, justice, correct behavior, and harmony.

Migdol A type of Syro-Palestinian fortification.

Mut Vulture goddess, wife of Amun, mother of Khonsu.

Nemes headdress Royal headdress like that worn by Tutankhamun on his gold mask, consisting of a piece of cloth covering the forehead, tied at the back, and hanging over the shoulders.

Nut Goddess of the sky whose body lay above the earth and who, each evening, swallowed the sun, Ra, and each morning gave birth.

Osirid pillar A pillar whose face is carved in the form of the mummiform god Osiris. Rows of such pillars usually surround a temple's forecourt or peristyle.

Ostracon (pl. *ostraca*, Greek for "potsherd") Small pieces of pottery or stone used by scribes for jotting down memos, lists, notes, letters, or sketches.

Papyrus A plant (*Cyperus papyrus*) from which sheets and rolls of writing material were made; the plant is a symbol of Lower Egypt.

Peristyle Open temple courtyard surrounded internally with a row of pillars or columns.

Ptah Mummiform creator god, especially worshipped at Memphis, and also associated with craftsmen.

Pylon "Gate" in Greek. A monumental, sloping-sided temple gate, the center

lower than its two towers, marking the entrance to a temple or one of its component parts. It represents the horizon, with two mountains and an intervening valley above which the sun rises each day.

Ra Solar god, especially worshipped at Heliopolis, in the New Kingdom joined with Amun as Amun-Ra.

Ramesside Period The 19th and 20th Dynasties in the New Kingdom when 11 of 17 rulers were named Rameses.

Sacred lake Pool of water within a temple compound used for sailing the sacred bark and as a source of water for religious rituals.

Shawabti (also ushabti, shabty) Small mummiform statuettes that magically performed work for the deceased in the Afterlife.

Shrine The most sacred part of a temple where the cult image of a god resided. Sometimes called a "naos." Also a small religious structure (see also "kiosk") or small box in which a statue might be palced.

Stele A flat stone or wooden slab on which inscriptions were carved or painted. Most stele are funerary or commemorative and were placed in tombs or temples.

Temenos A Greek term for the walled precinct in which a temple or other cult building lay.

Temple In dynastic Egypt, the residence of a deity or group of deities. It may consist of a building or a complex of buildings in which performed various cult activities. Temples were regularly considered the site on which creation had taken place.

Thoth God of knowledge, represented as a baboon or an ibis.

Uraeus A representation of a cobra heads worn on the forehead of pharaoh's crown or headdress as a protective symbol.

INDEX

BIBLIOGRAPHY

THEBES: A MODEL FOR EVERY CITY
and
THE EXPLORATION OF THEBES
Texts by Kent R. Weeks
Arnold, Dieter. *Gräber des Alten und Mittleren Reiches in El-Tarif* (Archäologische Veroffentlichungen, Deutsche Archäologisches Institut, 12). Mainz, 1976.
Assmann, Jan (ed.). *Theben.* Mainz am Rhein, 1983-96. Thirteen volumes publishing the decoration of Ramesside tombs.
Gardiner, Alan H. and Arthur E.P. Weigall. *A Topographical Catalogue of the Private Tombs of Thebes.* London, 1913.
Nims, Charles F. *Thebes of the Pharaohs: Pattern for Every City.* London, 1965.
Otto, Eberhard. *Topographie des Thebanischen Gaues* (Untersuchungen zur Geschichte und Altertumskunde Aegyptens, 16). Berlin, 1952.
Riefstahl, Elizabeth. *Thebes in the Time of Amunhotep III.* Norman, Oklahoma, 1964.
Strudwick, Nigel and Helen. *Thebes in Egypt: A Guide to the Tombs and Temples of Ancient Egypt.* London, 1994.
Thomas, Elizabeth. *The Royal Necropoleis of Thebes.* Princeton, 1966.

THE TEMPLE OF AMENHOTEP III
Text by Kent R. Weeks
Bickel, Susanne et al. *Untersuchungen im Totentempel des Merenptah in Theben, 3: Tore und andere wiederverwendete Bauteile Amenophis' III* (BÄBA, 16). Stuttgart, 1997.
Haent, Gerhard. *Untersuchungen im Totentempel Amenophis' III.* BÄBA 11 (1981).
Helck, Wolfgang. *Les Inscriptions grecques et latines du colosse de Memnon.* Bibliothèque d'Étude, 31. Cairo, 1960.
Kozloff, Arielle P. and Betsy M. Bryan. *Egypt's Dazzling Sun: Amenhotep III and his World.* Cleveland, 1992.
Petrie, William M.F. *Six Temples at Thebes.* London, 1897.

THE TEMPLE OF HATSHEPSUT
Text by Betsy M. Bryan
Dieter, Arnold. *Deir el-Bahari, in Lexikon der Ägyptologie I, 1017-1022*
Dieter Arnold in *Die Tempel Ägyptens* (Zurich, 1992) 134-141
Jadwiga Lipinska. *Deir el-Bahari, Vol. II, The Temple of Tuthmosis III.* Architecture (Warsaw 1977)
Edouard Naville. *Deir el Bahari,* 6 volumes (London 1895-1908)
Z. Wysocki. *The Result of research ... in the Hatshepsut Temple of Deir el-Bahari,* in MDAIK 40 (1984) 329-349; 41 (1985) 293-307; 42 (1986) 213-228.

THE TEMPLE OF SETI I
Text by Peter Brand
Peter Brand. *The Monuments of Seti I* (Leiden, 2000).
Kitchen, Kenneth A. *Pharaoh Triumphant. The Life and Times of Ramesses II King of Egypt.* Warminster 1981.
Murnane, William J. *Ancient Egyptian Coregencies* Chicago, 1977.
Osing, Jurgend. *Der Tempel Sethos 'I . in Gurna: Die Reliefs und Inschriften* (Mainz, 1977).
Seele, Keith. *The Coregency of Ramses II with Seti I and the date of the Great Hypostyle Hall at Karnak* (Chicago, 1947).

RAMESSEUM THE TEMPLE OF RAMESES II
Text by Christian Leblanc
Ch. Leblanc. *Diodore, le tombeau d'Osymandyas et la statuaire du Ramesseum.* Mélanges Gamal Eddin Mokhtar. Bibliothèque d'Etude de l'IFAO, tome 97/2, pp. 69-82 et pl. I-VI. Le Caire 1985.
Ch. Leblanc et F. Hassanein. *Le Ramesseum, temple de millions d'années à la gloire de Ramsès le Grand.* Les Dossiers Histoire et Archéologie, n° 136, pp. 36-45, Fontaine-lès-Dijon 1989..
Ch. Leblanc. *Le temple de millions d'années de Ramsès II à Thèbes. Histoire et sauvegarde du Ramesseum.* Bulletin du Cercle Lyonnais d'Egytologie Victor Loret. n° 7, pp. 63-76. Lyon 1993.

Ch. Leblanc. *Les sources grecques et les colosses de Ramsès-Rê-en-hekaou et de Touy, au Ramesseum.* Memnonia, tome IV-V, pp. 71-101 et pl. XVI-XX. Le Caire 1994.
Ch. Leblanc. *Quelques réflexions sur le programme iconographique et la fonction des temples de millions d'années,* in The Temple in ancient Egypt. New discoveries and recent research, Stephen Quirke ed., British Museum Press, pp. 49-56, Londres 1997. Article également publié dans: Memnonia, tome VIII, pp. 93-105. Le Caire 1997.
Ch. Leblanc, Ch. Barbotin, M. Nelson et G. Lecuyot. *Les monuments d'éternité de Ramsès II. Nouvelles fouilles thébaines.* Editions de la Réunion des Musées Nationaux. Coll. Les Dossiers du musée du Louvre. Paris 1999. 96 pp.
Ch. Leblanc. *Le Ramesseum et la tombe de Ramsès II. Recherches et travaux de mise en valeur.* Les Dossiers d'archéologie, n° 241, pp. 12-23. Dijon 1999.
Ch. Leblanc. *Ramses II e il Tempio di Milioni di Anni.* Archeologia Viva, n° 77, anno XVIII, pp. 18-31. Firenze [septembre-octobre] 1999.
Le Ramesseum. Collection scientifique du CEDAE, vol. I, IV, VI, IX-1, IX-2, X et XI parus. Le Caire 1973-1988.
Memnonia, Bulletin édité par l'Association pour la Sauvegarde du Ramesseum, vol. I-X. Le Caire 1990-1999.

THE TEMPLE OF RAMESES III
Text by Betsy M. Bryan
Uvo Hölscher. *The Mortuary Temple of Ramses III* (The Excavations of Medinet Habu, Vol. 4/5, Chicago, 1951, 1954).
R. Stadelmann. *Medinet Habu,* in Lexikon der Ägyptologie III, 1255-1271.
William J. Murnane, *United with Eternity: A concise guide to the monuments of Medinet Habu* (Chicago, Oriental Institute, University of Chicago, 1980).

INTRODUCTION TO THE VALLEY OF THE KINGS
by Kent R. Weeks

Hornung, Erik. *Tal der Könige: Die Ruhestatte der Pharaonen. Zurich, 1982.* Published in English as: Valley of the Kings: Horizon of Eternity. New York, 1990.
Romer, John. *Valley of the Kings.* London, 1981.
Thomas, Elizabeth. *Royal Necropoleis of Thebes.* Princeton, 1966.
Weeks, Kent R. (ed.). *Atlas of the Valley of the Kings* (Publications of the Theban Mapping Project, 1). Cairo, 2000.
Wilkinson, Richard and C. Nicholas Reeves. *The Complete Valley of the Kings.* London, 1996.

THE FUNERARY LITERATURE IN THE TOMBS OF THE VALLEY OF THE KINGS
by Erik Hornung
Funerary Literature
Hornung, Erik. *The Ancient Egyptian Books of the Afterlife,* Ithaca N.Y., 1999.
Clagett, M. *Ancient Egyptian Science: A Source Book,* Vol. I, Philadelphia 1989.
Hornung, E., *Die Unterweltsbücher der Ägypter,* Zurich 1992.
Amduat
Hornung, E. *Das Amduat. Die Schrift des Verborgenen Raumes,* 3 vols, Wiesbaden 1963-1967;
id. *Texte zum Amduat,* 3 vols, Geneva 1987-1994.
Schweizer, A. *Seelenführer durch den verborgenen Raum, Das Ägyptische Unterweltsbuch Amduat,* Munich 1994
Litany of Ra.
Piankoff, A. *The Litany of Re,* New York, 1964.
Hornung, E. *Das Buch der Anbetung des Re im Westen,* 2 vols, Geneva 1975-1976.
Book of Gates
Hornung, E. *Das Buch von den Pforten des Jenseits,* 2 vols, Geneva 1979-1984
Zeidler, J. *Pfortenbuchstudien,* 2 vols, Wiesbaden 1999.
On **Amduat** and **Book of Gates** see also:
Hornung, E. *Die Nachtfahrt der Sonne,* Zurich und Munich 1991.
Book of Caverns
Piankoff, A. *Le Livre des Quererts,* Cairo 1946.

Book of Earth
Piankoff, A. *La création du disque solaire*, Cairo 1953.
Books of Heavens
Piankoff, A. *Le Livre du jour et de la nuit*, Cairo 1942.
Roulin, G. *Le Livre de la Nuit*, 2 vols, Fribourg and Göttingen 1996.
Book of the Celestial Cow
Hornung, E. *Der ägyptische Mythos von der Himmelskuh*, 3rd ed. Fribourg and Göttingen 1997.

THE TOMB OF THUTMOSIS III
Text by Erik Hornung
Romer, J. *The Tomb of Thutmosis III*, in: Mitteilungen des Deutschen Archäolog. Instituts Kairo 31, 1975, 315-351.
Fornari, A. and Tosi, M. *Nella sede della verità*, Milano 1987.

THE TOMB OF AMENHOTEP II
Text by Erik Hornung
Bucher, P. *Les textes des tombes de Thutmosis III et d'Aménophis II*, Cairo 1932.

THE TOMB OF TUTANKHAMEN
Text by T.G.H. James
Carter, H. *The Tomb of Tut.ankh.Amen.* 3 vols. (vol. 1 with A. Mace). London, 1923-1933.
Desroches-Noblecourt, C. *Tutankhamen: Life and Death of a Pharaoh*. London, 1963.
James, T.G.H. *Howard Carter: The Path to Tutankhamun.* London, 2001
James, T.G.H. *Tutankhamun: The Ethernal Splendour of the Boy Pharaoh.* London, 2000.
Reeves, (C.) N. *The Complete Tutankhamun.* London, 1990.

THE TOMB OF AY
Text by T.G.H. James
Piankoff, A. 'Les peintures dans la tombe du roi Aï', in *Mitterilungen des Deutschen archäologischen Instituts für Ägyptische Altertumskunde in Kairo*, 16, pp. 247-51.
Reeves, (C.) N. and Wilkinson, R.H., *The Complete Valley of the Kings.* London, 1997.
Schaden, O.J. 'Clearance in the tomb of the king Ay (WV 23)' in *Journal of the American Research Center in Egypt*, 21, pp. 39-64. Boston, 1984.

THE TOMB OF HOREMHEB
Text by T.G.H. James
Davis, T.M. et al. *The Tomb of Harmhabi and Toutânkhamanou.* London, 1912.
Hari, R. *Horemheb et la Reine Moutnedjement.* Geneva, 1965.
Hornung, E., *Das Grab des Haremhab im Tal der Könige.* Bern, 1971.
Martin, G.T. *The Memphite Tomb of Horemheb, Commander-in-Chief of Tut'ankhamun.* Vol.1. London, 1989.

THE TOMB OF RAMESES I
Text by Erik Hornung
Piankoff, A. *La tombe de Ramsès Ier*, in: Bulletin de l'Institut français d'archéologie orientale 56, 1957, 189-200.

THE TOMB OF SETI I
Text by Erik Hornung
Burton, H. and Hornung, E. *The Tomb of the Pharaoh Seti I*, Zurich and Munich 1991.

THE TOMB OF RAMESES II
Text by Christian Leblanc
Ch. Leblanc. *Trois campagnes de fouille dans la tombe de Ramsès II. [KV.7] - Vallée des Rois 1993/1994/1995.* Memnonia, tome VII, pp. 185-211et pl. L-LVII. Le Caire 1996.
Ch. Leblanc. *The Tomb of Ramesses II and Remains of his Funerary Treasure.* Egyptian Archaeology, Bulletin of the Egypt Exploration Society, n° 10, pp. 11-13. Londres [mars] 1997.
Ch. Leblanc. *Nella tomba di Ramses II. Ultime scoperte in Egitto.* Archeologia Viva. n° 63, anno XVI, pp. 24-33. Firenze [mai-juin] 1997.
Ch. Leblanc, *Quatrième campagne de fouille dans la tombe de Ramsès II [KV.7] — 1996/1997.* Memnonia, tome VIII, pp. 151-172 et pl. XXXVII-XLVII. Le Caire 1997.
Ch. Leblanc. *Cinquième campagne de fouille dans la tombe de Ramsès II [KV.7] — 1997/1998.* Memnonia, tome IX, pp. 73-91et pl. V-X. Le Caire 1998.
Ch. Leblanc. *Les récentes découvertes dans la tombe de Ramsès II.* Bulletin de la Société Française d'Egyptologie, n° 141, pp. 20-35 et fig. 1-6. Paris [mars] 1998.
Ch. Leblanc et Ch. Barbotin. *Les monuments d'éternité de Ramsès II. Nouvelles fouilles thébaines.* Editions de la Réunion des Musées Nationaux. Coll. Les Dossiers du musée du Louvre". Paris 1999.
Ch. Leblanc. *Le Ramesseum et la tombe de Ramsès II. Recherches et travaux de mise en valeur.* Les Dossiers d'archéologie, n° 241, pp. 12-23. Dijon, mars 1999.
Ch. Leblanc. *Sixième et septième campagnes de fouille dans la tombe de Ramsès II [KV.7] — Années 1998/1999 et 1999/2000.* Memnonia, tome XI. Le Caire 2000.

THE TOMB OF MERENPTAH
Text by Edwin C. Brock
Assmann, Jan. *Die Inschriften auf den äusseren Sarcophagdeckel des Merenptah*, MDAIK 28 (1972), pp. 47-74.
Brock, Edwin C. *The Tomb of Merenptah and its Sarcophagi.* In: C. Nicholas Reeves (ed.), After Tut'ankhamun: Research and Excavation in the Royal Necropolis at Thebes, London, 1992, pp. 121-140.
Carter, Howard. *Report of Work Done in Upper Egypt (1903-1904)*, ASAE 6 (1906), pp. 116-119.
Lefébure, Eugène. *Les Hypogées royaux de Thèbes: notices des hypogées (MMAF III, 2)*, Paris, 1886, pp. 35-47.
Porter, Bertha, and Rosalind Moss. *Topographical Bibliography of Ancient Egyptian Hieroglyphic Texts, Reliefs and Paintings*, vol. I, pt. 2, The Theban Necropolis: Royal tombs and smaller cemeteries, Oxford, 1964, pp. 507-509, plán, p. 504.
Thomas, Elisabeth. *The Royal Necropoleis of Thebes*, Princeton,

1966, pp. 108-110.
Wilkinson, Richard H., and C. Nicholas Reeves. *The Complete Valley of the Kings*, London and New York, 1996, pp. 147-149.

THE TOMB OF TAUSERT AND SETNAKHT
Text by Harwig Altenmüller
B. Porter, R. Moss. *Topographical Bibliography of Ancient Egyptian Hieroglyphic Texts, Reliefs, and Paintings*, Oxford 1964, p. 527-532.
Hartwig Altenmueller. *Das Grab der Königin Tausret im Tal der Könige von Theben.* Studien zur Altaegyptischen Kultur 10, Hamburg 1983, p. 1-24.
Hartwig Altenmueller. *Bemerkungen zu den neu gefundenen Daten im Grab der Königin Twosre (KV 14) im Tal der Könige von Theben.* In: C.N. Reeves (ed.). After Tutankhamun: Research and Excavation in the Royal Necropolis at Thebes, London 1992, p. 141-164.
Hartwig Altenmueller. *Das Grab der Koenigin Tausret und des Sethnacht*, forthcoming.

THE TOMB OF RAMESES III
Text by Edwin C. Brock
Andrzejewski, Tadeusz. *Le Livre des Portes dans la salle de sarcophage du tombeau de Ramsès III*, ASAE 57 (1962), pp. 1-6.
Lefébure, Eugène. *Les Hypogées royaux de Thèbes: notices des hypogées (MMAF III, 2)*, Paris, 1886, pp. 87-120, pl. 58-656.
Marciniak, Marek. *Deux campagnes épigraphiques au tombeau de Ramsès III dans ka Vallée des Rois (no. 11)*, Études at Travaux 12 (1983), pp. 295-305.
Marciniak, Marek. *Réparations anciennes dans le tombeau de Ramsès III (no. 11) dans la Vallée des Rois*, Africana Bulletin 31 (1982), pp. 37-43.
Porter, Bertha and Rosalind Moss. *Topographical Bibliography of Ancient Egyptian Hieroglyphic Texts, Reliefs and Paintings*, vol. I, pt. 2, The Theban Necropolis: Royal tombs and smaller cemeteries, Oxford, 1964, pp. 518-527, plan, p. 510.
Thomas, Elisabeth. *The Royal Necropoleis of Thebes*, Princeton, 1966, pp. 125-126.
Wilkinson, Richard H. and C. Nicholas Reeves. *The Complete Valley of the Kings*, London and New York, 1996, pp. 163-168.

THE TOMB OF RAMESES IV
Text by Erik Hornung
Hornung, E. *Zwei ramessidische Königsgräber*: Ramese IV. und Ramese VII., Mainz 1990.

THE TOMB OF RAMESES VI
Text by Edwin C. Brock
Abitz, Fiedrich. *Baugeschichte und dekoration des Grabes Ramses' VI.* (OBO 89), Fribourg, Göttingen, 1989.
Aldred, Cyril. *More Light on the Ramesside tomb robberies.* In: J. Ruffle, G.A. Gaballa, K.A. Kitchen (eds.). Glimpses of Ancient Egypt. Studies in Honour of H.W. Fairman, Westminster,

1979, pp. 92-99.
Barguet, Paul. *Remarques sur quelques scènes de la salle du sarcophage de Ramsès VI*, RdE 30 (1978), pp. 51-56.
Brock, Edwin C. *Documenting the Sarcophagi of Rameses VI.* Canadian Mediterranean Institute Bulletin, 13.2 (April, 1993), p. 2.
Darressy, Georges. *Rapport sur le déblaiment des tombes 6 et 9 de Biban el Molouk.* ASAE 18 (1919), pp. 270-274.
Darressy, Georges. *Un Trace égyptienne d'une voute elliptique*, ASAE, 8 (1907), pp. 237-241.
Goebs, Katja. *Expressing Luminosity in Iconography: Features of the Solar Bark in the Tomb of Ramesses VI*, GM 165 (1998), pp. 57-71.
Grapow, Hermann and Heinrich Schäfer. *Zu den Deckenbild im Grabe Ramses des Sechsten mit dem Aufriesszeichnungen der Sonnenschife*, ZAS 81 (1956), pp. 24-28.
Hornung, Erik. *Zum Schutzbild im Grabe Ramses' VI.*, In: J. M. Kamstra, H. Milde, K. Wagtendonk (eds). Funerary Symbols and Religion. Essays dedicated to Professor M. S. H. G. Heerma van Voss on the occasion of his retirement from the Chair of the History of Ancient Religions at the University of Amsterdam, 1988, pp. 45-51.
Hornung, Erik. *Zum Turiner Grabplan.* In: John Baines et al. (eds) Pyramid Studies and Other Essays Presented to I. E. S. Edwards (EES Occasional Publications, 7), London, 1988, pp. 138-142.
Lefébure, Eugène. *Les Hypogées royaux de Thèbes: notices des hypogées (MMAF III, 2)*, Paris, E. Leroux, 1886, pp. 48-80, pl. 25-54.
Piankoff, Alexandre. *La création du disque solaire*, Cairo, 1953.
Piankoff, Alexandre and Charles Maystre. *Deux plafonds dans les tombes royales*, BIFAO 38 (1939), pp. 65-70, pl. V. VI.
Piankoff, Alexandre. *The Tomb of Ramesses VI* (Egyptian Religious Texts and Representations = Bolingen Series 40. 1,2) New York, 1954.
Porter, Bertha and Rosalind Moss. *Topographical Bibliography of Ancient Egyptian Hieroglyphic Texts, Reliefs and Paintings*, vol. I, pt. 2, The Theban Necropolis: Royal tombs and smaller cemeteries, Oxford, 1964, pp. 511-517, plan, p. 510.
Thomas, Elisabeth. *The Royal Necropoleis of Thebes*, Princeton, 1966, pp. 129-130.
Ventura, Raphael. *The Largest Project for a Royal Tomb in the Valley of the Kings*, JEA 74 (1988), pp. 137-156.
Wilkinson, Richard H., and C. Nicholas Reeves. *The Complete Valley of the Kings*, London and New York, 1996, pp. 164-165.

THE TOMB OF RAMESES IX
Text by Edwin C. Brock
Abitz, Friedrich. *Der Bauablauf und die Dekoration des Grabes Ramese IX.* SAK 17 (1990), pp. 1-40.
Abitz, Friedrich. *The Structure of the Decoration in the Tomb of Ramesses IX.* In: C. Nicholas Reeves (ed.). After

Tutankhamun: Research and Excavation in the Royal Necropolis at Thebes. London, 1992, pp. 165-185.

Daressy, Georges. *Rapport sur le déblaiment des tombes 6 et 9 be Biban el Molouk*. ASAE 18 (1919), pp. 270-274.

Guilmant, Felix. *La Tombeau de Rameses IX (MIFAO 15)*, Cairo IFAO, 1907.

Hornung, Erik. *Ein aenigmatische Wand im Grabe Ramses' IX*. In: Jurgen Ösing and Günther Dreyer (eds.). Form und Mass. Beiträge zur Literatur, Sprache und Kunst des alten Ägypten. Festschrift für Gerhard fecht zum 65. Geburtstag am 6. Februar 1987. (Ägyptens und Altes Testament. Studien zu Geschichte, Kultur und Religions Ägyptens und des Altes Testaments, 12). Wiesbaden, 1987, pp. 226-237.

Lefébure, Eugène. *Les Hypogées royaux de Thèbes:notices des hypogées (MMAF III, 2)*, Paris, 1886, pp. 16-30, pl. 4-23.

Porter, Bertha, and Rosalind Moss. *Topographical Bibliography of Ancient Egyptian Hieroglyphic Texts, Reliefs and Paintings, vol. I, pt. 2*, The Theban Necropolis: Royal tombs and smaller cemeteries, Oxford, 1964, pp. 501-505, plan, p. 498.

Thomas, Elisabeth. *The Royal Necropoleis of Thebes*, Princeton, 1966, pp. 131-132.

Wilkinson, Richard H., and C. Nicholas Reeves. *The Complete Valley of the Kings*, London ad New York, 1996, pp. 168-171.

WESTERN THEBES AND THE QUEENS OF THE TWO LANDS IN THE NEW KINGDOM
and
THE TOMB OF NEFERTARI
and
THE TOMBS OF THE SONS OF RAMESES III
and
THE TOMB OF AMENHERKHEPSHEF
and
THE TOMB OF KHAEMWASET
texts by Christian Leblanc

Abitz, F. *Ramses III. in den Gräbern seiner Söhne*, OBO 72, Göttingen 1986.

Cabrol, Agnès. *Aménophis III*, Monaco 2000.

Hassanien, Fathy et Nelson, Monique. *La tombe du prince Amon-(her)-khepchef [VdR n° 55]*, Collection scientifique du CEDAE, Le Caire 1976.

La tombe du prince Khaemouaset [VdR n° 44], Collection scientifique du CEDAE, Le Caire 1997.

Leblanc, Christian. *Le dégagement de la tombe de Ta-nedjemy. Une contribution à l'histoire de la Vallée des Reines*. Bulletin de la Société Française d'Egyptologie n° 89, Paris 1980, pp. 32-49.

Leblanc, Christian. *Henout-taouy et la tombe n° 73 de la Vallée des Reines*. Bulletin de l'Institut Français d'Archéologie Orientale 86, Le Caire 1986, pp. 203-226.

Leblanc, Christian. *L'identification de la tombe de Henout-mi-rê, fille et*

grande épouse royale de Ramsès II. Bulletin de l'Institut Français d'Archéologie Orientale 88, Le Caire 1988, pp. 131-146.

Leblanc, Christian. *Architecture et évolution chronologique des tombes de la Vallée des Reines*. Bulletin de l'Institut Français d'Archéologie Orientale 89, Le Caire 1989, pp. 227-247.

Leblanc, Christian. *Ta set neferou. Une nécropole de Thèbes-Ouest et son histoire*. I. Le Caire 1989. [II-V: en préparation]

Leblanc, Christian. *L'archéologie et l'histoire de la Vallée des Reines*. Les Dossiers d'archéologie, n° 149/150, Dijon 1990, pp. 22-29.

Leblanc, Christian. *The Valley of the Queens and Royal Children. History and Resurrection of an archaeological site*, in Art and Eternity. The Nofretari Wall Paintings Conservation Project [1986-1992], pp. 19-29. The Getty Conservation Institute, Santa Monica 1993.

Leblanc, Christian. *Nefertari, "l'Aimée-de-Mout". Epouses, filles et fils de Ramsès II*. Coll. Champollion. Monaco 1999.

Leblanc, Christian. *Reines, princesses et princes étrangers à la cour royale d'Egypte, durant le Nouvel Empire*, Dédale, n° 9-10, pp. 497-520, 4 fig. et 4 pl. Paris 1999.

Leblanc, Christian et Hassanein, Fathy. *La Vallée des Reines. Des tombes royales enfin identifiées*. Archéologia, n° 205, Dijon 1985, pp. 24-31.

Leblanc, Christian et Siliotti, Alberto *Nefertari e la Valle delle Regine*. Florence 1993. 200 pp. + planches photographiques en couleurs et en noir et blanc, dessins. Seconde édition revue et corrigée, Florence 1997.

Lecuyot, Guy. *Deir Roumi, monastère copte de la Vallée des Reines*. Les Dossiers Histoire et Archéologie, n° 136, Dijon 1989, pp. 60-63.

Lecuyot, Guy. *Un sanctuaire romain transformé en monastère : le Deir er-Roumi*. Atti del Sesto Congresso Internazionale di Egittologia, I, Turin 1992, pp. 383-390.

Lecuyot, Guy. *The Valley of the Queens in the Coptic Period*. Acts of the Fifth International Congress of Coptic Studies II/1, 1993, pp. 263-272.

Loyrette, Anne-Marie et Mohamed Sayed. *La tombe d'une princesse anonyme [N°36] de la Vallée des Reines*. Annales du Service des Antiquités de l'Egypte 72, Le Caire 1993, pp. 119-135.

Mahmoud Soliman, Ibrahim et Tosi, Mario. *La tombe de la reine Isis [VdR 51], grande épouse royale de Ramsès III*. Memnonia VII, Le Caire 1996, pp. 213-225 et pl. LVIII-LXI.

Mohamed Sayed, Sayed et Sesana, Angelo. *Les vestiges du mobilier funéraire de la reine Tyti, retrouvés dans la tombe n° 52 de la Vallée des Reines*. Memnonia VI, Le Caire 1995, pp. 215-228 et pl. XL-XLI.

Porter, Rosalind et Moss, Bertha. *Topographical Bibliography of*

Ancient Egyptian Hieroglyphic Texts, Reliefs and Paintings. I. The Theban Necropolis. Part 2. Royal Tombs and Smaller Cemeteries. Oxford 1964.

Schiaparelli, Ernesto. *Relazione sui lavori della Missione archeologica italiana in Egitto. I. Esplorazione della "Valle delle Regine" nella necropoli di Tebe*. Turin 1924.

Thausing, G. et Goedicke, Hans. *Nofretari. Eine Dokumentation der Wandgemälde ihres Grabes*. Graz 1971.

Thomas, Elisabeth. *The Royal Necropoleis of Thebes*. Princeton 1966.

Yoyotte, Jean. *The Tomb of a Prince Ramesses in the Valley of the Queens [N° 53]*. The Journal of Egyptian Archaeology 44, Londres 1958, pp. 26-30.

DEIR EL-MEDINA, A VILLAGE OF CRAFTSMEN
text by Mohamed A. el-Bialy

J. Cerny. *A Community of Workmen at Thebes in the Ramesside Period*. Bibliothèque d'Etude n°50, IFAO, Le Caire 1973.

B.G. Davies. *Who's Who at Deir el-Medina*. Uitgaven 13, Leiden 1999.

M. El-Bialy, *Une tombe de la XVIIIe dynastie découverte à Gournet Moura'i*, in Les Dossiers d'Archéologie, n°149/150, Dijon 1990, pp. 96-98.

I. El-Masry. *La nécropole d'El-Taref*, in Les Dossiers d'Archéologie, n°149/150, Dijon 1990, pp. 120-121.

Ch. Leblanc. *The Valley of the Queens and Royal Children. History and Resurrection of an archaeological site*, in Art and Eternity. The Nofretari Wall Paintings Conservation Project [1986-1992], pp. 19-29. The Getty Conservation Institute, Santa Monica 1993.

B. Porter and R. Moss. *Topographical Bibliography of Ancient Egyptian Egyptian Hieroglyphic Texts, Reliefs, and Paintings*. I. The Theban Necropolis. Part 1. Private Tombs. Oxford 1985.

D. Valbelle. *Les ouvriers de la Tombe. Deir el-Médinah à l'époque ramesside*. Bibliothèque d'Etude n° 96, IFAO, Le Caire 1995.

C. Vandersleyen. *L'Egypte et la Vallée du Nil*. Nouvelle Clio. PUF, Paris 1995.

THE TOMB OF SENNEDJEM
text by Morris L. Bierbreir

Bierbrier, M.L. *The Tomb-builders of the Pharaohs*, London 1982.

Bruyère, B. *La Tombe no 1 de Sennedjem*, Cairo, 1954.

Porte, B. and Moss, R. *Topographical Bibliography of Ancient Egyptian Hieroglyphic Texts, Reliefs and Painting I Part II*, new ed Oxford, 1960.

THE TOMB OF INHERKHAU
text by Morris L. Bierbreir

Bruyère, B. *Rapport sur les fouilles de Deir el-Médineh (1930)*. Cairo, 1933

Davies, B., *Who's Who at Deir el-Medina*. Leiden, 1999.

Porte, B. and Moss, R. *Topographical Bibliography of Ancient Egyptian Hieroglyphic Texts, Reliefs and Painting I Part II*, new ed Oxford, 1960.

THE TOMB OF PASHEDU
text by Morris L. Bierbreir

Alain-Pierre Zivie. *La Tombe de Pached à Deir el-Médineh*; Cairo 1979.

THE TOMB OF KHAEMHAT
text by Lyla Pinch-Brock

Betsy M. Bryan. *Private Relief Sculpture Outside Thebes and Its Relationship to Theban Relief Sculpture*, in Laurence M. Berman, ed. The Art of Amenhotep III: Art Historical Analysis, Cleveland, 1990, pp. 65–80.

Jean Capart and Marcelle Werbrouck *Thebes*, Brussels, 1926, pp. 286, 288, 290, figs. 183, 206.

Dows Dunham. *Note on Some Old Squeezes from Egyptian Monuments*, Journal of the American Oriental Society, vol. 56, (1936), pp. 173-177.

Victor Loret. *La Tombe de Khâ-m-bâ*, Memoirs de la Mission archéologique française au Caire, vol. i, 1884, pp.113-132.

Lisa Manniche. *The Tombs of the Nobles at Luxor*, Cairo, 1987, p. 50, pl. 24, 30.

Kazimierz Michalowski. *The Art of Ancient Egypt*, London,1969, figs. 437, 438.

Sir Robert Mond. *Report of Work in the Necropolis of Thebes During the Winter of 1903-1904*, Annales du Service des Antiquités de l'Égypte, vol. vi, 1905, pp. 66-67.

Bertha Porter and Rosalind L.B. Moss. *Topographical Bibliography of Ancient Egyptian Hieroglyphic Texts, Reliefs, and Paintings, I The Theban Necropolis, Part 1, Private Tombs*, 2nd ed., Oxford, 1960, pp.113-119.

THE TOMB OF SENNEFER
text by Lyla Pinch-Brock

Howard Carter. *Report on the Tomb of Sen-nefer found at Biban el Molouk near the Tomb of Thutmose II*, no. 34, Annales du Service des Antiquités de l'Égypte, vol. 2, 1901), pp. 196-200.

Jean Francois Champollion. *Notices descriptives, vol. 1*, Paris, 1844-1879, p. 505.

Norman de Garis Davies. *The Graphic Work of the Expedition*, Bulletin of the Metropolitan Museum of Art, vol. 24, 1929, pp. 35-49.

M. Eaton-Krauss. *The Fate of Sennefer and Senetnay at Karnak Temple and in the Valley of the Kings*, Journal of Egyptian Archaeology, vol. 85, 1999, pp. 113-130.

Rolf Gundlach. *Das Grab des Sennefer*; in Ägyptens Aufstieg zur Weltmacht, Arne Eggebrecht, ed., Mainz am Rhein, 1987, pp. 66-83.

Arpag Mekhitarian. *Egyptian Painting*, Geneva. 1954, pp. 53-56.

Bertha Porter and Rosalind L.B. Moss. *Topographical Bibliography of Ancient Egyptian Hieroglyphic Texts, Reliefs, and Paintings, I The Theban Necropolis, Part 1, Private Tombs*, 2nd ed., Oxford, 1960, pp. 197-203.

Charles K. Wilkinson and Marsha Hill. *Egyptian Wall Paintings*, New York, 1983, p. 110.

THE TOMB OF REKHMIRE
text by Rita E. Freed
Newberry, P. *The Life of Rekhmara*, Westminster, 1900
Davies, N. de G. *The Tomb of Rekhmi-re' at Thebes* New York, 1943.

THE TOMB OF NAKHT
text by Melinda K. Hartwig
Nadine Cherpion. *Quelques jalons pour une histoire de le peinture thebaine*, BSFÉ 110 (Octobre, 1987): 27-47.
Norman de Garis Davies. *The Tomb of Nakht at Thebes*, PMMA, Robb de Peyster Tytus Memorial Series I New York, 1917.
Selke Susan Eichler. *Die Verwaltung des "Haus des Amun" in der 18. Dynastie*, SAK Beihefte 7, Hamburg, 2000, 170.
Erhart Graefe. "*Talfest*," LÄ VI (1986): 187-189.
Melinda K. Hartwig. "*Painting*," The Oxford Encyclopedia of Ancient Egypt, vol. 3, editor-in-chief Donald B. Redford, Oxford and New York, 2001, 1-13.
Friederike Kampp. *Die Thebanische Nekropole: Zum Wandel des Grabgedankens von der XVIII. bis zur XX. Dynastie I*, Theben XIII, Mainz, 1996, 257-258.
Arielle Kozloff. "*Theban Tomb Paintings from the Reign of Amenhotep III: Problems in Iconography and Chronology*," in The Art of Amenhotep III: Art Historical Analysis, edited by Larry M. Berman, Cleveland, 1990, 55-64.
Dimitri Laboury. "*Une relecture de la tombe de Nakht (TT 52, Cheikh `Abd el-Gourna)*," in La Peinture Égyptienne Ancienne: Un monde de signes à préserver, Actes de colloque international de Bruxelles, Avril 1994, edited by Roland Tefnin, Monumenta

Aegyptiaca VII, Bruxelles, 1997, 49-81.
Gaston Maspero. "*Tombeau de Nakhti*," in Mémoires publiés par les Membres de la Mission Archéologie Français au Caire, V, 2, 1894, 469-485.
William J. Murnane. "*Paintings from the Tomb of Nakht at Thebes*," Field Museum of Natural History Bulletin 52, no. 10, November, 1981, 13-25
Arpag Mekhitarian. *Egyptian Painting*, Geneva, 1954, 67-72.
Abdel Ghaffar Shedid and Matthias Seidel. *The Tomb of Nakht*, translated by Marianne Eaton-Krauss, Mainz, 1996.
Dietrich Wildung. *Ägyptische Malerei. Das Grab des Nacht*, Zurich, 1978.

THE TOMB OF MENNA
text by Melinda K. Hartwig
Betsy M. Bryan. "*Evidence for Female Literacy from Theban tombs of the New Kingdom*," BES 6, 1984, 17-32.
Lanny Bell. "*The New Kingdom 'Divine' Temple: The Example of Luxor*," in Temples of Ancient Egypt, edited by B. Shafer, Ithaca, 1997, 136-137, 183-184.
Colin Campbell. *Two Theban Princes: Kha-em-uaset & Amenkhepesh sons of Rameses II; Menna, a Land-Steward and their Tombs*, London, 1910, 85-107.
Nadine Cherpion. "*Quelques jalons pour une histoire de le peinture thebaine*," BSFÉ 110, Octobre, 1987, 27-47.
Selke Susan Eichler. *Die Verwaltung des "Haus des Amun" in der 18. Dynastie*, SAK Beihefte 7, Hamburg, 2000, 56-72.
Martin Fitzenreiter. "*Totenverehrung und soziale Repräsentation im thebanischen Beamtengrab der 18. Dynastie*," SAK 22, 1995, 95-130.

Melinda K. Hartwig. "*Painting*," The Oxford Encyclopedia of Ancient Egypt, vol. 3, editor-in-chief Donald B. Redford, Oxford and New York, 2001, 1-13.
Jac J. Janssen. Review of I.A. Stuchevsky, Zemledel'tsy gosudarstvennogo khozyaïstva drevnego Egipta epokhi Ramessidov (The Cultivators of the State Economy in Ancient Egypt during the Ramesside Period), Moskava, Izadtel'stvo 'Nauka', 1982, in BiOr 3/4, May-July 1986, 352-366.
Friederike Kampp. *Die Thebanische Nekropole: Zum Wandel des Grabgedankens von der XVIII. bis zur XX. Dynastie I*, Theben XIII, Mainz, 1996, 294-297.
Arielle Kozloff. "*A Study of the Painters of the Tomb of Menna, No. 69*," in Acts, First International Conference of Egyptology, edited by Walter F. Reineke, Akademie der Wissenschaften der DDR Zentralinstitut für alte Geschichte und Archäologie XIV, Berlin, 1979, 395-402.
Arielle Kozloff. "*Theban Tomb Paintings from the Reign of Amenhotep III: Problems in Iconography and Chronology*," in The Art of Amenhotep III: Art Historical Analysis, edited by Larry M. Berman, Cleveland, 1990, 55-64.
Arpag Mekhitarian. *Egyptian Painting*, Geneva, 1954, 72-95.
Robert Mond, "*Report of Work in the Necropolis of Thebes during the Winter of 1903-1904*," ASAE 6, 1905, 88.

THE TOMB OF RAMOSE
text by Rita E. Freed
Davies, N. de G. *The Tomb of the Vizier Ramose*, London, 1941

THE TOMB OF USERHAT
text by Lyla Pinch-Brock
Lyla Pinch-Brock, "*Norman or Nina?*" Journal of the Society for the Study of Egyptian Antiquities, vol. XXVI, 1996, 2000, pp. 82- 92.
Norman de Garis Davies, *Two Ramesside Tombs at Thebes*, New York, 1924, pp. 3-30.
Arielle P. Kozloff, "*Theban Tomb Paintings from the Reign of Amenhotep III: Problems in Iconograph and Chronology*," in Laurence M. Berman, ed., The Art of Amenhotep III: Art Historical Analysis, Cleveland, 1990, pp. 55-64.
Arpag Mekhitarian, *Egyptian Painting*, Geneva 1954, pp. 131-137.
Sir Robert Mond, "*Report of Work in the Necropolis of Thebes During the Winter of 1903-1904*," Annales du Service des Antiquités de l'Égypte, vol. vi, 1905, pp. 67-71.
Bertha Porter and Rosalind L.B. Moss. *Topographical Bibliography of Ancient Egyptian Hieroglyphic Texts, Reliefs, and Paintings, I The Theban Necropolis, Part 1*, Private Tombs, 2nd ed., Oxford, 1960, pp. 97-99.
Charles K. Wilkinson and Marsha Hill. *Egyptian Wall Paintings*, New York, 1983, pp. 139-145.

THE TOMB OF KHERUEF
text by Rita E. Freed
University of Chicago. Oriental Institute. *Epigraphic Survey, The Tomb of Kheruef*: Theban Tomb 192, Chicago, 1980
Fakhry, A. "*A Note on the Tomb of Kheruef at Thebes*," ASAE 42, 1943, pp. 29ff.
Habachi, L. "*Clearance of the Tomb of Kheruef at Thebes (1957-1958)*," ASAE 55, 1958. pp. 28ff

PHOTOGRAPHIC CREDITS